Business-to-Business Marketing

Business-to-Business Marketing

Relationships, Networks & Strategies

Nick Ellis

OXFORD
UNIVERSITY PRESS

Great Clarendon Street, Oxford OX2 6DP

Oxford University Press is a department of the University of Oxford.
It furthers the University's objective of excellence in research, scholarship,
and education by publishing worldwide in

Oxford New York

Auckland Cape Town Dar es Salaam Hong Kong Karachi
Kuala Lumpur Madrid Melbourne Mexico City Nairobi
New Delhi Shanghai Taipei Toronto

With offices in

Argentina Austria Brazil Chile Czech Republic France Greece
Guatemala Hungary Italy Japan Poland Portugal Singapore
South Korea Switzerland Thailand Turkey Ukraine Vietnam

Oxford is a registered trade mark of Oxford University Press
in the UK and in certain other countries

Published in the United States
by Oxford University Press Inc., New York

British Library Cataloguing in Publication Data
Data available

Library of Congress Cataloging in Publication Data
Data available

ISBN 978–0–19–955168–2

10 9 8 7 6 5 4 3 2 1

Typeset by Glyph International, Bangalore, India
Printed in Italy
on acid-free paper by
L.E.G.O. S.p.A.—Lavis TN

To my mother, Karin Ellis

Preface

Aims

This book represents my desire to promote the wider teaching of business-to-business (B2B) marketing within higher education. Having worked, taught, and researched in the B2B field for several years, I share the view that any management student graduating without understanding how business or organizational markets work is missing something vitally important (Barclay et al, 2007). I have thus set out to raise readers' awareness of the significance of B2B marketing in contemporary economies, in both local and global contexts. With this in mind, the text is pitched at a highly accessible level in order to appeal simultaneously to British, European, and broader international readership.

The book provides a comprehensive introduction to the main theoretical and managerial issues in the area of B2B marketing. From the outset, I stress that for every consumer (or end-user) market there are typically several upstream organizations which must deal with each other in products and services before anything is ultimately consumed. The book aims to show that B2B marketing is about trying to manage the complex network of buying and selling relationships between these organizations. This is captured in its striking cover design: the links in the chain depicted can be seen as a metaphor for inter-organizational relationships, relationships that have a positive side in bonding organizations together for mutual benefit and strength, yet that also have a negative side in tying firms into networks where they can never be fully in control of their own destiny.

To help those readers thinking of a career in B2B marketing, I have included detailed discussions concerning the role of individual managers and the organizations they represent. As well as outlining possible managerial solutions to common B2B marketing dilemmas (such as the design and delivery of business products and services, and the selection of communication methods), the text also examines issues like e-commerce in B2B markets, key account management, and supply chain ethics. I am aware, however, that most students' original introduction to the study of marketing was probably conducted in the context of consumer (B2C) markets, and thus the approach I take allows for the necessary adjustment of perspective that readers may have to make.

Indeed, I deliberately use several B2C-related illustrations to capture readers' interest, and then move beyond consumer marketing issues to provide a host of real-life examples that focus on the challenges of marketing to organizational (or business) customers. A key aim is to make students aware of some of the tensions encountered by B2B marketing and purchasing managers as they go about their daily tasks. This is achieved through a careful interweaving of clearly explained, relevant theoretical discussion and a series of (short and long) case study examples. Conceptual material is drawn from marketing scholarship in US and European contexts, as well as some contributions from researchers working further afield. Empirical material is global in scope, with examples from organizations operating in a large number of international contexts.

Structure and Coverage

Figure A represents a structural overview of the book. The rationale behind this structure is to ensure comprehensive discussion of the important topics of marketing and organizational

Part One: The Organizational Marketing Context

1. The Significance of B2B Marketing
- Significance of B2B Marketing
- Supply/Demand Chains
- Organizational Markets
- Significance of Relationships & Networks
- Supply Chain Ethics

2. Organizational Buying Behaviour
- Types of Markets
- Organizational & Consumer Buyer Behaviour
- Influences on Demand
- Organizational Decision-Making

Part Two: Inter-Organizational Relationships & Networks

3. Inter-Organizational Relationships
- Market & Relational Exchange
- CRM
- Partnerships & Alliances
- How IORs 'Work' in Different Contexts

4. Marketing Channels & Supply Chains
- Structure & Role of Channels
- Flows & Blockages in Channels
- From Channels to Chains
- Marketing Logistics

5. Industrial Networks
- The Interaction Approach
- From Channels & Chains to Networks
- Learning from the Industrial Network View

Part Three: Business Marketing Planning

6. B2B Marketing Planning & Analysis
- Planning & S/DCM
- The Planning Process
- Situation Analysis
- Sources & Assessing Market Potential
- B2B Market Segmentation

7. B2B Strategies & Implementation
- Market Positioning
- B2B Branding
- Making Strategy Decisions
- Issues of Implementation

These 6 chapters can also be effectively combined as the 'marketing mix'

Part Four: Business Marketing Programmes

8. Business Products
- Classifying Business Products
- Managing Business Products
- New Product Development

9. Business Services
- Classifying Business Services
- Characteristics of Business Services
- B2B Services Marketing Management

10. Value & Pricing
- Value in Organizational Markets
- Making Pricing Decisions
- B2B Pricing Strategies (incl. Web-based activities)

11. Marketing Communications
- Communication Strategies
- Elements of the Communications Mix
- Relative Effectiveness of B2B Media (incl. the Internet)

12. Personal Selling & Sales Management
- Personal Selling in B2B Markets
- Organizing the Sales Force
- Key Account Management (KAM)

Figure A Book structure

buying in Part One, and of relationships, chains, and networks in Part Two. These topics inform the B2B planning processes covered in Part Three, before we move on to look at more specific managerial activities in Part Four. On further exploration of the book, it will be seen that I make frequent references throughout Parts Three and Four to the contextual inevitability of having to cope with managing in the inter-organizational relationships that link channels, chains, and networks.

In Part Three, some qualification of planning approaches has been necessary. This is because what is trying to be shown in this book is that, despite the managerially orientated exhortations of many marketing textbooks, B2B marketers do not necessarily choose their strategy and then conveniently plan their firm's relationships; rather, they are effectively embedded 'in' a series of relationships, chains, and networks before they start. Of course, they can try to manage in these situations, but making suitably reflective and responsive marketing plans relies on managers understanding this organizational market context from the outset.

The contents of Part Four do follow a '4Ps' structure to an extent, but only after affirming the significance of inter-firm relationships and an industrial network view. Incorporating the concepts of channels and chains in Chapter Four, instead of as part of a purely marketing mix 'place' discussion, ensures that students get a holistic picture of B2B issues, especially regarding upstream marketing and purchasing activities. Also, the channels and chains of Chapter Four form a conceptual link between the relationships discussed in Chapter Three and the networks of Chapter Five.

In adopting this approach, I am trying to get students to think a little differently about marketing management in the B2B context (for instance, by taking more of a European-inspired network perspective), hence the location of a slightly reduced traditional mix towards the end of the book. Nevertheless, as Figure A shows, I have also been mindful to reassure readers that one could view the five chapters of Part Four and Chapter Four together as the marketing mix for business markets if so desired.

There is no separate chapter on global B2B marketing since an integrated coverage of international marketing issues and examples is found throughout the text. Similar reasoning explains the lack of a stand-alone chapter devoted to the impact of information technology or the Internet on B2B marketing. Moreover, while there may be a case for separate chapters on topics such as B2B segmentation or market research, the deliberately accessible positioning of this book means that it cannot 'do everything' in quite the depth that some readers might wish. To counter this, each chapter contains a large number of supporting references and advice on more advanced academic reading. There will also be links on the companion website, where certain topics are discussed in more detail and further information sources provided.

Intended Readership

It is my firm belief that there is room for an accessible B2B marketing textbook written for the undergraduate market and for the postgraduate market where students often have no prior knowledge of the subject. The contextual focus of many B2B texts continues to be rather biased towards the US and, whilst some fine UK/European-based books have emerged recently, no B2B text has adequately catered for the high proportion of international students (for whom English is rarely their first language) that typically make up higher education business courses. This book intends to plug that major gap.

I have found that the subject of B2B marketing appeals to both management generalists and marketing students, many of whom recognize the greater employment potential in this field compared to the superficially more 'glamorous' area of B2C marketing. It is also worth noting that after a few years of commercial employment, people with initial training in non-marketing disciplines often gravitate to B2B roles where they can combine their technical know-how with an understanding of organizational markets gleaned from books such as this one. Thus, as well as helping readers with prior knowledge of general marketing concepts to specialize in the challenging yet rewarding area of B2B, this text will also be extremely useful for prospective managers with a more scientific/engineering background who are seeking to move into marketing-related jobs.

Indeed, with B2B-related issues such as the overseas sourcing of products of dubious quality, farmer/manufacturer/retailer relations in the food supply chain, and the concept of fair trade remaining extremely relevant to contemporary society, the demand for managers who have been taught something about these issues will surely grow, as will the demand from students who wish to become better informed about such high profile issues. The book has been slanted to attract the interest of students wanting to explore 'behind the scenes' of B2C marketing by analysing these sorts of B2B problems.

The overall approach taken in this book, and many of the teaching materials in it, have been 'road tested' on hundreds of students during my ten years'-plus experience of teaching B2B marketing. My ideas have been presented at academic conferences such as those of the Industrial Marketing and Purchasing (IMP) Group and the Academy of Marketing. Several lecturers from around the world have also drawn upon draft versions of my chapters in their teaching, including colleagues in the UK, North America, Africa, and the Far East. The feedback I have received from my students and my peers has enabled me to fine-tune my materials.

So Why Should You Read This Book?

It is a little risky to make claims about the uniqueness of any new text, especially as this book mirrors the strengths of most good textbooks. In other words:

- It has an accessible writing style.
- It is clearly and logically presented.
- It contains a large range of pedagogic features.
- It comes with extensive online support.

Nevertheless, I believe that the book is differentiated from other texts in the B2B area by uniquely incorporating *all* the following features in a single volume:

- It is pitched at an academic level suitable for the majority of final year undergraduate, postgraduate, and international students in marketing and management.
- It relates theory to practice via a wide range of case study illustrations, mid-chapter 'boxes', and discussion questions.
- It draws upon examples from cultural and trading contexts beyond the standard US and European scenarios and the large corporations that typically dominate marketing texts.
- It aims to capture students' imaginations by addressing 'hot' B2B-related topics such as fair trade, retailer power, overseas sourcing, and 'green' marketing.

- It facilitates students' understanding of the day-to-day challenges faced by B2B marketing and purchasing managers.

- It combines a broad US marketing management orientation with European industrial network academic perspectives.

- It remains focused on key B2B marketing issues and does not risk dilution (and excessive length) by unnecessary coverage of marketing concepts that can easily be found elsewhere.

- It contains extensive guidance regarding wider and deeper reading for students who wish to pursue further study in the area.

I hope it will be agreed that this combination of factors means that this is a book worthy of study. I am sure it will help readers make sense of the fascinating yet challenging world of B2B marketing!

Nick Ellis
University of Leicester

References

Barclay, D. W., Deutscher, T. H., & Vandenbosch, M. H. (2007) Business Marketing in Master's Programs: A Part of the Fabric, Journal of Business-to-Business Marketing, 14 (1), pp 31–51

Acknowledgements

My thanks go to the following guest contributors of case study material:

Peter J. Batt, Curtin University of Technology, Perth, Western Australia (Main Case Study, Chapter Eight)

Bella Butler, Curtin University of Technology, Perth, Western Australia (Box 6.6, Chapter Six)

Steve Carter, Leeds Metropolitan University, Leeds, UK (Main Case Study, Chapter Four; Box 5.5, Chapter 5)

Maurizio Catulli, Sustainable Business Process Research Group (SPRING), University of Hertfordshire, Hatfield, UK (Main Case Study, Chapter Ten)

Phil Cooper, Abbeysteel™, Stevenage, Hertfordshire, UK (Main Case Study, Chapter Ten)

Gillian Hopkinson, Lancaster University, Lancaster, UK (Main Case Study, Chapter Three; Main Case Study, Chapter Eleven)

Sylvie Lacoste, Advancia-Negocia Business School (run by the Paris Chamber of Commerce), Paris, France (Main Case Study, Chapter Two)

Sid Lowe, Kingston University, Kingston upon Thames, UK (Box 5.7, Chapter Five; Box 10.2, Chapter Ten)

Kevin Morris, Abbeysteel™, Stevenage, Hertfordshire, UK (Main Case Study, Chapter Ten)

Michel Rod, Carleton University, Ottawa, Canada (Main Case Study, Chapter Seven)

Sarena Saunders, Victoria University of Wellington, Wellington, New Zealand (Main Case Study, Chapter Seven)

Peter Svensson, Lund University, Lund, Sweden (Main Case Study, Chapter Nine)

Theingi, Assumption University, Bangkok, Thailand (Box 6.1, Chapter Six)

Natalia Tolstikova, University of Gloucestershire, Cheltenham, UK (Main Case Study, Chapter Eleven)

Ibrahim Umar, University of Leicester, Leicester, UK (Main Case Study, Chapter Five)

Angela Vickerstaff, Nottingham Trent University, Nottingham, UK (Main Case Study, Chapter Six)

The following copyright holders have kindly granted permission to use the material detailed below:

American Marketing Association, Chicago, US for: Figure 11.3 – adapted from Figure 1 on p 38 of J. Mohr & J. R. Nevin (1990) Communication Strategies in Marketing Channels, Journal of Marketing, 54 (4), pp 36–51

Cengage Learning Services Ltd, Andover, UK for: Figure 2.8 – adapted from Table 2.4 on p 50 of D. Wilson (1999) Organisational Marketing, International Thomson Business Press, London; Figure 5.3 – adapted from D. Ford (ed.) (2001) Understanding Business Markets and Purchasing, p 37, Thomson Learning, London

Elsevier Inc, New York, US for: Figure 3.8 – adapted from Figure 1 on p 84 of S. Wagner & R. Boutellier (2002) Capabilities for Managing a Portfolio of Supplier Relationships, Business Horizons, 45 (6), pp 79–88; Figure 6.1 – adapted from Table 2 on p 389 of U. Juttner, M. Christopher, & S. Baker (2007) Demand Chain Management – Integrating Marketing and SCM, Industrial Marketing Management, 36, pp 377–92; Figure 7.2 – adapted from Figure 1 on p 556 of E. Penttinen & J. Palmer (2007) Improving Firm Positioning through Enhanced Offerings and Buyer–Seller Relations, Industrial Marketing Management, 35, pp 552–64

Elsevier Ltd, Oxford, UK for: Figure 3.1 – adapted from Table on p 19 of M. Christopher, A. Payne, & D. Ballantyne (2002) Relationship Marketing: Creating Stakeholder Value, Butterworth-Heinemann, Oxford; Figure 3.3 – adapted from Figure 2.6 on p 48 of M. Christopher, A. Payne, & D. Ballantyne (2002) Relationship Marketing: Creating Stakeholder Value, Butterworth-Heinemann, Oxford; Figure 3.4 – adapted from Figure 1.1 on p 4 of M. Christopher, A. Payne, & D. Ballantyne (2002) Relationship Marketing: Creating Stakeholder Value, Butterworth-Heinemann, Oxford; Figure 3.6 – adapted from Figure 2.1 on p 40 of F. Buttle (2004) Customer Relationship Management: Concepts & Tools, Elsevier Butterworth-Heinemann; Figure 4.3 – adapted from Figure 4.5 on p 84 of M. Christopher (1997) Marketing Logistics, Butterworth-Heinemann, Oxford; Figure 4.8 – adapted from Figure 2.4 on p 37 of M. Christopher (1997) Marketing Logistics, Butterworth-Heinemann, Oxford; Figure 10.2 – adapted from Figure 3.2 on p 49 of M. Christopher (1997) Marketing Logistics, Butterworth-Heinemann, Oxford; Figure 10.3 – adapted from Figure 3.8 on p 67 of M. Christopher (1997) Marketing Logistics, Butterworth-Heinemann, Oxford

Emerald Group Publishing Ltd, Bingley, UK for: Figure 2.2 – adapted from Table 1 on p 8 of B. Cova & R. Salle (2008) The Industrial/Consumer Marketing Dichotomy Revisited, Journal of Business & Industrial Marketing, 23 (1) pp 3–11; Figure 12.3 – adapted from p 39 of D. W. Cravens, T. N. Ingram, & R. W. la Forge (1991) Evaluating Multiple Channel Strategies, Journal of Business & Industrial Marketing, 6 (3/4), pp 37–48

Ben Enis for: Figure 2.6 – adapted from M. B. Enis (1980) Marketing Principles, 3rd edn, Scott Foresman & Co, Glenview, IL

Pearson Education Ltd, Harlow, UK for: Figure 5.4 – adapted from p 112 of J. Egan (2001) Relationship Marketing: Exploring Relational Strategies in Marketing, FT-Prentice Hall, Harlow; Figure 5.5 – adapted from Figure 8.1 on p 155 of J. Egan (2001) Relationship Marketing: Exploring Relational Strategies in Marketing, FT-Prentice Hall, Harlow; Figure 7.3 – adapted from Figure 4.5 on p 93 of M. Christopher (1992) Logistics and Supply Chain Management, FT Pitman, London

Lynette Ryals for: Figure 12.5 – adapted from Table 3 on p 410 of L. J. Ryals & S. Holt (2007) Creating and Capturing Value in KAM Relationships, Journal of Strategic Marketing, 15, pp 403–20

Taylor & Francis for: Figure 12.5 – adapted from Table 3 on p 410 of L. J. Ryals & S. Holt (2007) Creating and Capturing Value in KAM Relationships, Journal of Strategic Marketing, 15, pp 403–20 (http://www.informaworld.com)

Wiley-Blackwell, Oxford, UK for: Figure 5.1 – adapted from p 24 of H. Håkansson (ed.) (1982) International Marketing & Purchasing of Industrial Goods: An Interaction Approach, John Wiley, Chichester

The publishers would be pleased to clear permission with any copyright holders that we have inadvertently failed, or been unable to contact.

I am also grateful for the conscientious manner in which the book's reviewers, all of whom were experienced B2B educators, commented on draft versions of the text. Although I could not respond to all their suggestions, the volume and depth of feedback received from these reviewers played a significant part in the book's development.

Finally, I would like to thank the editorial team at Oxford University Press, in particular my two commissioning editors, Claire Brewer and Nicki Sneath. Their advice and encouragement throughout this project have been much appreciated.

Outline Contents

Detailed Contents

Part Two: Inter-Organizational Relationships & Networks   63

3. Inter-Organizational Relationships   65

Part Four: Business Marketing Programmes   211

Guide to the book

Chapter-opening features

Introduction & Learning Objectives

Introduction & Learning Objectives

The purpose of this chapter is to show you how an in-depth understanding behaviour in business markets can facilitate attempts to manage the marketing/p interface between organizations. Organizational buying behaviour (OBB) is a key the relationships that a firm develops, either as part of a series of market-based (or transactions) or as closer, longer-term relational exchanges. The placing of the signing of contracts between organizations can confirm a current trading rel initiate a new relationship or perhaps signal the end of one. Thus, even in handlin

Each chapter begins with a brief introduction to the key issues and learning objectives that will be covered in the chapter.

Mini case

ment can influence the strength of many other B2B relationships, even those seem on the most rational purchase decision and for the most tangible of products.

Box 3.1 Mini case
Keeping business customers loyal

'In B2B markets more than anywhere else, people buy people', according to Ch the client service director of global marketing communications agency, Gyro Inter He says that as customers have many factors shaping their decisions, includin stant need to review prices, loyalty tends to come from the work done by th account managers who understand their clients' issues and resolve them quick

A topical mini case at the start of each chapter provides you with an introduction to the subject and helps to set the scene.

Chapter Aims

Chapter Aims

After completing this chapter, you should be able to:

- Recognize ways of classifying business services
- Appreciate how business services differ from business products in terms of s characteristics
- Understand some service management issues in organizational markets
- Reflect on the significance of personal relationships in professional business se

This feature highlights the key issues and concepts you should be able to understand and demonstrate by the end of the chapter.

In-text features

Each chapter contains four different features, each designed to enhance your learning and understanding.

Mini case

Box 9.5 Mini case
Business relationships in banking services

The commercial banking arm of the HSBC bank is keen to stress in its advertisi it understands how important relationships between business and their supplie be. In messages aimed at corporate clients during 2009, it even refers to its own sored research, contained in a report entitled, 'The Value of Relationships', to s this claim. The advertisements state that the bank is 'actively supporting busin ensuring that their Relationship Managers are 'proactively spending 30% mor

This feature illustrates key theoretical points made within the chapter, contextualize business-to-business marketing with real life examples from around the world, and represent SMEs and multinationals.

Food for thought

Box 4.5 Food for thought
The supply/demand chain for ethically sourced jewellery

Green Gold is a self-proclaimed 'ethical' jewellery business based in Chichester in but which has operations in Columbia where gold is mined. The firm is hoping fair trade certification for the gold panned from rivers each month by local miner ing together as the Association for Responsible Mining (ARM). The owners of Gre believe the ethical jewellery business is set to grow as a result of end-user demand, inspired by the movie *Blood Diamond*. However, they recognize that their business will only work if they can get sufficient certified supplies from groups like ARM. They

These are designed to get you to think beyond the 'common sense' approach to matters. They are often provocative and encourage you to examine alternative readings beyond the scope of the core textbook.

Box 9.4 Voices
Russian service firms 'onshoring' in the US

Offshore Russian suppliers of IT services face particular challenges when marketi
the onshore US marketplace. There is no link to Russia through the entrepreneurs
often return from the US to countries such as Taiwan or India, nor are there many
nizational links to large US firms that could facilitate outsourcing relationships.
makes it difficult for Russian service providers to establish a profile in the US as
frequently lack a social network to build upon. Software firms based in St Peters
have embarked on a number of activities across borders to create new linkages betw

Voices

This feature gives you the opportunity to hear practising B2B marketers, purchasing managers, and other stakeholders talk about the typical problems that they face in their day-to-day work.

resources, including money, time, and knowledge (i.e., the network understanding
the owner), which the firm has drawn upon to ensure success.

Box 7.1 Number crunching
The perfect mushroom

In 1996, the sugar mill opened by Nazem Ghandou's father in Tripoli, Lebanon to
cess high-grade imported beet closed after the price for sugar suddenly fell than
subsidies offered to domestic growers by the Lebanese Government. Having lo
father's business, Nazem opened two restaurants, hoping to exploit the economic b

Number crunching

These show the significance successful B2B marketing has on an organization through simple, quantitative means.

End-of-chapter features

those of another in order to move forward.

Summary

The key points to take from this chapter are as follows:

• How business marketing planning should go hand in hand with S/DCM in or
  customer needs.
• The main elements of a marketing plan for B2B organizations.
• Debates around the relevance of a formal planning approach to marketing 'ma
  in a network context.

Summary

Chapters conclude with a list of key points and concepts.

Discussion questions

1. How can a manufacturer of machinery for garment-making generate increas
   through its business service offerings?
2. What would you advise a newly appointed marketer representing a corporate
   venue about what they may need to take into account regarding the key chara
   business services?
3. Imagine you work in marketing for a large accountancy firm with many org
   clients. Explain to your human resources department why 'part-time marke
   important in B2B services marketing.
4. How do buyers of business services tend to evaluate the quality of wh

Discussion questions

At the end of each chapter you'll find a set of questions designed to test your knowledge and promote debate and the exchange of ideas.

Case study
Dongfeng Commercial Vehicle Company – EU Market Entry and Distribu

Steve Carter, Leeds Metropolitan University, Leeds, UK

Introduction

Dongfeng is a well-respected Chinese commercial vehicle company, whose over
department is based in Wuhan City, Hubei Province, China. Manufacturing an

Case study questions

1. In terms of meeting end-user organizational customer needs, why is a dealer netw
   so important to Dongfeng's ambitious plans for EU market entry?
2. What are the benefits of the firm's cautious 'sneaking in under the radar' appro
   to find distribution partners? Are there any risks with this strategy?
3. What logistical issues do you think Dongfeng will need to take into account? Are t
   any organizations from which it can get assistance in meeting these challenges?

Case study & Case study questions

These offer a longer and more in-depth examination of some of the key practical and theoretical concepts from the chapter. These are written by international academics and based upon their experiences in the B2B marketing field. These are accompanied by questions to engage you with the issues facing B2B practitioners.

Further Reading

Beverland, M. B. & Lindgreen, A. (2007) Implementing Marketing Orientation in Indu
A Multiple Case Study, Industrial Marketing Management, 36, pp 430–42
This study examines the creation of a market orientation (MO) in two New Zeala
tural organizations, identifying that moving the firms towards an MO involves cha
role of leadership, the use of market intelligence, and organizational learning st
pinned by supportive policies that form closer relationships between the organizati
marketplace.
Eng, T.-Y. (2008) Customer Portfolio Planning in a Business Network Context, Journal
Management, 24 (5/6), pp 567–87

Further Reading

This provides you with an extensive overview and guide to key articles to continue your study.

Guide to the Online Resource Centre

 www.oxfordtextbooks.co.uk/orc/ellis/

The Online Resource Centre (ORC) has material for students and lecturers.

End-of-chapter features

Web links

Find out more about B2B marketing with this range of useful online resources, from particular organizational examples of B2B marketing and trade associations, to sources of market information and B2B careers opportunities.

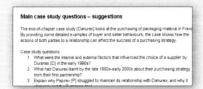

Additional case studies with questions

These additional case studies offer a chance to explore key B2B marketing issues in more depth. Cases come from around the world, a range of types of organizations, and a number of contributors; they give you a chance to engage at a more theoretical level with B2B marketing. The questions explore contexts and issues that could not be fully covered in the textbook itself and introduce you to contemporary research.

Wider reading

This feature represents examples of scholarly work on important aspects of B2B marketing and serves as a good starting point for further study.

Material available for lecturers

Lecture notes

After studying this chapter, your students should be able to:
- Recognize some key characteristics of organizational markets
- Compare and contrast consumer and organizational buyer behaviour (OBB)
- Appreciate the many influences on industrial purchasing decisions
- Understand processes of organizational decision making

The chapter begins by outlining the typical types of organizational markets to which suppliers of their products and services. These include markets comprising private and public sector organizational customers. The next section indicates the similarities as well as key differences between consumer buyer behaviour and OBB. While grasping some characteristics that distinguish B2B markets, students will also see what business marketers can learn from consu

Lecture notes

These are designed to help you organize and deliver your course. They include learning objectives, key points, and methods for teaching different types of courses on B2B marketing.

Summary questions – suggestions

1. List the major similarities and differences between organizational and consumer buyer behaviour? What insights into contemporary practices in OBB might we gain from the st of consumer culture theory?
   For some responses to this question, see the 'Learning from organizational and consumer buyer behaviour' section, especially Fig 2.3. For the second part of the question see Fig 2.2
2. What internal organizational influences are thought to affect a firm's purchasing decision How can the style of leadership within the DMU affect such decisions?
   See the 'Influences on organizational demand' section, including Fig 2.4, 'Interna influences' subsection, and Box 2.7. For the second question see 'Individual' an Relationship influences' subsections, particularly the last paragraph of the latter

Summary questions

These questions are geared to take an overview of the topic so you can test students' knowledge and come with guideline answers.

Main case study questions – suggestions

The end-of-chapter case study (Danurex) looks at the purchasing of packaging material in Fran By providing some detailed examples of buyer and seller behaviours, the case shows how the actions of both parties to a relationship can affect the success of a purchasing strategy.

Case study questions
1. What were the internal and external factors that influenced the choice of a supplier by Duranex (D) in the early 1990s?
2. What had Danurex learnt by the late 1990s-early 2000s about their purchasing strategy from their first partnership?
3. Explain why Papirex (P) struggled to maintain its relationship with Danurex, and why it ultimately lost the European deal.

Main case study questions

These suggest more focused and in-depth questions you can ask students about the main case study featured in each chapter of the book, along with suggested answers.

Additional seminar exercises

1. Voices from the textile machinery sector

Here are some further quotes from the managers in the main case study from Chapter 1 (W Perks). These quotes can be introduced to seminars to provoke **discussions** and to make students think back to this introductory case as they progress through the book

The first shows how customer firms view the risks involved in purchasing large capital items, wh the second illustrates the importance of understanding the DMU for WP's highly technical products.

a. Ian: 'The contract for this sale should have been signed months ago, but once you get t finance people and lawyers (from the customer firm) involved, it all drags on because the need to be sure of what they're doing.'

Additional seminar exercises

Each chapter is accompanied by a number of seminar exercises to help students engage and understand the key issues of B2B marketing. These are more complex and potentially group-based.

Assignment suggestion

Taking sources such as these articles as examples (as well as the Cova and Sale (2008) article cited in the textbook), students could be asked to write an **essay** debating the extent to which marketing scholarship should treat B2B and B2C contexts as fundamentally different

Fern, EF & Brown, JR (1984) The industrial/consumer marketing dichotomy: a case of insufficient justification, *Journal of Marketing*, 48 (Spring): pp 68-78

Lichtenthal, JD & Mummalaneni, V (2009) Commentary: Relative presence of business-business research in the marketing literature: review and future directions, *Journal of Business-to-Business Marketing*, 16 (1-2): pp 40-54

Assignment suggestion

For each chapter, there are also assignment suggestions for students to complete.

Examination question suggestions

1 Questions 3 and 4 from the Summary Questions at the end of Chapter 2 should constitute appropriate examination topics. Indeed, they could be combined by asking students to explain the concepts of both the DMU and Buy Phases for a particular purchase situation

2 An additional question that addresses some of the issues in this chapter Drawing on generic and/or specific examples, describe the different types of organizational customers that exist, and the many influences on industrial purchasing decisions may differ

Examination question suggestions

Examination questions allow you to give students a taste of what to expect from an exam so they are fully prepared.

Lecture notes

After studying this chapter, your students should be able to:
- Recognize some key characteristics of organizational markets
- Compare and contrast consumer and organizational buyer behaviour (OBB)
- Appreciate the many influences on industrial purchasing decisions
- Understand processes of organizational decision making

The chapter begins by outlining the typical types of organizational markets to which suppliers of their products and services. These include markets comprising private and public sector organizational customers. The next section indicates the similarities as well as key differences between consumer buyer behaviour and OBB. While grasping some characteristics that distinguish B2B markets, students will also see what business marketers can learn from consu

Lecture slides

A suite of customizable PowerPoint® slides has been provided to use in your lecture presentations.

Part One
The Organizational Marketing Context

Part One: The Organizational Marketing Context

1. The Significance of B2B Marketing
- Significance of B2B Marketing
- Supply/Demand Chains
- Organizational Markets
- Significance of Relationships & Networks
- Supply Chain Ethics

2. Organizational Buying Behaviour
- Types of Markets
- Organizational & Consumer Buyer Behaviour
- Influences on Demand
- Organizational Decision-Making

Part Two: Inter-Organizational Relationships & Networks

3. Inter-Organizational Relationships
- Market & Relational Exchange
- CRM
- Partnerships & Alliances
- How IORs 'Work' in Different Contexts

4. Marketing Channels & Supply Chains
- Structure & Role of Channels
- Flows & Blockages in Channels
- From Channels to Chains
- Marketing Logistics

5. Industrial Networks
- The Interaction Approach
- From Channels & Chains to Networks
- Learning from the Industrial Network View

Part Three: Business Marketing Planning

6. B2B Marketing Planning & Analysis
- Planning & S/DCM
- The Planning Process
- Situation Analysis
- Sources & Assessing Market Potential
- B2B Market Segmentation

7. B2B Strategies & Implementation
- Market Positioning
- B2B Branding
- Making Strategy Decisions
- Issues of Implementation

> These 6 chapters can also be effectively combined as the 'marketing mix'

Part Four: Business Marketing Programmes

8. Business Products
- Classifying Business Products
- Managing Business Products
- New Product Development

9. Business Services
- Classifying Business Services
- Characteristics of Business Services
- B2B Services Marketing Management

10. Value & Pricing
- Value in Organizational Markets
- Making Pricing Decisions
- B2B Pricing Strategies (incl. Web-based activities)

11. Marketing Communications
- Communication Strategies
- Elements of the Communications Mix
- Relative Effectiveness of B2B Media (incl. the Internet)

12. Personal Selling & Sales Management
- Personal Selling in B2B Markets
- Organizing the Sales Force
- Key Account Management (KAM)

Chapter 1
The Significance of B2B Marketing

Introduction & Learning Objectives

This book takes the view that business markets and business-to-business (B2B) marketing are quite simply part of what every aspiring manager needs to know. This claim stems from the fact that purchases by organizations account for well over half the economic activity in industrialized countries, with individual companies such as General Motors (www.gm.com) spending billions of dollars annually on goods and services. Indeed, some leading marketing writers estimate that in areas like e-commerce, B2B activity is 10 to 15 times greater than business-to-consumer (B2C) (Kotler, 2003). This suggests that any students graduating without understanding how these pervasive business markets work, how business purchases are made, and, crucially, how to market to organizational customers are somehow missing something (Barclay et al, 2007).

The purpose of this chapter is to introduce you to the field of B2B marketing and its importance in today's business environment. The chapter sets out the key issues we shall be exploring in greater detail as the book progresses. You might ask why a whole book on B2B marketing is needed – isn't it just another version of B2C marketing? Well, although there are similarities between B2B and B2C marketing, there are major differences too.

Consider the diamond industry in the Box 1.1 mini case. The significance of B2B marketing can be shown by considering that for every consumer (or 'end-user') market, there are typically several 'upstream' organizations which must deal with each other in products and services before anything is ultimately consumed. Sometimes, as in the case of diamonds, end users can be both consumers and other firms. The product has to pass through a chain of different organizations to reach both customer segments. Each of these organizations tries to 'add value' (see section 1.2) through processes like polishing and cutting, as well as designing and retailing, from the time the diamond is found in the ground to the point of sale.

Box 1.1 Mini case
The global diamond market

Diamond mining and distribution are big business. Among the world's biggest producers are Russia, Botswana, and Australia, each of which produces over 20 billion carats (a carat is a weight of 0.2 grammes) a year. It takes considerable investment: the time taken between discovering a diamond deposit and opening a mine is typically eight years.

Mining is just the start, however. Before they can be sold to a distributor or dealer, diamonds have to be cleaned and sorted: only about 20% actually go on to be used in jewellery manufacture, and thence down the marketing channel to retailers and the end consumer.

Organizational use takes up 80% of diamond production. The main industrial uses of diamonds include cutting tools, abrasives, and powder for grinding and polishing. Even though diamonds are expensive, the material is so long-lasting that it is worth the cost to the buying firm. Industrial diamonds are sold to companies working in the stone, ceramic, metal, and concrete industries. Diamonds are also used by manufacturers of pistons for aluminium-alloy car engines, computer chips, and surgical blades.

Thus, although marketing (via retailers) to consumers can be an important part of a diamond distributor's role (e.g. the famous 'a diamond is forever' advertising slogan, used by De Beers), knowing how to purchase and then resell the right sorts of diamonds from mining producers to satisfy the needs of a huge variety of organizational customers is actually a much more important set of activities for most distributors. Their business customers are far less likely to be persuaded by a stylish promotional message than is a consumer buying an engagement ring.

Source: Van der Gaag (2006); www.debeersgroup.com

The market for diamonds may be a slightly unusual example, given the current dominance of one company (De Beers) at various levels in the supply chain. Nevertheless, research shows that the significance of this 'cartel network' is lessening (Gupta et al, 2010). The bargaining power of intermediaries (such as distributors) is increasing, and external forces triggered by the illegal diamond trade, such as international regulatory constraints, no longer favour cartels like De Beers. This means that cartels which previously relied on hand-picked intermediaries in highly controlled networks to market their products are having to adopt a more flexible market-focused approach. These shifts in the commercial landscape illustrate why understanding B2B marketing is so important. This book aims to show how you might attempt to manage the complex network of buying and selling relationships between different types of organizations in business markets, organizations like the mining firms, distributors, manufacturers, and retailers highlighted in Box 1.1.

Chapter Aims

After completing this chapter, you should be able to:

- Understand the significance of B2B marketing in the global economy
- Explain the relevance of the supply/demand chain and value chain concepts for B2B marketers
- Recognize some key characteristics of business markets
- Appreciate the importance of inter-organizational relationships and networks in B2B marketing
- Debate how ethical issues in business marketing and purchasing can affect members of the supply chain.

1.1 The Significance of B2B Marketing

There are many reasons why B2B marketing knowledge should be important to students of management, not least of which is the fact that the majority of them will go on to work in firms whose primary customers are other organizations (Barclay et al, 2007). The importance of B2B marketing is also recognized by key business thinkers and practitioners. Listen to the opinion of leading management 'guru' Martha Rogers (co-founder of Peppers & Rogers Group, the partnership that coined the term 'customer relationship management'), who states: 'With the rise of customer focus, the B2C world has borrowed a lot from B2B. Now you can do for thousands of people what B2B has done for years' (*The Marketer*, 2008, p 50). Consider the profound shift in corporate mindset necessary when IBM (www.ibm.com) recently sold their entire personal computer division to the Chinese company, Lenovo, allowing one of their marketing directors, Lee Green, to announce to an audience that included the author of this textbook, 'We are a B2B company,' at a US seminar on innovation through collaboration (Green, 2008).

What might being a 'B2B company' entail? To set you thinking, here are some fascinating facts from the world of inter-organizational buying and selling:

- Organizational customers in the public sector have massive buying power. Purchased goods and services account for one-third of total public spending, or about 5–8% of GDP in most Organization for Economic Co-operation and Development (OECD) countries (Husted and Reinecke, 2009).

- Some B2B brands are also big spenders. Global management and technology consulting firm Anderson Consulting relaunched itself as 'Accenture' (www.accenture.com) at the start of this century at a cost of $175 million on advertising alone. This was thought to be the most expensive B2B rebranding in history (Gray, 2008).

- Speaking of history, B2B relationships have long been important in trade. The supply chain for frankincense and myrrh to the Mediterranean was controlled by an Arabian tribe, the Nabataeans, from the ancient city of Petra nearly 2,000 years ago. They managed a hub-and-spoke structure, with trading partnerships and value-added services in a striking resemblance to how supply chains are set up today (Hull, 2008).

Now, look at the organization outlined in Box 1.2. You may not have heard of this firm, but think of the strategic decisions Cargill must weigh up as it attempts to serve its many business markets. A detailed understanding is needed of the demand/supply chains for all these products and of the planning required to try to ensure their efficient function; yet, Cargill's B2B strategies are played out very much 'behind the scenes' of everyday consumer experiences.

Box 1.2 Mini case
The B2B activities behind Cargill's business

In recent years, Cargill has been the largest private company in the US, with revenues of around £55 billion in 2007. Although the firm does not comment on its market shares in what are predominantly B2B markets, reports suggest Cargill and its two largest rivals control nearly 75% of the global market in soya; and Cargill is the largest crusher of oilseed in the world. As one of its brochures asserts, 'We buy, trade, transport, blend, mill, crush, process, refine, season, distribute around the clock, around the globe.' The firm's products end up as flour in bread, wheat in noodles, corn in tortillas, oil in salad dressing, and the meat on people's tables. Yet, as Lawrence (2008, p 265) says, 'Cargill has no consumer face. Few people in Britain have heard of it.'

Source: Lawrence (2008); www.cargill.com

So, where does B2B marketing fit into this challenging (and often hidden) world of organizational markets?

Defining B2B marketing

The term 'business-to-business marketing' is used to describe the marketing activities of any kind of organization which has exchange relationships with other organizations or businesses (Turnbull, 1994). To explain some of the other terms that you will find in this book, we can plot the development of B2B marketing as a discipline within the broad field of marketing, roughly as depicted in Figure 1.1.

- The origins of B2B marketing as an area of academic research lie mainly in the study of marketing in an industrial (as opposed to consumer) context in the 1960s and 1970s when the subject was typically referred to as 'industrial marketing'.

- However, the term 'industrial' did not convey the scope of marketing between service organizations not engaged primarily in manufacturing, so during the 1980s and 1990s the title of 'business-to-business (B2B) marketing' emerged.

- More recently, it has been argued that the principles of marketing are appropriate to any organization, from charities and hospitals to government departments, and thus the term 'organizational marketing' is also becoming used across both private and public sectors.

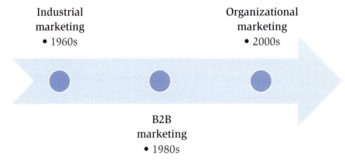

B2B marketing = *the marketing activities of any kind of organization which has exchange relationships with other organizations or businesses* (Turnbull, 1994)

Figure 1.1 The development of the B2B marketing discipline

This book will therefore generally use the term 'organization', but will also refer to a 'business' or a 'firm', especially when discussing buyers and sellers in industrial networks where goods and finances are typically exchanged in order to achieve a profit.

The context of most B2B marketing activities is the trade between the supplying and buying organizations that make up what is commonly called 'the supply chain', but which is becoming known as 'the demand chain' (see section 1.2). This metaphorical concept links the marketplace, the distribution network, the manufacturing process, and the procurement (or purchasing) activity, ideally in such a way that customers are serviced at higher levels and yet at a lower cost (see Chapter Four). Note that by 'customer' we mean the party who actually buys the products as distinct from the consumer. As Christopher (1997) states, the importance of this distinction is that much of marketing investment in the past has been aimed at consumers and not at the organizational customer. Because of the shift in the balance of power in distribution channels for most products, especially in Western grocery markets (i.e. from manufacturer to reseller), it is important that we recognize that customers (i.e. other organizations), not just consumers, have goals that they seek to achieve. The role of the supplier is to help their corporate customers achieve those goals. Thus we see the importance of B2B or organizational marketing.

An example of a B2B marketing success story with a direct impact on B2C marketing is provided in Box 1.3. Note here, too, how B2B marketing communication strategies can differ from B2C markets, as shown in the MD's attitude to TV advertising – more on these sorts of decisions will be found in Chapter Eleven.

The significance of B2B marketing for the customer and supplier organizations involved in such markets should be clear. You should also note the overall significance of organizational markets to national economies. For example, the Caribbean island of Dominica relies for 60% of its exports on bananas, marketed to buyers representing supermarkets in the

Box 1.3 Mini case

Ice-cream machinery

The Italian firm, Carpigiani, manufactures ice-cream-making machinery for organizational customers in over 100 countries. These include fast-food chains like Pizza Hut and McDonald's as well as several large franchise chains such as Cold Stone, which runs nearly 1,500 stores in America and East Asia. Carpigiani claims to have around half the global market for ice-cream makers, giving it profits of €163 million in 2006. It employs 500 people. The MD believes that this success is down to a recent focus on customer service, quality, and new product development. Pointedly, he has stopped television advertising, seeing it as what he terms 'an extravagance' for a machinery manufacturer. The firm uses outsourcing and its four factories are essentially assembly lines since few parts are made 'in-house'. An emphasis on Research and Development (R&D) has been especially important since poor materials from suppliers had caused problems in the past. This is vital in meeting the strict regulations for food-making machinery in countries like the US.

Source: The Economist (2007); www.carpigiani.com

US and Europe. The income of over 10% of the country's population is directly dependent on selling this crop. This requires significant effort from the marketing personnel who represent banana growers, exporters, and wholesalers/ripeners (Ransom, 2006). More information on the importance of these sorts of international issues can be found on the United Nation's Conference on Trade and Development website (www.unctad.org).

Ultimately, all organizations buy and sell goods and/or services in order to create their own offerings. Having added value in this way, firms then sell these products to other businesses which use them to create other products (as in the case of ice-cream-making machinery) or to resell as finished goods (as in the case of ripened bananas). Although much B2B marketing and purchasing are effectively carried out 'back stage' for the average consumer transaction, it is fair to say that business markets are generally larger than consumer markets; organizations trade in more products and services than consumers; and the B2B exchanges that occur between organizations have a greater impact on the lives of people than B2C transactions (see Box 1.4).

Of course, B2B markets don't just take the form of Western firms selling to customers in less-developed nations. For instance, you should remember that the majority of the world's manufacturing labour force is now situated in export-processing zones located in some of the most heavily populated regions of the globe. This means that millions of people work for organizations in Mexico and Central America, as well as the Philippines, Indonesia, and China, through to India, Pakistan, and Morocco, organizations which are dependent on the success of their B2B marketing efforts to other manufacturers and retailers worldwide. We shall encounter some of these firms as we progress through this book.

Box 1.4 Number crunching

Power generation in Africa

Providing electrical power is no easy matter in Africa: the continent accounts for over a sixth of the world's population but generates only 4% of global electricity. The demand for power grows as factories and shopping centres are constructed in countries like Nigeria where it is estimated that only 17 out of 79 power stations built in the 1970s and 1980s are still working. Power cuts are a frequent reality of life in Africa – inconvenient if you are trying to do your shopping, but catastrophic if you are facing hospital surgery. The impact of a firm supplying back-up generators to governments and power companies in such conditions is thus considerable.

Aggreko, based in Scotland, is the world's biggest supplier of temporary electricity in this form. It meets almost 50% of Uganda's power needs and 10% of those in Kenya and Tanzania. Thanks to the continuing demand for their products throughout the globe (in 90 countries at the last count), Aggreko's revenues soared by 42% in 2006–7. Further growth seems likely since developing counties continue to have infrastructure limitations in meeting power demands, while developed countries are holding ever-larger outdoor events such as the 2008 Olympic Games where Aggreko was the exclusive provider of temporary power.

Source: Dewson (2007); www.agrekko.com

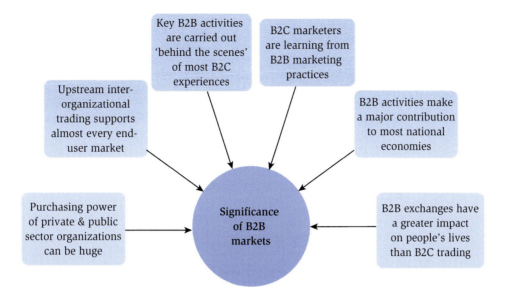

Figure 1.2 The significance of B2B markets

Some of the main points from the preceding discussion are summarized in Figure 1.2. The significance of B2B markets is so obvious that you might think it hardly needs to be stated, yet as Wilson has observed (1999, p 16), 'organizational marketing still seems to be treated as a peripheral variation of marketing in most textbooks, perhaps meriting a chapter or two once the more important issues of consumer marketing have been covered'. It is exactly this type of misperception that this book is designed to overcome!

B2B marketing management

The book assumes that B2B marketing is best understood in terms of evolving relationships between organizations, i.e. in terms of continuing interactions, rather than as a sequence of encounters where 'manipulative' suppliers engage with 'suspicious' customers. It treats organizations as social actors that effectively 'consume'. The buying and selling of goods on behalf of these organizations are carried out by interacting managers who do not consume the products and services themselves.

Underpinning this conceptualization is the recognition of marketing and purchasing managers as individuals with personal objectives, competing demands on their attention and some personal power, rather than the usual portrayal in the marketing literature of the manager as a strictly rational servant enacting corporate policies. This recognition is crucial in appreciating the difference between 'recommended best practice' (i.e. what some textbooks or theories claim) and 'optimal practice' (i.e. what can reasonably be expected from hard-pressed managers).

Indeed, an industrial network perspective (see Chapter Five) of business markets, with social actors (individuals and organizations) dependent on interactions with other actors all seeking different things from their relationships, suggests that B2B marketers and their firms

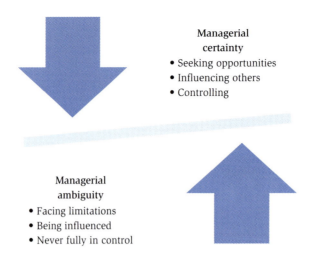

**Managerial
certainty**
- Seeking opportunities
- Influencing others
- Controlling

**Managerial
ambiguity**
- Facing limitations
- Being influenced
- Never fully in control

Figure 1.3 **Paradoxes facing managers and firms in industrial networks**

face three paradoxes (Håkansson and Ford, 2002). As Figure 1.3 indicates, these paradoxes render managers as social actors attempting to practise 'management' in situations that are characterized as simultaneously framed by a degree of certainty yet underpinned by a sense of ambiguity:

- Seeking opportunities and then facing limitations
- Influencing others and yet being influenced themselves
- Controlling but never being fully in control in network situations.

Coping with this context is clearly quite a challenge. So what do B2B marketing managers do, and where do they do it? Box 1.5 gives some examples of the sorts of jobs you might find yourself in if you decide to work in this fascinating field. These advertisements probably contain some marketing management terms that are familiar to you but others that are rather less so. Some of the roles entail knowledge that the average B2C marketer may never have to develop (for example, how many times do consumers ever buy plastic resin?). As we progress through this book, you will begin to see what some of these responsibilities mean in the context of B2B relationships within supply/demand chains and networks, and, furthermore, why these employers need people with such sophisticated skills.

Box 1.5 also shows how people with initial training in non-marketing disciplines often gravitate to B2B marketing roles, where they can combine their technical know-how with

Box 1.5 Food for thought

B2B job advertisements in the European business press

1. *VP Marketing, Software Solutions (via recruitment agency) (Marketing Week, 2007)*:
   This ad describes the recruiting firm as a global leader in software solutions for financial services, higher education, and the public sector. The role involves responsibility for researching industry reports, competitor analysis, 'positioning primary brands in the relevant market and creating sales tools', overseeing 'client communication, through

interactive marketing, newsletter, user groups, client conferences and meetings', developing 'business partnerships with consultants, hardware providers, industry bodies and other software vendors', and being capable of working closely with other areas of the business. Applicants need to have had exposure to complex B2B sales processes and the ability to write messages for technical audiences.

2. *Business Projects Manager, Home-Grown Cereals Authority (HGCA) (The Guardian, 2007)*: The HGCA is a private company whose mission is to improve the production and marketing of UK grain. It provides market information, promotes exports, and helps to develop products using cereals. It also 'informs UK growers, traders and plant breeders of overseas buyers' needs'. The advertised role involves 'co-ordinating cereal supply chain and marketing messages and communicating them to all parts of the cereals industry'. It adds, 'understanding the supply chain is essential to the role', along with 'direct knowledge of the agribusiness and food and drink industries', and a degree in food marketing or agribusiness.

3. *Graduate Training Programme, Resin Express (The Guardian, 2007)*: The firm describes itself as the UK division of the international plastics manufacturer, Ravago, which has a $5 billion worldwide turnover. The advertisement explains that the firm's customers are major manufacturing companies in the UK, including 'household names and Blue Chip companies' making a variety of products in the automotive, electronic, medical, consumer goods, and packaging industries. The firm's suppliers are international companies like GE and Dow. The role means 'you would be in daily contact with both customers and suppliers'. The company promises in-depth training at their Belgium head office and at their suppliers' headquarters. Candidates are expected to have a degree, 'preferably technical, chemistry, engineering etc', but it is not essential to be qualified in these disciplines.

an understanding of organizational markets gleaned from books such as this one. Hence, this book will help readers with prior knowledge of general marketing concepts to specialize in the challenging yet rewarding area of B2B; and it will also be extremely useful for prospective managers with a more scientific/engineering background who are seeking to move into marketing-related jobs.

1.2 The Significance of Supply/Demand & Value Chains

Supply/demand chains

As we have seen, a number of firms are typically linked through buying and selling activities in B2B markets. This is the case whether other firms are end users, or whether the end users ultimately comprise B2C markets. Although other terms are also used (such as 'channel' or 'pipeline', see Chapter Four), the business system represented by a series of inter-organizational relationships set up to support the buying and selling of goods has come to be termed the 'supply chain'. According to Svensson (2003, p 306), supply chain management (SCM) can be seen as 'a management philosophy that strives to integrate the dependent activities, actors, and resources into marketing channels between point-of-origin and the point-of-final-consumption'. We will discuss the concepts of activities, actors, and resources in more detail in Chapter Five when we turn our attention to industrial networks.

The idea of SCM was coined in the early 1980s by logistics consultants (Oliver and Webber, 1982), who viewed the chain as a single entity with strategic decision-making at the 'top' of the chain needed to manage it. This viewpoint is still shared by many channel theorists in marketing (Weitz and Jap, 1995), despite the growing power of 'downstream' channel actors such as retail supermarkets. Now, however, a new business model is emerging known as 'demand chain management' (DCM). DCM is more closely aligned to B2B marketing than SCM as it starts with specific customer needs and attempts to design the chain to serve those needs, instead of starting with the supplier/manufacturer and working 'forwards' as in SCM (Juttner et al, 2007). In order to reflect this customer-driven perspective, throughout this book we shall usually be referring to 'supply/demand chains' when we mean what many commentators would simply refer to as a supply chain. Similarly, instead of talking about SCM, we shall more often use the abbreviation S/DCM.

A typical supply/demand chain, here in the car (automobile) sector, might be represented as shown in Figure 1.4. The flow of goods linking this chain is from top to bottom. Other factors that serve to integrate the chain are flows of money and information, and attempts at managerial coordination and chain leadership by a focal firm. Note how B2B marketing takes place between all the actors in the chain, and how B2C marketing can also occur when the end user is a consumer, rather than an organizational, customer.

As well as the vertical depiction in Figure 1.4, it is also common to represent supply/ demand chains horizontally, with goods flowing from left to right. You will see this done in other parts of this book. Both ways of drawing supply chains are perfectly acceptable,

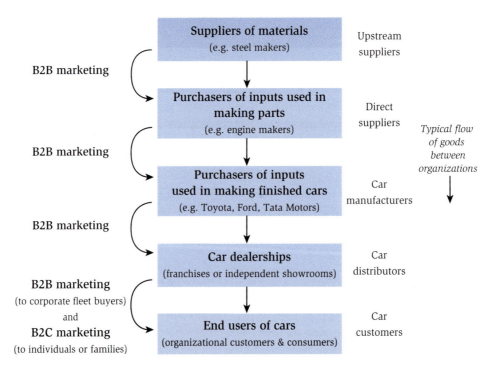

Figure 1.4 A supply/demand chain for cars

although a vertical representation lends itself better to notions of 'up' stream suppliers and 'down' stream distributors and customers in relation to the focal firm, typically a manufacturer. The vertical imagery also seems to be commonly utilized by managers to draw perceptual 'pictures' to help them make sense of the industrial networks that they believe their organization to be embedded in (Henneberg et al, 2006).

Value chains

A requirement of the supply/demand chain is that each participating firm adds value in some way to the goods flowing down it. We saw this in our opening discussion of the diamond case in Box 1.1. But why are these processes of adding value so important? For a business customer, value is determined by the net satisfaction derived from any transaction, and not simply the costs of obtaining the goods or services concerned. We will explore notions or value in more detail in Chapter Ten. For now, note that value is relative to the customer's expectations and experience of other offerings within any product category, such as alternative (perhaps cheaper) sources of goods or services. Competing firms attempt to offer enhanced value to their potential customers through activities such as product design, flexibility of production, marketing, and service in the form of delivery and after-sales support.

These activities are referred to by Porter (1985) as the 'value chain'. This model arranges key functional elements of the firm from left to right as goods pass through the organization, much like the horizontal representations of the supply chain we have just discussed. All the activities summarized in the idea of a value chain (see Figure 1.5) have the potential to incur

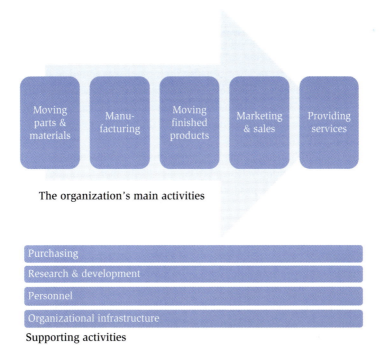

Figure 1.5 Elements of a typical value chain

cost but, crucially, also to create value. Thus, primary activities such as bringing materials or components into the firm, converting them into products or services, shipping them out to customers, and providing marketing and servicing facilities, along with secondary activities such as the appropriate purchasing of materials, should all be combined to reduce cost or improve performance, such that customers perceive they are gaining superior value.

Note how these activities are thought to happen inside the firm. The notion of the value chain can be taken beyond its original internal context to embrace how organizations can join together to provide a consistent stream of resources for their customers. In this way, a supply/demand chain is formed, a chain that offers each business within it the opportunity to gain value, e.g. upstream from lower costs and improved reliability of supply; to down-stream speed of servicing or access to new markets. For the B2B marketing manager, this means that a host of issues, like post-purchase support, pricing, marketing communications, and logistics, can be examined to see how they could improve the value perceptions of the organizational customer.

Value can also be destroyed by poor S/DCM, as the cases in Box 1.6 highlight. What responsibility do you think managers working in marketing and purchasing at the various links in these supply chains have for these incidents?

Box 1.6 Food for thought

What can happen when supply/demand chains are not properly managed

Headlines around the world announced the decision of the major toy manufacturer, Mattel, to recall over 18 million of its products in the middle of 2007. Sadly for suppliers in China who had spent years building up their reputations as good supply chain partners, the actions of some firms meant that relationships between business customers worldwide and their 8,000 Chinese suppliers were being called into question. The Mattel toys included die-cast cars from the Pixar film, *Cars*, recalled because their paint was found to contain lead. Also removed from retailers' shelves were toys containing small magnets that can come loose, such as Polly Pocket and Batman Magna sets. The company blamed the potentially danger-ous amount of lead in the paint on a subcontracted Chinese firm called Hong Li Da which used paint from unauthorized suppliers.

Given that so many other companies source in China, and the probability that the local paint supplier did not just supply Hong Li Da, it is likely that there are other companies which may be discovering their products have some serious shortcomings. Unfortunately, these supply chain scares were not confined to the toy market. A number of Chinese-manufactured products have caused alarm both at home and abroad, including pet food tainted with melamine, toothpaste with diethylene glycol and truck tyres with a fault that could cause blowouts.

The anonymous nature of firms like Hong Li Da's arrangements with its more high-profile customers enables the firm to win contracts from several competing foreign companies. It also suits their clients who do not always want consumers to know, for example, that a Taiwanese contractor named Yue Yuen produces shoes for Adidas, Puma, and Nike. The actions of some brand-name companies in demanding ever-lower prices and changes to pro-duction volume at short notice, without asking too many questions about how these targets are achieved, might even be contributing to the actions of their suppliers. Now, however, the issue of quality control may mean that some Chinese suppliers will be more open about their own supply chains in order to try to distinguish themselves from their more suspect rivals.

Source: BBC News (2007); Clark (2007); www.yueyuen.com

1.3 Some Characteristics of Organizational Markets

Fundamentally, B2B marketing managers must recognize that most organizational buyers are focused on helping their firms (or institutions) to increase sales or lower costs, often via improving efficiency or by purchasing cheaper goods or services. These, along with the frequent need to meet government regulations, are the driving forces behind most business markets. Recognizing these forces means that we can identify some of the key characteristics of such markets. More on this topic will be found in Chapter Two, but for now we briefly introduce several factors thought to contribute to the nature of the organizational market-place, and which lead to a number of implications for the skills set of B2B marketers.

The size of the market

From the cases you have already explored in Chapter One, you should have come to realize that the sheer number of transactions needed to provide end customers with a taken-for-granted product like a car or an ice cream means that the B2B market is larger than the B2C market. It is generally believed that in the US, more than half of all jobs and associated economic activities are in upstream markets (Lichtenthal, 2007). Of course, the good news for students studying B2B marketing is that there are therefore more job opportunities in the organizational marketing sector than in consumer marketing! For instance, even universities are starting to offer positions like the 'Head of Business to Business Marketing' recently advertised by Sheffield Hallam University in the UK, which is seeking a manager 'to work with small business, national and international blue chip companies to identify opportunities to market our research projects' (*Marketing*, 2008, p 46).

International aspects

B2B marketing is increasingly taking place on a global scale. Compared with B2C markets, where tastes and culture can have a massive impact on the acceptability of goods across borders, B2B products are much less diverse in terms of functionality and performance – industrial diamonds for cutting tools are a good example. Similarly, trading associations have been instrumental in setting agreed standards for certain industries across the world such as steel, plastics, and chemicals. For example, the International Council of Chemical Trade Associations represents over 1,500 chemical distributors globally, allowing them to exchange information and best practices (www.iccta.org). The technological influence of the Internet and other modes of communication have also facilitated international communication between trading organizations. All this offers firms considerable opportunities to market their goods and services to organizational customers worldwide, something that firms in the Philippines have been keen to take advantage of (see Box 1.7). Note how B2B activities in a variety of sectors are contributing to the nation's economic development.

Box 1.7 Number crunching

The Philippines economy and B2B markets

B2B exports from the Philippines, especially to China, are an important part of that nation's economic recovery. The economy has grown by at least 5% in each of the years since 2004. This growth has come from a number of sources. Texas Instruments recently chose the Philippines for a £600 million electronics factory, and Hanjin (a South Korean shipbuilder) plans to spend £1 billion on its Philippines shipyard. Mining firms have also begun to develop the islands' untapped mineral resources. In addition, firms in the country are becoming the main rivals to India's in providing business process outsourcing services, and now host call centres for many US organizations.

Source: The Economist (2007); www.hanjin.com; www.ti.com

Concentration of buyer power

Consumer markets can consist of millions of individuals, whereas far fewer customers make up organizational markets. It is quite common for a few of these customers to account for a large share of the spending in a particular segment. For instance, B2B marketers representing cocoa producers need to be aware of the concentration of organizational buying power in the English-speaking world, and what these firms want. Buyers representing the firms which dominate the UK marketplace for chocolate (Cadbury, Mars, and Nestlé) and the US (Hershey, Kraft, plus Mars, and Nestlé, too) are seeking a relatively cheap product with a low proportion of cocoa solids. Thanks to achieving 75% of the sales in these markets, the near-monopolistic power that these few firms have over the supply chain for commodities like cocoa is significant. Moreover, following the further consolidation in the chocolate sector seen by Kraft's (www.kraftfoods.co.uk) recent takeover of Cadbury, the influence of these firms is set to increase (Allen and Ridley, 2010) A similar concentration of buyer power is found in the UK coffee market, where just two firms, Nestlé (www.nestle.com) and Kraft General Foods, have over 78% market share between them (Ransom, 2006).

The nature of demand

Demand for many B2B products is derived from sales to the end user. If consumers of ice cream develop a preference for a certain type of low-fat ice cream or for food that is more hygienically produced, then ice-cream machine manufacturers will have to respond to these demands as they pass up the supply chain from retailers and restaurants. Whilst a company like Carpigiani may, as we have seen in Box 1.3, have the expertise to design new machinery to stimulate market demand, it can also find itself forced to do so to meet the wishes of its organizational customers as they ensure that their own customers' wishes are met. The impact of factors further beyond the control of such a manufacturer can also be significant, meaning that demand can be hugely variable: witness the disastrous sales of ice cream in Northern Europe in the summers of 2007 and 2009, when the lack of sunshine kept tourists away from ice-cream vendors who then saw no need to upgrade their equipment for those seasons.

Box 1.8 Mini case

Latin American business buying processes

The views of chief executives in Latin America reported in a recent survey suggest that the buying decisions made by their firms are underpinned by a high degree of risk. Most of these risks are due to the economic environment rather than concerns over the performance of suppliers. Nevertheless, they point to a need for B2B marketers to understand the implications for relationships between firms in countries like Brazil and Argentina. Fears amongst financial officers exist over hugely varying regulations (in areas such as licensing agreements and tax laws), foreign exchange rates, and fluctuations in commodity prices. These fears seem to reflect the prominence of cyclical, export-driven industries, like agriculture, mining, and energy, in the region's economy. To mitigate these perceived risks, purchasing managers commonly impose strict performance contracts on supplier organizations.

Source: Krishnan et al (2007)

Buying processes and decision-making

While the B2C buying process can be fairly complex over the purchase of things like a family holiday, B2B organizational buying processes typically involve more people than B2C purchases. Members of this group can include managers not directly involved with using the goods, but who have a particular financial perspective of the purchase – see Box 1.8, which shows that marketers selling to Latin American organizations may need to work hard to persuade finance officers of their firm's credibility.

Moreover, decisions are generally more rational in the business buying process than in B2C markets. As well as financial considerations, they are also usually driven by technical specifications. These issues will be analysed in more detail in Chapter Two. For the moment, a sense of the type of decisions made by organizational clients can be gained by examining the criteria contained in the bids for major contracts that are often put out by governments – see Box 1.9. Managers working for any prospective firms hoping to win this particular

---

Box 1.9 Food for thought

Bids in Tanzania

A full-page advertisement in a leading business magazine announced an Invitation for Bids issued by Tanzania's Ministry of Justice and Constitutional Affairs. The ad invited bids from organizations wishing to tender for the contract to digitize the paper records of the country's Registration, Insolvency and Trusteeship Agency (RITA). The government stressed that the digitization of these records was part of its 'business environment strengthening' programme, jointly funded by the World Bank. The ad listed a number of 'qualification requirements' for what it called Bid Number RITA/03, including: financial capability; audited financial statements; previous experience in carrying out similar assignments; a technical team; and, crucially, that the 'goods supplied have the capacity to scan in excess of ten million records over a period of three years'. Other requirements included the provision of signed CVs of key personnel, power of attorney and an 'anti-bribery statement'.

Source: The Economist (2007)

contract clearly have a lot of preparatory work to do in order to meet these demanding financial, technical, and legal criteria.

Implications for marketing management

The characteristics of B2B markets outlined in this section, as summarized in Figure 1.6, will affect how the traditional marketing mix (or 'the 4Ps', i.e. product, price, promotion, and place) is deployed by managers.

The classic elements of the marketing mix for organizational customers will mainly be discussed in Chapters Eight to Twelve of this book, where we shall look at strategies for managing products (goods and services), pricing (and value), and promotion (communications and personal selling). Marketing channels (effectively the place 'P') are covered a little earlier, in Chapter Four where distribution will be linked to supply/demand chain management.

Of equal importance to contemporary marketing managers, however, is the idea of relationship marketing. The management of inter-organizational relationships will be fully addressed in Chapter Three, and the challenges of 'managing' in networks explored in Chapter Five (with Chapters Six and Seven offering some resulting advice on devising B2B marketing strategy), but we introduce the topics of relationship and networks briefly in the following section.

Figure 1.6 Some general characteristics of B2B markets

1.4 The Significance of Relationships & Networks

It has been argued that the goal of marketing activity has now shifted from a transactional, short-term focus towards a need to seek and forge long-term relationships with targeted customers. Thinking more broadly in terms of business networks, this relational perspective can be extended to a variety of other social actors, sometimes known as 'stakeholders' or partners.

Relationships in B2B marketing

As you will see in Chapter Three, an understanding of the principles of relationship marketing (RM) can offer firms the potential to achieve sustainable competitive advantage in B2B markets. Instead of just manipulating the marketing mix, what we attempt to manage under RM is the relationships that are the context for trading. Inter-organizational relationship (IOR) management is thus an important part of strategy in business markets. Collaboration between firms over the development, supply, and support of products and services is a core element of B2B marketing and S/DCM (Cousins and Lawson, 2007).

Organizations worldwide (or more accurately, the managers who represent them) realize there is a need to build and sustain relationships with their customers, and with a network of other key stakeholders, even competitors – see Box 1.10. Note here how two firms which you might think of as international rivals have seen the benefits of cooperation in the Chinese marketplace.

The significance of social networks

To help them to manage IORs, global B2B marketers often need to study network cultures in different markets. A good example is that of *guanxi* networks in China. The *guanxi* approach

---

Box 1.10 Mini case

A car manufacturer partnership in China

General Motors (GM) has agreed to a 2 billion yuan joint venture with the Chinese state-owned carmaker, FAW, to manufacture light trucks and vans. The vehicles will be produced at existing FAW facilities in the cities of Changchun and Harbin. The Chinese marketplace offers great potential to GM, which sold over 800,000 vehicles there in the first half of 2009. Demand was especially strong for its minivans and other small vehicles. GM's managing director of Chinese operations said, 'For us in China, this is an important complement to the rest of our portfolio. We are well established in passenger vehicles (i.e. mainly B2C goods, but also bought by businesses and government officials) and mini commercial vehicles (i.e. entirely B2B goods) and we haven't had a presence in the truck segment,' a part of the B2B market that the partnership with FAW is clearly aiming for.

Source: BBC News (2009)

is a widely misunderstood concept, yet it has been the foundation of much Chinese commerce (Ambler, 1995). Important features here are reciprocity and the maintenance of social, rather than purely economic, relationships. While cultures in the West might rely on contract law to ensure that firms honour their obligations, this is not necessarily required in China. The relationship is built first, and then, if this is successful, transactions follow. So, in trying to build a commercially viable relationship, Western managers may fail because they have given insufficient attention to building personal relationships before moving on to complete a transaction.

Some suppliers are acutely aware of this. For instance, note the comments made by the manager in Box 1.11 who represents an Australian firm dealing with Pacific Rim companies. He clearly claims to value his staff's interpersonal skills.

As Gao et al (2010) observe, individual actors can only ever hope to craft strategies interactively with others over time in *guanxi*-orientated contexts. For relationships involving Western and Chinese organizations, B2B managers need to learn about the evolving social rules that exist at different levels of *guanxi*. These can be represented by concentric circles, ranging from tighter networks of 'expressive' (normally family) local ties, through 'intermediate' ties (typically with friends, and possibly involving intercultural relationships), to 'instrumental' ties with people who merely know each other (which is closer to the Western business model). Learning about these social nuances should enable Western managers to acquire the capabilities to engage in the appropriate strategies – and, of course, vice versa as Chinese managers become increasingly acquainted with Western cultural norms.

For more on these sorts of topics, see the extended discussions of interactions in industrial networks in Chapter Five and marketing planning in Chapters Six and Seven. Meanwhile, some of the themes of this section are summarized in Figure 1.7.

Interestingly, it has been suggested that global competition and the move to an urban society, with less emphasis on family connections, are tempering the influence of *guanxi* in China (Donaldson and O'Toole, 2002). Nevertheless, in Asian and other cultures worldwide, a seller should aim to encourage the development of a relationship with a buyer through:

- The way that the customer is treated by the organization (or, effectively, by its staff)
- The location (e.g. physical or 'cyberspace') where the interaction occurs
- The atmosphere (e.g. cooperative or adversarial) in which it takes place
- Attempts to raise the economic interaction to a socio-emotional level.

Box 1.11 Voices

Building relationships in the Australasian mining sector

'If you have quite personable people that are employed by us and customers have a relationship with those people, then their characters will begin to be recognised, and that forms part of that trust relationship. You try to build that rapport.' – sales manager, rubber products manufacturer.

Source: Ellis et al (2007)

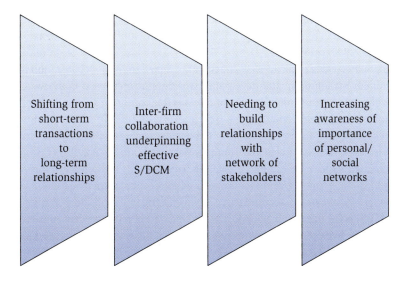

Figure 1.7 The significance of relationships and networks

1.5 Supply/Demand Chain Ethics

Ethical concerns are becoming an increasingly important element of B2B marketing and purchasing as organizational stakeholders begin to question how their firms have achieved their trading results. At first glance, you may wonder why this should be so. After all, more efficient supply chains mean that we (as reasonably sophisticated consumers) can continue to go shopping for ever-cheaper goods. Surely this is also good for producers since they can make greater profits and pay their workers accordingly – a classic 'win–win' situation? However, students the world over are starting to uncover things about modern S/DCM practices that make them feel uncomfortable about the functioning of organizational markets. It is important that you are aware of some of these issues – after all, you may have to defend, or even try to change, some of these practices once you enter your first management position.

The cost of supply chain efficiency?

If efficiency involves 'transporting a product away from where it was grown or made, packing it somewhere else, sending it to distribution centres somewhere else again, and then sending it to be sold at a gigantic warehouse that has destroyed many small businesses' (Parker, 2002, p 204), we might think about the environmental costs of efficiency more carefully. Moreover, in terms of the value chain, it may seem rather unfair that the supply chain members who probably add the most value through human interaction with the product, e.g. coffee farmers who plant, grow, pick, wash, and dry the beans, typically get only a tiny percentage of the price of a cup of coffee for their efforts. Indeed, some commentators argue that as IORs become increasingly globalized, the physical and social distance between consumers and producers has widened to too large a degree: 'This has increasingly left customers (perhaps wilfully) unaware of the social and ecological cost of their purchases, be it in rainforest destruction in Brazil . . . or the growth in child labour in the sweatshops of Manila' (Crane, 2000, p 13).

Marketing management practices are inextricably linked to these debates. Recent scandals regarding labour standards in the developing world associated with brands such as Nike and Levi's have meant that such issues are now on the corporate agenda in many Western nations. However, as Klein (2000) points out, at every link in the supply chain, B2B marketers representing manufacturers regularly bid against each other to drive down the price, and at every level, as we saw in the Hong Li Da paint case in Box 1.6, contractors and subcontractors struggle to earn their (frequently small) profit. At the end of this 'bid-down, contract-out' chain is the unfortunate worker, whether employed in garment factories in Bangaldesh or on banana plantations in Dominica. Organizations like Traidcraft (www. traidcraft.co.uk) point out that businesses' marketing and purchasing decisions have a direct effect on people's lives. They argue that Western firms have an obligation to manage their buying so as to enable better working conditions, for instance by not always insisting on the lowest price from foreign suppliers.

Some industries do seem to be responding to these problems, as we can see in the mini case in Box 1.12. Wearing your consumer 'hat' for a moment: would you seek to influence demand at the B2C end of the supply chain for cut flowers (or coffee, or bananas) by changing the way you purchase goods for your personal consumption? If so, then you are part of the derived demand factor to which B2B marketers must remain attuned if they are to help serve the ultimate customer's needs.

Fairness in supply/demand chains?

The commercial world is frequently portrayed as a ruthless one, with large firms exerting their power quite legitimately over smaller rivals or suppliers. It is perhaps naive of us to

---

Box 1.12 Mini case
Ethics in the cut-flower supply/demand chain

On a daily basis, British Airways carries thousands of flowers from the fields of Kenya to European cities. Within 24 hours, they can be found on the shelves of supermarkets and florists. The flower sector is the fastest-growing part of Kenya's economy, providing employment to around 50,000 workers. The industry depends heavily on migrant female workers who, despite the welcome job opportunities, still face exploitation. Following television coverage, Kenyan producers were implicated in facilitating the low cost of flowers to retailers by allegedly mistreating their staff. In response, UK supermarkets have attempted to improve their reputations by sourcing some of their cut-flower supplies in the form of 'fair trade' blooms from 'farms that have been specially selected for their high standards of worker welfare, community support and environmental awareness', according to one retailer. Despite the fact that such flowers cost more, this shift in relationships with suppliers seems to have worked: UK sales of fair trade flowers reached £4 million in 2005.

Source: Dolan (2007)

think the rational conduct of business could ever be otherwise. However, maybe the concept of fair trade can provide a solution to accusations of unfair practices in B2B markets. According to the Fairtrade Labelling Organizations (FLO) International, fair trade aims to guarantee fair prices to producers plus some adherence to principles of ethical purchasing. It also aims for long-term business relationships that are transparent throughout the supply chain (FLO, 2004). Fairtrade initiatives seek to create positive social change by altering what occurs at each end of the chain while shortening the social distance between producers and consumers (Shreck, 2002). This is relevant to B2B marketers since a relational perspective on marketing exchange (see Chapter Three) suggests a focus on issues of trust, mutuality, and fairness in IORs, a focus that would seem to match the aims of fairtrade (www.fairtrade. org.uk).

So, does Fairtrade work? In an interesting example, a 2004 press release saw the UK retailer Tesco (www.tescoplc.com) announce that its award of a Fairtrade label for a new line of products was 'good news for producers, who will benefit from the additional sales, and good news for consumers who will see a much greater choice of Fairtrade products in store'. As we noted at the start of this section, this sounds like a 'win–win' situation, but is the picture really that simple? In fact, shareholders at Tesco's annual meeting in 2007 voiced their anger over the low wage levels workers are still being paid in the developing world, especially compared with the massive pay increase proposed for the company's chief executive (see Box 1.13). The meeting was also addressed by a South African fruit picker and a Bangladeshi textile worker who claimed that workers are 'not being paid a living wage'. The fact that many shareholders of what is ultimately a commercial organization applauded these speeches indicates that life for those managers charged with managing supply/demand chains is far from simple. The Fairtrade debate shows that B2B marketers and purchasers need to remain sensitive to different perspectives on how to manage stakeholder relationships in the complex networks in which they find themselves operating (see Chapter Five).

It is worth reminding ourselves, too, that it is not always the organizational customer who is guilty of neglecting ethical issues in S/DCM. Sadly, B2B marketers can also be found wanting, as shown in the clause we saw in the Tanzanian government bid announcement (see Box 1.9) regarding the need for suppliers to provide an 'anti-bribery statement'. Too many developing countries have had state officials bribed by vendors desperate to close the deal (see Chapter Twelve for more examples).

Unethical practices are not confined simply to sales negotiations or to any particular culture, however. Even the most mundane business product marketed to one of the most

Box 1.13 Voices

Tesco's stakeholders speak out

'There is nothing that lowers a company more in the estimation of right-thinking people than a public display of executive greed in an affluent world going hand in hand with a display of corporate miserliness and indifference towards those at the bottom in an impoverished world who contribute so munificently to our corporate wealth.' – Ben Birnberg, retired solicitor, leader of shareholder revolt.

Source: Wray (2007)

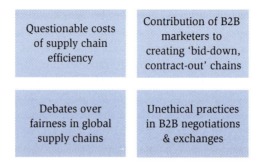

Figure 1.8 Some ethical issues in supply/demand chain management

powerful customers in the world can be subject to fraudulent dealings. This was highlighted when a US plumbing and electrical firm, C&D Distributors, which supplied parts to the US military, was found guilty of defrauding the Pentagon. Through the use of an automated-billing system designed to cut red tape, the company added hundreds of thousands of dollars to the cost of shipping parts. The most outrageous example of this fraud, which had been going on for ten years, was the $998,798 charged for two metal washers worth 19 US cents each (MacAskill, 2007).

Some of the ethical issues from this section are summarized in Figure 1.8. By now, it should be clear to you that the world of B2B marketing is full of fascinating challenges that require the application of a wide-ranging set of skills. It is the aim in the remainder of this book to introduce many of the tools and concepts that you can draw upon in your future managerial role, as well as make you think a little harder about what goes on in organizational markets and networks.

Before you leave this chapter, however, have a look at the end-of-chapter case study. It is designed to familiarize you with some of the issues facing managers trying to sell their firm's products and services in a typical international B2B market, that of textile machinery.

Summary

The key points to take from this chapter are as follows:

- The extent to which business-to-business (B2B) markets pervade the global and, indeed, local economy.

- How we define B2B marketing in terms of exchange activities between organizations, and what this may mean for marketing managers.

- How the concepts of the supply chain, the demand chain, and the value chain are inter-related in B2B marketing.

- The extent to which organizational markets differ from, and are also related to, consumer markets.

- How our thinking about B2B marketing encompasses relationships and networks as well as basic buyer–seller transactions.

- How ethical considerations can affect the management of supply/demand chain relationships.

Discussion questions

1. Explain why business-to-business (B2B) marketing is so significant to the functioning of the global economy.

2. What do we mean by 'the supply chain'? Why is the term 'demand chain' perhaps more appropriate to B2B marketing?

3. Think of a firm or institution in a B2B market, ideally your own. What range of other organizations does this organization deal with, both 'up' and 'down' stream? Draw the supply/demand chain for a key product or service marketed by this organization.

4. Why is relationship marketing important for B2B marketers attempting to cope with the characteristics of organizational markets?

5. Debate the issue of whether supply/demand chain ethics should matter to marketing managers.

Case study

B2B Marketing Challenges in the Textiles Sector

Introduction

W Perks Ltd (hereafter 'WP') is an exclusive distributor of textile-processing machinery to manufacturers. This study is based on interviews with the firm's managing director, Brian Jones, and one of its technical sales executives, Ian Stewart. All corporate and personal names have been disguised.

WP employs 30 staff in the UK at a head office that includes a 'Productivity Improvement Centre'. This allows WP to offer a full range of demonstration equipment in a simulated working environment. The average unit selling price for one of WP's machines is about £50,000, but some sell for £250,000 to £300,000. Following the firm's £500,000 investment in their premises in 2001, Brian stated, 'Becoming the number one choice distributor of innovatory cutting room solutions in each of the markets in which we operate is an achievable goal.'

The quotes which follow illustrate how WP sees the industrial network in which it is embedded. A number of B2B marketing strategies help WP cope with the challenges of this context, which are considerable when you realize that some of its rival distributors employ hundreds of staff.

Organizational markets and distribution networks

Brian claims, 'Wherever a roll of material is used, we get involved in the handling of it, the processing of it, and the cutting of it.' Ian adds, 'Our markets are companies making apparel (clothing), furniture, automotive trim, and airbags, and those in aerospace and motor racing.' He acknowledges, however, that WP's long-term aim is to move out of the apparel trade as margins are low in that sector. In targeting market segments, he explains, 'We try to predict where the manufacturer is going to be operating, which, given global shifts in production locations, isn't so easy. You've got the automotive industry which moves very quickly, and at the other end you have the aerospace industry which moves exceedingly slowly'.

The firm sees itself as 'quite a player in a global industry', and constantly monitors the business environment. For instance, Brian said, 'One of my managers is in Sri Lanka at the moment, doing a marketing audit covering the surrounding countries, with a view to setting up an office over there.' The firm has more than 300 customers world-wide, over 700 systems installed, and a distributor network covering 32 countries. For example, it has an agent in Germany who also covers Poland, Romania, and Austria.

The firm's competitors are machine manufacturers with their own subsidiaries and sales teams working in major markets, and independent distributors in smaller markets. Most of those distributors will have a portfolio of different suppliers. In fact, there is 'a huge network of competitor distributors', according to Ian, but he claims a high degree of loyalty, stating, 'We've never had a customer who's gone to another distributor yet.'

Members of WP's supply/demand chain

WP has identified the top 50 global apparel retailers and is in the process of establishing which firms manufacture on their behalf. If WP can get its equipment recommended for those organizations, then it can get a great deal of repeat business. For example, 85% of the manufacturers for European retailer 'N&T' have specified WP's quality control equipment. Brian is also aware of the end user's needs as he describes a machine that relaxes fabric prior to it being processed: 'This assists the manufacturers because if a fabric's going to stretch when the consumer wears it, it's going to stretch when manufacturers make it, and you know, in lingerie the difference between a size 32 and a 34 isn't a lot, but if you don't get that bit right, you've got a lot of uncomfortable ladies!'

On each of the machines supplied by WP is a 'partnership' logo with the suppliers' names quite prominent, along with WP's brand. Brian states, 'It's important that that relationship is there. I like to think our suppliers have the expertise in R&D and manufacturing, and we have the expertise in the marketing and after-sales side.' WP are conscious of their position in the supply network, as Ian points out: 'We've got eight different suppliers out there, and obviously they know that we have other partners who we work with and they want us to prioritize their products.' The firm appears to be attractive to suppliers as a route to market because 'It's very difficult for makers of these technical sort of products to find a good distributor as it's such specialized technology. Therefore they need to go through people like us.'

The organizational buying process

Some customers can be quite difficult to deal with. Brian believes, 'Automotive customers are now the most unfriendly organizations. Whereas in the past you could have relationships, they've sort of changed buyers around. They purposely don't want you to have any personal relationships.' The number of individuals involved for a major purchase in hi-tech sectors is also a challenge. Ian describes one project where there were 'probably 20 people who we sat down with at one point or another, like engineers on the utilities side, the IT people, the production people, the operations people, and the financial directors, and even the MD'. Different members of this group want different things: 'If it's an MD you're talking to, they're often more interested in the strategy of your organization than the actual product. Whereas the production guy whose head's on the line, all he cares about is whether the product works.'

WP's B2B marketing strategies

It is important for a small distributor like WP to stand out from its competitors. Ian believes that 'Customers buy from us because of our good reputation. WP doesn't have a huge brand name, and we don't have a huge advertising budget, so our main communication comes from word of mouth.' Brian explains further, 'What we're doing to make ourselves different is getting things like the people, the culture, and the premises right. Part of that is our Productivity Improvement Centre.'

WP's reputation is also built on its problem-solving expertise. As Ian says, 'Customers are looking for closer partnerships with people providing more complete technology. If you're providing a solution and you're using all the knowledge you've built up using the knowledge of your suppliers, then you start creating value in what you're offering.'

WP sometimes develops products in collaboration with key customers. Brian explains: 'This is usually done on the client's site because these machines need to be looked at in action. By working with customers in that way, we've often developed solutions that are unique, and obviously that keeps you ahead of the game as well.' For example, he points out, 'The cutting of the leather is very difficult because it doesn't come on a roll. It comes in a very irregular shape, you know, because cows aren't square! So we've developed a solution that enables manufacturers to get the best utilization out of a hide, saving companies a lot of money.'

WP offers lifetime service support on everything that it sells. The firm also offers external servicing. This involves persuading the client that if they are going to take out a service agreement on a WP-supplied machine, they might want WP to look after competitors' machines at the same site, too. Service contracts provide the firm with a regular income compared to what Brian describes as 'ups and downs of machine sales which can be bad for our cash flow'.

Some interesting contradictions emerge when discussing marketing communications strategies. Brian states that 'We find that our quarterly newsletter is a good method of communicating with our customers. We probably send 3,000 of those out, and we get some really good feedback,' whereas Ian counters: 'Actually the newsletter has not been a total success. It's been great for British customers, but if you send them abroad it's a very expensive exercise. So, we're considering electronic methods but there are so many e-newsletters now that they're all just irritating the clients.' Moreover, WP has never been comfortable advertising in trade magazines. Ian reckons, 'It's far more effective for me to sit down for half a day doing 30 phone calls than it is spending £2,000 on a page advert.'

Relationship marketing

WP seems to take the building of relationships with its customers very seriously. This can be seen in the firm's approach to negotiations, as Ian explains: 'As soon as you talk openly with a person, that's when you actually have constructive meetings. If two sides are holding back from each other, you'll never get an agreement; you'll never have formed any trust. And it's an old sales adage, but you still need some trust there.'

Brian tends to see customer relationship marketing as 'What a good salesperson does anyway. It's the guy that always remembers the customer's birthday, that he's got three kids, he plays golf.' He likes to formalize this sort of knowledge within the firm via a customer database which contains all customers' details, including 'information on equipment supplied and competitive equipment that he might use'. The database even tells WP 'which are the best engineers to send to service that machine'.

Nevertheless, some customers are keener to form a personal relationship than others. Ian claims that 'To accomplish something with any British company, you have to get in front of them and talk to them, whereas with the Scandinavians, you can achieve a lot by email. With a German person, you never get a relationship. You might build respect, you might lose respect, but you'll never have a relationship.' B2B marketing in the textiles sector, it appears, is a complicated undertaking.

Source: Ellis (2006); Ellis and Hopkinson (2010)

Case study questions

1. Which members of a typical supply/demand chain involving the use of textiles must be considered by WP's managers in formulating their strategies?

2. How has the firm ensured that it is an attractive distributor to its organizational customers and, indeed, to its suppliers?

3. Have conventional marketing communications been sufficient to target clients effectively? What other approaches has WP used to build its business?

Further Reading

Day, G. S. (2000) Managing Market Relationships, Journal of the Academy of Marketing Science, 28 (1), pp 24–30
This paper strongly argues that in an environment characterized by increased market diversity, intensifying competition, demanding and well-informed customers, and accelerating advances in technology, organizations must develop close and long-lasting relationships with their customers – relationships that are hard for rivals to understand, copy or displace.

Gao, H., Ballantyne, D., & Knight, J. C. (2010) Paradoxes and Guanxi Dilemmas in Emerging Chinese–Western Intercultural Relationships, Industrial Marketing Management, 39, pp 264–72
The authors integrate managerial paradoxes suggested by an industrial network perspective with additional Chinese–Western dilemmas associated with *guanxi*. These extra dilemmas are: those between strong personal ties and weak ones; between previous understandings and new learnings of *gaunxi* ties; and conflicting obligations between inner and outer circles of *quanxi* networks.

Juttner, U., Christopher, M., & Baker, S. (2007) Demand Chain Management – Integrating Marketing and Supply Chain Management, Industrial Marketing Management, 36, pp 377–92
This article endorses demand chain management (DCM) as a new business model aimed at creating value in the modern marketplace by combining marketing and supply chain competencies. The authors base their proposition for the role of marketing within DCM on a comprehensive literature review and their own findings from qualitative research with B2B marketing and purchasing professionals.

Wilkinson, I. F. & Young, L. C. (2002) On Co-operating: Firms, Relations and Networks, Journal of Business Research, 55, pp 123–32

These authors suggest that industrial networks present a challenge for management because firms are unable to control or direct relationships and networks. They believe that network structures and behaviours emerge as a result of the local interaction of network members in a 'bottom-up' way. The paper also considers some of the managerial implications of this perspective.

Wind, Y. (2006) Blurring the Lines: Is there a Need to Rethink Industrial Marketing? Journal of Business & Industrial Marketing, 21 (7), pp 474–81

In this paper, one of the 'fathers' of industrial marketing reflects on the evolution of the discipline. He plots a number of changes: advances in the Internet and the rise of small-to-medium sized enterprises (SMEs); the prevalence of outsourcing and the creation of value networks across firms and countries; customer involvement in R&D and manufacturing; functional integration within the firm; and the move towards a 'knowledge' economy.

References

Allen, P. & Ridley, J. (2010) Chocolate Wars: The Big Four, Guardian News & Media, online at http://guardian.co.uk/business/interactive, accessed January 2010

Ambler, T. (1995) Reflections on China: Re-orienting Images of Marketing, Marketing Management, 4 (1), pp 23–30

Barclay, D. W., Deutscher, T. H., & Vandenbosch, M. H. (2007) Business Marketing in Master's Programs: A Part of the Fabric, Journal of Business-to-Business Marketing, 14 (1), pp 31–51

BBC News (2007) Mattel Recalls Millions more Toys, online at http://www.news.bbc.co.uk, accessed September 2007

BBC News (2009) General Motors Expands in China, online at http://www.news.bbc.co.uk, accessed August 2009

Christopher, M. (1997) Marketing Logistics, Butterworth-Heinemann, Oxford

Clark, E. (2007) Playtime's over as Toys are Sent Home, The Guardian, 18 August, p 27

Cousins, P. D. & Lawson, B. (2007) Sourcing Strategy, Supplier Relationships and Firm Performance: An Empirical Investigation of UK Organizations, British Journal of Management, 18, pp 123–37

Crane, A. (2000) Marketing, Morality and the Natural Environment, Routledge, London

Dewson, A. (2007) Power-Hungry World Allows Aggreko to Put in Stellar Performance, The Independent, 14 September, p 59

Dolan, C. S. (2007) Market Affections: Moral Encounters with Kenyan Fairtrade Flowers, Ethno, 72 (2), pp 239–61

Donaldson, B. & O'Toole, T. (2002) Strategic Market Relationships: From Strategy to Implementation, John Wiley & Sons, Chichester

Economist (The) (2007) The Jeepney Economy Revs Up, 18 August, p 50

Ellis, N. (2006) (De)constructing Organizational Relationships, unpublished Ph.D. thesis, Lancaster University

Ellis, N. & Hopkinson, G. (2010) The Construction of Managerial Knowledge in Business Networks: Managers' Theories about Communication, Industrial Marketing Management, 39, pp tbc

Ellis, N., Purchase, S., & Lowe, S. (2007) The Discursive Construction of Organizational Boundaries in Traditional and Electronic Networks, 23rd Annual Conference of the Industrial Marketing & Purchasing Group, Manchester University, 4–6 September

Fairtrade Labelling Organizations (FLO) International (2004) Fair Trade – Overview, http://www. fairtrade.net, accessed September 2007

Gao, H., Ballantyne, D., & Knight, J. C. (2010) Paradoxes and Guanxi Dilemmas in Emerging Chinese–Western Intercultural Relationships, Industrial Marketing Management, 39, pp 264–72

Gray, R. (2008) Turnaround, The Marketer, February, pp 30–3

Green, L. (2008) Innovation through Collaboration at IBM, Keynote Presentation at 15th Conference on Multi-Organizational Partnerships, Alliances & Networks, Boston, 25–7 June

Guardian (The) (2007) 'Work' Section, 18 September, pp 8 & 15

Gupta, S., Polonsky, M., Woodside, A., & Webster, C. M. (2010) The Impact of External Forces on Cartel Network Dynamics: Direct Research in the Diamond Industry, Industrial Marketing Management, 38, pp 202–10

Håkansson, H. & Ford, D. (2002) How Should Companies Interact? Journal of Business Research, 55 (2), pp 133–9

Henneberg, S. C., Mouzas, S., & Naudé, P. (2006) Network Pictures: Concepts and Representations, European Journal of Marketing, 40 (3/4), pp 408–29

Hull, B. Z. (2008) Frankincense, Myrrh and Spices: The Oldest Global Supply Chain? Journal of Macromarketing, 28 (3), pp 275–88

Husted, C. & Reinecke, N. (2007) Improving Public Sector Purchasing, McKinsey Quarterly, online at http://www.mckinseyquarterly.com, accessed August 2009

Invitation for Bids (2007) The Economist, 18 August, p 39

Juttner, U., Christopher, M., & Baker, S. (2007) Demand Chain Management – Integrating Marketing and Supply Chain Management, Industrial Marketing Management, 36, pp 377–92

Klein, N. (2000) No Space, No Choice, No Jobs: No Logo, Flamingo, London

Kotler, P. (2003) Marketing Management, 11th edn, Prentice Hall Inc, Englewood Cliffs, NJ

Krishnan, M., Parente, E., & Shulman, J. A. (2007) Understanding Latin America's Supply Chain Risks, McKinsey Quarterly, online at http://www.mckinseyquarterly.com, accessed September 2007

Lawrence, F. (2008) Eat your Heart out: Why the Food Business is Bad for the Planet and your Health, Penguin, London

Lichtenthal, J. D. (2007) Advocating Business Marketing Education: Relevance and Rigor – Uttered as One, Journal of Business-to-Business Marketing, 14 (1), pp 1–12

MacAskill, E. (2007) Pentagon's $1m Bill for Washers, The Guardian, 18 August, p 12

Marketer (The) (2008) Big Shot: Martha Rogers, February, p 50

Marketing (2008) Recruitment Section, 6 August, p 46

Marketing Week (2007) Job Search, August, online at http://www.marketingweek.co.uk, accessed August 2007

Oliver, R. K. & Webber, M. D. (1982) Supply Chain Management: Logistics Catches up with Strategy, in Christopher, M. (ed.), Logistics: The Strategic Issues, Chapman & Hall, London, pp 63–75

Parker, M. (2002) Against Management, Polity Press, Oxford

Porter, M. E. (1985) Competitive Advantage: Creating and Sustaining Superior Performance, The Free Press, New York

Ransom, D. (2006) The No-Nonsense Guide to Fair Trade, New Internationalist Publications, Oxford

Shreck, A. (2002) Just Bananas? Fair Trade Production in the Dominican Republic, International Journal of Sociology of Agriculture and Food, 10 (20), pp 11–21

Svensson, G. (2003) Holistic and Cross-Disciplinary Deficiencies in the Theory Generation of Supply Chain Management, Supply Chain Management, 8 (4), pp 303–16

Turnbull, P. W. (1994) Business-to-Business Marketing: Organizational Buying Behaviour, in Baker, M. J. (ed.), The Marketing Book, 3rd edn, Butterworth Heinemann, Oxford, pp 216–37

Van der Gaag, N. (2006) Trigger Issues: Diamonds, New Internationalist Publications, Oxford

Weitz, B. A. & Jap, S. D. (1995) Relationship Marketing and Distribution Channels, Journal of the Academy of Marketing Science, 23, (4), pp 305–20

Wilson, D. (1999) Organizational Marketing, International Thompson Business Press, London

Wray, R. (2007) Tesco Rocked by Shareholders' Revolt, The Guardian, 30 June, p 38

Chapter 2
Organizational Buying Behaviour

Introduction & Learning Objectives

The purpose of this chapter is to show you how an in-depth understanding of buyer behaviour in business markets can facilitate attempts to manage the marketing/purchasing interface between organizations. Organizational buying behaviour (OBB) is a key element of the relationships that a firm develops, either as part of a series of market-based exchanges (or transactions) or as closer, longer-term relational exchanges. The placing of orders and the signing of contracts between organizations can confirm a current trading relationship, initiate a new relationship or perhaps signal the end of one. Thus, even in handling transactions that appear to be fairly 'hit-and-run', B2B marketers should consider the relationship potential in the exchange. In order to do this, they need to be able to make sense of some of the complex processes involved in OBB. For instance, think of how carefully a company like Danieli in Box 2.1 must manage its organizational purchasing.

Box 2.1 Mini case
The global sourcing of engineering goods

Danieli SpA is a world leader in the design and construction of industrial systems for the iron and steel industries. Its main centres are in Italy, Germany, and the US, where it employs a total of 3,000 workers. Danieli's sales in the year 2002 were approximately €1 billion. Almost all its profits come from exports, with 40% of its orders carried out in the Far East. In order to ensure high levels of engineering reliability, quality, and quick response times, the purchasing department of Danieli is constantly searching for suitably qualified suppliers. The company spends almost €500 million a year on raw materials, components, equipment, auxiliary systems, and services. Major supplying markets are Europe, South America, and the Far East. Approximately half the value of an entire industrial system derives from the production of machines designed by Danieli. Of this 50%, almost three-quarters is made at the company's own facilities, and one-quarter bought from international suppliers. The remaining 50% of total cost to customers comes from the purchase of technical products, such as motors, electrical components, security systems, and services.

Source: Nassimbeni and Sartor (2006); www.danieli.com

Chapter Aims

After completing this chapter, you should be able to:

- Recognize some key characteristics of organizational markets and customers
- Compare and contrast consumer and organizational buyer behaviour (OBB)
- Appreciate the many influences on industrial purchasing decisions
- Understand processes of organizational decision-making.

2.1 Types of Organizational Markets

We can identify a variety of different types of organizational customers with which B2B marketers may build relationships. Broadly speaking, these can be classified as commercial, institutional, or governmental sectors, as summarized in Figure 2.1. The first category comprises distributors, original equipment manufacturers (OEMs), users, and retailers; the second, not-for-profit (NFP) and community-based organizations; and the third, public sector organizations involved in delivering health, education, policing, transportation, defence, etc. The first category is not necessarily the largest market sector (some governmental budgets are huge) but it is probably the one that most students will associate with the practice of B2B marketing. Each of the main types of customer is described below.

Commercial customers

1. *Distributors*: distributors are also known as intermediaries. As their name suggests, they function in order to transfer products through the supply chain or channel, adding value as they do so. The key types of intermediary are wholesalers, distributors (or dealers), agents, and value-added resellers. Box 2.2 looks at wholesalers in more detail. It shows why this relatively unsung member of the marketing channel can still make a major contribution to developing economies.

Distributors' customers include both end-user business customers and OEMs (see below). Value-added resellers specialize in combining a variety of software and hardware products from different suppliers to design customized systems, often for large corporate clients. In

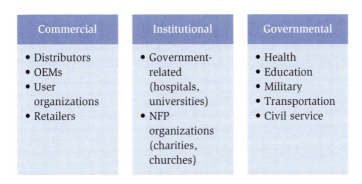

Figure 2.1 Types of organizational customer

Box 2.2 Food for thought

The role of wholesalers in developing countries

Although the role of wholesalers is not a particularly high-profile one in most economies, it is nevertheless important, especially in developing countries. In nations with only a basic infrastructure, manufacturing is limited mainly to cottage industries which are unable to reach their fragmented local markets. Wholesalers in these contexts can function to pull the entire supply system together. They can do so by drawing upon their marketing skills to deal with small retailers and cater for ultimate consumers, thus supporting the specialization of small local manufacturers. Wholesalers can contact a series of small-scale manufacturers scattered throughout the country and bring their various products together in a single location, thereby acting as a convenient 'one-stop shop' for retailers who typically lack the resources to maintain communication with all the manufacturers that might provide the necessary merchandise for their businesses to be able to satisfy consumer needs.

Source: Samli and El-Ansary (2007); www.foodstradeholding.com (2008)

this way, they can become a key node in a business network (see Chapter Five). Retailers are also technically intermediaries; however, due to their role as an effective end customer of many B2B supply chains, we shall discuss them separately later in this section.

2. *Original equipment manufacturers*: OEMs are firms which purchase materials or parts that they then make into products that are marketed, often with the manufacturer's brand name, to their customers. They are, in many ways, the classic business customer. A high-profile example is car manufacturers, such as General Motors (www.gm.com) and Toyota (www.toyotauk.com). From an analytical point of view, OEMs are typically seen as the 'focal firm' of a supply chain since they must deal upstream with suppliers and downstream with distributors. They thus become the organizational customer for suppliers of components and raw materials and, at the same time, the vendor of products to customers of their own. These customers can, of course, be either organizations or consumers. Computer manufacturers like Hewlett-Packard (www.hp.com) and Fujitsu Siemens (www.fujitsu.com) function in the same way.

3. *Users*: these organizations buy goods and services to support their production processes. This differs from the way component goods are bought since these materials do not appear in the final product offering, but are used up (or consumed) in its manufacture. Thus, an OEM can also be classified as a user but for a different set of goods from things like steering wheels and engine parts. Consumable goods include machine tools, lubricants, cleaning equipment, etc. We shall discuss different B2B product types in more detail in Chapter Eight, but note how important it is for marketing managers to know exactly how the buying organization intends to use the products they are trying to sell.

4. *Retailers*: retailers purchase goods to resell to consumers. They add value in a similar way to other intermediaries (see above), but often have more highly developed marketing functions, and, indeed, budgets, in managing their relationships with their customers. To meet the sophisticated demands of the consumer, the larger retailers have also become highly professional in handling their purchasing from suppliers. Many manufacturing organizations

have to sell to retailers in order to reach the end user. It can thus be vital for B2B marketers to understand the needs of this market and, if possible, to exert some sort of influence over their firm's relationships with retailers.

Relationships between manufacturers and retailers can be especially fraught in the fast-moving consumer goods (FMCG) sector. Historically, manufacturers attempted to attract consumers 'over the heads' of the retailer, whereas now supermarkets, with their close links to the end consumer, have the most power (Egan, 2001). The legacy of these changes has been one of often adversarial relationships within the retail supply chain, as the Wal-Mart case in Box 2.3 shows. For much more on inter-organizational relationships in this context see Chapter Three.

Institutional customers

While many of the bureaucratic procedures involved in buying under this heading, and the governmental (public sector) organizational category, may differ substantially from those of commercial firms in the preceding list, the principle of focusing on customer needs is still paramount, whether that ultimate 'customer' is a patient, passenger, or a student. Think of the numerous organizational purchases that have had to take place to ensure that your university is looking after your needs, e.g. computers, desks, library resources, etc. Universities are a good example of an institutional customer in terms of the products they must buy in order to keep operating. For instance, the University of Leicester's website outlines to prospective suppliers how its Purchasing Unit functions (www2.le.ac.uk/offices/purchasing). Other government-related examples include community-based organizations like schools, museums, and hospitals, although some of these institutions can, of course, be privately run or controlled by public–private partnerships.

NFP organizations such as charities and churches are also classified as institutions. As you can see, some institutions may be run on a profit-making basis but most are not. This does not, however, mean that their purchasing practices are any 'softer' than those of an OEM. In fact, restrictions on budgets can often be even tighter than in the private sector.

Box 2.3 Number crunching

The power of Wal-Mart

Some retailers are very powerful actors in the supply chain. The classic example is Wal-Mart. It is the largest company in the world, with $245 billion in sales in 2002. The firm's $12 billion in imports from China in that year accounted for a tenth of total US imports from that country and, moreover, its tough line on costs has forced many factories to move overseas. Wal-Mart's labour costs are 20% less than those at unionized supermarkets, and perhaps not unconnectedly, in 2001, its sales staff made less than, on average, the federal poverty level. In its relentless drive for lower prices and supply chain efficiency, Wal-Mart's relationships with its suppliers are subject to great scrutiny, including which products get developed, what they are made of, and how to price them. No wonder one consultant says the second-worst thing a manufacturer can do is to sign a contract with Wal-Mart, but the worst thing they can do is not to sign one!

Source: Bianco and Zellner (2003)

Governmental organizations

Governments are interesting customers to do business with. Different governments have different political priorities, as seen in their spending on health, education, and the military. This can happen even if you might think that their first concerns would be for the medical welfare and development of their populations. For instance, governments of these developing countries actually spend more on defence than on health and education combined: Oman, Burma, and Pakistan; and these countries spend more on the military than either health or education: Saudi Arabia, Turkey, China, Nigeria, and Cambodia (Burrows 2006). This is important information for B2B marketers working for arms manufacturers, however morally questionable some people may find their trade. Indeed, arms marketing to developing countries is a key component of several Western nations' exports, including the US (almost £9 billion from 1998 to 2001), the UK (£2.9 billion), and France (£2.1 billion). The arms industry provides employment for a lot of people, with over 1,100 companies producing weapons in 98 different countries, including Colt in the US, Beretta in Italy, and BAE Systems in the UK.

The area of healthcare makes an equally fascinating global B2B case. Health services bought and sold internationally have been estimated as being well over £3 trillion p.a. One way to facilitate healthcare worldwide may be the phenomenon of 'e-health', which is an umbrella term for telephone advice as well as more recent Internet applications that can be delivered 'live' or via 'store and forward' modes. The future of e-health initiatives depends on an increasing number of organizational stakeholders in the process. These include development banks; multilateral development agencies; NFP organizations such as international foundations, professional bodies, academic institutions; and last, but not least, the private sector that produces medical products, services, and IT. Each partner has its own priorities that may not coincide with the interests of communities and countries (Scott and Palacios, 2002). The issue of global inter-organizational relationship management thus arises, with governments having to recognize the growing influence of business partners in e-health service programmes.

2.2 Learning from Organizational & Consumer Buyer Behaviour

Ultimately, it is important for you to remember that although we have talked a lot about 'organizations' buying goods and services, these things we call organizations do not really make decisions: people do in the name of organizations. B2B marketers must try to understand how individual buyers in business markets tend to behave. If we take this perspective, then it becomes appropriate first to consider what we can learn from B2C markets about people's buying behaviour.

Similarities between B2B and B2C buying

While there are contrasts between consumer and organizational buying, there are also quite a number of similarities, especially when one realizes that the rationality associated with OBB is frequently misplaced: basically, if buyers are people too, then they can make decisions based on misperceptions, emotions, and peer pressure just as easily as consumers. Moreover, some consumer purchases involve a great deal of technical complexity and information searches, turning the supposed 'emotional' buying process claimed to be common in B2C markets into quite a rational, fact-based approach.

Indeed, the division between B2B and B2C marketing practices is not always clear-cut. For instance, Sun Microsystems (www.sun.com) gains market access through direct approaches to large business customers and indirect approaches through channel partners. It also, however, encourages groups of highly enthusiastic software developers to form communities of IT experts that can then sell integrated systems to customers in their own right. We thus see a key account management (KAM; see Chapter Twelve) style of working on the one hand, while on the other a type of 'brand community' developing, like those found in B2C marketing. Cova and Salle (2008) build on this observation to look more closely at contemporary B2B marketing studies and compare them with recent interpretive consumer research which they classify as Consumer Culture Theory (CCT). They compare the perspectives of the IMP (Industrial Marketing and Purchasing) Group on organizational markets with those held by CCT scholars. The IMP Group of scholars have greatly influenced the field of B2B marketing and we shall return to their ideas in much more detail in Chapter Five.

Cova and Salle argue that commonly asserted points of difference between B2B and B2C marketing are becoming increasingly blurred in several areas: seeing the brand as a relationship partner for the customer; accepting the customizing consumer as a producer, too; recognizing the potential for collective consumer action; and, analysing processes of consumption more deeply in their social and cultural contexts. The comparison is summarized in Figure 2.2, which shows how the marketing discipline could benefit by rethinking its theoretical perspectives in both B2B and B2C marketing on:

- notions of time
- the role of the customer
- market structure
- the unit of analysis.

Although it is the second shaded column in Figure 2.2 that concerns us most with its description of the B2B buying context, the columns on either side make for interesting reading, too. On the one hand, the first column captures traditional perspectives on B2C markets held by B2B researchers, and on the other, taken together, the second and third columns show just how much overlap there is between IMP-inspired B2B studies and CCT perspectives. This begins to explain some of the apparent contradictions in the approaches taken to marketing by firms like Sun.

Differences between B2B and B2C buying

Nevertheless, as we discovered in Chapter One, although there are some similarities between contemporary B2C and B2B marketing, there are major differences, too. For instance, consumer markets can consist of millions of individuals, whereas far fewer customers make up organizational markets. It is quite common for a small percentage of these customers to account for a large percentage of spending in a particular segment, giving them considerable purchasing power. This power is so great that the airline sector has long targeted the business customer, both in the traditional area of business class travel but also in the more rarefied field of personal aircraft. Some classic advertisements in the National Geographic magazine from 1976 illustrate this nicely, in language that we still find in B2B communications today: in the former case, we find Lufthansa (www.lufthansa.com) asserting that 'nothing can get you closer to the German market than Lufthansa: best connected with 10 German business centres'; and in the latter case, Beechcraft Aircraft Corporation (www.hawkerbeechcraft.com) offers light aircraft

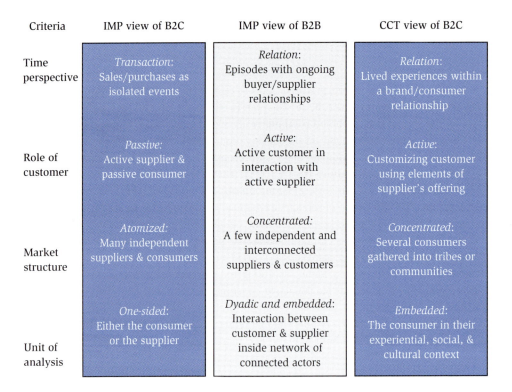

Criteria	IMP view of B2C	IMP view of B2B	CCT view of B2C
Time perspective	*Transaction*: Sales/purchases as isolated events	*Relation*: Episodes with ongoing buyer/supplier relationships	*Relation*: Lived experiences within a brand/consumer relationship
Role of customer	*Passive*: Active supplier & passive consumer	*Active*: Active customer in interaction with active supplier	*Active*: Customizing customer using elements of supplier's offering
Market structure	*Atomized*: Many independent suppliers & consumers	*Concentrated*: A few independent and interconnected suppliers & customers	*Concentrated*: Several consumers gathered into tribes or communities
Unit of analysis	*One-sided*: Either the consumer or the supplier	*Dyadic and embedded*: Interaction between customer & supplier inside network of connected actors	*Embedded*: The consumer in their experiential, social, & cultural context

Figure 2.2 B2C and B2B marketing as seen by IMP and CCT researchers
Source: Adapted with permission from Cova and Salle (2008, p 8)
B. Cova & R. Salle (2008) The Industrial/Consumer Marketing Dichotomy Revisited, Journal of
Business & Industrial Marketing, 23 (1), pp 3–11, Emerald Group Publishing Limited

giving 'years of dependable performance with a minimum of maintenance and a high degree of value retention' to 'businessmen [sic] and government officials around the world'.

In general, as the Beechcraft example shows (notwithstanding the status symbol of having one's own private plane, of course!), it is probably fair to say that decisions are more rational in the business buying process than in B2C markets. As well as financial considerations, they are also usually driven by technical specifications. Thus, in consumer markets, evaluative criteria are thought to be based on social issues (such as status) and level of utility (the extent to which the product meets the customer's practical needs), whereas in B2B markets, utility is still vitally important, but price and value are usually felt to be of greater importance than the buyer's ego. B2B marketers try to capture some of these criteria in their advertising. For example, in the pages of *Business Week* (2008) magazine, Sharp's document imaging products (photocopiers) promise to 'meet your everyday business needs' and to 'improve your productivity' (www.sharpusa.com/documents); while CDW, who supply IT hardware, offer 'the server solutions you need' thanks to the claim that their 'personal account managers know the needs of today's businesses' (www.CDW.com).

As you saw in the end-of-chapter case study in Chapter One, the organizational purchase process is often more complex than consumer buying (or perhaps it is more accurate to say, complex in a different way) due to the demanding technical issues so often associated with industrial goods. It can be triggered off by many people other than the actual purchaser

Box 2.4 Number crunching

The biggest street market in the world?

It is estimated that 80% of the world's Christmas decorations and 60% of its toys are made in China, with the majority of these being sold in the city of Yiwu. In the months before Christmas, more than 1,000 container loads of goods sold in its markets leave the city each day. The city is dominated by a series of huge covered markets containing 50,000 booths selling over 300,000 product lines, as well as whole streets dedicated to selling individual items ranging from calendars and picture frames to stationery and beads. Yet these products are not aimed at consumers. Instead, it is industrial buyers representing manufacturers and retailers that scan the streets of Yiwu. The city sells to the world's corporate buyers because it is surrounded by the cities of the province of Zhejiang, where firms produce an extraordinary variety of products. For instance, the town of Qiaotou has 200 factories making 60% of the world's buttons and zips, so a clothing manufacturer seeking a good deal on fasteners for a mass-produced line of clothing is likely to be drawn to this part of China to make their purchases.

Source: Pearce (2008)

or buyer in B2B markets (see the buying centre/decision-making unit discussion in section 2.4), and the information search is often longer in these contexts, too. The orders placed in business markets are also typically larger and of higher value than in consumer markets – note the scale of selling operations in the city of Yiwu in Box 2.4.

Some of the broad differences between B2C and B2B buying behaviours are summarized in Figure 2.3. You may note that this list is slightly more task-specific than the rather conceptual criteria highlighted earlier in Figure 2.2.

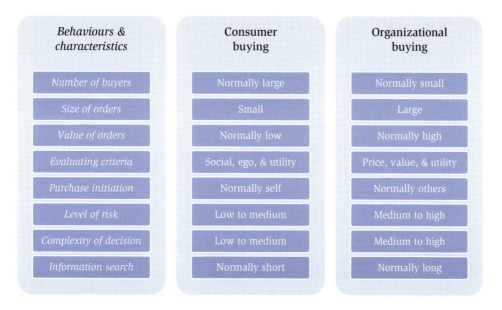

Behaviours & characteristics	Consumer buying	Organizational buying
Number of buyers	Normally large	Normally small
Size of orders	Small	Large
Value of orders	Normally low	Normally high
Evaluating criteria	Social, ego, & utility	Price, value, & utility
Purchase initiation	Normally self	Normally others
Level of risk	Low to medium	Medium to high
Complexity of decision	Low to medium	Medium to high
Information search	Normally short	Normally long

Figure 2.3 Broad differences between B2C and B2B buying behaviours

All these elements can mean that the risks involved in making an organizational buying decision are perceived as higher than those associated with consumer markets. To put it starkly, the ramifications (financial, legal, social, and ethical) for a buyer who purchases cheap but unsafe brake components for a car manufacturer are likely to be more significant than those arising from a parent's choice over which breakfast cereal to buy for their children.

This contrast captures what we have presented in this section in terms of a useful summary of some key OBB characteristics, stressing the significance of utilitarian and economic factors. Nevertheless, you should not forget that, while industrial buyers may not always admit it, they are susceptible to the social and ego-driven considerations of making the 'right' decision, too. A wise B2B marketer should always bear this in mind when planning their firm's marketing communications.

Let us now look at some of the influences on these organizational purchasing decisions.

2.3 Influences on Organizational Demand

There are many influences shaping OBB. Moving from a macro to a micro view, they can range from environmental factors that are external to the organization, through internal policy and structural issues, and on to personal factors affecting individual managers. What we term 'relationship factors' are also important. B2B marketers must appreciate that any or all of the forces summarized in Figure 2.4 may have the potential to influence a particular purchase decision.

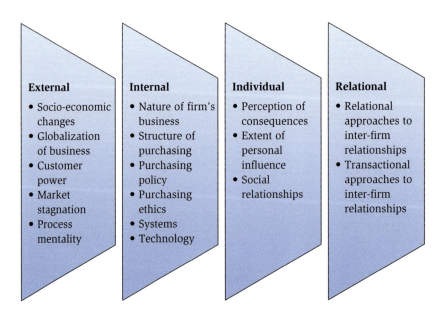

External
- Socio-economic changes
- Globalization of business
- Customer power
- Market stagnation
- Process mentality

Internal
- Nature of firm's business
- Structure of purchasing
- Purchasing policy
- Purchasing ethics
- Systems
- Technology

Individual
- Perception of consequences
- Extent of personal influence
- Social relationships

Relational
- Relational approaches to inter-firm relationships
- Transactional approaches to inter-firm relationships

Figure 2.4 **Influences on organizational purchasing decisions**

External influences

A number of forces affect the contemporary external environment in which companies make purchasing decisions:

1. *Socio-economic changes*: as B2B markets are based primarily on derived demand, organizations must remain attuned to the confidence of the end-user (often consumer) market. What happens here can affect the ability of firms further 'up' the supply/demand chain to purchase goods and services. For example, the recent global crisis of confidence in the banking system has had a huge impact on people's ability to obtain mortgages. The resulting downturn in the housing market has affected all those firms involved in this sector, such as those providing financial services, building materials, and engineering consultancy. Similarly, the large increase in the price of oil and subsequent fuel surcharges passed on to passengers over the last few years have badly affected the airline industry. Several operators have gone out of business, with resulting 'knock-on' effects on manufacturers of aircraft such as Boeing (www.boeing.com), and providers of in-flight services (like meals which are typically bought in by airlines from local food processors). Relationships between manufacturers and their business customers in other sectors have also been hit by rising oil prices, as Box 2.5 shows.

2. *The globalization of business*: many firms are in the process of developing efficient 'end-to-end' supply/demand chains from components supply to end-customer delivery. Such clients are seeking to work with logistics suppliers who can develop their own businesses globally and provide international product flow, as well as the information flow that comes with this, and a willingness to provide customized service where required. Good B2B marketers will try to ensure that their firms are similarly responsive, whatever the location of their customers (see Chapter Four for more on marketing logistics).

3. *Increasing customer sophistication and power*: customers are becoming ever more demanding in their expectations of quality, reliability, and compatibility in their relationships with supplier organizations. This has stemmed from a situation where customer firms tend to be better informed, and purchasing power is becoming more concentrated through takeovers and mergers. When Lenovo (www.lenovo.com) acquired IBM's personal computer division, for instance, the purchasing department of the newly merged companies was asked

---

Box 2.5 Voices
The pain of rising costs

Here is what Michael Morosin, who runs an electronics packaging company, PRT Manufacturing, in the Chinese city of Shenzhen has to say about the difficulties in keeping prices low when faced by increasing costs: 'Our customers have pushed for years to get the lowest possible price and they feel because it's made in China it's got to be cheap.' Unfortunately, PRT's main cost is plastic, which is derived from oil. Morosin goes on: 'The cost of oil is killing us, but we can never pass on more than 50% because on the other end of the phone you can hear these guys scream.'

Source: Garnaut (2008); www.prtml.com

to save them more than £100 million in direct-spending costs within 18 months (Hexter, 2008). Also, as customers become more demanding, they can often expect suppliers to cooperate in the transfer of people and knowledge across notional organizational boundaries.

4. *Market stagnation*: growth has all but ceased in mature markets such as North America and Europe. Here we find overcapacity, increased competition, and shrinking profit margins as customers expect better 'value for money' from a smaller portfolio of suppliers – see Chapter Ten for more on the issue of value. Sometimes, the nature of the added value that a supplier can bring is recognized by the customer firm in the way products are branded to the end user, as in the case of the processors found in laptop computers.

5. *A 'process', rather than a product, mentality*: many organizations are moving to a systems orientation underpinned by improved information handling capacity. This means suppliers are marketing less on the basis of a ready-made tangible product, and more on a marketing approach based on their reputation to meet strict client specifications in manufacturing and service delivery. Indeed, product- and service-related factors are now often not enough to differentiate a supplier. Differentiation now stems from the problem-solving and relational abilities that supplying firms can demonstrate – see Box 2.6 for a view on how this shift may affect purchasing policies.

Internal influences

Six factors pertaining to the buying firm can be identified:

1. *The nature of a firm's business*: an organization can be categorized depending on how it organizes its own activities; i.e. whether they are based on unit, mass or process production technology (Gadde and Håkansson, 2001). Although they are somewhat manufacturing-biased, these distinctions can help a selling firm understand what a buyer is looking for:

- In unit production, products are made to specific customer requirements, often extremely technologically complex and large in scale (as we saw in the Danieli case). A client firm engaged in this type of activity must draw heavily on its suppliers of materials and components for assistance in design and production know-how.

Box 2.6 Voices

The future of the purchasing function

Note how Qiao Song, Lenovo's chief procurement officer, views some likely changes in organizational purchasing in the global high-tech sector: 'Companies will have to differentiate their products in new ways – especially on the outside, in the look and feel of the product, as opposed to the inside, where there are fewer and fewer differences between competitors' offerings'. He believes that coming to terms with additional complexity and product diversity will be a central challenge for procurement managers in the technology sector in the next few years. Another issue is speed in the supply chain: 'Customers want everything to be faster and faster, and this creates challenges for supply continuity.'

Source: Hexter (2008)

- A mass-production company supplies high-volume standardized products (e.g. consumer groceries), and is more often focused on good value and production efficiency. In this case, suppliers to such a firm must ensure they can provide a consistently high quality of goods via the functioning of a smoothly running supply chain.

- A process production firm centres on the processing of material for use in other supply chains rather than the assembling of finished products. These firms typically buy via commodity markets, and can become fixated on price and availability in their buying decisions.

2. *The structure of purchasing*: some organizations choose to manage their purchasing from a centralized department in order to facilitate greater consistency and control. This approach can enable costs to be reduced by the buying power held by this department thanks to it being able to combine the orders of all the organization's operating units. This is common practice in public sector organizations such as the UK's National Health Service (e.g. www.hpc.nhs.uk). Decentralized purchasing, on the other hand, allows buyers to meet local needs more closely, both in terms of product modifications and response rates.

Centralized buying can cause frustrations for selling firms. For instance, a product manager of an oil additives supplier quoted by Ellis and Mayer (2001) has this to say about the tendency for multinational lubricant manufacturers to adopt centralized buying policies, thus reducing the possibility for his firm to appeal to local client needs: 'Some of the major customers have driven it too far. Their local operating units now, for example in Scandinavia where they have colder weather, and in South America where the end users haven't got the same level of technical sophistication, they need different things.'

3. *Purchasing policy*: a supplier's opportunity for increased business can be affected by the customer organization's plans to adopt certain strategies, such as lean manufacturing (where stocks of parts are held at a minimum), or to shift responsibility for all buying decisions to be 'signed off' by senior management only (often in response to concerns about overspending). It will be important for the B2B marketer to appreciate what the buying firm expects the purchasing function to contribute to that firm's performance: whether it is driven by a desire for the best value from the supply chain or simply to get the best deal, which often means, basically, low cost.

In the former case, a marketer must be confident that relationships within the supply/demand chain will be able to guarantee the buyer consistent, reliable delivery. In the latter case, marketers must try to influence the opinion of appropriate members of the organization, typically the senior finance officer, of their firm's ability to keep prices low. The impact of a fully fledged 'strategic' approach on purchasing and marketing is discussed in Box 2.7. Note how much depends on the perceptions held by the buying firm.

Box 2.7 Food for thought
What B2B marketers should know about strategic purchasing

The adoption of a strategic purchasing orientation means that firms scrutinize their supply relationships across a broad range of criteria and, in addition to issues such as quality and delivery, they emphasize 'fit' between buyer and supplier. This refers to the match between the competitive strategy (e.g. premium positioning) and the organizational culture (e.g. a market orientation) of the supplying and buying firms. Customers are basically seeking 'people who we can work with'. If this fit is felt to be lacking, it can lead to relationship failure. B2B marketers can show how their firm 'fits' by ensuring they are believed by the customer organization to have the ability to adapt their capabilities to meet the changing needs of the buyer. This means convincing buyers of the supplier's ability to innovate in processes and product development, be prepared to invest in joint technology, and actively contribute to the customer's strategy.

Source: Pressey et al (2007)

4. *Purchasing ethics*: it is increasingly common for ethical considerations to be incorporated into purchasing decision-making, and for this to be done in quite a high-profile manner by purchasing firms. For example, we may observe claims of 'partnership', 'commitment', and 'valuing all people', respectively (as cited by Maignan and McAlister, 2003) in organizational statements in publications such as Levi's 'Sourcing & Operating Guidelines', B&Q's corporate website, and Conoco's 'Supplier Diversity Program' (see corporate websites: www. levistrauss.com; www.kingfisher.co.uk; www.conocophillipscareers.com). It can be difficult for any stakeholder (not simply the representative of a supplier) to determine the extent to which these claims are just made for public relations purposes, but it would be foolish for any B2B marketer to ignore them.

Senior management in some organizations certainly appear to be sending a signal to staff in purchasing departments over ethical practices, as shown in this extract from the Buyer's Guide of a large UK engine manufacturer: 'All staff are expected to have good professional relationships with suppliers, based on mutual respect and a recognition of a common interest to maintain a satisfactory association to the benefit of both companies; Staff employed in Procurement occupy positions of trust and have to establish high standards of integrity' (as quoted in Ellis and Higgins, 2006). It is worth noting that although the benefits for the client of interdependence are emphasized, the identification of what constitutes benefits or satisfaction, or who assesses these, remains under-defined – some skilful reading of such codes of ethics is required by marketers.

5. *Purchasing systems*: where the pace of change in many sectors is accelerating, this encourages companies to compete in terms of how quickly they can deliver products to the marketplace. Such demands can arise beyond sectors driven by high-tech product innovation; think of the need for suppliers to be responsive to the buying needs of 'fast-fashion' retailers like Zara (www.zara.com) or H&M (www.hm.com). Suppliers that can help their clients to react to marketplace changes faster than the competition via information systems that support approaches such as just-in-time (JIT) production techniques can therefore differentiate themselves – see Chapter Four.

6. *Purchasing technology*: the Internet has had a huge influence on the ways in which organizations communicate and trade with each other. There has been a significant growth in the number of transactions taking place within electronic marketplaces. For an illustration of the scale of some of these systems see Box 2.8. The Internet facilitates the search by customers for potential suppliers; it allows firms to become networked with other firms in related industries, thereby combining their product requirements and enabling them to deal with suppliers from a position of greater purchasing power; and it can enable the running of electronic auctions. For more on this topic, see Chapter Ten on pricing strategies.

Box 2.8 Number crunching

The growth of an online marketplace

For 2008, the global online marketplace operator, Alibaba.com, reported first-quarter net profits up by 112% to HK$335 million. This was due to the rate at which it was adding new paying members whose numbers jumped 7% in the same period. The self-styled 'world's largest online B2B marketplace' said that it saw increased buyer activities in its international marketplace, despite the slowdown of the US economy. Alibaba announced that it planned to continue to develop its mainland marketplace where Chinese firms sell to other Chinese companies, and would also focus on industries and regions less likely to be affected by any further declines in Western economies.

Source: Scent (2008); www.alibaba.com

Individual influences

Three factors are thought to affect purchasing managers' personal decisions:

1. *Perception of consequences*: many different individuals can be involved in the process of organizational purchasing. The extent to which people take part in buying decisions is affected by their perceptions of personal responsibility for that decision: the more that an individual believes they may be praised or blamed for a decision, the greater is likely to be their level of participation and their attempts to influence the direction followed by their colleagues. Such pressures are not helped by the downsizing that has occurred in many purchasing departments, with the result that overworked staff feel their decisions are being made under conditions of ever-increasing uncertainty (Lewin, 2001). Blame in a B2B context can have serious consequences: if a decision results in a firm wasting money or manufacturing shoddy goods, then the buyer can be at risk of, at best, 'losing face' and, at worst, losing their job. In some cultures, of course, the former loss can be a very serious issue in itself.

2. *Extent of personal influence*: how power is shared (or not) across the 'decision-making unit' (DMU, see section 2.4) for purchases can have a significant impact on decisions. Some managers have greater control of the flow of information and the resources available inside a firm, thus enabling them to have a disproportionate effect on how the DMU functions. In general, purchasing managers are most important in repetitive purchases, while senior management or board members become more influential in high-risk, 'one-off'' purchases such as a new production line or business premises. Making sense of where the power is held in the DMU can be difficult for industrial sales people.

3. *Social relationships*: some managers may develop close personal relationships with suppliers, either via activities outside the work context, or simply through liking a particular individual who represents the supplying firm (see Chapter Twelve for more on personal selling). Internal social relationships, for instance when a manager sets out to 'score points' over a rival for promotion by driving the hardest bargain, can also come into play. These personal relationships can sometimes override inter-firm relationships in decision-making processes, hopefully still making them run smoothly, but sometimes running the risk of distorting them if personal allegiances are allowed to obscure other more objective criteria.

Relationship influences

This factor refers to the relationships between the client organization and other stakeholders in the industrial network in which the organization is embedded. The key topic of the relationships between firms is one we shall discuss in more detail in Chapter Three. As we shall see, the nature of the exchange relationship and the style of communication between parties will influence buying decisions. For now, and for ease of illustration, two approaches to relationships and buying behaviour can be contrasted:

1. *Relational approaches*: relationships that are based on a long-term commitment and are trusting and mutually supportive tend to foster (and be fostered by) DMUs that behave in a highly cooperative and constructive manner.

2. *Transactional approaches*: relationships that are short term in outlook, and where exchanges are sometimes built on suspicion and are generally unsupportive, tend to exhibit buying behaviours that may be described as 'polite but distant', or 'arm's length'.

The nature of relationships between firms can be influenced by the leadership styles of the managers charged with inbound purchases. It is believed that 'transformational' leaders (i.e. those who try to raise awareness of others and promote significant positive changes in individuals, departments, and organizations) will influence the performance of supply chains beyond their own firm most positively in turbulent environments. In contrast, 'transactional' leaders (who attempt to meet current needs by focusing on maintaining standards within market exchanges) are not so well suited to managing within the trusting relationships demanded by dynamic operating contexts. The transactional style of leadership, where formality and centralized decision-making are more common, seems to lend itself better to stable business settings where the status quo in day-to-day purchasing by more powerful customers is necessary for success (Hult et al, 2007). The latter style appears to be evident in the food supply/demand chain, as seen in Box 2.9. Note how one of the manufacturers seems to believe that end-user demand may help to counter this trend.

Box 2.9 Mini case
Relationships in the grocery supply/demand chain

The growth in store 'own brands' (or private labels) amongst retailers has resulted in relationships with suppliers in the grocery sector increasingly exhibiting transactional characteristics. For example, Australian pie-maker Mrs Mac's recently revealed that it was 'told' by a major retailer, thought to be the Coles chain, that its products would soon be replaced by own-branded goods. The firm recognized the right of retailers to make this decision, but saw it as a worrying sign of what was happening in the marketplace. Mrs Mac's had been given the opportunity to tender for a contract for the replacement own-brand range of goods, but had declined as they argued that they were 'in the business of developing our own (manufacturer) brands and not anybody else's'. One of Australia's biggest food manufacturers, George Weston Foods, claimed that the rise in own brands was being fuelled by a 'delisting process' by which powerful retailers were steadily shedding the number of their suppliers. Many of these were firms with

---

whom they had been doing business for a considerable time, and who were argued to be 'trusted by customers around Australia' who might not welcome these stocking policy changes.

Source: Thomson (2008); www.mrsmacs.com.au; www.georgewestonfoods.com.au

2.4 Organizational Decision-Making

Now, let us learn more about how organizations make their buying decisions, both in terms of the people thought to be involved, and the processes by which decisions are believed to be made. A number of marketing scholars have developed quite sophisticated models for these activities, including Hill (1972), Sheth (1973), and Johnston and Bonoma (1981). The best known of these, and the frameworks that appear to have stayed longest in managerial imaginations, are the intuitively attractive ideas of the buying centre and the Buygrid, which owe much to the work of Webster and Wind (1972) and Robinson et al (1967).

The buying centre or decision-making unit

While the B2C buying process can certainly be fairly complex over the purchase of goods like a family car, B2B organizational buying processes typically involve more people than B2C purchases, in what is known as the 'buying centre' or decision-making unit (DMU). Key members of this group can include managers not directly involved with using the goods or materials purchased, but who have a strategic or financial perspective of the organization as a whole (see Figure 2.5).

There are often a large number of people involved in a business purchase decision, with the actual purchasing department sometimes performing a less significant role than one might expect. You should note the different parties (Webster and Wind, 1972), which can include:

- Initiators, who make the first request for the purchase of a product or service. They thereby propel the buying decision process. The initiator is frequently a role taken by

Figure 2.5 Potential members of the buying centre/DMU

one of the other members of the DMU listed below, such as the user. Indeed, in many firms, a single individual can occupy more than one of these roles simultaneously.

- Buyers (also known as purchasers), who are the actual buyers with the formal authority to order products from a supplier. They are often based in a specialist purchasing department within the customer organization. Depending on the firm's attitude to purchasing as a strategic issue, their role can range from a relatively administrative one for more basic items to being a key player in making buying recommendations to senior management over major purchases.

- Influencers affect the decision-making process by providing information and sometimes criteria for evaluating alternatives. They can be internal or external to the client firm. An example of the former could be an engineer with specialist knowledge of competitive offers, while the latter could be an IT consultant employed to advise over the purchase of a major computer system.

- Decision makers are those with the authority to approve purchases. In complex purchases this is likely to be a senior manager, although in more routine situations the buyer (or purchaser) is often the decider. Since this authority may not always be formalized, it can be difficult for B2B marketers to identify these members of the DMU.

- Users are the people who will ultimately use the product or service. The role of the user can be continuous, especially in providing feedback on the performance of a purchase. Selling firms will often try to influence these employees by the provision of after-sales support in the case of a technically demanding product, sometimes to such a degree that these concerns can override issues like price and delivery times for the DMU.

- Gatekeepers can control the flow of information to other managers within the buying organization. Typical gatekeepers include buyers who have the authority to prevent sales people from seeing users and deciders, as well as technical personnel or personal secretaries. Industrial marketers will thus often attempt to build relationships with organizational gatekeepers (who, of course, are usually not literally guards at the factory gates!).

It is crucial for a selling firm to understand the composition of the buying centre/DMU, whose members can be drawn from all functional areas of the customer firm, including purchasing, operations R&D, finance, and even marketing (for instance, when the buying firm needs to ensure that what goes into their products is going to be valued by their own downstream customers). The supplying company's marketing efforts must try to reflect the individual interests of the group's members as well as overall group dynamics. This can often mean making trade-offs in order to meet the collective concerns of the DMU, such that the most critical benefits sought by the buying firm are addressed. Thus, while a buyer (purchasing manager) may be seeking the lowest price, for instance for an industrial lubricant, if the influencer is a production manager keen to ensure that the specification of the product is of a high standard to facilitate a sensitive manufacturing process, then this influencer may have the biggest say in affecting the ultimate decision.

Suppliers need to take such issues into careful consideration, especially when facing stiff competition from global rivals, as Box 2.10 shows. Do you think the advice given here will help US suppliers?

You should appreciate that, although we have discussed DMU roles in some detail, it is rare that a proper committee with designated roles is actually formed to drive this process

Box 2.10 Food for thought

How should US auto-component suppliers compete with China?

One way these suppliers could maintain their profitability is to focus on the more complex product needs of their customers. For instance, for parts such as hand-sewn seat covers, where labour accounts for almost half the total cost, Chinese suppliers will have a significant advantage. However, this should still allow US suppliers to concentrate on making components for which they have a technological edge; or material-intensive parts such as steering knuckles, a front suspension component for which direct labour costs represent only about 5% of the total.

Source: Knupfer and Mercer (2005)

(although this can happen sometimes – see the enterprise resource planning (ERP) acquisition mini case in Box 2.11). It is much more common for the buying centre to be an informal, fluctuating group of people. The dynamic nature of the decision-making process can mean that the composition and behaviour of the DMU can vary over time. This is especially likely for complex evaluation decisions over, say, the installation of a new piece of production machinery and the resulting ongoing training needs for an entire organization. B2B marketers need to try and keep track of the communication and influence patterns inside the DMU over the entire cycle of the purchase process, and to provide the appropriate information at various stages. The aim is to make as many of the DMU members as possible into advocates of the selling firm. For instance, this is how the MD of the textile machinery supplier we encountered at the end of Chapter One describes working with machine operators (i.e. end users) in a client organization: 'If you get them on your side, you build them up, the machine goes in, and you hit the ground running' (Ellis and Ybema, 2010).

The decision-making process

One of the most widely recognized models of OBB is the classic 'Buygrid framework' (Robinson et al, 1967) which combines the nature of the buying situation with the stages gone through in the decision process. The notion of situational 'buyclasses' varies according to the degree of familiarity the buyer has with the need or problem that the purchase is meant to solve. The notion of 'buyphases' portrays the decision-making process as passing through a series of sequential stages.

A criticism of the Buygrid is that it considers only the 'newness' of the buying task, while not really addressing issues like the purchasing orientation of the firm, and broader network considerations such as the choice of suppliers open to the client. Nevertheless, although organizational buying decisions will consequently vary a great deal, it is worth noting the differences between these three main types of buyclass situations, since recognizing them should enable the B2B marketer to begin to target their efforts appropriately:

- New task purchase – here, a company will be buying a particular product or service for the first time. This typically means that the client has no experience of supplier capabilities or performance evaluation. For purchases with great potential cost or risk, such as an ERP software package capable of coordinating the firm's entire operations, the DMU will often be larger, along with the informational requirements, and the time taken to reach a decision will be longer – see the mini case in Box 2.11 and note how a customer's buying plans can get very complicated indeed.

The new-task situation should represent the B2B marketer's greatest opportunity to gain business by influencing members of the DMU more convincingly than the competition. This is ideally done at as early a stage of the decision-making process as possible via, for instance, obtaining information regarding the nature of the particular problem a customer is trying to address and identifying their specific product or delivery requirements. Alert 'in-suppliers' who already trade with the customer clearly have an advantage here over the competition ('out-suppliers').

- Modified rebuy – although in this case the buying organization will have some experience of the product involved, the particular purchasing situation requires some degree of customization, perhaps in the product specification, price or faster delivery. There is less perception of risk than in new-task situations in such purchases and correspondingly often a simpler DMU. It is possible that the firm will look amongst its list of existing suppliers to find potential alternatives to meet its needs. This allows approved suppliers to make a better offer than the incumbent supplier in order to win new business, but it also runs the risk of alienating an existing in-supplier who had believed they were in a committed relationship. Marketers representing out-suppliers in this situation will often try to establish some of the issues that have led to the customer seeking modifications: for instance, did the quality of the in-supplier's goods deteriorate, or were there problems in reliability of supply?

Box 2.11 Mini case

The acquisition of ERP systems

ERP systems integrate databases between upstream and downstream operations and their internal and external supply chains (i.e. those that join manufacturing to purchasing departments, for example, and those that link suppliers to purchasers). While such a system has the potential to streamline operations and make considerable cost savings, an ERP package can cost millions of pounds, and the purchase can be fraught with risk and uncertainty. This is because, if an inappropriate acquisition is made, it can affect the entire organization, as a number of firms have discovered. For instance, Volkswagen and the Hershey Food Corporation both experienced processing problems resulting in stock shortages as a consequence of unexpected issues with their SAP 'R/3' (a popular software system) implementation. The sheer volume of issues that require consideration when buying an ERP package means the needs and behaviours of many individuals involved directly or indirectly with the purchase must be accommodated. Thanks to the cost and the potential impact on the buying organization, it is a situation demanding considerable planning. Planning activities typically involve project-team formation (i.e. a formalized DMU), definition of requirements, establishment of evaluation criteria, marketplace analysis, choice of purchasing strategies, and anticipation of purchasing issues.

Source: Verville et al (2007); www.sap.com

- Straight rebuy – here, we encounter repeat purchases where the buyer reorders without requesting any modifications. In this normally routine situation, for example for basic goods such as cleaning equipment or for relatively mundane components such as screws, the supplying firm is chosen based on past buying satisfaction. The supplier may be confident enough of customer loyalty to suggest the use of an automated reordering system via electronic data interchange (EDI) or the Internet to save purchasing time and reduce the chance of losing this regular business. In-suppliers in this situation are, nevertheless, advised to maintain regular contact with the customer firm to resolve any potential problems before they escalate.

Figure 2.6 provides some product examples of typical organizational buying classifications. In this diagram, the nature of the product will typically determine the extent to which either complete negotiation or pure routine dominates the purchase decision. For example, commodity items like bulk chemicals sit in the 'straight rebuy' end of the continuum, whereas major construction projects are usually 'new tasks'.

It can be argued that relatively few truly new task scenarios actually occur in B2B markets. The development of collaborative approaches like partnership sourcing involves situations where purchasing decisions become much more a matter of supply management achieved via relationship handling. When this occurs, the role of the DMU is ambiguous since the fundamental purchase decision has already been made, with subsequent issues relating largely to adjusting and developing the exchange of goods and services between the two organizations.

Nevertheless, for analytical purposes, it is helpful to appreciate that the decision-making process in B2B markets can be quite formal. It is thought to go through as many as eight different stages (or buyphases) in the case of a new task purchase:

1. *Problem recognition*: this can include changing business needs (perhaps to meet a new government regulation, or to target a new market), a supplier review or dissatisfaction with current service provision.

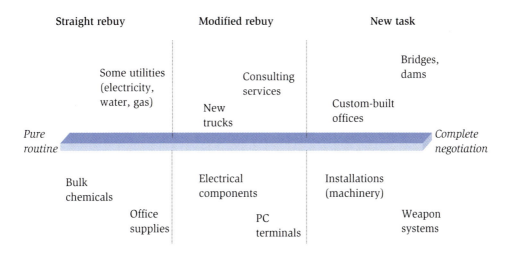

Figure 2.6 Typical organizational buying classifications
Source: Adapted with permission from Enis (1980)
M. B. Enis (1980) Marketing Principles, 3rd edn, Scott Foresman & Co, Glenview, IL

2. *General need description*: this may spring from an innovation (and a need for particular new components), the need to achieve cost savings or the desire for improved performance. Marketers need to react to these needs. For instance, when suppliers to the Royal Malaysian Navy became aware in 2009 that it was looking for a multirole support ship to replace a vessel destroyed by fire, the South Korean firm Hanjin Heavy Industries sent one of their ships to Malaysia to show it to naval officials (*New Straits Times*, 2009).

3. *Specification*: this often necessitates buyer/supplier dialogue, and the setting of 'qualifying' and 'differentiating' criteria to evaluate suppliers (see Box 2.12). If a supplier can become involved in agreeing a specification, it will have an advantage over potential competitors.

4. *Supplier search*: here, the risk of the purchase is profiled, information is gathered, and a 'consideration set' of suppliers arrived at. Clearly, those supplying firms already part of the client's network of contacts will have more chance to create an impression at this stage.

5. *Proposals submission*: suppliers are qualified, resulting in a 'choice set' (rather like the 'evoked set' found in consumer buying behaviour), and proposals solicited from those last few suppliers under consideration.

6. *Supplier selection*: here, proposals are reviewed and evaluated, and negotiations may take place between buyers and sellers, leading to the selection and ratification of a supplier. Sometimes, of course, several suppliers may be confirmed to avoid 'having too many eggs in one basket'.

7. *Order process specification*: this involves the drawing up of an order or contract, agreement over order fulfilment procedures (typically by the purchasing department), and the initiation of the relationship between the buying and selling firms.

8. *Performance review*: the supplier's performance is benchmarked and evaluated, with a decision taken to endorse, modify or discontinue the relationship. The opinions of the users in the DMU can be crucial during this stage. As Box 2.12 shows, similar criteria can be used at this stage to those considered at the specification stage. Note how, despite some suggestions that relational issues are becoming ever more crucial in B2B purchasing, it is rational criteria that tend to be rated as the most important by these customers.

Although the buying process looks like a simple linear progression (as summarized in Figure 2.7), in practice the stages are rarely this neat. Sometimes, they may occur simultaneously or out of sequence. Modified or straight rebuys will often omit some of these stages, especially stages 1 and 2, and quite possibly stages 4 to 7. Some players may only be involved at certain stages, such as a logistics manager called upon to advise over the hiring of a haulage firm whose views are pertinent at the start of the process where needs are identified, and again at the end during service evaluation, but who is perhaps less likely to be involved during the search for suppliers and order process specification stages.

Generally, however, it is safe to assume that the greater the risk associated with the organizational purchase, the more complex the DMU and the longer (and often the more stressful, for both buyer and seller) the decision-making process; and buyer–supplier relationships and communication networks become more important in fostering an atmosphere of cooperation. One way of overcoming the complexity of the buying decision process is for selling firms to adopt a team selling approach, fronted by a key account manager who looks after the inter-firm relationship and who can draw on other specialists from the supplier to facilitate

Box 2.12 Food for thought

Evaluating suppliers

In a study of European firms outsourcing to Asian markets, including those involved in manufacturing textiles, office furniture, woodworking machinery, and electrical components, the following criteria were ranked in order of importance to buyers on average (5 = very important and 1 = not important).

Selection criterion	Average importance
Quality	4.8
Price	4.2
Delivery reliability	3.5
Technical know-how	3.0
Product mix	2.8
Relations consolidated over time	2.5
Geographical location	2.3
After-sales service	2.3

Source: Nassimbeni and Sartor (2006)

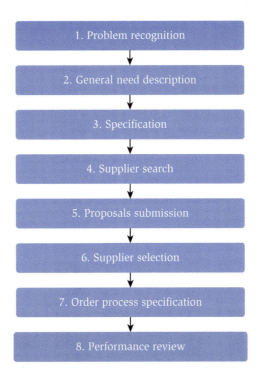

Figure 2.7 Potential stages in the organizational buying process

the needs of each DMU member and each stage in the buying process when required (see Chapter Twelve).

2.5 Buying Decisions in Relationships

The practical use of theoretical models is that they can help to structure people's perceptions of 'the world' and thereby the problems faced by managers. Taking into consideration some of the above buying frameworks, as well as the ideas about B2B markets contained in Figures 2.2 and 2.3 at the start of this chapter, we can identify two groups of problems:

1. *Limitation problems*: concerning the extent of the firm's activities in certain relationships, and the extent to which different customers should be treated differently.

2. *Handling problems*: in the long term over balancing power with dependence and conflict with cooperation, and in the short term over attaining an efficient way of handling the different exchange processes.

For purchasing managers, we see the same set of handling problems as for marketing management, but also the problem of decisions over an appropriate structure of suppliers. There is a need for a balance between internal and external resources, sometimes characterized as the 'make or buy' decision. For example, can the firm manufacture its own components, or should it source them externally? If the latter is the more appropriate strategy, (typically depending on the firm's core capabilities), then from how many suppliers should the component be sourced?

Such considerations can affect purchasing managers' attitudes to the optimal number of firms with which the buying firm should deal. Figure 2.8 lists some of the contrasting issues which a manager may have to ponder when debating whether to pursue a strategy of single or multiple sourcing. As you can see, there are a number of potential advantages with each approach. Thus, it would not be fair to say that one approach or the other is always 'right': much depends on the context facing the buying organization and its attitude to risk.

Some customer organizations adopt what is effectively a multiple-sourcing policy, but do so in a way that tries to develop a sense of belonging among the suppliers to the firm, even going as far as heralding the supplier network as a 'community' (see also section 2.2). This is the case for Ferrari (www.ferrari.co.uk), which introduced their 'Partner' supplier portal with an awareness of the need to maintain close relationships with each of its suppliers. A supplier portal provides the technology for improving the efficiency of transactions between firms by promoting the electronic sharing of information and the coordination of logistics flows. Thus, despite the fact that such portals can allow customers to make better-informed and potentially tougher buying decisions by easily comparing different offers, strong leadership was provided by Ferrari's senior management during the implementation phase of the portal to encourage suppliers' involvement. Information was disseminated to all suppliers regarding the skills needed to interact effectively through the portal, support was provided to aid recovery in the event of any technological disruption, and suppliers' level of satisfaction with the portal was closely monitored (Baglieri et al, 2007). The social side of such relationships is at least as important as the technology side, as Box 2.13 illustrates.

It has been important in this chapter for us to think about the implications of a relational approach for the study of buying decisions since it is so pertinent to the context of OBB.

Multiple sourcing advantages | Single sourcing advantages

Avoids supplier dependence

Bargaining leverage
(to maintain low prices)

Insurance against disrupted
supply

Not limited to capacity of
single supplier

Access to more supplier data

Stimulus to competition

Greater prompt to innovation

One relationship to manage

Greater commitment

Clearer responsibilities

More leverage over supplier

Simplified monitoring

Easier supplier training

Cheaper tooling costs

Simplified scheduling

Figure 2.8 Single vs multiple sourcing
Source: Adapted with permission from Wilson (1999, p 50)
D. Wilson (1999) Organisational Marketing, p 50, Cengage Learning

There is much more to the understanding of relationships in B2B markets than this, however, and so inter-organizational relationships (or IORs) will be addressed in greater detail in Chapter Three.

Now, turn to the end-of-chapter case study on the purchasing of packaging material in France. By providing some detailed examples of buyer and seller behaviours, the case shows how the actions of both parties to a relationship can affect the success of a purchasing strategy.

Box 2.13 Food for thought

Electronically-mediated B2B relationships

For collaboration to work, information must be readily exchanged between partner organizations. The document transmission technology of Internet-based EDI solutions is transforming this process. This makes it easier for companies like General Electric, for example, to liaise with all of its 45,000 suppliers. Nevertheless, research suggests that managers wishing to develop strong partnerships based on trust should invest effort in face-to-face interactions too. This is especially important in the early stages of relationship building, while thereafter the electronically mediated frequent and open exchange of information should be seen as a relationship-enabling factor.

Source: Myhr and Spekman (2005); www.ge.com

Summary

The key points to take from this chapter are as follows:

- The types of organizational customers that exist, and how their buying needs may differ.

- What scholars of organizational buying behaviour (OBB) can learn from studies of consumer buying behaviour.

- The wide range of macro and micro influences on organizational decision-making in B2B markets.

- The level of perceived risk and personal consequences faced by organizational buyers, and how these individuals try to cope with this risk.

- The different roles taken up by members of the buying centre/decision-making unit (DMU) in organizational purchase decisions.

- The stages that the buying decision process is thought to go through, and how these stages may vary depending on the novelty of the buying situation.

- How an appreciation of inter-organizational relationships can potentially improve buying decisions.

Discussion questions

1. List the major similarities and differences between organizational and consumer buyer behaviour. What insights into contemporary practices in OBB might we gain from the study of consumer culture theory?

2. What internal organizational influences are thought to affect a firm's purchasing decisions? How can the style of leadership within the DMU/buying centre affect such decisions?

3. If you were the sales manager for a firm supplying photocopiers to business customers, how would you explain the significance of the DMU in B2B markets to a new recruit to your sales force?

4. Describe the decision-making process that is likely to be undertaken by a governmental organization facing a new-task purchase of an organization-wide PC-based computer system.

5. What sort of criteria would be appropriate for a customer firm to use to evaluate potential suppliers of a key component in the manufacture of automobiles? How might these criteria differ for the same customer organization, this time as it considers suppliers of cleaning services?

6. Consider the following statement: 'It is always best to deal with as many suppliers as possible.' Do you agree or disagree? Support your arguments with examples where possible.

Case study

'Did you Say "Partnership"?' Tensions in the Purchase of Packaging

Sylvie Lacoste, Advancia-Negocia Business School (run by the Paris Chamber of Commerce), Paris, France

Introduction

'Danurex' is a multinational company (MNC), based in a European country. It manufactures fast-moving consumer goods (FMCG) and owns several brands popular in France (the names of the company and the other firms in this case have been disguised). As France was a key foreign market for the firm, in the early 1990s the top management decided it was time to merge their various separate French business offices into one single 'Danurex France' head office and to rationalize managerial practices. They decided that all local companies were to move to a new office built in the suburbs of Paris. Behind the symbolic merging of all the brand businesses into a single location, there was also a desire to create a single corporate culture and to eradicate some historical but very local brands, in order to bring most products under the umbrella brand of Danurex.

Challenges of restructuring

This strategic move was difficult to undertake. The French management of Danurex thought that one way of succeeding was to change their purchasing strategy. A new department was created gathering dozens of buyers from the different local companies. There was now to be one sourcing manager per line of products, headed by one purchasing director for the entire French market. It was further decided to launch a major 'Partnership Project', the goal of which was to select a very limited number of suppliers that would supply one line of products to all of Danurex's businesses. Instead of each local company having their own (and different!) suppliers, the idea was to bring them together with a few dedicated suppliers. A director of partnerships was appointed to lead the project. Of course, a second goal of the project was to reduce supply costs.

As so many new changes were introduced at the same time, it was decided to implement the partnership concept gradually, and to start with a product that had little impact on the parent company's brands: the packaging used for transportation, made of corrugated cardboard.

The supply of packaging materials

The aim was to reduce the number of corrugated cardboard suppliers to two, each of which would supply an equal share of Danurex's packaging needs, for which the firm was promising a five-year exclusivity contract. At that time, the different businesses' requirements were covered by a large supplier ('Manurex') as well as a number of much smaller sellers.

A major Scandinavian packaging supplier ('Papirex') saw the possibility of increasing significantly its market share in France. Although a big player in Europe, this firm happened not to supply any French Danurex plants. Papirex had just set up a European key accounts team and the ambitious team leader saw this possible deal as a way to promote his own career. So, the team leader (whom we shall call Pierre) wanted to have the deal at all costs; and 'all costs' was not a euphemism, as he decided to undercut market prices by 25% to make sure Manurex would not win the contract. As Pierre was also aware that the weak position of his company in the French market was a major hurdle, he decided to improve the offer by promising to build a new state-of-the-art manufacturing plant, and to seek further cost reductions for Danurex's packaging of as much as 12%.

Danurex could not resist all those great promises and Papirex became one of their two preferred suppliers, whereas Manurex's contract was terminated.

The buyer/supplier relationship

Pierre was appointed manager of the existing French plant that was going to supply Danurex and he was also to be their key account manager. Upon moving from the Papirex European head office to France, he decided to settle in the same village as the Danurex partnership director, to build up closer links. Around the same time, this director, who was an aristocrat, started to have his castle roof repaired. That was enough for the rumour to begin that Papirex had bribed Danurex to get the deal. Furthermore, many Danurex workers, who had been working with Manurex for a very long time, had not been involved in the choice of the new supplier, and started to rebel against the choice of Papirex. Any flaw in products or deliveries led to product rejections. Thus, the relationship quickly became riddled with conflict.

On the Papirex side, the French plant was not prepared for handling such a demanding key account, as their usual customers were smaller, local packaging dealers. The cost of poor quality and customized services led the plant to fall into the red. Papirex's European president became aware that a lot of hidden costs were involved in the deal and Pierre had not been internally transparent on all his promises. Pierre got sacked and was replaced by an experienced plant manager, Jean, and a key account manager, Paul, dedicated to Danurex. Both men had the challenge of making the partnership work while minimizing the costs for Papirex.

On the Danurex side, senior management were satisfied that Manurex had been let go, as they wanted a strong symbol for the change of company culture, but the partnership director was aware that the change was not for the better operationally and they may have relied too hastily on Pierre's promises. A new purchasing manager was appointed and the signal to Papirex was clear: this new 'partnership' had to work. So, to release the tensions, Paul decided to invite the partnership director to visit Papirex's head offices in Scandinavia, where a lot of social activities were planned between office and plant visits. One of these was a sauna session, but Paul soon realized that finding himself and his customer nude in a sauna was not his ideal vision of key account management, especially as this was the moment the partnership director chose to tell him, 'Do not force us to kick you out.'

Saving the partnership?

Back from Scandinavia, Paul and Jean decided to take the warning seriously and to address the relationship. A quality improvement programme was undertaken in the French plant and a dedicated team set up under Paul's leadership to work on Danurex packing productivity and to deliver the promised relational benefits. After three years of hard work, the relationship began to show signs of progress. Paul was relieved, but anxious about the renewal of the partnership due in less than two years: some people in Danurex had still not accepted the change in supplier and were convinced that corruption had been involved. Moreover, the promised state-of-the-art plant had never been built. Internally, the situation was not much better: a new European corrugated product president was frowning at the improved, but still low level of, profitability of the account.

Paul decided to take another job within Papirex and Corinne, an experienced key account manager, took over. The challenge was now to prepare the renewal of the partnership. Corinne was aware that the focus should be on improving profitability as when the renewal tender was launched, Danurex's purchasing department would expect a visible lowering of prices to legitimate their choice. For the next two years, Danurex was still a 'captive' customer and during the five-year partnership, no price negotiation took place. Under the 'partnership' arrangements, new products could be introduced at a high price range, as no benchmarking or competitive pressures were imposed by Danurex. Corinne decided to go for a large decrease in prices to secure renewal and, more important to her, 75 jobs in the Papirex plant. Under great pressure, she offered a double-digit price decrease, and the contract was renewed to her relief; but the stress was too great and she resigned.

The buying firm's perspective

On the Danurex side, the renewal of the contract was not so much based on the price decrease, as the prospect of a further change in organizational structure. Five years after having merged the French organization into one corporate culture, Danurex had decided to stabilize its supply base, before getting ready to set up a European-wide purchase system. Shortly after the renewal of the contract, senior management decided to have European lead buyers for a category spend (e.g. corrugated cases), who would be appointed in the country where the category spend was the highest. These lead buyers would coordinate a network of local buyers for country-specific projects. Danurex also decided to have buyers dedicated to their different businesses, so that supplier choice would be dictated by the businesses' marketing needs rather than the sole category spend. Thus, if a Danurex business required sophisticated retail-ready packaging, it could choose a specific supplier, but if another business was under strong competitive pressure and just needed standard cases at the lowest cost, it could choose another supplier.

The overall purchasing aim was no longer to split corporate spending among a small number of suppliers, nor to go for a pan-European supplier, but to get the best fit between the specific needs of each business with specific suppliers. Danurex wanted to have a continuum of European suppliers, ranging from 'low-cost' suppliers to 'strategic' ones. Last, but not least, it was judged inappropriate ever again to be a 'captive' customer and so all new product developments had to include at least two competing suppliers.

When this European approach was formalized via tenders in the early 2000s, Papirex lost most of its business share, whereas Manurex came back as a 'strategic' supplier, a position they still have today, fulfilling almost 100% of Duranex's needs for packaging in the French market.

Case study questions

1. What were the internal and external factors that influenced the choice of a supplier by Darunex in the early 1990s?

2. What had Danurex learnt by the late 1990s–early 2000s about their purchasing strategy from their first partnership?

3. Explain why Papirex struggled to maintain its relationship with Danurex, and why it ultimately lost the European deal.

Further Reading

Borghini, S., Golfetto, F., & Rinallo, D. (2006) Ongoing Search among Industrial Buyers, Industrial Marketing Management, 59, pp 1151–9

This paper looks at information search activities by buyers that are independent of specific purchase decisions. It does so by examining closely, via ethnographic methods, the behaviours of trade show visitors. The study gives B2B marketers a more nuanced idea of how best to select and manage their return on investment in such events.

Ellis, N., Tadajewski, M., & Pressey, A. (eds) (2011) Major Works in Business-to-Business Marketing, Vols 1–4, Sage, London, forthcoming

Volume 1 of this edited collection focuses on some classic early works in OBB and purchasing, including original papers by Lewis from the 1930s and authors like Fearon, Sheth, Webster and Wind, and Johnston and Bonoma from the 1960s to 1980s. It also provides some more recent readings, including work by IMP scholars Araujo, Dubois, and Gadde.

Guillet de Monthoux, P. B. L. (1975) Organizational Mating and Industrial Marketing Conservatism – Some Reasons why Industrial Marketing Managers Resist Marketing Theory, Industrial Marketing Management, 4, pp 25–36

In this iconoclastic piece, the author argues that what he terms 'the spell of economic theory and the decision-making approach' must be cast aside in favour of alternative approaches in order to obtain greater insight into inter-organizational relationships. He is one of the first scholars to adopt the 'marriage' metaphor for B2B relationships as he explores how marketing managers perceive their roles.

Moon, J. & Tikoo, S. (2002) Buying Decision Approaches of Organizational Buyers and Users, Journal of Business Research, 55, pp 293–9

These authors show how the classic decision-making models of OBB still appear to be highly relevant to B2B marketing. They compare buying activities and the impact of buying situational variables on the use of a buying decision approach by organizational purchasers and users in Korea. Their results provide some empirical support for the Buygrid model.

Pache, G. (2007), Private Label Development: The Large Food Retailer Faced with the Supplier's Opportunism, Service Industries Journal, 27 (2), pp 175–88

This paper uses a number of case studies to highlight how the buying strategies of large retailers have had to adapt in order to cope with potentially opportunistic behaviour by manufacturers of 'own-brand' goods. It concludes that purchasing managers will need to combine sophisticated skills in logistics, technical issues, and commercial assessment.

References

Baglieri, E., Secchi, R., & Croom, S. (2007) Exploring the Impact of a Supplier Portal on the Buyer–Supplier Relationship: The Case of Ferrari Auto, Industrial Marketing Management, 36, pp 1010–17

Bianco, A. & Zellner, W. (2003) Is Wal-Mart too Powerful? Business Week, 6 October, pp 46–53

Burrows, G. (2006) Trigger Issues: Kalashnikov AK47, New Internationalist Publications, Oxford

Business Week (2008) 18 August, pp 7 and 16

Cova, B. & Salle, R. (2008) The Industrial/Consumer Marketing Dichotomy Revisited: A Case of Outdated Justification? Journal of Business & Industrial Marketing, 23 (1) pp 3–11

Egan, J. (2001) Relationship Marketing: Exploring Relational Strategies in Marketing, Financial Times/Prentice Hall, Harlow

Ellis, N. & Higgins, M. (2006) Recatechizing Codes of Practice in Supply Chain Relationships: Discourse, Identity and Otherness, Journal of Strategic Marketing, 14, pp 327–50

Ellis, N. & Mayer, R. (2001) Inter-Organizational Relationships and Strategy Development in an Evolving Industrial Network: Mapping Structure and Process, Journal of Marketing Management, 17 (1/2), pp 183–222

Ellis, N. & Ybema, S. (2010) Marketing Identities: Shifting Circles of Identification in Inter-Organizational Relationships, Organization Studies, 31, pp 279–305

Enis, B. M. (1980), Marketing Principles, 3rd edn, Scott Foresman & Co., Glenview, IL

Gadde, L.-E. & Håkansson, H. (2001) Supply Network Strategies, Wiley, Chichester

Garnaut, J. (2008) China's Costly Leap Forward, The Sydney Morning Herald, 15 March, p 43

Hexter, J. R. (2008) Integrating Purchasing in M&A: An Interview with Lenovo's Chief Procurement Officer, McKinsey Quarterly, online at http://www.mckinseyquarterly.com, accessed May 2008

Hill, R. W. (1972) The Nature of Industrial Buying Decisions, Industrial Marketing Management, 2 (1), pp 45–56

Hult, G. T. M., Ketchen, D. J., & Chabowski, B. R. (2007) Leadership, the Buying Centre and Supply Chain Performance: A Study of Linked Users, Buyers and Suppliers, Industrial Marketing Management, 26, pp 393–403

Johnston, W. J. & Bonoma, T. V. (1981) The Buying Centre: Structure and Interaction Patterns, Journal of Marketing, 45 (Summer), pp 143–56

Knupfer, S. & Mercer, G. (2005) Can US Auto Suppliers Stay ahead of Chinese Rivals? McKinsey Quarterly, online at http://www.mckinseyquarterly.com, accessed September 2005

Lewin, J. E. (2001) The Effects of Downsizing on Organizational Buying Behaviour: An Empirical Investigation, Journal of the Academy of Marketing Science, 29 (2), pp 151–64

Maignan, I. & McAlister, D. T. (2003) Socially Responsible Organizational Buying: How Can Stakeholders Dictate Purchasing Policies? Journal of Macromarketing, 23 (2), pp 78–89

Myhr, N. & Spekman, R. E. (2005) Collaborative Supply-Chain Partnerships Built upon Trust and Electronically Mediated Exchange, Journal of Business & Industrial Marketing, 20 (4/5), pp 179–86

Nassimbeni, G. & Sartor, M. (2006) Sourcing in China: Strategies, Methods and Experiences, Palgrave Macmillan, Houndmills

National Geographic (1976) 150 (3), pp 415 and 420

New Straits Times (2009) On a Mission to Woo Malaysia, 4 December, p 13

Pearce, F. (2008) Confessions of an Eco-Sinner: Travels to Find where my Stuff Comes from, Eden Project Books, London

Pressey, A., Tzokas, N., & Winklhofer, H. (2007) Strategic Purchasing and the Evaluation of 'Problem' Key Suppliers: What do Key Suppliers Need to Know? Journal of Business & Industrial Marketing, 22 (5), pp 282–94

Robinson, P. J., Faris, C. W., & Wind, Y. (1967) Industrial Buying and Marketing, Allyn & Bacon, Boston

Samli, A. C. & El-Ansary, A. I. (2007) The Role of Wholesalers in Developing Countries, International Review of Retail, Distribution and Consumer Research, 17 (4), pp 353–8

Scent, B. (2008) New Paying Members Drive Alibaba, The [Hong Kong] Standard, 7 May, p 11

Scott, R. E. & Palacios, M. F. (2002) E-Health: Challenges of Going Global, in Scott, C. E. & Thurston, W. E. (eds), Collaboration in Context, University of Calgary, Calgary, pp 45–55

Sheth, J. N. (1973) A Model of Industrial Buyer Behaviour, Journal of Marketing, 37, pp 50–6

Thomson, J. (2008) Pie Maker a Home Brand Victim, The West Australian, 28 April, p 3

Verville, J., Palanisamy, R., Bernadas, C., & Halingten, A. (2007) ERP Acquisition Planning: A Critical Dimension for Making the Right Choice, Long Range Planning, 40, pp 45–63

Webster, F. E. & Wind, Y. (1972) Organizational Buying Behaviour, Prentice Hall, Englewood Cliffs, NJ

Wilson, D. (1999) Organizational Marketing, International Thompson Business Press, London

Part Two

Inter-Organizational Relationships & Networks

Part One: The Organizational Marketing Context

1. The Significance of B2B Marketing
- Significance of B2B Marketing
- Supply/Demand Chains
- Organizational Markets
- Significance of Relationships & Networks
- Supply Chain Ethics

2. Organizational Buying Behaviour
- Types of Markets
- Organizational & Consumer Buyer Behaviour
- Influences on Demand
- Organizational Decision-Making

Part Two: Inter-Organizational Relationships & Networks

3. Inter-Organizational Relationships
- Market & Relational Exchange
- CRM
- Partnerships & Alliances
- How IORs 'Work' in Different Contexts

4. Marketing Channels & Supply Chains
- Structure & Role of Channels
- Flows & Blockages in Channels
- From Channels to Chains
- Marketing Logistics

5. Industrial Networks
- The Interaction Approach
- From Channels & Chains to Networks
- Learning from the Industrial Network View

Part Three: Business Marketing Planning

6. B2B Marketing Planning & Analysis
- Planning & S/DCM
- The Planning Process
- Situation Analysis
- Sources & Assessing Market Potential
- B2B Market Segmentation

7. B2B Strategies & Implementation
- Market Positioning
- B2B Branding
- Making Strategy Decisions
- Issues of Implementation

> These 6 chapters can also be effectively combined as the 'marketing mix'

Part Four: Business Marketing Programmes

8. Business Products
- Classifying Business Products
- Managing Business Products
- New Product Development

9. Business Services
- Classifying Business Services
- Characteristics of Business Services
- B2B Services Marketing Management

10. Value & Pricing
- Value in Organizational Markets
- Making Pricing Decisions
- B2B Pricing Strategies (incl. Web-based activities)

11. Marketing Communications
- Communication Strategies
- Elements of the Communications Mix
- Relative Effectiveness of B2B Media (incl. the Internet)

12. Personal Selling & Sales Management
- Personal Selling in B2B Markets
- Organizing the Sales Force
- Key Account Management (KAM)

Chapter 3
Inter-Organizational Relationships

Introduction & Learning Objectives

This chapter considers the significance of relationship marketing (RM) in B2B marketing thought and practice. The argument will be put forward that competitiveness is about winning and retaining customers, not about exploiting them for short-term gain. The chapter will show how managers representing supplier firms should be asking the questions: how loyal are our customers, and how can we build and manage our relationships with them? The answers to such questions are far from simple and require an appreciation that inter-organizational relationships (IORs) involve many different elements.

For instance, the mini cases in Box 3.1 highlight what business service providers believe the social and communication elements of a relationship mean to their customers, as well as economic elements and notions of reliability. The 'people' side of an IOR in an intangible service context (see Chapter Nine) is clearly important but, as we shall see, this social element can influence the strength of many other B2B relationships, even those seemingly built on the most rational purchase decision and for the most tangible of products.

Box 3.1 Mini case
Keeping business customers loyal

'In B2B markets more than anywhere else, people buy people,' according to Chris Hare, the client service director of global marketing communications agency, Gyro International. He says that as customers have many factors shaping their decisions, including a constant need to review prices, loyalty tends to come from the work done by the firm's account managers who understand their clients' issues and resolve them quickly.

Another company proud of how its reputation for good service has built customer loyalty is Star Technology. This firm is an Internet service provider which focuses on the SME market, with 3,800 clients throughout the UK. Kevin Wright, the firm's London customer service manager, explains how client relationships are maintained. First, the company sees itself as 'local', by keeping regional offices serving nearby customers. Second, they have face-to-face meetings with their major customers at least quarterly to draw up support plans for them. Finally, every Star customer is given an 'escalation document' which contains the mobile telephone numbers of the regional and operations directors, enabling them to pursue any problems until they are solved.

Source: Dye (2008); www.gyrointernational.com; www.star.co.uk

---

Chapter Aims

After completing this chapter, you should be able to:

- Contrast market (discrete) and relational exchange in inter-organizational relationships (IORs)

- Appreciate the significance of trust and commitment in relationship marketing (RM), as well as the importance of relative power and dependence

- Recognize the elements of successful customer relationship management (CRM)

- Understand some key reasons for the formation (and dissolution) of partnerships and alliances.

3.1 From Market Transactions to Relational Exchange

We begin by asking: just how 'new' is RM? There has always been some sort of relationship between buyers and sellers in B2B markets. However, with a few notable exceptions (see Tadajewski and Saren, 2009), it is fair to say that the critical significance of these relationships has only relatively recently been considered by marketing scholars. Before the widespread acceptance of RM ideas, most marketing thought was devoted to analysing products sold in single, discrete market transactions (often described as 'material' and/or 'economic exchange').

Of course, a purely market-based approach can be legitimate for certain situations, especially when the customer is driven by price comparisons, as happens sometimes in 'spot' markets for commodities such as gravel and cement in the construction industry where the interaction between parties is minimal. Unfortunately, both buyers and sellers have been accused of taking advantage of each other in such 'arms length' trading arrangements as they seek a short-term goal at the expense of all other considerations. This is known as 'opportunistic' behaviour and can involve cheating, dishonesty, distorting data, hiding issues, making false promises, and withholding information. The consequences of such behaviour can be damaging, as Box 3.2 explains.

However, as we saw in Chapter One, it is now generally accepted that managers representing firms interacting in the supply/demand chain must plan together in order to achieve a seamless stream of products to satisfy customers and provide a good profit for chain members. Thus, it seems obvious that good inter-firm relations are something that B2B marketing

---

Box 3.2 Food for thought

Opportunistic behaviour in IORs

If suppliers or customers behave opportunistically in IORs and just seek to maximize the return from an individual deal at the expense of the other party, their actions can have both legal and ethical consequences. In other words, they may be sued for breach of contract or, even if they have behaved within the law, they may have to weigh up a moral decision not to let their partner down. This can be important since, if an organization develops a reputation for taking advantage of their trading partners, it may find it difficult to set up any future deals with companies that prefer cooperative relationships. This area is complex as one person's perception of inappropriate behaviour may differ from another's. For instance, merely negoti-ating aggressively or adopting a transaction-orientated business model is not necessarily the same as behaving opportunistically. In this way, a buyer's use of reverse auctions (see Chapter Ten) might simply be a tool to help gain the best possible price from a range of suppliers, although it runs the risk of being perceived as a mechanism for squeezing a better price from an existing supplier, with no intention of awarding the contract to the auction 'winner'.

Source: Hawkins et al (2008)

---

and purchasing managers should strive for, yet managers in different companies often do not trust each other sufficiently. Moreover, some firms have more power than others and can promote their own needs rather than working with their partners to optimize the entire chain. Independent companies are rarely used to working closely together. So, to allow for the tough negotiations they anticipate with powerful customers, managers representing suppliers will often keep product and cost information to themselves or, if pushed to reduce prices, they will provide inflated estimates 'to be on the safe side'. This can result in adver-sarial relationships rather than relational contracts. Understanding the nature of long-term relationships between people and between firms becomes important if we are to overcome some of these hurdles.

Some conceptual views of business relationships

An evocative way of capturing relationship behaviours is the metaphor of IORs as 'marriages' between firms. This metaphor is not without its problems, since it makes many assumptions about the way marriages work and typically takes an overly Western perspective of such arrangements, but it does help us to remember the more intangible and long-term elements of exchanges between organizations. This is reflected in the language used by managers themselves to describe IORs. It is common to hear talk of 'courtship', 'marriage', and even, when relationships have run their course, 'divorce'. Within the area of organizational mar-keting, Guillet de Monthoux (1975, p 35) appears to have been the first author specifically to apply the marriage analogy to IORs, as he explored 'how industrial marketing managers perceived the job of marketing within such stable matrimonies'. Note how relationships are described as 'stable', indicating a long-term orientation.

In marketing studies from the 1980s, there was an ever-greater focus on the conceptualiza-tion of a relationship, rather than solely on the buying decisions so commonly considered under organizational buying behaviour (OBB – see Chapter Two): for instance, Wilson and Mummalaneni (1986, p 44) commented that for some scholars, 'relationships constitute the very essence of industrial marketing'; and Dwyer et al (1987) suggested that even the simplest model of discrete economic or material exchange must also acknowledge a social element. Such was the impact of RM on marketing thought, that within a few years, Webster (1992, p 10) concluded that the focus of research in industrial marketing had shifted 'from products and firms as units to people, organizations, and the social processes that bind actors together in ongoing relationships'. Later, in an article that has greatly influenced the theoretical development of RM, Morgan and Hunt (1994, p 22) drew upon a variety of disciplines to argue that 'the presence of relationship commitment and trust is central to successful RM, not power and its ability to "condition others"'. These are significant claims and we shall return to these concepts in the next section.

Having listed a number of key thinkers in IORs whose work appeared in the latter part of the last century, we should not forget that commentators on marketing management have long been aware of RM issues. Indeed, Tadajewski and Saren (2009) point to several writers from the 1920s and 1930s who encouraged marketers to embrace notions of relationships, supply chain partnerships, and even the wider industrial network. Nevertheless, we can say that, overall, the trend in IOR research has moved from a portrayal of buying organizations as relatively passive recipients of 'marketing mix' elements from selling firms (and to which they are thought to react and thus decide to buy) to an interactive view that examines all the links that can extend back and forth between organizations. A further group of scholars, the IMP (Industrial Marketing and Purchasing) Group, have made the interactive nature of relationships the focus of their studies. They have brought some valuable insights to our understanding of IORs and industrial networks that move beyond an RM perspective – see Chapter Five, where more of the theoretical underpinnings of contemporary IOR theory will be briefly discussed.

For now, we shall focus on the implications of RM for B2B marketers. The concepts mentioned above have helped the marketing discipline shift its focus from transactional (single) exchanges between trading participants to relational (multiple) exchanges. Just how much contemporary RM differs from the transactional perspective of marketing is captured in Figure 3.1.

RM embodies the following elements: it involves a managerial shift in perspective from purely economic transactions to the 'fuzzier' boundaries of socio-economic exchange (i.e. recognizing that relationships involve people); it understands the economics of customer retention, as opposed to just attracting customers; it recognizes the need for quality,

Transactional marketing	Relationship marketing
✓ Focus on single sales ✓ Focus on volume ✓ Short-term timescales ✓ Emphasis on product features and quality ✓ Little emphasis on customer service ✓ Moderate but discontinuous customer contact	✓ Focus on customer retention ✓ Focus on customer value ✓ Long-term timescales ✓ Emphasis on relationship quality ✓ High emphasis on customer service ✓ High level of continuous customer contact

Figure 3.1 Comparing transactional marketing with RM
Source: Adapted with permission from Christopher et al (2002, p 19)
M. Christopher, A. Payne, & D. Ballantyne (2002) Relationship Marketing: Creating Stakeholder Value, p 19, copyright Elsevier

customer service, and marketing to be closely integrated; it extends the principles of relationship management to a range of market domains (at least in some of its variants – see Chapter Five); and it highlights the role of internal marketing in achieving external marketing success and ensures that marketing is considered cross-functionally (Christopher et al, 2002).

These themes will all be addressed as we progress through this chapter, and the two chapters which follow, on marketing channels and supply chains, and networks.

Key elements of relationship marketing

Although you should not be too concerned about distilling the essence of relationship management into a simple sentence, a couple of popular definitions of RM are worth repeating here. Reflecting the notion of lifetime value in managing relationships, Gordon (1998, p 9) describes RM as: 'The process of identifying and creating new value with individual customers and then sharing the benefits of this over the lifetime of association.' Another of the most widely cited definitions of RM is that of Gronroos (1994, p 9), in which he describes the objectives of RM as to: 'Identify and establish, maintain and enhance and, when necessary, terminate relationships with customers and other stakeholders, at a profit so that the objectives of all parties involved are met; and this is done by mutual exchange and fulfilment of promises.' No definition is ever perfect, but this one, with its reference to a series of stakeholders, will suffice for the purposes of this book. One caveat should be added, however: the achievement of 'profit' is not necessarily an objective of the NFP organizations that can sometimes be members of supply/demand chains and networks.

We now need to consider what a B2B marketer must take into account when attempting to manage relationships. As summarized in Figure 3.2, key issues include taking a long-term perspective, being trustworthy, showing commitment, managing communications, organizing for service quality, and ensuring mutual benefits.

1. *Long-term perspective*: a fundamental tenet of RM is an emphasis on long-term relationships via strategies that aim to retain customers, and thus improve their profitability. This occurs because it is thought to cost more to attract a new customer than it does to persuade

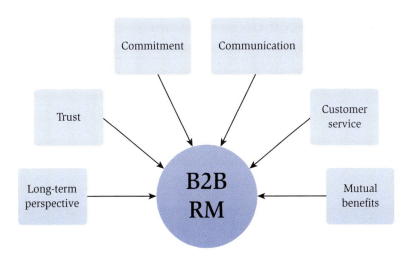

Figure 3.2 Key issues in B2B relationship marketing

existing customers repeatedly to spend more with you (Varey, 2002). While not all clients prove to be profitable over time (especially some of the more demanding yet cost-conscious ones), a belief in the value of customer retention is common. It can be seen with the way Boeing attempts to look after one of its key customers, the UK Ministry of Defence. The company runs what it terms a 'Through Life' customer support programme, believing that by 'working side by side' with the MOD to 'ensure the UK's fleet of CH-47 Chinook helicopters stands ready', they will maintain their relationship. Indeed, Boeing are keen to stress their 34-year-long commitment to what they call this 'partnership' in their advertising (www.boeing.co.uk). It is also likely that Boeing will gain from being associated with such a prestigious customer, even if the profitability of the relationship is not that great.

In order for a relationship to flourish over time, there should be trust, commitment, and communication between the interested parties. The first two of these elements are pretty much inseparable.

2. *Trust*: trust within business is a hugely complex area, but has been defined by Blois (1997, p 58) as 'An acceptance of vulnerability to another's possible, but not expected, ill will or lack of good will'. Trust can be viewed as a relationship 'atmosphere' that results from cooperation, based on predictability, dependability, and faith. It appears to reduce risk perception in relationships; in other words, each party believes that the other will not take unfair advantage. Trust that develops through social interaction between individuals can often be more important than legally binding contracts. For example, if the export manager of a Caribbean banana producer is confident that a US supermarket product buyer will not ruthlessly exploit their powerful position in the marketing channel (perhaps by constantly demanding unreasonable price cuts), a good relationship has the chance to develop.

For more on trust at the level of individual buyers and sellers, see Box 3.3 in this chapter and the discussion of social capital in Chapter Five. It is also common to talk of trust between organizations (as the related discussion of commitment below shows), yet it could be argued that organizations are not really things that can trust each other, as it is people that do this. Perhaps viewing firms as more or less 'trustworthy' in terms of how they try to build their corporate reputation is a more helpful conceptualization (Blois, 1999).

3. *Commitment*: commitment has been defined by Morgan and Hunt (1994, p 230) as 'An exchange partner believing that an ongoing relationship with another is so important as to warrant maximum efforts at maintaining it'. Commitment motivates partners' efforts to preserve an IOR and to resist alternative offers. It is actually not clear whether commitment is the outcome of growing trust or whether trust develops from the decision to commit to one supplier. Nevertheless, trust and commitment are required for firms to consider adaptations to meet partner needs. For instance, Toyota UK may request that a European component supplier radically redesigns its production line in order to fulfil orders for a new car model, such as the Avensis (www.toyotauk.com). Without a belief that Toyota UK will remain a loyal customer, the supplier will be reluctant to invest in adapting its facilities accordingly. Trust and commitment also provide a barrier to a customer leaving the relationship in favour of short-term (possibly cheaper) supply.

In general, we can identify several categories of commitment or what we can view as a form of loyalty between actors. These are shown as rungs of a loyalty 'ladder' in Figure 3.3. The model is relevant for all elements of a firm's channel to market: company buyers, intermediaries, and end users. The idea is for sellers to try to move a customer up the ladder,

Partner: somebody in a mutual partnership with your organization

Member: somebody with a great affinity to your organization, and who is truly loyal

Advocate: somebody who actively recommends your organization to others

Supporter: somebody who is positive towards your organization, but only passively

Client: somebody who has done repeat business with you, but may be neutral or even negative towards your organization

Customer: somebody who has done business with you, but only once

Prospect: somebody who may be persuaded to do business with your organization

Figure 3.3 A relationship ladder of loyalty
Source: Adapted with permission from Christopher et al (2002, p 48)
M. Christopher, A. Payne, & D. Ballantyne (2002) Relationship Marketing, p 48,
copyright Elsevier

ideally from being merely a prospect, through the customer stage, and on to becoming a partner, or at least an advocate. In this representation of IORs:

- Prospects can become customers following a transaction.
- Clients may emerge after several transactions, but are not especially committed to any one supplier.
- While supporters may passively recognize a seller's worth, they do not spread positive word of mouth (WOM) about the seller, and may not be able to enter into regular purchases.
- Advocates, though, support the firm and recommend it to others.
- Partners extend the same amount of trust and commitment to the selling organization as it does to them.

Such metaphors are, of course, somewhat simplistic, but the resulting categories do afford the marketing manager one potentially useful way of segmenting customers based on their perceived (or ideally actual) level of commitment and then positioning the firm's offering accordingly (see Chapter Six). You should realize, however, that commitment can be attitude- and/or behaviour-based. In other words, the former is a belief about a social actor's intentions, whereas the latter is concerned more with what the actor actually does. Attitudinal commitment is portrayed most often in RM studies, but sometimes intention and behaviour do not necessarily match.

4. *Communication*: it is largely through communication that trust and commitment are developed. Whatever source of communication is being employed (see Chapter Eleven), consistency is the key. Firms should focus on creating a 'relationship dialogue'. This will enable both the firm and the customer to 'reason' together and eventually develop a 'knowledge platform' that will add value to customers as well as forge the relationship (Gronroos, 2000). For example, the computer manufacturer, Lenovo, has set up a Web-based 'Partner Network' which is aimed at its resellers. The network provides free access to sales and marketing tools, as well as training courses to all registered members. For high-performing dealers, there is the opportunity to attain the 'Premium' level of membership which makes the reseller eligible to apply for the status of authorized warranty service provider (www. pc.ibm.com/partnerworld).

5. *Customer service*: as we saw in the cases at the start of this chapter, customer service is also important in forging relationships. There is, after all, little point encouraging dialogue in a relationship if all the feedback you get from your customer is how annoyed they are with your poor service.

This understanding is reflected in the so-called 'service-dominant logic' (SDL) paradigm that some scholars have put forward for both B2C and B2B markets (e.g. Vargo and Lusch, 2004). SDL appears to be a synthesis of our knowledge of the significance of the service element of product offerings (see Chapters Eight and Nine), the co-creation of value with customers, and how this impacts on buyer–seller relationships. As such, it serves as a useful reminder to B2B managers of the linkages between these issues. However, like RM, there is considerable debate about how new SDL actually is. For instance, Brown (2007, p 293) points out that in 1972, Levitt was proclaiming that 'there are only industries whose service components are greater or less than those of other industries. Everybody is in service'; and Wooliscroft (2008) argues that the fundamental principles of SDL are all present in the work of Alderson (1965), a leading scholar on marketing channels.

Nevertheless, it is fair to say that an ongoing challenge to most RM-orientated organizations has been to align marketing, quality, and customer service strategies closely (Christopher et al, 2002). Organizational structures that allow diverse functions such as production, sales, and logistics to interact with a common goal of fulfilling customer relationship maintenance are essential (see Chapter Seven). A broad transition reflecting these organizational changes from a TM to an RM orientation is summarized in Figure 3.4. Note how it emphasizes the efforts of people beyond the marketing department.

6. *Mutual benefits*: a strong IOR is characterized by shared benefits and a sense of mutuality (Varey, 2002). For most selling organizations, the benefit is, of course, revenue. For organizational customers, benefits are typically those derived from ownership and/or access to a good-quality product or service. For purchasing managers, they can also include emotional benefits such as reduced anxiety, recognition, or preferential treatment. Mutuality implies that relationships should be 'win–win' reciprocal situations where each partner provides for the other through exchange. Each exchange interaction will be affected by what has gone before and what may happen in the future. Thus, the 'hit-and-run' mentality of transactional marketing has severe limitations in a relationship-building context. For example,

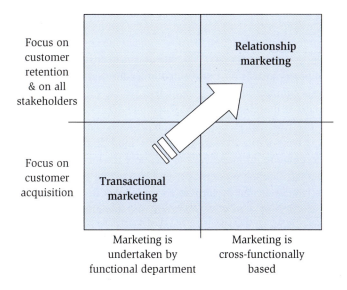

Figure 3.4 **The transition to RM**
Source: Adapted with permission from Christopher et al (2002, p 4)
M. Christopher, A. Payne, & D. Ballantyne (2002) Relationship Marketing, p 4,
copyright Elsevier

you may employ an aggressive, high-pressure industrial salesperson who always achieves their monthly sales volume targets, but if this is done by misleading clients over what the product can actually deliver, what will be the cost for your firm's long-term income stream?

The mutual benefits brought about by honesty between people and the organizations they represent is shown in Box 3.3. Note how the situation reveals the importance of trust and loyalty between the IOR participants. The incident also shows that material performance is not unimportant. Consistently bad performance, in other words, would make the establishment of trust impossible since achieving promises is an important element in giving and receiving 'face' in long-term relationships.

Box 3.3 Number crunching

The benefits of an open relationship in Hong Kong

Sid Lowe, Kingston University

Mr Cheung (not his real name) was managing director of the Hong Kong subsidiary of a large British electrical engineering firm. In 1994, it was discovered from records that an electrical cable which had been supplied from the parent company was faulty and had been laid as an underground supply for a major company in Hong Kong. The fault was not serious but could induce failure in electrical supplies under certain circumstances. The penalties under the contract decreased year by year due to straight-line depreciation but the potential disruption to the customer of total supply failure was considerable.

After heated discussion within the organization, Mr Cheung decided to go along to the customer and 'confess' about the fault. This resulted in the customer requesting replacement of the cable, which cost HK$200,000 plus overhead costs.

The outcome, however, was an unexpected order from the customer less than four months later for a contract to supply equipment to the value of over HK$5 million. Mr Cheung considered that the act of confession had dramatically improved *shun yum* (trust) between the two parties and that whereas his own *mien-tzu* (reputation for achievement) was temporarily damaged, this was more than compensated for by an increase in *lien* (reputation for integrity) and therefore the incident had given him 'face' with the customer. Mr Cheung was quick to emphasize that this new status was fragile and that further failures in the performance of products in the HK$5 million project would mean destruction of *shun yum*, *mien-tzu*, and *lien* and that, as a result, he was committed to supervising personally the contract throughout 1995.

One further managerial implication resulting from an RM approach to B2B marketing is the realization that managers trained under a competitive and hierarchical management philosophy may require a different set of skills to achieve cooperation amongst supply chain partners. Basically, a greater understanding of the mutual needs of the relationship partner, whether at the organizational or the personal level, is essential. While this point simply reinforces the most basic advice given in most marketing textbooks on 'marketing orientation', true RM demands more interaction than just simple customer awareness. For instance, it will be important for managers to consult partners before acting in any decision process, such as a consumer goods manufacturer's plans to launch a new brand. Will it fit with the plans for the own-label ranges of the firm's main retail customers? Furthermore, negotiated outcomes in relationships should represent compromises that lead to 'win–win' outcomes for all parties. Thus, can an agreement be reached for the manufacturer to produce certain own-label goods at low cost for the retailers, who then also agree to stock the manufacturer's new brand in prominent in-store locations?

Understanding partner needs in IORs is also important in markets comprising institutional buyers, such as those for medical equipment, as the international case in Box 3.4 shows.

Box 3.4 Mini case

Fisher & Paykel Healthcare Ltd in India

New Zealand company Fisher & Paykel Healthcare (FPH) has existed for over 30 years, producing respiratory-based products. Currently FPH employs around 1,000 staff (300 or more offshore), and has a turnover of about US$160 million, exporting products to most countries in the world. Essentially, the company sells to hospitals and to dealers in healthcare equipment.

The company first entered the Indian market about 20 years ago. The company accepted that as India could be a large potential market for it in the future, it had to commit resources to it. So, the company appointed its own representative who has intensified its knowledge of the market and helped it deal with regulatory issues and Indian bureaucracy, and indicated to key players in India that it is there for the long haul. Two years ago, the company moved to opening a warehouse in India, and held stock there. This greatly assisted its many distributors – it has about 90 of them who operate at the local level and for whom importing stock would be a major difficulty. FPH's Indian sales staff are also regularly brought over to New Zealand, as the company finds this develops their loyalty.

FPH is now experiencing rapid growth in India. Although the company considers that the only significant error it has made so far in India was in not putting stock into the market earlier, even an experienced exporter like it has taken at least ten years to get up to speed. FPH's success shows the benefits of adopting a long-term view of market development: currently, India only spends about US$1 billion on medical devices, whereas Australia spends US$1.7 billion.

Source: Next Stop India (2006); www.fphcare.com

3.2 Customer Relationship Management (CRM)

The practice of marketing is never as clear-cut as any one textbook definition of RM would suggest. In fact, marketing managers themselves confirm that there may be four different types of marketing being practised by contemporary organizations, sometimes simultaneously (Brodie et al, 1997). These range from transactional marketing (TM) to three separate types of RM: database marketing; interactive marketing; and network marketing. There is a degree of overlap between the terms and the strategies used, but we can describe these forms of RM more generally as: direct marketing; relationship marketing (B2C); and relationship marketing (B2B), respectively (Egan, 2001). It is, of course, the third of these that concerns us most. The value of seeing B2B RM as network marketing is explained in more detail in Chapter Five when we shall discuss the importance of industrial networks.

It is thus too simplistic to see marketing strategy merely as TM versus RM. It is typically only possible to have close relations with a limited number of business customers. This applies equally to managing relationships with suppliers. A hybrid managerial approach incorporating elements of both RM and TM may be the most appropriate response to prevailing market circumstances. Thus, rather than suggesting that, say, a highly interactive 'one-to-one' form of RM should take over as a firm's single new marketing strategy, a more viable approach is to develop a portfolio of relationships (see Chapters Five and Six).

As part of an overall strategic plan, the extension of the RM concept to that of 'customer relationship management' (CRM) now appears to be the dominant perspective for many marketers (Tanner, 2005). This is despite the probability that no IOR can ever be fully 'managed' – social actors are far too complex for that. But marketers constantly seek ways in which this 'management' may be made possible, and CRM approaches are certainly popular in helping them make sense of all the uncertainties inherent in IORs.

The extent to which firms commit to CRM is variable, however. Some people view CRM as a 'bottom-up' practice that focuses on the intelligent mining of customer data for tactical purposes (rather like the direct or database marketing variant of RM mentioned above), while others take more of a 'top-down' view that sees CRM as a core customer-centric business strategy that aims to win and keep profitable customers. A further take on CRM is an operational one, where automation becomes a key part of service delivery or sales force management (Buttle, 2004).

Technology can play an important part in CRM practices. CRM software systems aim to provide all staff who interact with customers access to real-time customer information and a complete history of all customer interactions with the selling firm. This enables staff to answer external questions about order status and quotations as well as internal questions regarding sales forecasts and relationship potential. The Internet also provides B2B marketers with opportunities to enhance their CRM activities. Even though the Internet may also make it easier for customers to search for and compare alternative suppliers, a recent study (Day and Bens, 2005) showed that managers viewed the Internet as a medium for encouraging customer dialogue and one that permitted the personalization of marketing messages (see also Chapter Eleven). For instance, hospital radiologists using General Electric's CT scanners and MRI machines can use the company's website to test new software that increases the efficiency of spinal examinations. If these expert members of the DMU like what they see, they can get their purchasing officer to order the software for $65,000 without the need to see a salesperson (www.ge.com). Another example of the financial impact of CRM facilitated by the Internet is given in Box 3.5.

Despite the promise of CRM systems that can manage loyalty schemes, cleanse databases or improve call centre performance, there is often a lack of perspective on the overall management of customers. Buttle (2004) outlines some common misunderstandings about CRM, as summarized in Figure 3.5.

- First, that it is just database marketing – while many firms do, indeed, build and exploit customer databases, CRM is much wider in scope.

- Second, it is purely a marketing process – while this seems to be, at first glance, quite true, a customer-centric perspective to planning needs to be held by many different functional areas as well (see Chapter Seven).

Box 3.5 Number crunching

Myaccount@dow

Dow Chemicals offers its customers 24-hours-a-day access to product information and detailed specification ('spec') sheets. Customers benefit by gaining the information they need much more quickly and easily than before, when the firm had relied on a phone-based system and the postal service to handle queries. Dow benefits, too: in 2000, the company is thought to have saved $1 million per month by not having to print and mail spec sheets to customers. Their website, myaccount@dow, allows customer-specific information to be accessed by the customer and Dow, for instance in the secure Internet monitoring of customer chemical tank levels. Reordering is automatically triggered when tanks reach predetermined levels.

Source: Day and Bens (2005); www.dow.com

Figure 3.5 Common misconceptions about CRM

- Third, it is just an IT issue – not all CRM initiatives involve investing in computerized systems. Behavioural changes by frontline staff may be far more important.

- Fourth, it is all about building loyalty – although firms like airlines use loyalty schemes quite successfully, CRM is much more than giving customers 'rewards' for their spending.

- Fifth, it can be implemented by any organization – while a CRM strategy is viable (and arguably essential) for any firm, the resources required to implement a data-based and/ or an automated approach to CRM may not be viable for all.

Moreover, while there are many reputable CRM consultants offering their services (e.g. Customer Connect Australia – www.customerconnect.com.au – whose clients include office automation suppliers Ricoh), some firms buying CRM packages are seduced by IT consultants into thinking that a fancy new computerized tool will ameliorate any other problems with the customer interface. It is all very well being able to warn a customer that their new machine tool will be delivered two months late, but far better to have ensured the product was ready by the promised time in the first place.

In response to such concerns, recent thinking in CRM argues for the interaction of a number of business processes which, if managed collectively, should avoid the fragmentation problems usually encountered during implementation (Payne, 2000). These include the recommendation that strategy development should be concerned with aligning both the selling organization's and customer's strategies. Also, the selling firm should strive for three-fold value creation, which consists of the actual value delivered to customers (see Chapter Ten), the value realized by the organization, and the lifetime value of particular customer segments. Such is the importance of value to relationship management that a value chain approach to CRM which captures these strategic processes has been put forward, as shown in Figure 3.6.

The model suggests five primary stages in the development and implementation of a CRM strategy. These sequential stages are as follows:

- Stage 1, customer portfolio analysis: To identify the actual and potential customers to service in the future.

- Stage 2, customer intimacy: To explore the profile, history, expectations, and preferences of these customers.

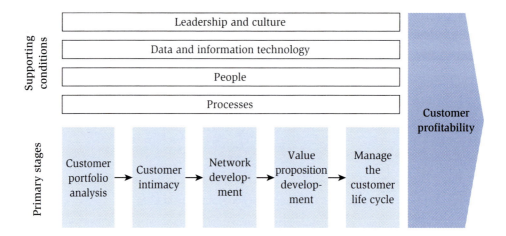

Figure 3.6 **The CRM value chain**
Source: Adapted with permission from Buttle (2004, p 40)
F. Buttle (2004) Customer Relationship Management: Concepts & Tools, p 40,
copyright Elsevier

- Stage 3, network development: To manage relationships with the individuals and organizations that contribute to the value creation for the chosen customers (for more on this topic, see Chapter Five).

- Stage 4, value proposition development: To identify sources of value for customers that meet their expectations and even exceed them (see Chapter Ten).

- Stage 5, manage the customer life cycle: By considering processes of customer acquisition, retention and development, and structural questions about how the firm is organized (see below).

This is not a one-off series of stages: they are iterative in the sense that the five stages are repetitive and continuous, especially in highly dynamic markets where the firm may need to respond to unexpected competitor activity; and reflexive in the sense that there is interdependence between the stages such that, for example, if Stage 4 reveals the firm's core competences do not match Stage 2's determining of customer needs, the firm may need to review its target market decisions (Buttle, 2004).

Relationship life cycles

Since lifetime value is an important element of CRM, it would be helpful if managers could somehow plot the progression of a relationship. This is far from easy, but Dwyer et al (1987) propose the idea of an IOR life cycle, suggesting that customer relationships can be broken down into four (idealistic) phases of development:

- First, the awareness stage: The buying and selling organizations independently consider each other as an exchange partner, perhaps by observing trade press advertisements or corporate websites.

- Second, the exploration stage: The parties begin to probe and test each other, perhaps by arranging sales calls or making an initial purchase. A number of processes can enable the relationship to develop at this point. They include attraction (the degree to which the interaction yields both buyer and seller some sort of payoff, whether this is tangible or intangible); negotiation (typically involving disclosures from each party over their longer-term desires and ability to compromise); the exercise of power and justice (with the latter arising from a fair use of the former); development of norms (standards of behaviour by which the parties interact); and expectations (including trust over the ability of each party to meet their obligations). The mini case in Box 3.6 shows a typical exploration stage in an IOR.

- Third, the expansion stage: The IOR moves to a greater exchange of rewards and an enlarging of the scope of exchange between the two organizations. This can be manifested in account development and the 'up-selling' by the supplier of additional higher-value goods and services. This stage involves increasing dependence between the partners.

- Fourth, the commitment stage: This is reached when both parties show a lasting desire to maintain a valued relationship. The two firms will exchange significant resources, including those dedicated to the preservation of the relationship. This may involve the dedication of equipment and systems to goods and services that are customer-specific, and even the swapping of employees between supplier and buyer to facilitate learning.

- Extra stage: If the parties decide that the IOR is no longer mutually beneficial, then they may (together or unilaterally) dissolve the relationship. Dissolution is easier at the early stages of the relationship life cycle. At the advanced stages, ending a relationship can make assets dedicated to the partnership obsolete and the termination can require additional search, negotiation, and set-up costs for both parties. Some organizations remain in less than desirable IORs because exit is too costly or there is no alternative partner in the marketplace.

One useful skill a firm can possess at this stage is project-ending competence. Done effectively, this can secure future business opportunities, as shown in the case of the Mitsubishi Motor Australia Ltd's (MMLA) car-manufacturing plant in South Australia (Havila and Medlin, 2009). Once the parent company had decided in 2004 to withdraw from making the 380 model in Adelaide, careful negotiations were necessary between MMLA and its local

---

Box 3.6 Mini case

Aggreko and an oil-rig customer

The global supplier of generators, Aggreko, prides itself in inspiring confidence in its customers worldwide in order to build relationships. A few years ago, a Gulf of Mexico-based oil rig experienced problems with its on-board generators, resulting in emergency shut-downs. For the oil company, restoring power was essential to maintain production. Aggreko was able to deliver and install eight 8000kW 480V generators in less than two days. The speed of the supplier's response impressed the customer so much that, although the firm used Aggreko as an emergency solution to begin with, the contract was eventually converted to a long-term lease.

Source: www.aggreko.com

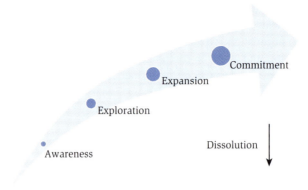

Figure 3.7 Potential relationship life-cycle stages

component suppliers. This involved terminating over 130 relationships and ensuring that suppliers who had built up stocks of parts were fairly compensated. The situation was handled so well that the brand name of Mitsubishi does not seem to have suffered in Australia, where import sales actually rose in 2008.

The life-cycle conceptualization of an IOR can guide mangers broadly over what to do next in a relationship at the strategic level but, like the well-known product life-cycle model (see Chapter Eight), it can oversimplify things since not all relationships will follow the cycle through the five stages represented in Figure 3.7 in the predicted way. Indeed, many relationships will 'stall' some way before the later stages are reached. For more on this, see Chapter Twelve for a discussion of key account management (KAM) development. There is a risk that managers may allow the model to desensitize them to the complexity of what is actually going on in day-to-day interactions, and even to the actions of other organizations in the overall network (i.e. operating in the same marketplace but outside the particular relationship).

Of course, sometimes the best-laid plans in B2B markets can come unstuck, especially when your firm is over-reliant on a key IOR that looks like it may fail to live up to its initial promise (see Box 3.7). In such circumstances, what would you advise the selling firm to do – curtail the relationship or be patient?

Box 3.7 Number crunching

The importance of an air conditioning contract

Worthington Nicholls, a British air conditioning provider, warned in 2007 that it had been hit by flooded clients and contract delays. The most significant of these was slow progress towards the signing of a contract with a large hotel firm to supply air conditioning for over 1,000 bedrooms. Water damage due to the flooding in certain parts of the UK led to installation work at three hotel sites being postponed. Worthington Nicholls' chief executive explained that the nature of its business relationships meant that the company was exposed to what he termed 'contract slippage'. As a result of these problems, the firm was predicting zero profits, representing a fall of £6.3 million from the previous year. In fact, the *Daily Telegraph* went as far as to describe the company's position as 'beleaguered' following a sharp fall in the firm's share price as a result of its poorly performing maintenance business. Long-term relationships in this sector are clearly crucial to underpinning a company's future.

Sources: Bland (2008), Bowers (2007)

3.3 Partnerships & Alliances

You should note that every relationship is ultimately different, and some will become more important than others. Wagner and Boutellier (2002) suggest that the development of relationships is dependent on a number of internal and external factors. The former include the nature of the product, the degree of technological sophistication, and the firm's core competencies. The latter include the environment, the market, and the competitive situation. When combined with an understanding of the strategic importance of the supplier's goods and the ease with which the supplying firm could be substituted, these factors result in four possibilities for IOR formation, as outlined in Figure 3.8. This diagram uses the example of

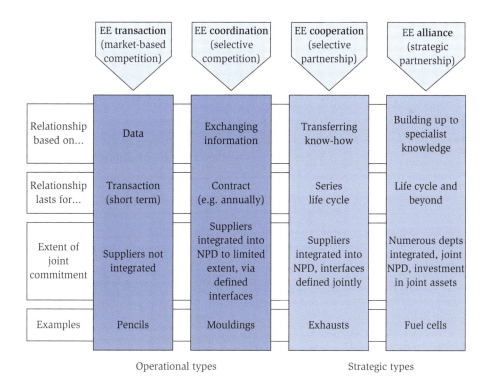

	EE transaction (market-based competition)	EE coordination (selective competition)	EE cooperation (selective partnership)	EE alliance (strategic partnership)
Relationship based on...	Data	Exchanging information	Transferring know-how	Building up to specialist knowledge
Relationship lasts for...	Transaction (short term)	Contract (e.g. annually)	Series life cycle	Life cycle and beyond
Extent of joint commitment	Suppliers not integrated	Suppliers integrated into NPD to limited extent, via defined interfaces	Suppliers integrated into NPD, interfaces defined jointly	Numerous depts integrated, joint NPD, investment in joint assets
Examples	Pencils	Mouldings	Exhausts	Fuel cells

Operational types   Strategic types

Figure 3.8 Types of relationship at DaimlerChrysler
Source: Adapted with permission from Wagner and Boutellier (2002, p 84)
S. Wagner & R. Boutellier (2002) Capabilities for Managing a Portfolio of Supplier Relationships,
Business Horizons, 45 (6), pp 79–88, copyright Elsevier

a German–US car manufacturer (known since 2007 as Daimler AG; www.daimler.com) to illustrate different 'extended enterprise' (EE) types. Note how it may not always be appropriate to form a close relationship with every supplier, with a hierarchy of 'closeness' being suggested, ranging from the operational levels of transaction and coordination to the more strategic levels of cooperation and alliance.

Terms like strategic alliance, or business partnership, or joint venture (JV) describe the ways in which some organizations have tried to gain competitive advantage by developing committed working partnerships, such as the 'code sharing' arrangement made between airlines like BA and American Airlines which entailed the two carriers coordinating routes, schedules, and reservation systems. Advantages can be gained through both partners agreeing to share the benefits of pooling their complementary resources. A key benefit of this approach is that it can allow firms to reduce the uncertainties that come with developing channel structures and roles (see Chapter Four). Cooperation enables partners to strengthen their market positions while sharing the burden of managing the supply chain. For instance, small biotechnology firms may partner large pharmaceutical companies. The former gain access to larger markets and distribution resources while the latter develop knowledge in cutting-edge research carried out by the smaller specialist firm (Lerner and Merges, 1997).

Perhaps surprisingly, alliances can occur between competing organizations, as well as between non-competing firms (Dussauge and Garrette, 1999). In the non-competitive arena, strategic motives for alliance formation include:

- International expansion (e.g. Renault forming a JV with Diesel Nacional, SA – www. dina.com.mx – to enter the Mexican market)

- Vertical integration (e.g. Aerospatia and Thompson working together to design and manufacture equipment for the aerospace sector)

- Diversification (e.g. BMW and Rolls-Royce – www.rolls-royce.com – collaborating to enable BMW to enter the aircraft engine market).

IOR scenarios involving apparent competitors include:

- Shared supplier alliances (e.g. Volkswagen and Renault jointly manufacturing automatic gearboxes to gain economies of scale)

- Quasi-concentration alliances where competitors collaborate to create a product that the consortium then offers to the market, but in other non-consortium activities the parties compete as usual (e.g. the development of the Tornado fighter jet by BAE, DASA, and Alenia – www.aeronautica.alenia.it – achieved by pooling the huge capital costs required)

- Complementary alliances, where partners bring different competencies to the collaboration (e.g. when Chrysler distributed Mitsubishi cars in the US, they sold only those models that complemented Chrysler's product line).

Alliances are not simple things to manage, however, and for a supplier or competitor to achieve partnership status, a number of things will typically need to be in place. These include: the development of the relationship at the personal as well as the organizational level; the ongoing, active management of the relationship; the ability of the supplier to provide bespoke (made-to-order) products where relevant; the ability to contribute to NPD processes; and, ideally, the location of the supplier close to the manufacturer for interaction and delivery purposes (Lemke et al, 2003), or the location of a distributor in the appropriate

Box 3.8 Voices

Celebrating the alliance between UMW and Toyota

The Malaysian company UMW (United Motor Works) advertises its strategic alliance with Toyota on its website and in trade journals. It is clearly proud of what it calls its 'close relationship' with Toyota Motor Corporation of Japan, dating back almost 25 years. In the company's words, 'this partnership has culminated in manufacturing, assembling, marketing and distribution of Toyota vehicles in Malaysia'. UMW attributes the success of the IOR to the trust and commitment UMW shows to its partners, and claims that the proof of its strategic approach is in the doubling of its share value over the previous two years.

Source: Advertorial, Vision Four Malaysia (2008); www.umw.com.my

marketplace, as in the case of UMW in Box 3.8. Note how the corporate 'voice' of UMW celebrates this IOR.

3.4 How IORs May 'Work' in Different Contexts

We close this chapter by considering some aspects of IORs that are not so often talked about in the majority of mainstream writings on RM. IORs are complex: they can function in unexpected ways in different contexts, and there are always external and internal forces acting, which mean relationships do not always 'work' as well as we hope they might. Some reasons why IORs may not function as expected are summarized in Figure 3.9.

First, we must remain aware of the relative importance of social and economic exchange. Despite the significance of social exchange between most organizations, the importance of economic performance should not be forgotten – as we saw in the Hong Kong case of Mr Cheung in Box 3.3. Even in cultures like China, where personal connections (also known

Figure 3.9 Some reasons why IORs may not work

as *guanxi* – see Chapter One) have long been held to be vital in IORs, recent research shows that industrialization and modernization have reduced the importance of traditional forms of *guanxi*. In the search for and appraisal of local suppliers, Millington et al (2006) found that UK and US manufacturers with subsidiaries in China looked for business rather than family or community connections to identity suitable supply partners. Formal relational contracts in long-term buyer–supplier relationships were found to be far more important than *guanxi* processes.

Second, we need to accept the likelihood of conflict in IORs. If we think of some contemporary B2B marketing issues such as high-profile cases of poor-quality goods sourced from China, the tensions that exist between farmers and supermarkets, or the growth of fair trade initiatives, we can see that the potential for conflict can be great, up and down supply chains. There is no escaping the fact that the commercial world is frequently perceived as a ruthless one, with large firms exerting their power quite legitimately over smaller rivals or suppliers. It is perhaps naive of us to think that the rational conduct of business could ever be otherwise. Thus, the B2B marketer must know something about managing inter-firm conflict (for more on this, see Chapter Four).

Third, the issue of power has not miraculously vanished just because firms have all supposedly embraced RM. Despite commonly espoused claims that collaborative IORs are the way forward for B2B marketers, you should not forget that differences in commercial power and dependency are still central to any purchasing relationship. These issues will be likely to have a significant effect on the nature and longevity of buyer–supplier interaction. Moreover, as the end-of-chapter case study shows, there can be a great difference between the rhetoric of cooperation in supply chains expressed by buyers and the reality of commercial exploitation faced by suppliers and the marketing managers who represent them.

Having said this, it is worth noting that relationships between organizations need not always be geared around buying and selling, as Box 3.9 suggests. However cynical you might be about a private firm's motives in linking up with a charitable cause, it can be hard to deny the benefits that can accrue to the receiving organization.

Box 3.9 Food for thought

Non-trading-based relationships

For many companies, the management of relationships with non-governmental organizations (NGOs) and other non-profit agencies such as charities is a key capability. This is because dialogue with different stakeholders is often an important element of the company's Corporate Social Responsibility (CSR) commitments. If such relationships are well handled, then the NGO can benefit from donations or work in-kind offered by the firm, and the firm can gain from the public relations value attached to these links. These IORs need to be carefully planned, however. For instance, cement company Lafarge was proudly supporting the Worldwide Fund for Nature (WWF) at the same time as it was trying to develop a quarry in Scotland against strong local environmental opposition, resulting in the WWF being widely criticized and Lafarge's green credentials being questioned.

Source: Rabin (2004); Valor and Merino de Deigo (2009); www.lafarge.com

Fourth, we should consider whether all customers actually want relationships with selling organizations. Outside the following sets of circumstances, it is possible that a business customer may just be looking for a simple transaction. Longer-term relationships are more likely to be sought when: the product or its applications are complicated; the product is strategically important for the customer; there are downstream service requirements; financial risk is high; or when reciprocity is expected. For instance, a financial audit practice may develop a relationship with a management consultancy so that each firm can benefit from referrals by the other (Buttle, 2004).

Indeed, customer firms have expressed several concerns over establishing closer relationships with their suppliers (Biong et al, 1997), including:

- Fear of dependency: such as worries that the supplier may act opportunistically, as well as the loss of flexibility to choose alternative suppliers.

- Lack of perceived value in the relationship: such as not believing that the relationship will create a competitive advantage.

- Lack of credibility in the proposed partners: customers may feel that the supplier is too small, or has a poor reputation for quality.

- Lack of relational orientation in the buying firm: the buying culture of the firm may be transactional (see Chapter Two).

- The pace of technological change: committing to one supplier may mean missing out on innovations available via alternative relationships.

IORs under pressure

Finally, rather than just celebrating IOR successes as we have tended to do in this chapter, it is important to recognize that many relationships will fail. Remember that it is people that represent organizations, and these managerial actors can make mistakes all too easily. They may forget, for instance, that the process of adaptation between partners in IORs should ideally be one of benign adjustment in the best interests of the parties involved and be founded on mutual trust. It is important for managers to have modest expectations at the start of a collaborative relationship and not to allow short-term tactical issues to overshadow long-term strategic interests. Thus, individual and organizational behaviours can have a strong bearing on perceptions of trust. Perceived selfish exploitation of one partner by the other (e.g. by raising prices during a period of high demand) is likely to have a detrimental impact on the development of closer relations.

Thus, although alliance partners should benefit mutually from the relationship by learning new skills and capabilities or gaining exposure to new markets, while at the same time focusing on their respective areas of distinctive competence, things do not always work out that way. As Dalton (2009) points out, some partners adopt unreasonable and unrealistic positions, often failing to take ownership for their complicity in a relationship's dissolution, thus leaving all parties in an untenable position. Instead, it may be necessary to accept that a particular strategy is no longer viable and that sunk costs are unrecoverable. Sometimes, forces in the wider marketplace can impact negatively on a partnership. For instance, Hour Glass, a Singapore retailer that sells fine watches, signed a market entry alliance with an Indonesian partner prior to the economic crisis that hit Asia in the late 1990s. It then found that the market was less attractive as a result of sudden falling demand and it no longer needed the partner's contacts in the distribution network and within government (Pangarkar, 2007). This meant that the partnership had to be terminated, causing resentment and potentially jeopardizing any future market entry plans for Indonesia that Hour Glass may still harbour.

If the rationale for a supposed 'strategic fit' between alliance partners is not well analysed, the partnership can fall apart. This problem affected the JV outlined in Box 3.10.

As we can see from the GE/Cisco case, things can become complicated for individual managers working in an IOR, especially when colleagues at different hierarchical levels in each organization have different perceptions. Attitudes can also vary during the course of an alliance where firms commit employees to inter-organizational project teams to solve particularly complex problems over things like NPD. If cooperation is strong, careful relationship management is vital, since complications can arise when the collaboration entity (i.e. the project) may elicit internal staff loyalties that supersede loyalties to the parent organizations. In this way, staff might temporarily 'forget' who actually pays their wages!

Of course, problems also arise when cooperation is not so strong. A final example of an IOR under pressure is that attempted by Alza and Ciba Geigy in the US in the 1990s. Here, collaboration was undermined by managers' behaviour. Alza was an entrepreneurial start-up company and Ciba Geigy a long-established pharmaceutical firm (now known as Novartis – www.novartis.com). The plan was for the partnership to develop new products within two or three years. To try to make things happen quickly, Alza attempted to bypass the hierarchical structure in CG, but this was not well received by CG managers, one of whom said, 'Alza never let confidence develop, they made constant criticisms and attacks on people . . . close personal collaboration was very rare'. As a result, the partners' expectations that NPD would be rapid were not met and the alliance was eventually terminated (Kumar and Das, 2007).

An end-of-chapter case study on IORs in a retail supply chain is provided in order to highlight a number of important relationship-management challenges for a food supplier dealing with a very powerful retail customer. Once you are familiar with some of the key issues in IORs, turn to Chapter Four to discover more on the ways relationships link

Box 3.10 Mini case

A disappointing IOR between General Electric and Cisco

The stimulus for this alliance came from the close personal relationship between the CEOs of both firms, who had met on the golf course. At the outset, trust was strong between the two companies due to this social bond as well as each firm's good brand reputation. GE managers were encouraged to think of ideas of how GE and Cisco (a leading supplier of networking equipment) could work together, including a mooted JV to sell Ethernet-based products and services for manufacturing companies. Unfortunately, after the JV was announced in 2000, the alliance floundered partly because the deal proposed did not fit Cisco's formal way of working in other alliances, and because they were reluctant to assign quality employees to the project. The external factor of a downturn in US manufacturing in late 2001 exacerbated the tensions in the relationship.

Source: Bierly and Gallagher (2007); www.cisco.com

organizations in marketing channels and supply chains, and to Chapter Five for more on network linkages.

Summary

The key points to take from this chapter are as follows:

- How market transactions and relational exchange in inter-organizational relationships (IORs) can be contrasted.

- How relationship marketing (RM) thinking has developed over the last century.

- The key elements of RM, including a long-term perspective, trust, commitment, communication, service quality, and mutual benefits.

- The importance of relative power and dependence in IORs such that economic and material exchange are as vital to consider as the social elements of relationships.

- The complexity of undertaking a strategy of successful customer relationship management (CRM).

- The utility of taking a relationship life-cycle perspective and what each stage indicates about the activities likely to be taking place in the IOR.

- Why partnerships and alliances may form between organizations, and how we can classify these types of IOR.

- Some of the internal and external reasons why IORs may fail.

Discussion questions

1. Explain the main differences between transactional and relational exchanges in a B2B context.

2. While some authors argue that trust and commitment are central to relationship marketing success, others have suggested that power is the key factor. Explain which elements of IORs you think are the most important, and why.

3. Write a series of events that might typify the stages in a developing relationship between an office-furniture dealer with several sites and a computer-system vendor. Repeat this for the same furniture dealer and a growing investment bank, thinking of how the relationship might develop differently in this case.

4. What advice would you give to the director of an SME supplying specialist electronic components to the motor sector who was considering the purchase of an IT-based CRM system?

5. Give an example of a collaborative relationship (ideally, a reasonably close one) between your organization (or one with which you are familiar) and another, either upstream or downstream, or even a competitor, in the supply/demand chain. How essential to the competitive advantage of your organization is the strength of this IOR?

6. Could any other organizations (e.g. alternative suppliers or distributors) in the surrounding network adequately replace either your firm or your partner firm in this IOR? If so, what factors do you believe are keeping the two firms together?

Case study

Working with a Powerful Customer: IORs in the Retail Supply Chain

Gillian Hopkinson, Lancaster University, Lancaster, UK

Introduction

In the UK, four companies or 'grocery multiples' (so called because of their multiple retail outlets), Tesco, Sainsbury's, Asda, and Morrisons, dominate the retailing of grocery products with a combined total of over 70% of market share. The UK public have what seems to be a love–hate relationship with these organizations. The product and service offerings of the giant retailers seem well matched to consumer preferences. The concentration of the market, however, has also led to widespread suspicion as demonstrated, for example, on the website www.Tescopoly.com.

The competition authorities are also concerned about the concentration in the grocery retail market and the most recent Competition Commission enquiry that addressed these concerns was initiated in May 2006 and reported in April 2008. One area this enquiry addressed was the effect of concentration at the retail level on the entire grocery supply chain. By the time of the provisional report in 2007, the Commission had noted that they had received only sparse evidence regarding specific practices from primary producers or farmers. Noting a likely 'climate of fear' amongst the farmers, the commission promised them anonymity. William Hudson, however, required no anonymity as a former strawberry farmer who attributed the collapse of his business to what he perceives as the malpractices of the multiples. These malpractices include payments extracted for promotions, the use of retrospective discounts, and of pay-to-stay fees. Mr Hudson was quoted in *The Times* newspaper on the day the commission finally reported: 'Buy one get one free? The grower has to pay for those and gets no say in it' and 'In the food chain it's always the supermarket that does best.'

However, this picture of supply chain abuse is not supported in all the evidence provided by supply chain participants. Some submissions to the commission point to the role of the multiples in the growth and development of supplier organizations. Branston Ltd provides one such account which serves as an example through which we can explore a business relationship.

Supplying Tesco with potatoes

'Potatoes are our business,' according to Branston Ltd. The company was founded in 1968 as a business owned by farmers and is now a leading player in the 'buying, packing, distribution and marketing' of potatoes. Whilst you are unlikely to be familiar with the name, you have probably eaten its product – at least if you live in the UK. In the late 1980s, Branston noted the increasing importance of the supermarkets in the fresh produce area and thus sought close involvement with key retail organizations. To this end, it invested heavily in high-quality facilities that would enable it to meet the demands of retail customers. In turn, this allowed it to commence supply to Tesco in 1990. At that time, Branston was the smallest of Tesco's 19 potato suppliers. From those small beginnings, a relationship has developed in which Branston now supplies 65% (260,000 tonnes per annum) of Tesco's potatoes. These are largely retailed as own brands in ranges including 'Tesco Finest' and 'Tesco Value'. For Branston, this generates sales in excess of £100 million per annum, 85% of the company's turnover.

Branston's Managing Director, Graeme Beattie, played an important role in initiating the relationship, which he is careful not to romanticize. Evidence he presented to the Commission speaks of 'ups and downs', occasional 'unreasonable demands', and the continuous push on production costs made by Tesco, 'a challenging customer'. Tensions notwithstanding, Branston insists that its priority is to understand and respond to customer needs.

Potatoes were once a commoditized product but a trip to a large grocery retailer confirms that differentiation and product proliferation have brought complexity to those customer needs. Supermarkets now offer a range of varieties and price points and increasingly sell packaged, rather than loose, potatoes, and this creates valuable branding opportunities. Potatoes have moved from traditional locations in the fresh produce stand or the freezer section to occupy space in the chiller cabinet as well. Prepared and semi-prepared offerings are predominantly own (retailer) brand and include microwavable mash, stuffed mini-jackets, croquettes, and easy-steam baby new potatoes. Branston is at the forefront in the development of such innovative products and, as Branston says, [we now] 'wash, peel, slice, dice, wedge, core and fill, coat, dress, flavour, and season so that our customers don't have to.'

How the IOR affects and is affected by end-user markets

The highly developed market-sensing abilities of the major multiples and their pursuit of market share have been key factors in the development of innovative, value-added potato products. An example can be drawn from the summer of 2008, when Tesco, which has a higher than average value shopper segment, sought responses to consumer concerns over rapidly escalating food prices. Tesco suggested the launch of a microwavable herb-and-butter pack of potatoes in the value range. This product was developed and delivered by Branston in just five weeks and hit the chiller cabinets in August 2008, just weeks before the 'credit crunch' entered Western consumers' daily vocabulary. Perhaps this successful product launch contributed to the awarding later in the year of 'Tesco Vegetable Supplier of the Year' to Branston.

The market-shaping and market-growing abilities of the grocery multiples can clearly be attractive to those suppliers that are able to find ways to collaborate with these giant companies. Collaboration, however, does place immense demands upon suppliers in terms of abilities, investments, and organization. Collaboration spans many functional areas, and at Branston, specialists in logistics, product development, quality control, and account management work with relevant counterparts within the customer organization. Investments are ongoing and include the construction of a new £3.5 million factory 'to meet the increasing demands of retail customers' in 2008. Branston needs to be able to work effectively with packaging companies and logistics providers in order to deliver complex products.

Upstream impacts of the IOR

The volume, range, and reliability that Tesco requires have also led Branston to expand its own supplier base. In turn, in order to be able to deliver volume efficiently, many of Branston's suppliers cooperate in groupings. For example, the 3Ms group (3 Musketeers) in fact comprises five farming businesses in Suffolk that initiated collaboration upon being approached individually by Branston in 2002. Further afield, the Majorcan Esplet cooperative comprises 25 potato growers. They had been exporting potatoes to the UK since 1924 and in the late 1990s worked directly with both Marks & Spencer and Waitrose. In 1998, they commenced supply to Branston, believing that the addition of a level to the supply chain would allow them to expand their UK presence and, specifically, offer a channel for their product into Tesco. Esplet enjoys the security that supply to Branston brings but would like to see more marketing from its partner focusing on the specific attributes of Majorcan potatoes.

What security does Tesco bring to Branston and its suppliers? Branston has no contract with Tesco but dedicates 85% of the activity of the firm to this organizational customer. The lack of a contract may be seen as placing Branston in a vulnerable position. This argument must be balanced with consideration of the ability of Tesco to source elsewhere in a manner that offers the efficiency, volume, and innovation that Branston provides. Graeme Beattie told the Competition Commission: 'Tesco has put a huge amount of faith in us to supply them with 65% of their potato volume. They need us – but they need us to be efficient. If we run a low-cost, efficient business which delivers Tesco and their customers what they want – then we have all the security a contract could deliver.' Branston does, however, offer contracts to its suppliers in order to provide them with security and lower risk and give them the confidence to invest in their businesses.

Signs of independence?

Despite the benefits that Tesco brings to Branston, should Branston have so many of its eggs (or potatoes) in one basket? In 2007, Branston made its first moves to produce a consumer-facing brand (it had previously had brands aimed at the wholesale market, thereby extending its customer network beyond Tesco). Under the name of the Real Potato Company, it sought to respond to consumer demand for fresh, quality, and contemporary potatoes and bring a wider range of varieties to a broader customer audience. Nevertheless, this product launch was, to an extent, coordinated with Tesco. The brand was stocked in 250 Tesco stores and Tesco was given exclusivity with respect to two new varieties, the Bellini and Piccolo potatoes.

Source: Branston (www.branston.com); Tesco (www.tescofarming.com); Potato Council (www. potato.org.uk); Competition Commission (www.competition-commission.org.uk); Tescopoly (www.tescopoly.org); The Times (2008) 30 April, p 20

Case study questions

1. Considering the various B2B exchanges mentioned in the case study, identify features that would lead you to see these exchanges as either predominantly transactional or relational.

2. On the basis of the evidence provided in this case study, do you think that Branston has too many potatoes in the Tesco basket? In light of your answer, what actions would you advise Branston to take now?

3. Visit the Competition Commission website (below) and locate evidence submitted by farmers that is critical of the supermarkets (from Mr Hudson or others). Taking one submission, critically consider whether you think the farmer could do anything (and, if so, what) to develop a satisfactory way of working with the multiple grocers. www.competition-commission.org.uk/inquiries/ref2006/grocery/third_party_submissions_farmers.htm

Further Reading

Blois, K. J. (1998) Don't all Firms have Relationships? Journal of Business & Industrial Marketing, 13 (3), pp 1–11

This paper discusses the need for suppliers to determine carefully the form of IOR appropriate for their business. Two firms are considered, one of which is successful because it does not develop close relationships, while the other each year applies a sophisticated classification scheme to determine what type of relationship will be most profitable.

Bresnen, M. (1996) An Organizational Perspective on Changing Buyer–Supplier Relations: A Critical Review of the Evidence, Organization, 3 (2), pp 121–46

The author critiques research in IORs in three respects: the over-concentration of research effort in particular industrial sectors; the underplaying of the roles of perceptions and choice on the part of supplier organizations; and the absence of any real consideration of the impact of intra-organizational structures and processes. It is interesting to ponder whether these criticisms are still relevant today.

Fuller, T. & Lewis, J. (2002) 'Relationships Mean Everything': A Typology of Small-Business Relationship Strategies in a Reflexive Context, British Journal of Management, 13 (4), pp 317–36

This paper investigates the meaning of relationships to owner-managers of small firms, and how differences in meaning are implicated in the strategy of these organizations. The analysis reveals that IORs are conceptualized as the mechanism that links the firm to its environment and also as causal to the impact that changes in the environment have on the firm.

Hingley, M., Leek, S., & Lindgreen, A. (2008) Business Relationships the Morrissey Way, British Food Journal, 110 (1), pp 128–43

Using the lyrics of English singer Morrissey (formerly of The Smiths) to introduce a variety of IOR concepts, these authors investigate the 'human factor' inherent in B2B relationships. They argue that business decisions can owe as much to the more emotional world of personal relations as to rational corporate thinking, and conclude that there is rarely a 'right' way to engage in IORs.

Möller, K. & Halinen, A. (2000) Relationship Marketing Theory: Its Roots and Direction, Journal of Marketing Management, 16 (1), pp 81–94

This paper argues that RM does not form a general theory of marketing, and that actually two types of relationship theory exist: market-based, more consumer-orientated RM, and network-based, more inter-organizationally-orientated RM. The fundamental differences between these two types of theory are identified and discussed.

References

Alderson, W. (1965) Dynamic Marketing Behavior: A Functionalist Theory of Marketing, Richard D. Irwin, Homewood, IL

Bierly, P. E. & Gallagher, S. (2007) Explaining Alliance Partner Selection: Fit, Trust and Strategic Expediency, Long Range Planning, 40, pp 134–53

Biong, H., Wathne, K., & Parvatiyar, A. (1997) Why do Some Companies not Want to Engage in Partnering Relationships? in Gemunden, H. G., Ritter, T., & Walter, A. (eds), Relationships and Networks in International Markets, Pergamon, Oxford, pp 91–108

Bland, B. (2008) LSE may Investigate Worthington Nicholls Float, online at http://www.telegraph.co.uk, accessed August 2008

Blois, K. J. (1997) When is a Relationship a Relationship? in Gemunden, H. G., Ritter, T., and Walter, A. (eds), Relationships and Networks in International Markets, Elsevier, Oxford, pp 53–64

Blois, K. J. (1999) Trust in Business-to-Business Relationships: An Evaluation of its Status, Journal of Management Studies, 36 (2), pp 197–215

Bowers, S. (2007) Cooler Weather and Floods Stem Profits at Air-Conditioning Firm, The Guardian, 18 August, p 35

Brodie, R. J., Coviello, N. E., Brookes, R. W., & Little, V. (1997) Towards a Paradigm Shift in Marketing: An Examination of Current Marketing Practices, Journal of Marketing Management, 13 (5), pp 383–406

Brown, S. (2007) Are we nearly there yet? On the Retro-Dominant Logic of Marketing, Marketing Theory, 7 (3), pp 291–300

Buttle, F. (2004) Customer Relationship Management: Concepts and Tools, Elsevier Butterworth Heinemann, Oxford

Christopher, M., Payne, A., & Ballantyne, D. (2002) Relationship Marketing: Creating Stakeholder Value, Butterworth-Heinemann, Oxford

Dalton, C. M. (2009) Strategic Alliances: There are Battles and there is the War, Business Horizons, 52, pp 105–8

Day, G. S. & Bens, K. J. (2005) Capitalizing on the Internet Opportunity, Journal of Business & Industrial Marketing, 20 (4/5), pp 160–8

Dussauge, P. & Garrette, B. (1999) Cooperative Strategy: Competing Successfully through Strategic Alliances, John Wiley, Chichester

Dwyer, F. R., Shurr, P. H., & Oh, S. (1987) Developing Buyer–Seller Relationships, Journal of Marketing, 51 (April), pp 11–27

Dye, P. (2008) How to Pamper your Customer, The Marketer, June, pp 32–7

Egan, J. (2001), Relationship Marketing: Exploring Relational Strategies in Marketing, Financial Times/Prentice Hall, Harlow

Gordon, I. (1998) Relationship Marketing: New Strategies, Techniques and Technologies to Win the Customers you Want and Keep them Forever, Wiley, Ontario

Gronroos, C. (1994) From Marketing Mix to Relationship Marketing: Towards a Paradigm Shift in Marketing, Management Decision, 32 (2), pp 4–20

Gronroos, C. (2000) Creating a Relationship Dialogue: Communication, Interaction and Value, Marketing Review, 1 (1), pp 1–14

Guillet de Monthoux, P. B. L. (1975) Organizational Mating and Industrial Marketing Conservatism – Some Reasons why Industrial Marketing Managers Resist Marketing Theory, Industrial Marketing Management, 4, pp 2536

Havila, V. & Medlin, C. J. (2009) Project-Ending Competence: Supplier Relationships Ending and Maintaining Trust with External Actors, Paper presented at 4th Meeting of the IMP Group in Asia, Kuala Lumpur, 10–12 December

Hawkins, T. G., Wittmann, C. M., & Beyerlein, M. M. (2008) Antecedents and Consequences in Buyer–Seller Relations: Research Synthesis and New Frontiers, Industrial Marketing Management, 37, pp 895–909

Kumar, R. & Das, T. K. (2007) Interpartner Legitimacy in the Alliance Development Process, Journal of Management Studies, 44, pp 1425–53

Lemke, F., Goffin, K., & Szwejczewski, M. (2003) Investigating the Meaning of Supplier–Manufacturer Partnerships, International Journal of Physical Distribution and Logistics Management, 33 (1), pp 12–35

Lerner, J. & Merges, R. P. (1997) The Control of Strategic Alliances: An Empirical Analysis of Biotechnology Collaborations, Working Paper 6014, National Bureau of Economic Research, Cambridge, MA

Levitt, T. (1972) Production-Line Approach to Service, Harvard Business Review, 50 (September/October), pp 41–52

Millington, A., Eberhardt, M., & Wilkinson, B. (2006) Guanxi and Supplier Search Mechanisms in China, Human Relations, 59 (4), pp 501–31

Morgan, R. and Hunt, S. (1994) The Commitment-Trust Theory of Relationship Marketing, Journal of Marketing, 58 (July), pp 317–51

Next Stop India: A Guide for New Zealand Business (2006) A Report to the Asia New Zealand Foundation, School of Marketing and International Business, Victoria University of Wellington

Pangarkar, N. (2007) Survival during a Crisis: Alliances by Singapore Firms, British Journal of Management, 18, pp 209–23

Payne, A. (2000) Relationship Marketing: Managing Multiple Markets, in Cranfield School of Management (eds), Marketing Management: A Relationship Marketing Perspective, MacMillan, Basingstoke, pp 16–30

Rabin, E. (2004) Business/NGO Partnerships – What's the Payback? online at http://www.greenbiz.com/feature/2004/05/03, accessed March 2009

Tadajewski, M. & Saren, M. (2009) Rethinking the Emergence of Relationship Marketing, Journal of Macromarketing, 29 (2), pp 193–206

Tanner, J. (2005) Customer Relationship Management: A Fad or a Field? Journal of Marketing Research, May, pp 240–2

The Times (2008) 30 April, p 20

Valor, C. & Merino de Deigo, A. (2009) Relationships of Business and NGOs: An Empirical Analysis of Strategies and Mediators of their Private Relationship, Business Ethics: A European Review, 18 (2), pp 110–26

Varey, R. J. (2002) Relationship Marketing: Dialogue and Networks in the E-Commerce Era, John Wiley, Chichester

Vargo, S. L. & Lusch, R. F. (2004) Evolving to a New Dominant Logic for Marketing, Journal of Marketing, 69, pp 1–17

Vision Four Malaysia (2008) UMW Advertorial: Beyond Boundaries, September, pp 24–5

Wagner, S. & Boutellier, R. (2002) Capabilities for Managing a Portfolio of Supplier Relationships, Business Horizons, 45 (6), pp 79–88

Webster, F. E. (1992) The Changing Role of Marketing in the Corporation, Journal of Marketing, 56 (October), pp 1–17

Wilson, D. T. & Mummalaneni, V. (1986) Bonding and Commitment in Buyer–Seller Relationships: A Preliminary Conceptualisation, Industrial Marketing & Purchasing, 1 (3), pp 44–58

Wooliscroft, B. (2008) Re-inventing Wroe? Marketing Theory, 8 (4), pp 367–85

Chapter 4
Marketing Channels & Supply Chains

Introduction & Learning Objectives

This chapter considers the importance of marketing channels and supply chains in B2B marketing. It explores some further issues of relationship management in the light of our discussion of inter-organizational relationships (IORs) in Chapter Three. We shall examine the various flows up and down marketing channels (i.e. those that typically extend 'downstream' from manufacturing firms to customers) and the main roles assumed by channel participants. As we shift our attention beyond downstream relationships to those extending upstream as well, we begin to take on board the idea of supply chain management (SCM). As we explained in Chapter One, however, we shall usually be referring to 'supply/demand chains' in order to accommodate a demand chain management (DCM) view (Heikkila, 2002). So, instead of SCM, we often use the abbreviation S/DCM.

The importance of taking a holistic view of the supply chain is shown in Box 4.1. Manufacturer De-Ta SpA and its component suppliers need their Taiwanese intermediary

---

Box 4.1 Mini case
Upstream intermediaries in China

Since 2000, the second-largest producer of office chairs in Europe, De-Ta SpA of Italy, has purchased spring suspensions from Korean and Taiwanese companies which have relocated their production to China. The price, quantity, payment terms, and delivery times for these components are negotiated with a Taiwanese intermediary. The intermediary then deals with their Chinese suppliers to ensure deliveries according to agreed schedules and technical specifications. The Taiwanese origin of the intermediary's representative is important for supplier IORs since he can speak Chinese and understands the relational context of the country. He also understands Western business practices and appreciates the need for warranties to assuage De-Ta's concerns that some suppliers may become preoccupied with reducing costs to meet their price demands by altering technical specifications. From an S/DCM perspective, product quality is something the firm cannot afford to compromise if it is to maintain its reputation for high-quality furniture with end-user organizations.

Source: Nassimbeni and Sartor (2006); www.detadesign.com

to ensure that relationships run smoothly so that De-Ta's end-user customers are satisfied. Without the skills of the intermediary organization, this chain would probably not function.

Chapter Aims

After completing this chapter, you should be able to:

- Identify the contribution of marketing channels to B2B marketing strategy
- Analyse key channel participants, activities, and flows
- Appreciate upstream and downstream supply chain issues
- Recognize how marketing logistics can support B2B marketing.

4.1 Structure & Role of Marketing Channels

Marketing channels (also known as distribution channels) have not always gained the attention they deserve, but in recent years this has been changing due to the recognition that they offer a way of gaining a sustainable competitive advantage (Narus and Anderson, 1996). There are several reasons why this advantage is hard to copy:

- First, channel strategy is long term: Setting up and maintaining channels for making products available to customers usually takes quite a long time to plan and implement.
- Second, channel strategy can be complicated: It generally involves some sort of structure comprising organizations and individuals.
- Third, channel strategy is based on relationships and people: A channel is not an inanimate 'thing', but is best seen as a collection of people interacting with each other in different organizations (Robicheaux and Coleman, 1994).

Some of the following B2B-orientated discussion of channels will be familiar to those of you who have studied the 'place' P of the marketing mix, although it is likely that you will have discussed it from the point of view of a high-profile brand producer trying to market to end users in the form of a mass of consumers. Our take on channels is somewhat broader than this, however, in that it embraces the B2B marketing that is necessary between manufacturer and retailer as part of an ultimate B2C channel, but mainly considers the B2B channels used to get industrial goods to organizational customers. In both these views, every organization is a customer to the previous organization in the value chain – see Figure 1.4 in Chapter One.

Channel management

A classic definition of a channel has been provided by Coughlin et al (2006, p 2) as: 'a set of interdependent organizations involved in the process of making a product or service available for use or consumption'. This seems pretty straightforward, but the concept can be interpreted differently by different channel members. For the manufacturer, the channel may mean the movement of products through different intermediaries (or 'middlemen', to use an old-fashioned term) needed to get to the end customer. Intermediaries themselves may perceive the channel in terms of the flow of title (or ownership) of goods. The end customer may simply view the channel as a host of profit-taking intermediaries between them and the manufacturer.

We must try to grasp the channel concept from a perspective that makes sense to the pro-spective B2B marketer. Thus, like Rosenbloom (1999, p 9), this chapter takes a managerial decision-making view of the channel. This means looking 'through the eyes of marketing management in producing and manufacturing firms' such that the channel is defined as: 'the external contactual organization that management operates to achieve its distribution objectives'. The term 'contactual' indicates that there are core functions being performed by linked channel members, such as the buying and selling of products. Other firms, such as transportation providers and insurance companies, perform non-core functions which largely exclude them from our channel considerations.

An important principle of channel management is the allocation of distribution tasks. These tasks can be summarized under four headings as shown in Figure 4.1.

1. *Reducing complexity*: the first of these tasks is to reduce complexity in terms of the number of market interactions. In order to reach their individual customers in a marketplace, each producer needs to ensure exchanges can take place with each customer. Manufacturers can choose to go direct, perhaps via the Internet and mail order/catalogues, or via their own sales forces or sales branch (see Chapter Twelve). However, without the use of an inter-mediary, the number of separate exchanges that would be required may be huge. With an intermediary, such as a wholesaler acting in the channel, several manufacturers can sell to this organization which, in turn, collects a variety of different products which it then makes available to all its customers. These customers benefit by only needing to interact with the wholesaler instead of every manufacturer separately.

2. *Increasing value*: producing firms often rely on intermediaries to provide a level of added value that meets customers' requirements better than those thought to be offered by competitors. Due to their proximity to the market, intermediaries are felt to be better placed to understand and deliver the value that end users desire. For instance, organizations that produce computing, telecom, and networking equipment are advised to work with distribu-tors when seeking growth in emerging markets – see Box 4.2. Note how manufacturers are given a number of recommendations for building their relationships with distributors in the channel to ensure that the ultimate customer gets the best value added. The resulting IORs are necessary for SME clients to be properly serviced.

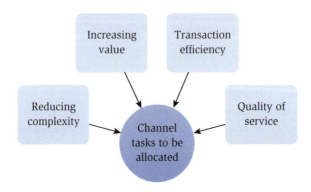

Figure 4.1 Distribution channel tasks

> ## Box 4.2 Mini case
> ### Distribution for high-tech equipment
>
> Although many high-tech original equipment manufacturers (OEMs) have turned to their sales forces and the Internet to service their large customers in developed economies, they should not ignore the possibilities of using so-called 'two-tier' distributors (the name arises because they buy from manufacturers and sell to resellers) in new markets. Such distributors can help manufacturers sell to SMEs as they typically control over 40% of all distribution to that market segment. They succeed because most deals are smaller, so the cost of a suppliers' direct sales force can be prohibitive compared with the cost of using a distributor. They also have well-established links with value-added resellers (VARs) who focus on specific regions and industries. SMEs tend to prefer purchasing from these smaller resellers, who understand their requirements and are conveniently located.
>
> Manufacturers should thus view these two-tier distributors as a strategic asset and invest in them to build channel partnerships. For example, when credit is restricted, manufacturers can extend more generous terms to assist distributors in stocking a larger inventory. They can also work with distributors to develop product 'bundles' or solutions aimed at particular markets. Finally, if distributors and VARs are concerned over potential channel conflict, an OEM can declare certain segments off limits to its own sales force.
>
> *Source: Doctorow et al (2008)*

3. *Transaction efficiency*: third, members of the distribution channel attempt to achieve routinization, that is, the standardization of transaction processes. This can be achieved by, for instance, regulating order size, delivery cycles, and payment frequency, as well as by automating ordering and distribution processes so as to lower operational costs. Logistics management has a key role to play here (see section 4.4).

4. *Quality of service*: finally, the provision of services like specialist training of end-user personnel, frequent deliveries, and credit facilities can represent considerable value to some customer organizations. Intermediaries must also be skilled in accumulating, sorting, and breaking down bulk quantities of all the goods provided by different manufacturers. This service allows end-user customers, whether they are other firms or consumers, to select products in quantities and formats that suit their purchasing needs.

Types of intermediary

Rather confusingly, the title 'distributor' is used by managers and scholars as an umbrella term for several different types of channel intermediary, as well as for a specific type of intermediary. We shall make sure we differentiate between the two uses of the term in this section. As their name suggests, these organizations function in order to transfer products through the channel, adding value as they do so, for example by providing storage, repair, or credit facilities. In B2B markets, the main types of intermediary are wholesalers, distributors (or dealers), agents, and value-added resellers. Retailers are also technically intermediaries (i.e. between producers and consumers) in what are ultimately B2C markets.

Distributors/intermediaries perform several important upstream and downstream channel tasks. Upstream, they serve manufacturers in a number of ways (Rosenbloom, 1999). They are, of course, key organizational customers of manufacturers as they usually purchase and hold stock (or inventory). In this way, the manufacturer is relieved of a good deal of the financial and logistical risk of holding stock itself. This is because distributors may share credit risk with the manufacturer. They do this by offering credit to their own customers, in addition to the credit that the manufacturer may extend to them as distributors. They also take on most of the selling risk since they have committed to buying the products. Distributors should be able to forecast market demand and provide information about potential new product needs better than manufacturers since they are closer to the end customer.

Distributors add value downstream in the channel by giving assistance and rapid response to customers. They serve customers by providing fast local delivery from their stock holdings and give local credit, product information, and buying advice. They can also supply a wide range of products that fit the needs of a particular customer segment, for instance builders' merchants that stock a variety of construction and home improvement products aimed at the SME trades like plumbers and joiners (Ellis et al, 1999). These sources of value will hopefully generate a committed set of end-user customers to which the manufacturer has targeted its products.

It is important to be aware of the differences between the activities carried out by types of intermediaries. For instance:

- A wholesaler differs from an actual 'distributor' (or dealer) in that the former provides products to other intermediaries, whereas the latter tends to sell directly to end-user customers, typically organizations.

- Moreover, distributors can be contrasted with 'agents'. Distributors/dealers typically take title of (i.e. purchase) the goods being sold, whereas agents do not. Instead, they will have on their books a number of products, often from a range of manufacturers, on which they gain commission should a sale take place downstream. You should think of what this might mean in terms of an intermediary's commitment to an IOR with a supplier: any intermediary firm that actually buys a manufacturer's products is probably going to expend more effort in selling it on to the next level in the value chain.

- Industrial distributors/dealers are often used when a manufacturer has many geographically dispersed customers or makes goods that are bought in small quantities on a local basis. They are thus common in sectors such as office stationery or building supplies.

- Agents are popular amongst manufacturers who want to act more quickly than the time it takes to negotiate with a distributor, or who do not have the resources to maintain their own sales force. In international markets, agents can search for potential overseas distributors and provide specialist support in exporting and promotion.

Channel structure

It is very likely that a B2B marketer will attempt to employ a multi-channel strategy to ensure that all their customer segments' needs are met. Such a strategy may involve both direct and indirect channels as well as a mixture of different intermediaries. Managers need to consider the appropriate length and breadth of what they typically come to see as 'their' channels. Some issues in trying to design channel structures are summarized in Figure 4.2.

Channel length concerns the optimum number of levels in the channel to ensure the desired service outputs for the end user. It can be common practice in some sectors for purchases to be made from a particular type of intermediary (like electronic parts for repairs or maintenance from specialist distributors), meaning that established approaches must be adopted. In other sectors, there may be opportunities to develop new types of channels that fulfil hitherto unexplored customer needs (such as 24-hour availability of parts).

The issue of breadth concerns the numbers of each type of intermediary to be used: the greater the number, the greater the intensity of distribution. Usually, the more customers sought by a producer, the more intermediaries required to service them. This intensive approach may be suitable for some goods, typically those sold at lower prices to mass markets (e.g. industrial fastenings), but other more technical products with higher margins may necessitate selective or even exclusive distribution with only a few carefully appointed dealers (e.g. computer systems).

Another consideration regarding high channel intensity is that this may bring greater sales but it can reduce the influence of the manufacturer over their channel partners, as well as increase the potential for inter-firm conflict. Moreover, a multi-channel strategy does not always guarantee reaching more customers. Segments that patronize any new channels may comprise mainly customers who have switched from the firm's prior channels (say, from 'bricks' to 'clicks', i.e. from conventional stores to the Internet), resulting in channel cannibalization rather than new business (Rosenbloom, 2006). See Chapter Eleven for more on the use of the Internet for B2B trading and communicating with customers.

As Box 4.3 shows, for a product with which some of you will be very familiar, channels are dynamic systems prone to change depending on the needs of their members. The case illustrates how intermediaries can effectively be 'squeezed' from above by an aggressive brewery and from below by consumer preferences. Whether fair or not, the combination of B2B and B2C marketing practices here has had a massive impact on a rival brewer.

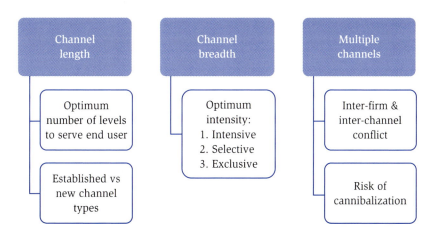

Figure 4.2 Some issues of channel structure

Box 4.3 Food for thought

Channel choices in Thailand

In the 1930s, the Thai government gave a virtual monopoly for what became known as the 'national' beer, Singha, to the Boon Rawd Brewery Company of Bangkok. In 1993, Singha had 90% of the market. Yet, within ten years, it was left with only 11% and a newcomer called Chang had achieved a 70% market share. How this was done is a story of ruthless channel management. It has lessons for marketing managers in how channel IORs can be handled in highly productive, though not necessarily entirely ethical, ways.

The family firm behind Singha was never seriously challenged until it encountered a company that had been given its own monopoly, for distilling rice 'whisky' (actually, rum). A brand of whisky called Mekhong was the preferred drink in rural Thailand, where 70% of the population lived. The owner of this firm, Charoen Sirivadhanabhakdi, formed a partnership with the European brewer, Carlsberg, when it was given permission to enter Thailand. Charoen's sales force was instructed to promote Carlsberg along with their whiskies, and to tell any Singha agent (or retailer) that if it declined to stock Carlsberg then it couldn't buy the popular Mekhong brand. Boon Rawd then informed its 10,000 agents countrywide that if they sold any bottles of Carlsberg, they would lose the right to sell Singha. However, rural retailers recognized that, if they couldn't get the whisky the consumer wanted they would go out of business, so the IORs that had sustained the Singha distribution system collapsed.

Then in 1994, Charoen obtained a licence to produce beer locally and promptly launched a Thai-made beer called 'Chang'. It did so at a deliberately low price by raising the price of whisky and bundling the sales of whisky and beer together to the poor intermediary. Channel relationships were thus further stretched as retailers who wanted to purchase 20 litres of the popular whisky also had to buy four cases of Chang. Charoen's bargaining power was such that, by 1996, Chang's market share stood at 60%, prompting Boon Rawd to complain to the newly formed Trade Competition Board in Thailand. Unfortunately for Boon Rawd, while what Charoen had done may have been unfair, it was not clear to the Board that it was illegal. Chang's market share continued to grow and, in 2003, Chaeron's businesses became incorporated as the Thai Beverage Public Company.

Source: Hopkins (2005); www.boonrawd.co.th; www.thaibev.com

4.2 Flows & Blockages in Channels

How channels work is the subject of some debate, so before we move on to consider the nature of the various 'flows' through the channel, we shall summarize some theoretical ideas about marketing channels.

The notion of goods flowing downstream from producers, through distributing firms, and on to consumers is captured in the metaphoric term 'channel' or 'pipeline' (Saunders, 1995). Marketing channels research is predominantly based on the firm and its immediate two-way (or dyadic) relationships, with a focus on how channel structure facilitates flows (Weitz and Jap, 1995). The basic interest is in economic exchange and its efficiency (Möller and Halinen, 2000). Having said that, an important theoretical perspective on channels involves seeing them as social systems, much like the social exchange perspective on IORs encountered in Chapter Three. This is important, since marketing channels are not simply rationally ordered economic systems devoid of social interaction. It means that B2B marketers must be aware of the behavioural and perceptual dimensions of channels (John, 1984; Stern and Brown, 1969).

However, there is confusion over power and conflict in channels research. Largely because of this confusion, many researchers embracing the relationship marketing (RM) paradigm have criticized power as having only negative effects of channel relationships. However, Frazier (1999) believes that, while a word like power can conjure up negative images, as Frazier and Antia (1995) note, control is not inherently evil. Appropriate and skilful control exerted by one dominant channel member can have positive effects on another firm's goal attainment.

All the above economic, material, and social considerations affect our understanding of channel flows.

Channel flows

Despite the common perception that the only flow involved in a channel is that of physical goods moving downstream, there are many other flows to consider. For instance, B2B marketing communications (see Chapter Eleven) also flow downstream, while payment and orders flow upstream. Moreover, negotiation over such issues as maintenance arrangements, and finance in terms of credit extensions, can flow both ways. Information also flows both ways in a well-organized channel, such that retailers are kept informed of manufacturers' plans for new product launches, say, while manufacturers are kept abreast of marketplace changes via the feedback provided by retailers. A further flow, of goods back up the channel, is discussed later in this chapter when we examine 'reverse logistics'.

Two key flows in achieving what is termed 'quick response' logistics in the US garment (clothing) channel are illustrated in Figure 4.3. Quick response refers to the speed at which

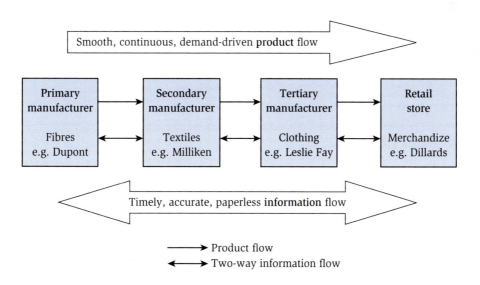

Figure 4.3 Quick response in a US garment industry channel
Source: Adapted with permission from Christopher (1997, p 84)
M. Christopher (1997) Marketing Logistics, p 84, copyright Elsevier

information about changing market demands can be passed up the supply/demand chain and then goods produced and shipped down the chain in response to those demands (e.g. a new trend in clothing fashion). Similar thinking underpins what is known as efficient consumer response (ECR) in the grocery sector, where channel decisions are often less about what to manufacture and more about how many units to manufacture and when to make them available. The information flows made possible via ECR enable the appropriate response from manufacturers to consumer sales promotions via continuous replenishment programmes (Zhao et al, 2002). While both these examples are ultimately about serving B2C markets, you should note that it is still a series of IORs that supports this process. Only with good management of B2B relations 'behind the scenes' is a positive end-user outcome possible.

The impact of technology on channel flows has been considerable in a number of areas. For instance, the physical flow represented by transportation and storage of goods between channel members can be undertaken more efficiently with advances in technology. The appropriate temperatures for the storage of foodstuffs and flammable chemicals, for example, can now be more closely regulated. Order processing flow is now often undertaken electronically via electronic data interchange (EDI). This can speed up delivery times as well as improve the accuracy of order specifications, which assists in production scheduling and stock control. Negotiation flows have been improved by reducing the need for physical travel between the managers representing organizations in the channel. Online systems and electronic-document transfers facilitate faster negotiations. Electronic transfer of funds has had a similar impact on financial flows.

In recent years, it has also been recognized that marketers can draw on new technologies to facilitate the design and management of multiple channels and integrate the Internet into existing channel structures (Narayandas, 2007). Some scholars believe that increasing the number of interactions between manufacturers and end users can be beneficial, thus somewhat contradicting the basic beliefs about how channel intermediaries should reduce complexity (see section 4.1 above). The increased use of direct marketing and online selling and Internet-based B2B auction sites can provide a range of communication flows with the supplier that gives end users greater choice. There is a risk, however, that stock availability and service levels can diminish for end users as the number of intermediaries falls (Mudambi and Aggarwal, 2003), thus negatively impacting physical flows.

Blockages or conflict in marketing channels

We should remind ourselves that organizations exchange because it is mutually beneficial to do so. Thus, a distributor will carry a line of products that it believes will sell in the industries it serves. The supplier concedes the distributors' margin as payment for the distribution functions performed. It is likely to take the distributor and supplier several months to ascertain accurately the benefits of their exchanges. The scale of investment that each party makes in such areas as inventories, delivery systems, product knowledge, sales training, systems integration, and brand image, as well as any termination clauses in contracts, means that channel interaction is generally relational.

Nevertheless, as we highlighted in Chapter Three, conflict has to be acknowledged in IORs. In the context of the social systems we call marketing channels, conflict exists when one member of the channel perceives another's actions to be impeding the achievement of their goals (Gaski, 1984). Conflict should not, however, be confused with competition. In a conflict situation, it is not competitive market forces that organizations attempt to overcome, but other organizations in the system or channel. As well as disagreements over economic factors such as margins, performance standards, and purchase terms, there are social factors to take into account.

We can classify conflict in channels as follows (see Figure 4.4). Note that all of these conflict types could potentially coexist in a single relationship.

- First, there can be goal conflict, where manufacturers typically care more about the sale of their products than also allowing for the distributor's overall growth through a reasonable level of profitability.

- Second, there is means conflict, which arises when channel members disagree over how things will be implemented, such as the introduction of an EDI system, how customer complaints are handled, or who will service Internet customers. It can be difficult for one party to know that these tasks are being done properly by the other.

- Third, there can be conflicting perceptions, especially when there are difficulties in monitoring other channel members' performance. For instance, if a distributor feels that the sales leads generated at the manufacturer level by a B2B marketer's marketing communications efforts are weak, they may choose not to follow them up. Similar disparate views may exist over issues such as how much inventory it is appropriate to carry or how many sales calls a key customer should receive from the distributor's representatives.

- Finally, conflict can occur when existing channel members fear being bypassed by channel innovations such as the Internet (Rosenbloom, 2006).

The consequences of such conflicts need not always be negative. If they are addressed positively, then constructive outcomes should be possible, with both organizations learning from the experience. For instance, firms launching Internet B2B trading sites can reassure distributors that they still have a role to play because personal interaction with customers

Figure 4.4 Classifying channel conflict

will remain part of a firm's channel strategy for certain products while less high-tech goods are redirected through a Web-based channel. However, if the parties continue to try to work together while holding vastly different world views, then coordination may become impossible, and competing channels will have the opportunity to take over the marketplace. An example of a firm that overcame potential conflict (both externally with its corporate customers and internally with its direct sales force) when it changed its channel configuration is provided in Box 4.4. Note how Grainger overcame the sheer scale of the changes it needed to do so successfully that Internet sales leapt by 500%.

So, how else can managers respond to channel conflict? We can identify a combination of informal and formal mechanisms.

1. *Informal mechanisms*: five potential reactions to conflict that are not necessarily formalized have been suggested (Graham, 1986):

- First, exit: This entails leaving an IOR. It is an extreme response, but may be the best way forward if there are irreconcilable differences. The threat of exit can also be used as signal to the other party who may react in time to prevent the relationship dissolving.

- Second, voice: This involves some way of articulating dissatisfaction. It can be a crucial process for uncovering the origins of a conflict. If we go back to the issue raised above over perceived low-quality sales leads, it would be unlikely that the manufacturer deliberately set out to generate weak leads, but perhaps was generating a high volume but low quality of potential buyers. The distributor should recognize that it benefits from the leads, too. Thus, as IOR goals and means appear to be shared, the conflict may well have arisen from incomplete information about promotional objectives being exchanged between the two parties – some sort of communication is clearly necessary.

- Third, loyalty: This relational approach represents perseverance in the face of the tension in the conflict. It involves the hope over the long term that the other party will eventually change their behaviour, even when their current actions suggest a clash of roles.

Box 4.4 Number crunching
The positive impact of careful channel management

When WW Grainger, a large US distributor of maintenance, repair, and operations (MRO) parts planned to migrate customers from its sales staff to the Internet in order to cut costs, it had to do so without them perceiving any lowering of service levels. To achieve this, the firm ensured that its 1,200 sales personnel visited customers to demonstrate how to order parts via the new Web-based system. Moreover, Grainger gained the commitment of its sales force to these training activities by adjusting its compensation scheme to give them credit for all sales in their territories, regardless of channel. Now sales reps spend most of their time on finding new prospects and building customer loyalty. The firm has seen its e-commerce sales rise from $100 million to nearly $500 million in the five years to 2003. Grainger has also differentiated itself from its competitors through this channel strategy.

Source: Myers et al (2005); www.grainger.com

- Fourth, aggression: Here, one party acts with the intention of harming the other. This can involve retaliatory business practices that accelerate a downward spiral of trust, such as delaying payments or shipments, or selling into another party's assigned customer territories. It is often very difficult to rescue an IOR from such behaviours.

- Fifth, neglect: This means leaving the conflict unresolved, perhaps by allowing the IOR to fade in significance. Trading may still take place but will often comprise only a small percentage of a party's overall sales. This differs from loyalty in that it merely indicates a minimal interest in the conflict.

2. *Formal mechanisms*: in addition to any informal managerial reaction to conflict, there are also formal mechanisms that can be employed. These include the manufacturer setting up a distributor council by enlisting representatives from several intermediaries which acts as a forum for all distributors to air complaints and flag up opportunities or potential threats to the channel. Some channel members take this approach further and appoint a third-party referee to seek mediated solutions to conflicts. Other ways forward include manufacturers and distributors joining each others' trade associations, or even exchanging personnel where, for instance, manufacturers send production managers into the field with the distributor's sales reps to better gauge customer perceptions of their products. The various mechanisms for handling channel conflict are summarized in Figure 4.5.

Ultimately, however, not all channel improvements benefit every member equally, and thus some conflicts will always revolve around the distribution of a system's profits

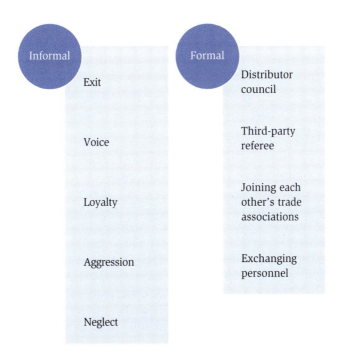

Figure 4.5 Mechanisms for responding to channel conflict

105

(or, indeed, losses). This reminds us that the way in which power is exercised in IORs is crucial to channel success (see Chapter Three). The 'leadership' of a channel is not a foregone conclusion. An S/DCM perspective tends to suggest that supermarkets are the practical leader of most supply chains, at least in Western B2C markets, whereas perhaps 30 years ago, manufacturers would have held the power. It is debatable which level of focal firm is the 'best' suited to channel leadership, but some commentators are convinced that retailers are too short term and adversarial in their upstream relations to be afforded this position (Sadler, 2007). Moreover, Chang (2009) shows how some upstream B2B firms still effectively control integrated supply chains in the Taiwanese steel, plastics, and semiconductor industries, even when demand originates downstream. Also, manufacturers can choose to behave differently in IORs upstream from those downstream. Apple, for example, collaborates closely with its suppliers to increase access to the best product design skills, but is wary when dealing with retail organizations because it seeks tight control over all aspects of product launches (Grover et al, 2008; www.apple.com).

4.3 From Channels to Chains

We now move from a channels perspective to encompass supply/demand chain thinking. Although terms like 'distribution channel' are still widely used by B2B marketers and, indeed, channel considerations remain vital to most B2B strategies, this book argues for a wider grasp of the interactions required to serve a marketplace. For this chapter, the management of the business system represented by all of the IORs set up to support the buying and selling of goods will be known as 'supply/demand chain management' (S/DCM). This approach strives to integrate dependent trading activities, organizational actors, and their resources into chains linking the point of origin and the point of final consumption.

It helps to consider this shift in perspective in the following way. While it can be argued that marketing channels are mainly concerned with the added value IORs can bring in matching finished goods to customer needs, the supply-chain side of S/DCM is more commonly discussed in terms of managing a number of business activities required, upstream as well as downstream, to 'get the right product to the right place, to the right customer, at the right time'. This SCM-informed view also addresses concerns that marketing has not always properly considered the full range of organizational structures, operations, and processes necessary to serve contemporary markets (Heikkila, 2002).

We shall now explore the components of SCM as they affect the role of the B2B marketer. As with our managerial take on channel management, we assume that a basic supply chain comprises a focal firm which produces goods or service for a set of end users, plus a range of distributors which deliver the goods to customers, and a range of suppliers of raw materials and components (as we saw in Chapter One's Figure 1.4). This assumption places the B2B marketer with the focal (manufacturing) firm, though you should remember that supply/demand chains can be driven at other levels in the chain, as the case in Box 4.5 shows. While ethical jewellery firms are attempting to set the agenda, they are heavily dependent on the notional top and bottom of their chain for survival. Thus, good B2B relationships must be maintained upstream with mining and processing firms, and sensitive B2C relations downstream with the consumer who has the ultimate buying discretion in the chain.

Box 4.5 Food for thought

The supply/demand chain for ethically sourced jewellery

Green Gold is a self-proclaimed 'ethical' jewellery business based in Chichester in the UK, but which has operations in Columbia where gold is mined. The firm is hoping to gain fair trade certification for the gold panned from rivers each month by local miners working together as the Association for Responsible Mining (ARM). The owners of Green Gold believe the ethical jewellery business is set to grow as a result of end-user demand, in part inspired by the movie *Blood Diamond*. However, they recognize that their business model will only work if they can get sufficient certified supplies from groups like ARM. They intend to apply strict rules for the kinds of suppliers they will work with. This means making commitments about methods of mining that do not harm local environments or communities. Green Gold also intends to keep a close eye on its entire supply chain, including the mine casters, refiners, and manufacturers who supply the gold which the company then finishes in its own workshops. Other firms are offering the same value to consumers; for instance, Ingle & Rhode of London stresses that its products contain 'only conflict-free diamonds and fair trade gold'. These manufacturers have to be able to show complete supply-chain 'transparency' to ensure that consumers buying a ring can be confident that its original materials have been as fairly and sustainably sourced as possible.

Source: Pearce (2008); www.ingleandrhode.co.uk

Managing IORs as part of SCM

IORs in supply/demand chains can extend from arm's length, transactional relationships to vertical integration, between which lie a range of partnership types (see Figure 4.6). Lambert et al (1996) differentiate between the various levels of supply partnership in terms of closeness:

- Type 1 partnerships coordinate activities and planning on a limited basis, typically with a relatively short-term focus and involving only one functional area with each organization.

- Type II partners move beyond coordination to integration of activities, with a longer-term horizon. Multiple divisions and functions within each firm are involved.

- Type III partnership organization share a significant level of integration, with each party viewing the other as an 'extension' of their own firm, and with no set end-date involved for the IOR. For example, the top suppliers of Texas Instruments are 'rewarded' for exceptional service and support in press releases highlighting the granting of the firm's annual Supplier Excellence Awards. In this way, the manufacturer recognizes the contributions made by suppliers such as Hamada Heavy Industries Inc. that help Texas better serve its customers (http://focus.ti.com/pr).

Despite the growth of relationship marketing, Lambert et al (1996) believe that the majority of a firm's supply chain relationships will be arm's length and Type I partnerships.

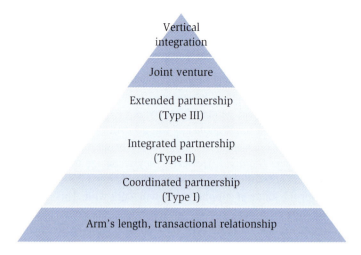

Figure 4.6 Types of supply chain IORs

This is possibly due to the overriding operational focus in traditional SCM thinking on asset/cost efficiency (such as reducing distribution and handling costs or improving asset utilization), such that the more customer service-driven objectives of DCM are not always as prominent in a supply chain manager's mind as they might be.

B2B marketers representing manufacturers who embrace an S/DCM perspective need to manage IORs with suppliers as well as with customers in order to service properly those customers. Moreover, if the selling firm plans to target new customer segments, this could involve dealing with new suppliers. The firm may have to be prepared to change some of its working practices in order to fit into the existing economic and social system, where behavioural norms (rules and practices) are well established. If B2B marketers are assigned an S/DCM-related role, as can be likely in an SME, then they are faced with quite a challenge: are they able to balance their IOR behaviours such that they are consistently fair in both 'directions', and treat suppliers with the same respect as customers?

You may feel that they should not even have to worry about such issues, but it is more than just an ethical question to ponder. It can be argued that as the contribution of suppliers forms such an integral part of a firm's competitive edge, maintaining positive buyer–supplier relationships even during difficult economic times is vital, however hard this may prove (Handfield and Nichols, 2004). This is particularly challenging when the buying firm's market conditions suggest the need for price reductions that may have to be passed on to the supply base, potentially driving them out of business. Things a forward-thinking customer firm can do in these circumstances include: establishing parameters for negotiations prior to issuing any requests for a quotation to ensure a fair process; avoiding making unreasonable demands; maintaining confidentiality regarding proprietary information and the supplier's terms; and achieving a prompt and open resolution of any problems. Sometimes, of course, such practices may not be enough. External forces like severely depressed consumer demand can have a devastating effect on suppliers, as seen in Box 4.6.

Box 4.6 Voices

The impact on a supply chain of a fall in derived demand

In 2009, the Visteon car-parts factory in Belfast, Northern Ireland, was closed after the administrators conceded that 'the entire automotive supply chain has been under pressure for a number of years. In the current economic downturn, car sales have dropped dramatically, which has caused further severe pressure on parts suppliers'. Trade union leaders described the way in which the plant's 200 job cuts were announced as 'brutal', leading to the occupation of the plant by disgruntled workers.

Source: BBC News (2009)

Other key elements of SCM

It is important for the implementation of B2B marketing strategies to ensure excellent SCM. When firms make mistakes anywhere within a supply chain, the effects can ripple through the chain in both directions (Flint, 2004). These effects include disruption to production, forecasting errors, inventory imbalances, stock-outs or damaged goods, all of which usually result in increased costs that may have to be passed on to end users, thus reducing their satisfaction and loyalty. Some important considerations for SCM are summarized in Figure 4.7.

Four central SCM goals have been identified by Brewer and Speh (2000):

1. *Waste reduction*: the aim here is to lower levels of duplicated and excess stock (inventory) in the chain. This can lower the costs of holding inventory (e.g. warehousing, security, insurance), as well as impact positively on the working capital of firms. Maintaining

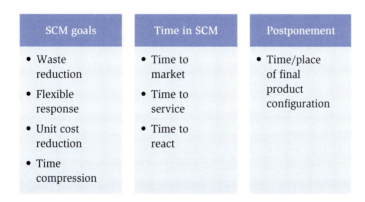

Figure 4.7 **Some key elements of SCM**

higher stock levels may afford better opportunities to meet increased customer orders, but can tie up considerable funds.

2. *Flexible response*: this aims to meet specific customer requirements through managing aspects of order processing, including size, timing, and handling to increase convenience for the customer.

3. *Unit cost reduction*: this involves understanding the levels of service required by the customer and then minimizing the costs entailed in meeting those standards. Note how these previous two goals coincide closely with core channel tasks (see section 4.1 above).

4. *Time compression*: by reducing the order-to-delivery cycle time, efficiency and customer service gains can be made. As well as giving higher levels of customer satisfaction, this should result in less stock being carried in the chain and faster cash flows.

In fact, time has become such an important issue in SCM that it is worth considering it in a little more detail. For many clients, both consumer and organizational, a key question when ordering a product is, basically, 'Can we have it now?' In other words, time reduction is crucial in S/DCM, especially in market conditions of ever-fluctuating demand. There are thought to be three dimensions to time-based competition that organizations should try to manage (Christopher, 1997). All these dimensions will normally require close cooperation between chain members:

- The first is 'time to market': How long does it take the organization to recognize a market opportunity and to translate this into a product/service, and to bring it to the market?

- The second is 'time to serve': How long does it take to capture a customer's order and to deliver or install the product to the customer's satisfaction?

- The third element is 'time to react': How long does it take to adjust the output of the business in response to volatile demand?

Even if a firm manages to improve its timely market response, a remaining challenge in S/DCM is that, despite trends towards globalization, there are still considerable differences in local tastes and requirements. A number of issues for B2B marketers to consider are raised by the need to 'localize' products (Christopher, 1997): can the final configuration or assembly of the product be delayed until real demand is ascertained; at what level in the supply chain should inventory be held and where should the final configuration take place; and where should the forecast be made – in the local market or at the centre?

These issues matter because it usually costs more to hold finished goods in stock than unfinished goods, which can be stored more easily. Ideally, manufacturers aim to withhold final production until the last moment. For example, the construction-equipment manufacturer JCB will postpone the final configuring of its machines until it has been appraised of local safety requirements in the intended marketplace, sometimes over quite a small matter such as the need for particular sets of additional warning lights in Scandinavian countries (www.jcb.com). Sometimes, customer demands for short order-to-delivery cycle times mean that this sort of postponement is not possible, and inventory has to be carried in finished form by intermediaries (or the producers' own sales branches) closer to the local market.

4.4 Marketing Logistics

In the contemporary marketplace, leading organizations are those which are the most responsive, i.e. those which can speed up the rate of innovation, bring new products and services to the marketplace faster, and replenish demand with shorter lead times and greater reliability: this is the arena of marketing logistics (Christopher, 1997). Thus, the attention of management has to include the processes through which customer demand is met. Logistics-related areas of S/DCM include purchasing, stock control, stores, and distribution, and can extend to after-sales maintenance and the replacement of parts. All of these activities can be crucial in helping a manufacturer achieve market share. Any upstream supplier that can enhance their organizational customer's performance (i.e. the manufacturer's or intermediary's performance) in these key areas is likely to have a competitive advantage.

In the supply chain context, one key way to gain customer loyalty and develop closer relationships, and thus profitability, is via improved marketing logistics. This line of thinking is captured in Figure 4.8. If a firm has a good level of support from its supply chain partners, and is able to ensure this support is passed downstream in the form of enhanced logistics service, then this advantage should be communicated to the firm's customers.

In making sense of their customers' buying behaviour, B2B marketers need to realize that the role of purchasing in most firms has shifted from a clerical/administrative function to a strategic level. This reflects the fact that the supply side of organizations has become more

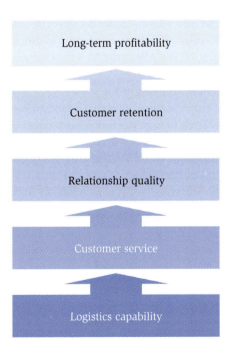

Figure 4.8 **The key drivers of long-term profitability in supply chains**
Source: Adapted with permission from Christopher (1997, p 37)
M. Christopher (1997) Marketing Logistics, p 37, copyright Elsevier

important in recent years as firms strive to become more competitive. This is because the cost of purchased goods and services often represents 60–80% of total costs, and thus a reduction in the cost of components can have a significant impact on profits. Also, shorter life cycles and broader assortments driven by consumer demands (e.g. for high-tech goods such as global positioning systems) mean that the need for coordinating supply chain activities is growing.

Moreover, as manufacturers cannot always afford the investments necessary in R&D to stay abreast of all the required technologies in their production processes, suppliers are increasingly being asked to contribute to the technical development of new products (Persson and Håkansson, 2007). Note how the marketing manager in Box 4.7 relies on his suppliers in this regard, even in a relatively 'low-tech' sector like animal feeds.

Taking a combined channels and SCM view, the most important aspects of logistics management for the B2B marketer are place, time, and service. Other functions within the supply/demand chain such as IT systems, transportation, and warehousing can be seen as supporting links to ensure logistics arrangements meet the needs of the chain. Thus, third-party shipping and trucking firms such as Federal Express (www.fedex.com) and UPS (www.ups.com) are redefining themselves as 'logistics facilitators' and explicitly emphasizing their skills in 'time and space management' for other firms (Curry and Kenney, 1999). B2B managers should be encouraging logistics personnel within manufacturing firms to work with these organizations in a number of key areas. These include: collaborating downstream with physical distribution providers and resellers over after-sales servicing and returning faulty products, as well as developing delivery schedules; organizing internal storage-area layouts and optimizing material flow with factories; and selecting upstream suppliers of materials and components and even developing packaging to meet channel needs for strength, safety, and recycling.

We shall now consider three important marketing logistics issues (summarized in Figure 4.9) in more detail.

Inventory and just-in-time approaches

Inventory acts like a safety buffer in the supply chain. Stockholding is needed because production and demand rarely match exactly. By stockpiling products, they can be released onto the market in periods when demand begins to outstrip supply. A key question then becomes: where in the chain should this stock be held? Some customer organizations have introduced just-in-time (JIT) purchasing and production, which means that they do not hold any inventory, but expect suppliers to deliver materials or components from their own stocks as and

---

Box 4.7 Voices

How suppliers can help B2B marketing managers

This is what the marketing manager of a European animal-feed manufacturer has to say: 'A lot of sources for USPs [unique selling points] for our products will come from our suppliers. I've got this guy coming to give me the full information on this new raw material, lactose, which has a strong USP for us. I can then turn it into information sheets to commercialize it for our farm customers.'

Source: Ellis et al (2005)

> **Inventory & JIT approaches**
>
> - How much stock to hold to meet demand?
> - Where should stock be held in the chain?
> - Implications of adopting a just-in-time approach
>
> **Logistics information flow**
>
> - Supply chain transparency for rapid response
> - Complexity in achieving speedy, clear information flows
>
> **Reverse logistics**
>
> - Moving goods 'backwards' up the chain
> - Recapture value (by recycling) or dispose of goods properly
> - Can cut costs and help the environment

Figure 4.9 **Some marketing logistics issues**

when they are needed. JIT is more a philosophy of doing business than a specific technique. It is arguably a good example of DCM since it involves initiating a 'pull' system of manufacturing where production is matched to known demand and nothing is made or ordered until it is needed in the system. The practice is common amongst Japanese-owned companies such as Nissan whose UK automotive factory requires its suppliers to hold a certain amount of inventory at warehouses close to its location in Sunderland (www.nissan.co.uk).

Suppliers may have to accept JIT demands from key customers even though JIT can be difficult to implement, as it often calls for changes in the suppliers' systems of production, storage, and order processing and frequency of deliveries at precise times. Close communication is essential, with suppliers being given long-range insight into the buyer's production schedule. IORs in JIT systems thus tend to be based on long-term, single-source contracts. A B2B marketer representing the supplier might be pleased to gain such a contract, but a downside is that it tends merely to shift the problem of excess inventory upstream where, in the end, someone will have to pay for it in terms of increased prices from suppliers who now have to absorb stockholding costs themselves. The need for more frequent deliveries under JIT can also be problematic when it comes to arranging cost-effective transportation.

Nevertheless, suppliers should be ready to respond to any impact on their supply chain of decisions by customer organizations to change production methods. This is shown by the case of the Italian division of Black & Decker (B&D), the producer of electrical tools, where suppliers and a key intermediary set up by B&D have coped admirably with the challenges they faced – see Box 4.8.

Box 4.8 Mini case
The impact of reconfiguring manufacturing on a global supply chain

Black & Decker Italy SpA has a manufacturing unit in Perugia. This unit specializes in producing stationary machines for woodworking targeted largely at professional users under the B2B De Walt brand to distinguish it from the consumer brand, Black & Decker (B&D). B&D formed a separate enterprise in Hong Kong known as Global Purchasing Asia (GPA) in 1987, in order to explore the possibilities for purchasing components and finished goods from China. GPA was much in evidence when B&D moved during the mid 1990s towards a lean manufacturing system that required internal changes as well as some reorganization of the supply chain. This system involved JIT principles for stock replenishment, so initial preference was given to local suppliers (those within 100 km of the Perugia unit) in order to meet delivery requirements.

However, the manufacturing unit also rapidly increased its purchasing from China, moving from ten component types in 2002 to almost 130 a year later. The challenge was how to benefit from the lower cost associated with Chinese goods while maintaining the high levels of supply chain service and flexibility required by production in Italy. GPA undertook a comprehensive sourcing project involving a detailed analysis of product costs, subdividing different components into various categories, searches, and appraisals of Chinese suppliers for each category, and the ultimate selection of certain suppliers. Weekly deliveries were scheduled in order to minimize stock. This was achieved by aggregating various orders in order to reach the critical volume for shipments from the Far East. Agreements were also signed with transportation firms to guarantee the security and traceability of deliveries. Based on the quality and timing requirements of B&D, GPA staff verify information on component stock levels in the suppliers' warehouses.

Interestingly, in spite of all these improvements in the management of the Chinese supply chain, a local supplier in Perugia is maintained for every component in case of problems with defects or delays.

Source: Nassimbeni and Sartor (2006), www.blackanddecker.com; www.dewalt.com

Logistics information flow

Recall that a key aim of S/DCM is to be able to respond to customer demands in good time and at an acceptable cost. This sort of flexible response requires the ability to 'see' from one end of the supply pipeline to the other. A rapid, clear flow of accurate information is thus vital, both for the transparency claimed for the jewellery supply chains we saw in Box 4.5 and the JIT approaches that underpin many contemporary logistics practices.

Maintaining such flows is no easy matter, however. According to Handfield and Nichols (2004), a typical commercial shipment can involve nine different organizations, 20 separate documents, 35 buyer–seller interactions, and multiple modes of transport, sometimes over multiple international borders. This can result in plenty of opportunities for miscommunication. For instance, these authors report a study based on General Motors' (GM) forecasts which were passed sequentially, firm-by-firm, upstream through a textile supply chain for car seating. It was found that while the forecast error for the immediate (first tier) supplier could be as low as 5%, it degenerated to 22% and 30% at suppliers furthest upstream. To overcome these problems GM were recommended to adopt a 20-week forecast shared with all parties in the chain.

Reverse logistics

Finally, we will consider a relatively recent phenomenon in which logistics has a key role to play in giving firms a competitive advantage: 'reverse logistics'. This involves moving goods from their typical final destination in order to recapture value (by recycling components or materials) or to dispose of them properly. Genchev (2009) reports that the value of returns is estimated to be an average of 15–20% of all goods sold. This backward flow can occur when defective goods reach the end user, repairs are needed, unsold merchandise arises from overstocking, or when goods have the potential to be recycled.

Although historically not given much prominence in most organizations, reverse logistics practised efficiently and effectively can cut costs as well as display the firm's environmental credentials in handling such eventualities. To set up an appropriate programme will usually entail: gaining senior management support to turn reverse logistics into a company-wide initiative; involving customers in the process; assigning responsibility and giving recognition to staff in the organization who handle returns; and developing carefully written rules over handling returned goods. The time invested in implementing these initiatives could pay rich dividends as end-user customers become increasingly concerned over environmental issues – an excellent example of S/DCM thinking.

A longer case study on the distribution of trucks from China to Europe concludes the chapter. This shows the relational and logistical challenges (including the notion of vehicle returns) of establishing a dealer network to support a manufacturer's products in a highly competitive marketplace.

Summary

The key points to take from this chapter are as follows:

- How downstream distribution channels and the intermediaries that make up such channels contribute to B2B marketing.

- Some key tasks performed by channel intermediaries, such as reducing complexity, increasing value, improving transaction efficiency and quality of service.

- How to evaluate the suitability of some of the different channel management options open to manufacturers supplying both organizational and consumer end users.

- The importance of the various flows that occur up and down marketing channels and how to address potential channel conflicts.

- What an expansion of a channel perspective to one embracing the entire supply/ demand chain up and downstream from the focal firm means for the B2B marketing manager.

- The key elements of SCM, including partnerships, waste reduction, and time reduction.

- How marketing logistics can support B2B marketing by enabling suppliers to build their customers' competitive advantage through superior logistics service.

- The impact on the supply chain of certain manufacturing and purchasing approaches like JIT and reverse logistics.

Discussion questions

1. Select an industrial sector (it might be your own or one with which you are familiar) facing changes in the structure of its typical distribution channels. Explain how these changes affect B2B marketing practices.

2. What is the best distribution strategy for a manufacturer of: (*a*) office stationery; and (*b*) machine tools such as industrial lathes? How would you design the channels for each of these firms?

3. Why might the existence of several different organizations along a marketing channel or supply/demand chain make it more difficult to ensure the smooth flow of goods to customers?

4. Discuss the key aims and considerations that make up an SCM view and explain how it differs from a marketing channel perspective.

5. 'A well-managed supply/demand chain is one that has swapped information for inventory.' Discuss this statement from the point of view of a marketing manager of a supplier of components to the electronics sector.

6. What are the pros and cons (for both customer and supplier organizations) of JIT-based approaches in supply chains?

Case study

Dongfeng Commercial Vehicle Company – EU Market Entry and Distribution

Steve Carter, Leeds Metropolitan University, Leeds, UK

Introduction

Dongfeng is a well-respected Chinese commercial vehicle company, whose overseas department is based in Wuhan City, Hubei Province, China. Manufacturing actually takes place in Shiyan City, in north-west Hubei, the largest manufacturing base of commercial vehicles in China. A company called SAW, established in 1969, was the predecessor of Dongfeng, which in June 2003 entered into a joint investment with the Japanese Nissan Motor Corporation. This venture saw the start of a new globalization chapter for Dongfeng.

Dongfeng Commercial Vehicle Company is one of the strategic business units of the Dongfeng Motor Company and mainly engages in R&D, manufacturing and marketing of medium- and heavy-duty commercial vehicles. It comprises one technical centre, seven manufacturing plants, and nine subsidiaries with a marketing and service network located China-wide. The company claims that its integrated value chain focuses on markets and customers, improving its quality continuously, and providing specialized transport solutions to its corporate customers.

An example of its products is the Dongfeng Kinland truck which has recently become China's fastest-selling heavy-duty truck with its emphasis on integrating global technologies giving advantages in technology, safety, reliability, economic efficiency, and comfort. It also includes some of the latest developments in environmental protection, including energy-saving components.

Collaborating and competing globally

Incorporating the truck-manufacturing experience of Dongfeng and the management method of Nissan, Dongfeng is striving to improve its brand image and global position.

After entry into the new century and China's entry to the World Trade Organization (WTO) in 2001, the national auto industry in China faced unprecedented competition. However, with the Nissan joint venture, in 2003 output and sales volume of Dongfeng's medium-heavy duty trucks were ranked second in the world. In 2006, with Renault's world-leading engine technology, the Kinland truck and the Dongfeng T-lift Truck (with a completely newly designed driving cab) were introduced and seen as the spearhead of establishing Dongfeng's competitive position globally.

With its internationally competitive products, Dongfeng saw a bright international future. In fact, Dongfeng's medium- and heavy-duty trucks are now exported to more than 20 countries, with markets in Iran and Russia still growing rapidly. It has a sales and service network in place across most regions of the world, including countries as far apart as Mongolia, Pakistan, Saudi Arabia, South Africa, Ghana, and Venezuela (www.dfcv.com.cn). With this supporting infrastructure, Dongfeng Commercial Vehicle Company's objective is to be China's number-one truck manufacturer and one of the world's top three across all products. However, one large and hyper-competitive market remains untouched – the European Union (EU).

The EU marketplace

The EU is a tough market to crack, with its high levels of competition and strict environmental laws, particularly on the recycling of obsolete vehicles and CO_2 emissions. April 2009 also saw the introduction by the EU of 'Whole Vehicle Type Approval' (ECWVTA). For the UK, the UK Vehicle Certification Agency is responsible for implementing the ECWVTA. This agency, and others EU-wide, help would-be market entrants to identify and validate changes in design requirements to ensure compliance to legislation. Similarly, the UK Department for Transport can help prospective entrants to examine all current and relevant EC directives pertaining to European import legislation.

The UK spends about £70 billion transporting goods by road and rail, with about 84% of UK freight being moved by road. The UK market is an open market and, despite the recession and the consequent economic slowdown, truck sales in 2008 increased over 2007. UK registrations up to September 2008 were 44,117, and 22.2% up on the previous year, according to motor industry statistics (www.smmt.co.uk). Despite the intense competition from local manufacturers like Volvo, DAF, MAN, Mercedes Benz, Iveco, Renault, and others, it is possible to gain market share in the EU. For instance, Hino trucks (a Toyota subsidiary), and a relative newcomer, achieved a small growth in 2008 of 528 unit sales, making it the 12th largest supplier. It achieved this partly by introducing new unit types but also by building up its dealer network. A truck-dealer network, offering a 'total service' to end-user customers, is key to market entry and distribution success. It is here that Dongfeng needs to look carefully.

Truck distribution channels

Trucks, depending on the type, weight, and build-state can easily cost upwards of £100,000. A truck can thus be much more expensive per unit than the average car and is distributed in a variety of ways. Marketing and distribution can take many forms, depending on the customer requirements, type, and state of vehicle build. Large fleet owners like UK haulier Eddie Stobart or truck rental firms like Salford Van Hire may buy in bulk direct. Small transporters may lease from vehicle importers or large dealers. Trucks may also be sold from the manufacturer in 'knocked-down form' and assembled by other vehicle builders. This was the case for British truck manufacturer ERF, which sold knock-down units to Zimbabwe in the 1990s under an aid scheme, where they were assembled and sold by Hubert Davies, a Zimbabwean engineering company. Manufacturers may sell chassis and engines to a specialized body builder, which adds value to the original product in order to meet end-customer specifications, e.g. Carmichael, who make fire engines.

The marketing and distribution chain can therefore be very complicated. As well as manufacturers, distributors, and dealers selling individual trucks to customers, a number of organizations, like Hill Hire of Bradford in the UK, buy trucks in bulk and hire them out to smaller transport contractors on a lease or hire basis. In this way, smaller transporters need not expend a lot of money on purchasing the truck, and this scheme helps those who do not have the capital for outright purchase in the first place. To take advantage of this route to market, the Japanese manufacturer Isuzu has just launched a new product with an explicitly 'European flavour', involving a technical specification designed to appeal to the UK rental sector (Milnes, 2009). To increase its distribution intensity, Isuzu has also appointed three new agents in the UK Midlands.

It is not only the distribution of trucks as original equipment from the OEM companies that is handled by channel members, but the channel (and, indeed, the entire supply chain) is also very important in terms of after-sales service, parts availability, and truck servicing. As shown by its competitors' activities, Dongfeng realizes that a reliable supplier of a 'total distribution service', from truck delivery to provision of the financing package to servicing and parts availability, is a must for successful distribution.

Dongfeng's strategy

Within this channel context, and competitive and legislative scenario, Dongfeng has had to find a way to enter the market and distribute its products, both trucks and parts. A base in continental Europe makes much sense as it is a bigger market than the UK, but it is equally ferociously competitive. Compared with the traditional transactional approach to using either direct or indirect exporting, Dongfeng is employing rather different ways to attempt to enter the EU, and the UK market in particular. This is totally in keeping with the Chinese way of doing business, i.e. carefully building a long-term lasting relationship with a distributor rather than pushing for a series of mere transactions.

In military strategy terminology, one of Dongfeng's approaches could be seen as 'sneaking in under the radar'. Chinese agents for Dongfeng, sometimes working with other Chinese nationals, have been coming to the UK for lengthy periods of time. Some have visited, it has to be said, on educational courses, and between their studies have been engaging in market intelligence and sensing activities, including prospecting potential UK distributors and dealers and hiring market research agencies. An example of the type of company under scrutiny might be IT Fleet who boast of their specialism in distributing vehicles 'from the smallest . . . van to the largest and most complicated trucks on the road' (www.itfleet.co.uk). IT Fleet offers what it calls a 'cradle to grave' service, including: specifying vehicles for customers; managing their acquisition, their build process and, if necessary, return; providing rescue and repair; and supplying relief vehicles.

Dongfeng's market sensing of prospective distributors, or 'behavioural monitoring' in modern academic jargon, is no different to UK executives spending large amounts of time in a potential country of entry (see Ambler and Styles, 2000). In this way, the sensing activity is low profile yet powerful, in that market behaviour can be observed over a period of time in detail and many potential contacts can be gained through a 'snowballing' mode of enquiry. Having identified a potential dealer and/or agent in this way, a relationship can be built up (an essential ingredient of Chinese business, where trust and long-term confidence must be established) which, over time, could lead to the establishment of a dealer/distributor network.

Source: Ambler and Styles (2000); Dongfeng Commercial Vehicle Company (2008); Milnes (2009); www.dfcv.com.cn; www.itfleet.co.uk; www.smmt.co.uk – all websites accessed May 2009

Case study questions

1. In terms of meeting end-user organizational customer needs, why is a dealer network so important to Dongfeng's ambitious plans for EU market entry?

2. What are the benefits of the firm's cautious 'sneaking in under the radar' approach to find distribution partners? Are there any risks with this strategy?

3. What logistical issues do you think Dongfeng will need to take into account? Are there any organizations from which it can get assistance in meeting these challenges?

Further Reading

Bello, D. C., Lohtia, R., & Sangati, V. (2004) An Institutional Analysis of Supply Chain Innovations in Global Marketing Channels, Industrial Marketing Management, 33, pp 57–64
The authors note how the adoption of sophisticated supply-chain innovations by trading partners in global channels of distribution are often limited by the regulatory, normative, and cultural-cognitive elements of institutional environments. They develop a conceptual model to explain the role of institutions (here, they mean the rules and environment for exchange) in the successful deployment of innovations in global marketing channels.

Cox, A. (1999) A Research Agenda for Supply Chain and Business Management Thinking, Supply Chain Management, 4 (4), pp 209–11
This paper demonstrates that there is no best way to manage supply chains. It concludes that the key to success is based on recognizing the types of supply chains that exist and aligning strategy and operational practice with the specific properties of the supply chain that the company is positioned within. The paper argues that this way of thinking about procurement and supply competence is underdeveloped in business management thinking.

Frazier, G. L. & Antia, K. D. (1995) Exchange Relationships and Interfirm Power in Channels of Distribution, Journal of the Academy of Marketing Science, 23, pp 321–7
These authors note that, while words like 'power' conjure up negative images, they stress that the control that can be exerted via inter-firm power is not inherently 'evil'. It can have positive effects on another firm's goal attainment. Thus, the trend towards espousal of 'close relationships' in most discourses of channels marketing does not mean that our need to understand uses of power is becoming less important.

Hausman, A. & Haytko, D. L. (2003) Cross-Border Supply Chain Relationships: Interpretive Research of Maquiladora Realized Strategies, Journal of Business & Industrial Marketing, 18 (6/7), pp 545–63

Maquiladora plants are foreign-owned plants operating in Mexico that provide cheap labour for US manufacturers. This interpretive study shows how internal relationships (with both management and line employees) and external relationships (both organizational and governmental) have contributed to the success (and failure) of maquiladora-realized strategies.

New, S. & Westbrook, R. (eds) (2004) Understanding Supply Chains: Concepts, Critiques and Futures, Oxford University Press, Oxford

The editors compile a wide range of contributions from leading thinkers in S/DCM to survey the key theoretical concepts of supply chain management and present critical evaluations of these underlying ideas and approaches. The book is accessibly written and provides plenty of food for thought for people studying, researching, and applying the ideas of supply chain management.

References

Ambler, T. and Styles, C. (2000) The Silk Road to International Marketing, Financial Times/ Prentice Hall, London

BBC News (2009) Sacked Workers Occupy Car Factory, on line at http://www.bbc.co.uk, accessed March 2009

Brewer, P. C. & Speh, T. W. (2000) Using the Balanced Scorecard to Measure Supply Chain Performance, Journal of Business Logistics, 21 (1), pp 75–95

Chang, H. H. (2009) An Empirical Study of Evaluating Supply Chain Management Integration Using the Balanced Sorecard in Taiwan, Service Industries Journal, 29 (2), pp 185–202

Christopher, M. (1997) Marketing Logistics, Butterworth-Heinemann: Oxford

Coughlin, A. T., Anderson, E., Stern, L. W., & El-Ansary, A. I. (2006) Marketing Channels, 7th edn,, Prentice Hall, Upper Saddle River, NJ

Curry, J. & Kenney, M. (1999) Beating the Clock: Corporate Responses to Rapid Changes in the PC Industry, California Management Review, 42 (1), pp 8–36

Doctorow, D., Lippert, M., and Srivatsan, V. N. (2008) Rethinking High-Tech Distribution, McKinsey Quarterly, online at http://www.mckinseyquarterly.com, accessed December 2008

Dongfeng Commercial Vehicle Company (2008) Product Catalogue, Overseas Business Department, Dongfeng, Wuhan City

Ellis, N., Higgins, M., & Jack, G. (2005) (De)constructing the Market for Animal Feeds: A Discursive Study, Journal of Marketing Management, 21, pp 117–46.

Ellis, N., Mayer, R., & Radford, V. (1999) Managing Trade Marketing Relationships in Non FMCG Sectors: A Case Study, International Journal of Customer Relationship Management, 2 (3), pp 205–16

Flint, D. J. (2004) Strategic Marketing in Global Supply Chains: Four Challenges, Industrial Marketing Management, 33, pp 45–50

Frazier, G. L. (1999) Organising and Managing Channels of Distribution, Journal of the Academy of Marketing Science, 27 (2), pp 226–40

Frazier, G. L. & Antia, K. D. (1995) Exchange Relationships and Interfirm Power in Channels of Distribution, Journal of the Academy of Marketing Science, 23, pp 321–7

Gaski, J. F. (1984) The Theory of Power and Conflict in Channels of Distribution, Journal of Marketing, Summer, 9–29

Genchev, S. E. (2009) Reverse Logistics Program Design: A Company Study, Business Horizons, 52, pp 139–48

Graham, J. (1986) The Problem-Solving Approach to Negotiations in Industrial Marketing, Journal of Business Research, 14, pp 549–66

Grover, G., Lau, E., & Sharma, V. (2008) Building Better Links in High-Tech Supply Chains, McKinsey Quarterly, online at http://www.mckinseyquarterly.com, accessed December 2008

Handfield, R. B. & Nichols, E. L. (2004) Key Issues in Global Supply Base Management, Industrial Marketing Management, 33, pp 29–35

Heikkila, J. (2002) From Supply Chain Management to Demand Chain Management: Efficiency and Customer Satisfaction, Journal of Operations Management, 20, pp 74667

Hopkins, J. (2005) Thailand Confidential, Periplus Editions Ltd, Singapore

John, G. (1984) An Empirical Investigation of Some Antecedents of Opportunism in a Marketing Channel, Journal of Marketing Research, 21 (August), pp 27889

Lambert, D. M., Emmelhainz, M. A., & Gardner, J. T. (1996) Developing and Implementing Supply Chain Partnerships, International Journal of Logistics Management, 7 (2), pp 1–17

Milnes, J. (2009) Isuzu Forward Enters 18-Tonne Market, online at http://www.roadtransport.com/articles, accessed May 2009

Möller, K. & Halinen, A. (2000) Relationship Marketing Theory: Its Roots and Direction, Journal of Marketing Management, 16 (1), pp 8194

Mudambi, S. & Aggarwal, R. (2003) Industrial Distributors: Can they Survive in the New Economy? Industrial Marketing Management, 32 (4), pp 317–25

Myers, J. B., Pickersgill, A. D., & Van Metre, E. S. (2005) Steering Customers to the Right Channels, McKinsey Quarterly, online at http://www.mckinseyquarterly.com, accessed July 2005

Narayandas, D. (2007) Trends in Executive Education in Business Marketing, Journal of Business-to-Business Marketing, 14 (1), pp 23–30

Narus, J. A. & Anderson, J. C. (1996) Rethinking Distribution, Harvard Business Review, July–August, pp 112–20

Nassimbeni, G. & Sartor, M. (2006) Sourcing in China: Strategies, Methods and Experiences, Palgrave Macmillan, Houndsmill

Pearce, F. (2008) Confessions of an Eco-Sinner: Travels to Find where my Stuff Comes From, Eden Project Books, London

Persson, G. & Håkansson, H. (2007) Supplier Segmentation: 'When Supplier Relationships Matter', IMP Journal, 1 (3), pp 26–41

Robicheaux, R. A. & Coleman, J. E. (1994) The Structure of Marketing Channel Relationships, Journal of the Academy of Marketing Science, Winter, pp 38–51

Rosenbloom, B. (1999) Marketing Channels: A Management View, 6th edn, The Dryden Press, Fort Worth

Rosenbloom, B. (2006) Multi-Channel Strategy in Business-to-Business Markets: Prospects and Problems, Industrial Marketing Management, 35, pp 4–9

Sadler, I. (2007) Logistics and Supply Chain Integration, Sage, London

Saunders, M. J. (1995) Chains, Pipelines and Value Streams: The Role, Nature and Value of Such Metaphors, in Kemp, R. A. & Lamming, R. C. (eds), Proceedings of Worldwide Research Symposium on Purchasing and Supply Chain Management, Arizona State University, March 23–5

Stern, L. W. & Brown, J. W. (1969) Distribution Channels: A Social Systems Approach, in Distribution Channels: Behavioural Dimensions, in Stern, L. W. (ed.), Houghton Mifflin, New York, pp 6–19

Weitz, B. A. & Jap, S. D. (1995) Relationship Marketing and Distribution Channels, Journal of the Academy of Marketing Science, 23, (4), pp 305–20

Zhao, X., Xie, J., & Zhang, W. J. (2002) The Impact of Sharing and Ordering Co-ordination on Supply Chain Performance, Supply Chain Management, 17 (1), pp 24–40

Chapter 5
Industrial Networks

Introduction & Learning Objectives

In Chapters Three and Four we saw the importance of inter-organizational relationships (IORs) in distribution channels and supply/demand chains. However, it is actually quite rare for a firm to function simply as a member of a linear supply chain. After all, how many companies just rely on a single supplier for all their parts or materials, and how many companies just sell all their goods to one customer? Relationships are much more likely to happen between more than two firms at any one point in the chain, especially upstream with several suppliers for the manufacture of a complex product, or downstream with a range of distributors serving end-user markets. Moreover, in order to facilitate the core supplier–customer relationship, other parties often have to be involved in IORs with a focal firm, such as providers of finance, advertising agencies, and specialist advisors. In these ways, what we term 'industrial networks' are formed by patterns of IORs between collaborating and sometimes competing firms.

The case in Box 5.1 introduces the network concept via a particular kind of network, one that facilitates the transfer of knowledge about a manufacturing material. We shall explore several other industrial network forms in this chapter to show how relationships between members are crucial to the success of individual firms.

Box 5.1 Mini case
Knowledge transfer networks

Knowledge transfer networks (KTNs) are rather like 'open sourcing' in a community of firms, where a group of organizations collaborate in order to develop core technologies and specific applications that can then be accessed by any member of the network. For example, in 2004, the UK government's Department of Trade and Industry (DTI) launched a KTN focusing on high-tech composites. Composites are hybrid materials created by a combination of plastics, metals, ceramics, etc., designed to provide enhanced structural qualities (e.g. increased strength, reduced weight) compared with traditional materials. Applications include automotive disc brakes and carbon-fibre bicycle frames.

The network, known as the National Composites Network (NCN), comprised a large variety of organizations including: end-user manufacturers (such as aircraft, boat, and

---

car manufacturers), suppliers of raw materials and components, and industrial and academic research laboratories. Their aim was to share existing knowledge and create new technical insights relating to composites that could spread throughout the supply chain. Although particular firms were seen as leading edge, smaller suppliers were often perceived as 'metal bashers' that needed to educate themselves to stay in the fast-moving market. The DTI wanted to create a mechanism with the NCN for the different participants to learn from each other, thereby transferring knowledge form the world-class capabilities residing in individual firms and research centres. End users were incentivized to join the network as it was felt that the network links would improve the capabilities of their supply chains and thus their international competiveness.

Source: Bond et al (2008); www.ncn-uk.co.uk

Chapter Aims

After completing this chapter, you should be able to:

- Understand IORs from an interaction point of view
- Appreciate how the metaphor of channels/chains in business markets can be extended to one of networks
- Explain the broadening of relationship marketing thinking from a focus on customer partnerships to a wider stakeholder perspective
- Compare different types of industrial networks, as well as vertical, horizontal, and diagonal relationships between organizations
- Recognize the complexity of analysing a firm's network position via what is known as the ARA Model, and the difficulties in defining the boundaries of a network.

5.1 The Interaction Approach

We begin our exploration of industrial networks by thinking once again about how customer organizations make their purchases. Although models of organizational buying behaviour (OBB) like the Buygrid framework remain popular (see Chapter Two), some people believe that they do not capture the complexities of the phenomenon very well. It can be argued, for instance, that customers relate purchase decisions to a number of highly personalized factors, including: their particular problems; their experience of dealing with similar problems in the past, and within each of their current IORs; their expectations of the future of those relationships; their own organization and its resources; and their view of the sector in which their firm operates (Turnbull et al, 1996).

These factors usually result in organizational customers beginning their search for answers to their purchasing problems within their existing supplier relationships. This continuity makes sense if we consider that an existing IOR can often involve large financial exchanges and/or contribute to either party's technical development. Such relationships tend to be long term since a customer may make strenuous efforts to find the right partner in the first place. It does not, however, preclude the customer from seeking continuous improvements in the level of service it receives from the in-supplier. Moreover, if the customer is not satisfied with the in-supplier's performance, or if new demands arise from the external environment, then the search may begin outside existing IORs, with the customer taking notice of other potential suppliers in the sector.

The IMP Group's contribution

We thus see once again the significance of relationships in business markets. Indeed, work by the Industrial Marketing & Purchasing (IMP) Group of researchers suggests that insights into the buying process may be gained by taking the relationship between organizations as the focus of attention (Håkansson, 1982; Ford, 1997). They have developed what is known as the Interaction Model of the relationships between buying and selling organizations.

The origins of the Interaction Model in a variety of disciplines shows how the marketing discipline can benefit by incorporating ideas from more general organization theory and from economics. This serves as a valuable reminder that good managers should never think that 'their' discipline has all the answers! The IMP model drew initially on inter-organizational theory, which complemented the existing marketing literature in three areas: organization-based studies, which illustrate dilemmas over the organization–environment connection; studies where the firm is seen to develop relations with other firms in a network in order to obtain resources; and studies of the organization in a societal context, where the organization is seen as an integrated part of a larger social system. The second theoretical area drawn upon was that part of economics known as 'the New Institutionalism', which involves an awareness of the following concepts: market (external) transaction costs versus hierarchical (internal) transactions, and opportunism (see Chapter Three) and checks on that opportunism.

The key elements of the Interaction Model are summarized in Figure 5.1. The concept of institutionalization mentioned under 'Long-term relationships' in the figure refers to the process (and the outcome of the process), whereby social activities become so regular and routine that they are perceived by people as stable, social-structural features. An example of institutionalization in B2B interactions is the mutual recognition of a committed 'partnership' or 'alliance' status designated to the relationship between two firms.

Understanding IORs from an interaction perspective

The IMP approach is a powerful way of conceptualizing inter-firm exchanges since it views B2B marketing and purchasing in the following ways:

- Relationships in organizational markets are conducted over time and are built up through cumulative 'exchange episodes' involving mutual exchange of purchases, remuneration, information, and socialization (rather like the channel flows highlighted in Chapter Four).

- Specific purchasing decisions can be thought of as 'punctuation' in a continuing stream of interaction, and are best understood in the long-term context of the relationship. This perspective is fundamentally different from earlier OBB models, which tended to see purchasing decisions as atomistic (or discrete) events to be explained solely in terms of the situational issues prevailing at the time – see Chapter Two.

- Long-established and habitual relationships can be hugely important to the efficiency and effectiveness of purchasing. The switching costs in changing supplier can often explain the conservatism found in IORs.

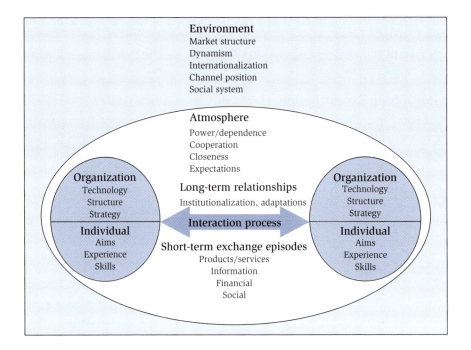

Figure 5.1 The Interaction Model
Source: Adapted with permission from Håkansson (ed.) (1982, p 24)
H. Håkansson (ed.) (1982) International Marketing & Purchasing of Industrial Goods:
An Interaction Approach, p 24, John Wiley & Sons

- Participants in exchanges are both organizations and individuals, and a large number of variables will affect their behaviour.

- The active role of the supplier in IORs is recognized (this is sometimes overlooked in studies that focus on buying decisions), in a balanced perspective that also avoids implying that the buyer is somehow just a passive recipient of marketing inputs.

- Exchange takes place within an 'atmosphere' formed by the experience of those involved and the previous history of the relationship (see below).

- The whole of the interaction process is surrounded by the macro-environmental features that can affect the sector.

The relationship 'atmosphere' can be described in terms of the power–dependence relationship which exists between firms, the state of conflict or cooperation, and the overall closeness or distance of the relationship, as well by the companies' mutual expectations. The atmosphere is a product of the relationship, and it also mediates the influence of the groups of factors listed in Figure 5.1 on the relationship. There is not necessarily a single atmosphere affecting (and affected by) the actions of a focal firm. As IMP authors point out, it is quite possible for an organization to have one relationship with a particular firm which is characterized by cooperation, whilst at the same time the organization can have a relationship with another firm which is characterized by frequent conflict.

So, although the Interaction Model presents a 'two-way' relationship for simplification, in reality any organization is likely to be involved in a wide range of relationships with

Box 5.2 Mini case

Networks in the Hong Kong clothing sector

Hong Kong is seen as the global sourcing hub for corporate clothing buyers. In the last few decades, however, clothing manufacturers there have had to respond to increased demands to deliver quality garments in short lead times to foreign importers and retailers. One way of handling these demands is the development of strategic networks with fabric suppliers. Three strategies in particular have been adopted by Hong Kong clothing manufacturers. First, investing in transaction-specific assets to protect network IORs, although the fabric suppliers have proved more willing to invest in physical assets (such as specialized equipment for manufacturing) as well as in human assets (such as specific skills and knowledge) than their client firms. Second, committing to long-term IORs, with an average duration of over four years, enabling customer firms to establish systems with which to track the performance of their suppliers. Third, maintaining a small supplier base, typically with three to eight suppliers, which helps the clothing manufacturer to stabilize network IORs and enhance the efficiency of purchasing. Only by working together with their networked fabric suppliers can these manufacturers meet the targets of their customers.

Source: Lau and Moon (2008)

other firms. Interactions between individual firms have the potential to cause a 'ripple effect' of events throughout a series of other organizations also interacting in different ways with each other. This results in a network of mutually influential IORs, the implications of which we shall address in the rest of this chapter.

To illustrate the idea of network interactions, Box 5.2 shows how clothing manufacturers are affected by relations with their corporate clients and, in turn, pass on these effects through the IORs they develop with their networks of suppliers.

5.2 From the Metaphor of Channels & Chains to Networks

A key point made by the IMP Group is that the distinction between 'marketing' (i.e. by suppliers) and 'purchasing' (i.e. by customers) is not a helpful way to describe what is essentially a seamless and iterative process. Purchasing can overlap with activities like product development, production management, and marketing planning. This will typically happen between more than just two firms at any one point, especially for a complex product or service-based exchange. In this way, what are termed 'industrial networks' are formed by patterns of IORs between firms engaging in these activities, and thereby exchanging a variety of resources (including products, money, and information).

Thus, despite the rather simplified view of IORs that we used in Chapter Three in order to explain how IORs 'work', virtually no relationship exists in isolation but forms part of a connected and interdependent set of relationships. Our understanding of IORs now extends from downstream channels to up and downstream chains, and then on to interlocking channels/chains in the form of networks. The metaphor of a 'net' seeks to capture the many links up, down, and 'across' an industrial sector as different firms strive together to reach the market. Basically, as well as being the links in the supply chain, IORs also connect organizational nodes in the net – see Figure 5.2.

This perspective renders the popular marriage metaphor of IORs as a little inadequate to represent the complexity of industrial network relations. Instead, we might consider using an 'extended family' metaphor (Johnston and Hausman, 2006). So, as well as considering relationship stages (like the life cycle we discussed in Chapter Three) in terms of, say, court-ship, honeymoon, and divorce, etc., we might also think of other people participating in the relationship, however indirectly, such as children, parents, grandparents, and uncles. What happens in the core marital relationship can affect these social actors, and in turn what they do can affect the marriage. The metaphor also accentuates the constant change that is part of a network perspective. As with extended families, participants will enter and leave the network, individual participants will experience changes in power, and may also change their position. In this way, firms can occupy several roles simultaneously within the network; they may be equal peers in some IORs, dominant elders in others, and respectful minors in yet other partnerships, depending on the atmosphere of the relationship. B2B managers must adapt to different ways of interacting with each member of the network.

Sometimes, the extended family is not a happy one. Box 5.3 shows what can happen to other network members when the dominant family member, here the UK retailer Marks & Spencer (M&S), changes its mind. The global impact of this customer organization's decision over its product sourcing was dramatic. As a result a powerful actor, previously perceived in Turkey as a benevolent 'patriarch' (i.e. M&S) arguably turned into the 'black sheep' of this network family, however economically legitimate its decision may have been.

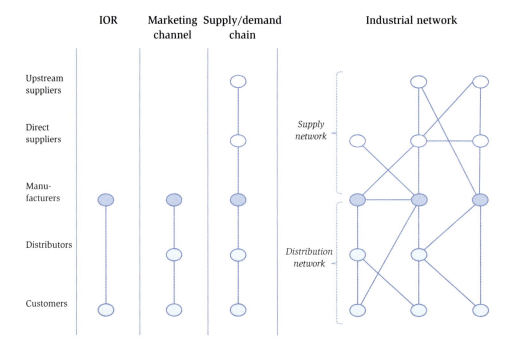

Figure 5.2 From IOR to channel to chain to network

Box 5.3 Voices

Relationships in the supply network for M&S

In the early 2000s, several of M&S's UK-based garment suppliers began to invest in Turkey. However, things did not work out well, partly due to the power M&S held over its exclusive suppliers and the speed with which it decided to terminate a key IOR. The retailer has always been proud of its history of loyal relationships with its suppliers, but recently these have been affected by concerns over costs. Desmonds, the retailer's biggest supplier of casual wear, came to Turkey because it was encouraged by M&S to do so in order to maintain quality but at a lower price of production than was possible in the UK. In addition to working with four Turkish manufacturers as subcontractors, Desmonds also transferred some of its previous Northern Ireland-based activities to Turkey. Here is how a Turkish productivity consultant describes what happened next: 'And then one day M&S said "It's over," [the contract with Desmonds] and all was over. The entire empire of Desmonds with eight factories in Ireland . . . one jointly owned factory in Turkey, eight factories in Sri Lanka . . . all collapsed like dominoes. They all closed down.'

Sources: Tokatli et al (2008); http://corporate.marksandspencer.com

An example of an industrial network can be seen in Figure 5.3 which tries to capture some of the members, and the links between them, of a distribution network in the computer-manufacturing sector. Note how managers within IBM need to remain aware of a number of issues, including: managing relationships in the firm's own multiple distribution channels to reach the end users; the rival channels used by its competitors, some of whom may trade with the same intermediary as IBM; the fact that suppliers can provide parts directly to the end customer, circumventing IBM and its distributors; and the fact that these suppliers supply both IBM and its competitors; plus the input of other organizations such as software houses and installers (www.ibm.com/partnerworld).

Types of industrial networks

Three main types of network have been identified that probably affect B2B marketing managers the most (Ford et al, 2006). These are supplier networks (as we saw in the M&S case in Box 5.3), distribution networks (as for IBM above), and product development networks (rather like the KTN we saw for composite materials at the start of this chapter):

- First, supplier networks: Taking an example of a car manufacturer like Toyota (www. toyotauk.com), we can see how the firm would be unable to work with all of the 50,000 suppliers that contribute components and materials to its final products. Thus, Toyota chooses to work closely with a small number of 'system suppliers', each responsible for the design and production of a certain part or system, such as a steering mechanism or door. Each system supplier deals with a limited number of suppliers that deliver key parts of the system concerned. These suppliers are in turn serviced by a further level of suppliers that provide standardized components to Toyota's suppliers and to other companies in the wider network for motor parts. The network structure allows the

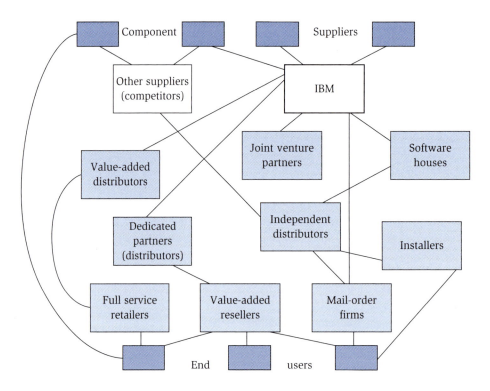

Figure 5.3 IBM's distribution network
Source: Adapted with permission from Ford (ed.) (2001)
D. Ford (ed.) (2001) Understanding Business Markets and Purchasing, p 37, Cengage Learning

customer firm to be indirectly linked to a large variety of suppliers, both technologically and geographically, even though it may only have direct contact with a few of them. The IORs involved in such a network take many years to set up, however, and it can be difficult for Toyota to ensure that all of them are working effectively. It is only when all the IORs linking nodes in the net are working well simultaneously that they create significant value for the customer firm. This example also shows how a large organiza- tion can play a major role in the development of a network, but you should remember that the perspective we have just provided is entirely from Toyota's end of the supply net (Blenkhorn and Noori, 1999). Suppliers at different levels will have a different view of 'their' network.

• Second, distribution networks: Returning to our example of IBM in Figure 5.3, we may observe how a number of different types of organization seem to be performing roughly the same activity, that is selling computers. These distributing organizations vary in their IORs with IBM and with their own suppliers, as well as in their customer IORs. As we saw in Chapter Four, this is because they provide a series of different customer solutions. Manufacturers like IBM need to select the appropriate distributors to work with for each customer segment and then manage a variety of relationships downstream with these intermediaries. The extent of such a network shows how hard it can be for even a large manufacturer to control the membership of a network or how the members should relate to each other.

- Third, product development networks: These networks tend to be larger and more complex than more conventional supply or distribution networks, especially for high-tech goods. To be able to conduct product or service development effectively, it is often necessary to draw upon the resources of, and appreciate the needs of, many different types of organization. In the case of an Internet-ready mobile phone, for example, innovation almost always involves more than one organization and more than one technology. Moreover, links with non-business members of the network can be crucial, including regulatory authorities and standards bodies. Such a network will be difficult for a single organization to coordinate, and although a network structure may allow one firm to influence (directly and indirectly) a large number of others, it also means that the firm can be influenced by those companies in turn.

Many different IORs and relationship atmospheres are likely to have to be negotiated if product innovation is to be successful – see the case in Box 5.4. This sector offers some nice examples of the importance of non-customer IORs in networks. Note how the first two of the three relationships identified relate directly to the core value creation process, while the third refers to relations with supporting network members. All are important.

Network stakeholder relationships

How does a network perspective affect how we see IORs? For some scholars, the relationship marketing (RM) thinking portrayed in Chapter Three has developed away from a strictly

Box 5.4 Food for thought

Different relationships in networks of software SMEs

The networks of many SMEs in the computer software sector can be their most important assets. These networks are drawn upon by smaller firms to gain access to resources that they do not possess in order to remain competitive and to take advantage of new market opportunities. As well as the crucial customer relationships in the network, three other types of relationship can be indentified: (1) those involving R&D activities (e.g. with universities); (2) those involving marketing and distribution activities (e.g. with network members offering after-sales service); and (3) those that facilitate the business of the firm (e.g. partners providing financial resources). The networks that form in all three categories can include both individual and organizational participants.

From the point of view of the software SME, managers exploring Type (1) links need to identify and evaluate their own and their potential partners' competence regarding key technologies (e.g. innovativeness, flexibility, and adaptability), and the extent to which these resources can be shared. For Type (2) links, managers need to monitor the end customers' requirements and identify the right partners with whom to forge the appropriate value proposition, ensuring that information is shared effectively throughout the channel. To make the most out of Type (3) links, managers are recommended to join entrepreneurial networks of industry associations and to invite professionals with the specific knowledge required (e.g. legal, financial) to join the board of directors of the SME.

Source: Westerlund and Svahn (2008)

two-way dialogue between supplier and customer. It has come to represent the whole series of relationships that a firm undertakes as part of its commercial dealings. In order to facilitate the supplier–customer relationship, other parties have to be involved in the RM process. Each organization in a network has to establish the appropriate connections between its different relationships.

There is thus much to be said for managers embracing a stakeholder perspective (Freeman, 1984) towards strategy. Stakeholders are parties with a 'stake', or interest, in a particular firm's activities. They can include customers, suppliers, employees, and shareholders. If we picture the firm as embedded in a network of relationships with a series of stakeholders or 'markets' (Ballantyne et al, 2003), then we can see that actions in the customer market, say, will have an impact on the supplier market, and beyond. For instance, if in response to consumer demand and government incentives, a car manufacturer intends to produce more recyclable cars, then some component suppliers will inevitably have to be persuaded to change their manufacturing practices and even their suppliers of raw materials. Furthermore, independent consumer agencies may wish to check that any 'green' claims are really true, particularly when suppliers are located internationally.

Whilst it is clear to marketers that the customer is a key stakeholder, we should not forget the other potential partners in a company's relationship portfolio. For instance, in service sectors like business consulting, where the quality of a customer's experience can be significantly affected by staff performance, the front-line employees are particularly important stakeholders (see Chapter Nine). This is also the case in the IT-based service sector where much business processing work has been outsourced to India. Time differences between customers in countries worldwide and Indian call centres result in long hours, an intense work pace, and health problems for night-shift workers (Nadeem, 2009). Firms drawing on these services in global networks should attempt to minimize these impacts if they are to respect all their network members.

Other important service providers in a network can be government departments, as the case below shows. Look at the amount of funding at BDC's disposal to deliver its core service to business customers and in the other products/services/markets in which it operates (see Box 5.5). Firms seeking to work in Botswana would probably need to forge relations with this key stakeholder.

Box 5.5 Number crunching

The Botswana Development Corporation (BDC)

Steve Carter, Leeds Metropolitan University, Leeds, UK

BDC, the primary Botswana government investment organization, was incorporated in 1970 and provides equity and long-term loans to viable business ventures sponsored by both local and foreign investors. The Botswana economy is generally in good shape, with real GDP growth which had been forecast at 4.5% for 2006–10. However, the economy is still heavily dependent on the mining sector. Botswana is one of the world's largest producers of high-quality diamonds. Future growth is based on airport and infrastructure development, investment in financial services, development of tourist destinations, and a plan to build a power generation capacity which would serve the southern African region based on the country's abundant coal deposits.

BDC's aims include promoting citizen (native Batswana) participation in business ventures; and identifying opportunities and implementing investments directly, or in partnership with other institutions, which impact on Botswana's economic and social development. To deliver these aims, BDC has one major advantage in that it has access to government funds, for example a total of 121 million pula (6 pula = £1) in 2008, projected to grow to 186 million by 2011. But it also has other strengths, including sound financial management, brand management in terms of the BDC name being generally well known, flexibility in 'product packaging' including long-term financing and product mixing, 'green-field' financing, and risk management expertise.

BDC has a number of external-facing functional areas. These include: (a) property development and management where BDC owns its own domestic housing and commercial property and rents or lets these out to individuals or companies; (b) industry where BDC has invested in a certain number of sectors like clay ware, canning, and artefacts. Some of these were 'social' investments and have to be financially supported year on year; (c) invoice discounting, which is a relatively new venture for the company. It involves buying up invoices from companies at a discounted rate, thus helping the seller's cash flow. BDC then collects the money itself from the seller; and (d) agribusiness and services where BDC offers agricultural services, including contract tractor power to small-scale farmers who cannot afford to buy a tractor themselves.

Categorizing network relationships

The B2B marketing manager is clearly faced with an operating environment of considerable complexity. So how might we classify these relationships in order to make any sense of all the possibilities open to us? A common ground between various models of stakeholder relations is that RM should accommodate notions of the focal firm and its partnerships. These are known variously as 'six markets' (Christopher et al, 1991), 'four partnerships and ten relationships' (Morgan and Hunt, 1994) or the '30Rs' (Gummesson, 1999). See Figure 5.4 for a summary.

Comprehensive though the 30Rs classification certainly is, a combination of the other two models probably offers the most convenient way to help managers keep track of the full set of network relationships. Thus, we may consider:

- Customer (or vertical downstream) partnerships, including B2B and B2C

- Supplier (or vertical upstream) partnerships for goods and services

- Lateral (or horizontal) partnerships, including competitor alliances, NGOs, NFP organizations, governments and shareholders

- Internal (horizontal) partnerships, including employees and functional departments.

Under a demand chain management perspective, the actions and opinions of the end consumer can have a significant impact on links throughout the network, sometimes in unexpected ways. Consider, for instance, the problems that can afflict firms which decide to relocate their factories overseas to reduce labour costs. This strategy may make sense financially in terms of network efficiency, but a holistic marketing orientation can identify potential risks. In many industrialized countries, rising unemployment is blamed on the

	VERTICAL		HORIZONTAL	
	Customer relationships	Supplier relationships	External relationships	Internal relationships
Morgan & Hunt (1994)	**Buyer partnerships** Intermediaries End consumers	**Supplier partnerships** Goods suppliers Service suppliers	Lateral partnerships Competitors Non-profit orgs Government	Internal partnerships Business units Functional depts Employees
Christopher et al (1991)	**Customer markets**	**Supplier markets**	Influence market incl. shareholders Referral market	Internal market Employee market
Gummesson (1999) *Selected '30Rs'*	**Classic market relationships** Dyad (customer/supplier) Triad (above plus competitor) Network (distribution channels) **Special Market Relationships** The service encounter Customer's customer relationship Monopoly relationship Electronic relationship Non-commercial relationship (etc.)		Mega relationships Personal/social relationships Mega relationships (e.g. government) Mega alliances (e.g. NAFTA) Mass media	Meta relationships Profit centres Quality Employee Marketing services Owner/financiers

Figure 5.4 **Classifying the network relationships of the focal firm**
Source: Adapted with permission from Egan (2001, p 112)
J. Egan (2001) Relationship Marketing: Exploring Relational Strategies in Marketing, p 112,
copyright Pearson Education Limited

cost-driven relocation strategies of multinational corporations. The resulting loss of goodwill towards a manufacturer's brands can be exacerbated when local factories have been part of a region's self-image (such as the Raleigh bicycle factory in Nottingham, UK, which was closed in 2002 and production was shifted to the Far East – www.raleigh.co.uk). In response, consumers may join a boycott of the firm's products to demand greater social responsibility (Hoffmann and Muller, 2009). Decisions over relocation thus need to be handled sensitively. Failure to do so could result in long-term negative reputation and reduction in brand value. Public relations management will have a part to play (see Chapter Eleven).

Moving back from the consumer stakeholder, let us refocus on relations with other organizations. As we saw in Chapter Four, vertical relationships represent those that integrate parts of the supply chain (or channel). Horizontal relationships include those with organizations at the same level in the chain who may seek to collaborate for mutual benefit (see Figure 5.5). Diagonal relationships indicate links between nodes in the network that form part of other horizontal or vertical 'strands' of the web. They commonly occur, for example, when a supplier sells to two or more different customer firms, or when several selling firms (perhaps supplying products and services) share the same downstream customer (see back to Figure 5.2). As in Box 5.4, on software SMEs, horizontal or diagonal relationships can also be ways of bringing supporting organizations, such as advisors or sources of funds, into the network.

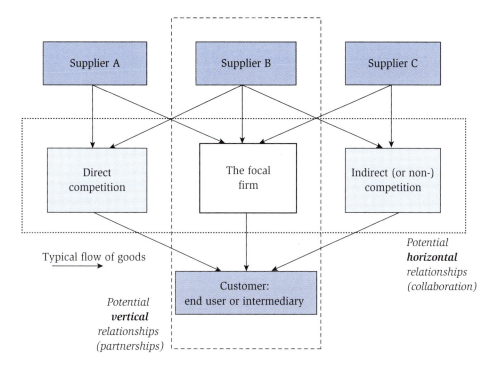

Figure 5.5 Horizontal and vertical network relationships
Source: Adapted with permission from Egan (2001, p 155)
J. Egan (2001) Relationship Marketing: Exploring Relational Strategies in Marketing, p 155,
copyright Pearson Education Limited

We can classify the formation of networks based on the goals their members are seeking to achieve (de Man, 2004). Networks based on vertical relationships tend to reflect supply chain arrangements (e.g. Dell's links with its suppliers – www.dell.com). Networks that comprise primarily horizontal relationships are often aimed at achieving market power, drawing on the complementary resources of member organizations (e.g. airline alliances – www.oneworld.com). Horizontal networks also exist when firms seek to provide solutions to specific customer needs. These 'solution networks' can be client initiated and frequently take in diagonal relationships, too, (e.g. Schwab financial services – www.charlesschwab.co.uk). Technology-orientated networks adopt a similar pattern with a mixture of horizontal and diagonal links across the network (e.g. Sematech's semiconductor research – www.sematech.org/corporate). These sorts of webs also develop in 'standardization networks' where firms try to set a dominant technology in product or service sector (e.g. the WAP Forum amongst telephone operating system providers – www.openmobilealliance.org). Moreover, as we saw in the opening case in this chapter, vertical relationships can form important parts of such 'knowledge transfer networks' as well.

The importance of different network relationship directions in the textile sector is shown in Box 5.6. Note how a B2B marketer representing the Cotton Cooperative has to remain attuned to IORs in both vertical and horizontal directions.

Box 5.6 Food for thought

Horizontal and vertical relationships in the cotton network

More than 30 US family farms in Texas have been attempting to promote the virtues of organic cotton. They claim its production can reduce the number of agricultural pollutants typically dumped into the environment through normal farming methods. To increase the impact of their marketing efforts, they formed the Texas Organic Cotton Marketing Cooperative in 2003. This group of horizontally linked organizations produces about 3,000 quarter-ton bales of organic cotton a year. While it has formed a close vertical relationship with an organization called Cotton Plus which sells a wide range of organic cotton fabrics, the Cooperative realizes that it needs more downstream allies to achieve market success. It is thus seeking a series of vertical relationships with garment manufacturers, retailers, and consumers who value organic cotton. It will be quite a struggle: organics formed less than 1% of the total US cotton grown in 2007, showing that the network as a whole views a shift to organic production as a risky venture.

Source: Wells (2007); www.texasorganic.com

5.3 Learning from the Industrial Network View

Easton and Araujo (1994, p 82) describe the theoretical background of the industrial network approach as being located 'half-way between economics and sociology'. This theoretical perspective helps to illuminate a series of B2B marketing issues, summarized in Figure 5.6: the significance of embeddedness and social capital in networks; analysing network position using what is known as the ARA Model; attempting to define the boundaries of a network; and the complexity of networks that extend across international borders.

Network embeddedness

As Håkansson and Snehota (2000, p 79) explain, 'Companies are embedded in multi-dimensional ways into their counterparts [and] into their counterparts' contexts. . . . Every

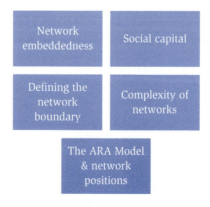

Figure 5.6 Considerations in B2B marketing from a network perspective

relationship is not only a bridge between two actors but also a reflector or a projection of other relationships.' However, the embedded nature of individual relationships is only treated to a limited extent in RM theorizing. For instance, a firm is often regarded as pursuing a relational strategy in the RM approach without considering that other firms may be involved in similar relational strategies with the same customers (Mattsson, 1997).

The network perspective recognizes this interconnectedness. It views structures of industrial networks as conditioned by technical and cultural factors, but formed and modified primarily through continuous, multiple interactions. In this way, network structure can be seen as the result of history (Håkansson and Johanson, 1993). This approach acknowledges that managers and firms are unlikely to act in IORs without a sense of what has gone before and what may occur in the future. In other words, an embeddedness approach tries to take into account the ever-changing social context of organizational activities (Grabher, 1993).

Such a view recognizes that something called 'social capital' can be an important resource in industrial networks. It is based on an individual person's embeddedness in social structures, such as their personal reputation amongst their colleagues. All relationships, whether they are business or personally orientated, can potentially be used for benefit. Social capital can be seen as a 'lubricant' in IORs, helping to make networks work through trust. Although not the same sort of 'capital' as money, it is often a crucial component of conducting business, particularly in Asian cultures. Social capital means that individual relationships developed in the past or present can be drawn on for future business purposes. Western managers are quite likely to be asked by Asian friends for favours, and they would normally be expected to reciprocate and request support from within their own social network (Theingi et al, 2008).

While drawing on social capital can benefit IORs, the social element of networks can sometimes represent a problem, as the case in Box 5.7 shows. The incident described confirms that trust is a key component of relationship coordination in the minds of many Hong Kong Chinese network members, but also reveals that trust is quite a complex and often contradictory factor.

Box 5.7 Mini case
Changing attitudes to trust and honour in a network

Sid Lowe, Kingston University, Kingston Upon Thames, UK

Stephen is the 60-year-old General Manager of a Hong Kong company manufacturing fashion garments mainly for the American market. The company was started by his father (who in 1995 was still alive and 'actively participating' in the business) and a partner who had died. Stephen explained that, in 1995, the company was in a period of recovery after an acrimonious break-up with the partner's son who had 'betrayed' the trust between the two families by 'double-dealing'. The partner's son had traded on the company's behalf with a friend who was a representative of another trading company. Generous credit terms had been agreed with this friend, despite the rumour that this party was in financial difficulty. On discovering the deal, Stephen questioned the partner's son but he claimed that his friend was solvent and invoked the responsibility of Stephen to give him 'face' in supporting his friend.

Under this obligation and on the advice of his father (who supported the venture on the basis of obligation to the memory of his partner), Stephen had agreed to the credit agreement. The friend of the partner's son then reneged on the deal and emigrated, and on the same day the partner's son left to join another company. This left Stephen with a HK$0.5 million unsecured debt which he did not expect to recover. Apparently, the partner's son and his friend had secured a cash sale for the goods and shared the revenue between them. Stephen complained that this kind of betrayal was increasingly common and attributed it to the general immorality of the younger generation who were prepared to abandon their reputation for fair dealing, reciprocal trust, and honouring their word for the seductive allure of living an 'easy life in a foreign country'.

The ARA Model

As you may have noticed from the chapter thus far, underpinning many industrial network studies are the concepts of 'actors', 'resources', and 'activities' (as depicted in Figure 5.7). For the IMP Group, these coexist in what is known as the ARA Model, a framework which is very useful in order to get some idea of the relative positions of the organizations making up a network. Actors in a network can be individuals, departments, a whole company or a group of companies. Each actor controls certain activities and resources directly, but due to interdependencies, actors may have an indirect control (or at least, influence) over their counterparts' activities and resources. Håkansson and Snehota (1995, p 26) outline these concepts in a relational sense as follows:

- Actor bonds 'connect actors and influence how actors perceive each other and form their identities in relation to each other' – e.g. IORs (see Chapter Three) or supply chains (Chapter Four).

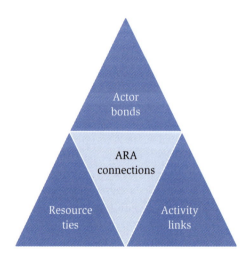

Figure 5.7 Elements of the ARA Model

- Resource ties 'connect various resource elements (technological, material, knowledge resources and other intangibles)' – often manifested as products (Chapter Eight) or services (Chapter Nine).

- Activity links 'regard technical, administrative, commercial and other activities of a company that can be connected' – e.g. purchasing (Chapter Two) or marketing communications (Chapter Eleven).

The concepts provide marketers with a model of what happens in business networks (Ford, 1997). An ARA-based analysis will typically begin at the point of the focal firm (i.e. the one the manager represents) and try to identify actor bonds emanating from there, as well as all the organizations and people that have economic or social bonds with other network actors. This type of analysis should show the degree of centrality of the firm to the network: does it function like a kind of 'hub' organization, or is it on the periphery of the other actors involved? The classic activity links between actors are those that underpin buying/selling interactions, but other activities may be important to recognize, such as joint R&D efforts. This sort of mapping can show the extent to which the focal firm contributes to the range of activities taking place in the network. While some resources will be used by solo actors (such as specific manufacturing machinery), resource ties occur when they are combined with resources from other network actors to create a shared resource. For instance, the sharing of data resources is increasingly facilitated by IT, as we saw in the supply-chain information flows discussed in Chapter Four. Such an analysis enables the firm to determine the degree to which it is reliant on its network partners' resources.

Combining these A, R, and A analyses allows managers to get a sense of whether their firm is in a desirable position or whether it needs to change some of the IORs it is involved with. Trying to become more central to a network may not, however, always be the best way forward: some firms may be major manufacturers requiring extensive horizontal, vertical, and diagonal connections, but others may be niche suppliers who function perfectly well by marketing to just a few organizational customers on the 'edge' of the network. Also, of course, your network position is not just up to you: changing it may require coordinating changes in the resource and activities of other actors. In fact, as Wilkinson (2006) explains, positions are constantly being established and re-established via the interactions that take place, including the transactions, knowledge flows, resources created and used up, and the bonds created and drawn upon by actors. The overall patterns of behaviour that emerge in the network shape its development and how it adapts to environmental events.

For example, note how the newspaper report in Box 5.8 describes the aims of a global network of stakeholders in the palm oil sector. What these actors decide to do could significantly change the ARA make-up of this industry.

Box 5.8 Voices

Multiple actor discussions on the future of palm oil

A local Malaysian newspaper announced that 'international players' in the palm oil sector are to meet in London for the World Sustainable Palm Oil Conference. These players include representatives from Malaysia and Indonesia, who together produce 85% of the world's palm oil, including corporate strategists from firms such as Kuala Lumpur Kepong and United Plantations, research bodies, and governmental organizations. The conference was described in a statement from the Malaysian Palm Oil Council as an opportunity for 'stakeholders in the palm oil supply chain to discuss critical issues with senior government decision makers and industry leaders'. The statement went on: 'it will encourage dialogue between civil society groups, end users and producers'. This dialogue aimed to clarify responsible practices in the industry, as well as share experiences in increasing productivity and offering new products.

Source: New Straits Times (2008); www.mpoc.org.my; www.unitedplantations.com

Defining the network

With all the different types of relationships that exist across a network, businesses often find themselves operating in loose-knit stakeholder networks that may be very hard to define. Part of the struggle for actors trying to manage the activities in a network comes from the fact that networks are opaque and unbounded. It is probably impossible to specify the limits of a supply chain or network for analytical purposes. This can make strategic decisions difficult. Managers will attempt to gain comprehension by building a cognitive model of the network structure (Håkansson and Johanson, 1993). One way of delimiting a network is to draw boundaries around it, but all such boundaries are effectively arbitrary since they are the result of people's interpretations.

In order to try to plan their marketing efforts (see Chapter Six), managers need to consider which actors have the greatest impact on the network they are examining. Consider, for example, a B2B trade marketer working for a US manufacture of consumer shavers for the European market, such as Gillette, now part of Procter & Gamble (www.uk.pg.com). This manager's analytical decisions will depend on the range of their responsibilities which are likely to be heavily channel-orientated. To simplify their task, they might decide to erect an imaginary boundary around the network based on the fact that they can effectively disregard international suppliers since they are mainly located outside Europe, as well as end consumers since they must choose from a range of non-customised shavers available in retail stores (Sadler, 2007).

As pictured in Figure 5.8, the key elements of the network for this B2B marketer to try to understand are then reduced to the IORs involving:

- The European HQ of the manufacturer
- Its European assembly plants
- Its range of distributors (some of which may be subsidiaries)
- The retailers who form the firm's organizational customers
- Any necessary transportation providers
- Plus, of course, the B2B activities of the firm's competitors.

The marketer will clearly still need to liaise with their SCM and B2C brand development colleagues, but their immediate remit would involve this more 'manageable' network of firms within the distribution channel, rather like the IBM network illustrated in Figure 5.3. For a related perspective on making sense of networks, see Leek and Mason (2009) who provide a series of managers' 'network pictures'. Further discussion of the usefulness of

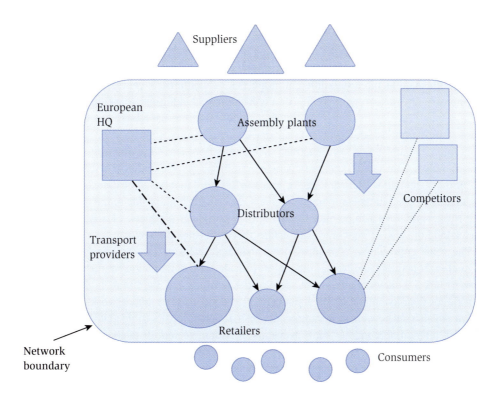

Figure 5.8 A possible network picture

the network pictures concept can be found in Chapter Seven (see also the explanation of Figure 1.4 back in Chapter One).

One point to ponder is where ethical responsibility begins and ends in an industrial network. Some commentators feel that ethical considerations should extend across a firm's network to an extent that embraces stakeholders not always included in supply chain codes of practice. For instance, Grein and Gould (2007, pp 298–9) examine the codes of Nike and Mattel regarding globally integrated marketing communications over production practices affecting workers and the environment. They cite Nike's website (www.nike.com), which states that the firm believes 'consumers must be able to reward brands and suppliers using fact-based information. . . . Disclosure of our supply chain is done in an effort to jump-start disclosure and collaboration throughout the industry.' Mattel's website (www.mattel.com) says that upstream it has 'developed country-specific standards that govern our operations and those of the companies that manufacture and assemble our products', while down-stream, it aims to 'create products that respect our global customer base and the diversity of cultures'.

Grein and Gould comment that the values and principles expressed in relation to marketing in both firms' statements are positive, but the companies are rather vague with regard to taking a proactive approach. They go on (2007, p 300), 'codes need to be broadened to include the entire extra-corporate network, i.e. agents, distributors, retailers, advertising agencies etc.'. This an interesting argument: just how far can (or should) a firm influence the network of organizations of which it is part?

Complexity in global networks

As we have seen, the supply network for a product like a family saloon car can be incredibly complicated and actually comprises several different chains, all supplying the automobile manufacturer with different products, or sometimes, of course, the same product via increasingly intense competition. For a typical car sold in Europe, these firms can be situated globally. The components they supply include glass from Canada, radios from Belgium, hose clamps from Sweden, valves from the US, wheel nuts from Mexico, steering shafts from India, radiator hoses from Australia, alternators from France, switches from Indonesia, starter motors from Japan, and body panels from Brazil, all leading to final assembly in the UK or the Netherlands (Ransom, 2006). Imagine the work that has to be done by the marketing managers of all these component suppliers to persuade high-profile brand manufacturers like Nissan and Toyota to commit to buying their particular products. Clearly, they have to understand the web of network relationships that permeates the sector.

The same appreciation is required from managers working for firms located upstream from global operators like Nokia, the largest provider of mobile phones in the world, as the case in Box 5.9 shows. Look at the scale of the network and the numbers of people that depend for their livelihood on the managerial decisions made in this network.

We can also see how an appreciation of industrial network IORs could guide a firm seeking to make international market entry decisions. A strong element of relationship assessment at each stage of the process would be advisable. For example, a large firm might begin with macro-level assessments of horizontal partnerships with governments and state agencies in the countries considered. A smaller firm might look vertically to its contacts in its current

---

Box 5.9 Mini case
Nokia's web of suppliers

Nokia and its subcontractors like the Taiwanese firm, Foxconn, assemble phones in 19 factories throughout the globe. Nokia's manufacturing web involves the sourcing of 400 different components. The subcontractors in this network handle around 100 billion display screens, buttons, batteries, motherboards, capacitors, and other parts each year. Foxconn's Chinese plant in Shenzhen employs 70,000 people. It is serviced by dozens of local component manufacturers such as Delta, which is based in Dongguan and employs a further 20,000 workers, and Hua Tong, based in Huizhou, which makes Nokia's circuit boards. Delta, which is also Taiwanese owned, is the world's biggest manufacturer of adaptors and capacitors for computers and mobile phones, so has other corporate clients besides Nokia. Servicing the needs of these component makers are the metals and plastics sectors, with firms mining, refining, and moulding the raw materials that go into the components. Suppliers of iron, copper, and tin, plus glass, ceramics, and various chemicals all feed into the web and must all manage their relationships with customer firms downstream. Thus, behind high-profile consumer products like cars and mobile phones are business networks of great size and complexity. No wonder there are so many firms needing good B2B marketing managers!

Source: Pearce (2008); www.nokia.com; www.foxconn.com

network of buyers and suppliers, or horizontally to its competitors (Donaldson and O'Toole, 2002). The firm's ability to develop network relationships will often determine its success in a foreign market, as illustrated by the Chinese consumer electronics manufacturer TCL (www.tclelectronics.com.au) which has formed an alliance with the French group Thomson. This agreement gives TCL effective control of Thomson's television plants in France, Poland, and Thailand, and provides cover against any possible protectionist trade actions from customer nations against China (Chandler, 2004). IORs are also crucial to doing business with partners in Middle East markets. For instance, research shows purchasing managers from Saudi Arabian SMEs seek long-term relationships with selling firms (Sohail and Alashban, 2009). As in so many of the contexts we have encountered over the last three chapters of this book, this research confirms how the development of long-established IORs is positively related to trust and dependence between network actors.

The wide-ranging nature of industrial networks means that many of the examples that have been provided in this chapter are global in their reach, often showing how non-commercial partners or stakeholders beyond the main customer/supplier IOR can exert considerable network influence. The chapter concludes with a case study which illustrates this by looking at the actors making up the industrial network surrounding the Nigerian oil sector.

Summary

The key points to take from this chapter are as follows:

- The way that the different elements of the Interaction Model are affected by (and affect) relationship atmosphere.

- How a network perspective captures the interconnectedness of business interactions more comprehensively than notions of a channel or supply chain.

- The need to broaden relationship marketing thinking from the customer/supplier IOR to a stakeholder perspective.

- How a focal firm can be embedded in a number of different types of industrial networks at the same time.

- Ways of classifying network partnerships and the idea of vertical, horizontal, and diagonal links between organizations.

- The significance of social capital in industrial networks, and potential problems with the social element of network links.

- How the concepts of actors, resources, and activities can help us make sense of industrial networks.

- What an industrial network perspective entails for the way we view IORs in global markets and supply chains.

Discussion questions

1. Think back to Chapter Two and debate whether the IMP Group's Interaction Model is any more useful to B2B marketers than more traditional models of OBB.

2. What are the main contributions of industrial network theory to our understanding of the interconnected nature of IORs?

3. Identify the key stakeholders with which a manufacturer of FMCGs seeking to trade in foreign markets may have to build relationships.

4. Why are horizontal partnerships as important as vertical ones in a network relationship approach?

5. How could an appreciation of social capital assist a marketing manager representing a Western SME specializing in pipeline testing equipment seeking to penetrate markets in Asia?

6. Draw an industrial network for a focal firm of your choice. Explain the decisions you have had to make in determining where the boundaries of this network lie.

Case study
Stakeholder Networks in the Nigerian Oil Sector

Ibrahim Umar, University of Leicester, Leicester, UK

Introduction

Shell's fuel products are used by organizational and individual consumers in more than 40 countries. An important part of this multinational corporation is its stake in the Shell Petroleum Development Company of Nigeria Limited (SPDC). SPDC commenced oil production in the West African country in 1957. The partners that make up the joint venture company account for more than 40% of Nigeria's total oil production (about 899,000 barrels a day), of which the Nigeria National Petroleum Corporation (NNPC) claims a 55% share, the Dutch/British firm Shell 30%, French Total 10%, and Italian Agip 5%. The company's operations cover upstream oil and gas production as well as downstream sales of oil and chemical products.

Stakeholders in SPDC's network

Shell Nigeria has numerous stakeholders who can affect or are being affected by the company's existence and operations. They include the following:

1. *Principal partners*: in this case, the NNPC, Shell itself, plus the Total and Agip oil companies. These organizational shareholders are primarily concerned with increasing the share value of their stocks. In the unlikely event that the SPDC is not making the expected returns, any of the partners may decide to opt out of the joint venture. This is unlikely, however, given their commitments to this capital- and technology-intensive sector where Shell, for instance, supports its fuel products with extensive R&D carried out in Europe, the US, and Singapore by 150 scientists (www.shell.com). The company owes its stockholders the responsibility of making a fair return on their investment in areas like extraction, refining, and research. In turn, these big equity holders like Shell are effectively made up

of small individual and corporate investors who may also increase, dispose of, or maintain their shareholdings for different reasons.

2. *Customers*: these include countries, refineries, and gas stations, and end users to whom the company offers a series of benefits including fuel economy, enhanced equipment performance, and reduced emissions.

(*a*) At the national level, countries around the world consume Nigerian oil, including the US, India, Spain, South Africa, the Netherlands, France, Brazil, Cuba, Argentina, Netherlands Antilles, Peru, Trinidad and Tobago, Germany, Portugal, Sweden, the UK, Indonesia, Malaysia, and China.

(*b*) Corporate customers include the refineries and gas stations (some of which are vertically integrated as part of the oil companies' marketing channels) that retail oil and other lubricants. These organizations rely on Shell for the supply of crude oil. Since upstream oil production is dominated by relatively few powerful national and multinational companies, the vertical relationship between Shell and its organizational customers is characterized by the need for both sets of actors to maintain a steady, reliable supply.

(*c*) Shell's customers also include the final users of their products such as factories that consume energy and even motorists in far-away Japanese towns. At the company level, we may note that Shell claims that, 'our products power heavy industrial companies worldwide – whether a mining company, paper factory or a cement plant' and that its offerings will help customers 'keep pace with advanced product specifications and environmental regulations' (www.shell.com). At the individual level, during his fieldwork trip to Shell facilities in the Niger Delta, the author of this case study came across a crew from a Japanese television station producing a documentary on the kidnapping of expatriate oil workers in the Niger Delta and other militant activities in the region against Shell and its facilities. They explained that the audience would be Japanese consumers who will be shown how events in remote African communities can affect their daily lives by disrupting oil supplies to the Japanese economy.

3. *Suppliers*: these are companies who provide goods, services, and facilities to Shell. They include both local and foreign organizations. Unfortunately for Nigerian firms keen to add value to Shell's operations, high levels of technical capabilities and experience are demanded by the challenges of development and cost-reduction pressures on the multinational oil companies. This makes it difficult for firms that are not already part of what is a fairly closely knit international supply chain to become an 'in-supplier'. Foreign-based companies tend to dominate the industry. For instance, one of the major oil service companies operating in Nigeria is the renowned multinational, Halliburton. A smaller, but still vital, supplier is Brazilian outfit Smar, which is an automation contractor for SPDC's oil flow stations.

4. *Employees*: including the National Union of Petroleum and Gas Workers (NUPENG) representing the junior staff workers and the Petroleum and Natural Gas Senior Staff Association of Nigeria (PENGASSAN) representing the senior workers.

There is also another additional category of contract employees who are supplied by recruitment agencies who do not belong to these two unions. The contract staff are greater in number than the permanent staff.

5. *Host communities*: SPDC has many host communities, from those whose land hosts the actual oil wells to those hosting its pipelines and flow stations. According to Shell (2006), the SPDC joint venture remains the biggest single player in the region, producing 43% of Nigeria's oil and controlling a drilling area of about 31,000 square kilometres of land with over 1,000 wells, eight gas plants, and 87 flow stations and a network of about 6,000 kilometres of pipelines across the Niger Delta. The Delta consists of nine states from Bayelsa to Ondo. In turn, each of these states are made up of several local government areas. In this respect, the company considers the states and its local components as a series of stakeholders, although more and more oil is now being found in Nigeria's territorial waters, deep in the Atlantic, which no community can logically lay claim to. The Niger Delta has been inconsistently defined using hydrological, ecological, and political boundaries; however, the Niger Delta Development Commission estimates that it has an area of 112,000 square kilometres (Shell, 2006, p 9). The nine states, which produce about 70% of Nigeria's oil, have an estimated population of 20 million people, with 40 ethnic groups.

6. *The Nigerian State*: the national government relies on oil revenue to sustain its economy. Oil accounts for more than 90% of Nigeria's export earnings and 85% of government revenues. This stakeholder can be affected by any increases or decreases in the supply and price of oil. In the period 2005–8, SPDC contributed more than $3.4 billion in taxes and other payments (www.shell.com) to the government. Thanks to such revenues, the government will be able to fulfil its commitment to its citizens and international obligations such as peacekeeping in war-torn nations.

7. *Competitors*: as well as Shell's partners in SPDC (i.e. Total and Agip), the other major foreign oil companies that operate in Nigeria are the US multinationals, Chevron and ExxonMobil. Shell's competitors will expect the company to abide by fair rules of competition in the industry. In fact, these oil companies are generally benign towards each other. Each has its own concession as well as market outlets. Even in the downstream context, there is hardly any serious competition. It appears to be more a case of sharing the market among themselves rather than engaging in any stiff horizontal competition.

8. *OPEC*: the Organization of Petroleum Exporting Countries (OPEC) is an association of oil-producing governments. Global oil prices in general are determined not only by demand and supply, but also by the decisions of OPEC members (which allots production quotas to its members), increasing oil consumption by growing economies such as China and India, and political pressure from powerful governments such as that of the US which believes that any hike in oil prices will affect its economic growth. Both OPEC and, historically, multinational oil companies have been accused of operating a cartel to set oil prices. Interestingly, Nigeria is a member of OPEC while the US, which is a major oil producer in its own right, is not.

Discussion

The parties listed above are the principal stakeholders of SPDC. They qualify for this designation because they can affect or will be affected by the company's operations. Clearly, not all these stakeholders get equal treatment from the management of the company. The network described in this case is particularly interesting if we consider the non-traditional supply chain elements (i.e. those beyond the supplier–customer links in the supply/demand chain for oil).

For example, Shell's shareholders generally get good returns on their investment and make hardly any complaints about the company. This is not the case with Shell's host communities in the Niger Delta who are always at loggerheads with SPDC. As a result, many militant groups have emerged from these disgruntled communities. They are now literally holding the company to ransom by kidnapping its expatriate workers and demanding money, as well as engaging in sabotage activities against Shell's facilities such as blowing up its pipelines. Similarly, while the workers under the two respective unions are some of the best paid in any industry in Nigeria, the contract workers have been complaining of low wages and unfair conditions of service.

Handling relationships with these multiple stakeholders is a task that the management of SPDC has constantly to grapple with.

Source: Umar (2008) material collected as part of unpublished Ph.D. thesis, University of Leicester; www.shell.com (accessed February 2010); The Shell Sustainability Report (2006), online at http:// sustainabilityreport.shell.com

Case study questions

1. Provide an analysis of SPDC's network position by using the ARA Model. Try to map some of the principal stakeholders (i.e. actors) in the case context in terms of the activities and resources that link them vertically and horizontally.

2. How should SPDC fairly prioritize its stakeholder relationships? That is to say, on which actors, and with what resources and activities, should the company focus most of its attention, and why?

3. Are there any ethical issues regarding anti-competitive practices amongst certain actors within the oil sector? Could this be seen as a 'dark side' of network collaboration?

Further Reading

Axelsson, B. & Easton, G. (eds) (1992) Industrial Networks: A New View of Reality, Routledge, London
This collection of chapters by a number of leading IMP scholars captures a wide spectrum of perspectives on industrial networks. Topics covered include: a conceptual background to network studies; approaches to network analysis; issues of change within networks; the relationship between strategy and industrial networks; and suggestions for future research possibilities within the field, many of which remain pertinent.

Ellis, N. & Mayer, R. (2001) Inter-Organizational Relationships and Strategy Development in an Evolving Industrial Network: Mapping Structure & Process, Journal of Marketing Management, 17 (1/2), pp 183–222

The authors augment the RM literature with insights from sociology and organizational studies in order to explore IORs in the global chemicals market. Analysis is presented in the form of 'before' and 'after' scenarios that highlight factors which can redirect an organization's activities away from any intended relationship building and towards a transactional orientation, with consequences for all the network members.

Hite, J. M. (2003) Patterns of Multidimensionality among Embedded Network Ties: A Typology of Relational Embeddedness in Emerging Entrepreneurial Firms, Strategic Organization, 1 (1), pp 9–49

This paper posits that network ties embedded within social relationships influence economic actions and represent a strategic form of organizing for emerging entrepreneurial firms. It uses case study methods to examine external network ties of eight firms in the computer industry to produce a classification of relational embeddedness.

Mattsson, L.-G. (1997) 'Relationship Marketing' and the 'Markets-as-Networks Approach' – A Comparative Analysis of Two Evolving Streams of Research, Journal of Marketing Management, 13, pp 447–61

This article analyses the similarities and the differences between relationship marketing studies and network studies. The conclusion is that RM in its limited interpretation is just a development within the marketing mix approach. Relationship marketing in its extended interpretation could become close to the markets-as-networks approach, however, the basic attribute in network studies of embeddedness is largely missing in RM.

Ottessen, G. G., Foss, L., & Gronhaug, K. (2004) Exploring the Accuracy of SME Managers' Network Perceptions, European Journal of Marketing, 38 (5/6), pp 593–607

This paper studies the accuracy of small- to medium-sized (SME) company managers' perceptions of their information exchanges with important market actors such as customers, competitors, and suppliers. By comparing managers' perceptions with an 'objective' tracking of their actual behaviour, it reveals substantial perceptual errors, the implications of which are highlighted.

References

Ballantyne, D., Christopher, M., & Payne, A. (2003) Relationship Marketing: Looking Back, Looking Forward, Marketing Theory, 3 (1), pp 159–66

Blenkhorn, D. & Noori, A. H. (1999) What it Takes to Supply Japanese OEMs, Industrial Marketing Management, 19 (1), pp 21–31

Bond, E. U., Houston, M. B. & Tang, Y. (2008) Establishing a High-Technology Knowledge Transfer Network: The Practical and Symbolic Roles of Identification, Industrial Marketing Management, 37, pp 641–52

Chandler, C. (2004) TV's Mr Big, The Business, 8/9 (February), p 10

Christopher, M., Payne, A., and Ballantyne, D. (1991) Relationship Marketing, Butterworth Heinemann, Oxford

de Man, A.-P. (2004) The Network Economy: Strategy, Structure and Management, Edward Elgar, Cheltenham

Donaldson, B. and O'Toole, T. (2002) Strategic Market Relationships: From Strategy to Implementation, John Wiley & Sons, Cheltenham

Easton, G. & Araujo, L. (1994) Market Exchange, Social Structures and Time, European Journal of Marketing, 28 (3), pp 72–84

Egan, J. (2001) Relationship Marketing: Exploring Relational Strategies in Marketing, Financial Times/Prentice Hall, Harlow

Ford, D. (ed.) (1997) Understanding Business Markets: Interaction, Relationships and Networks, 2nd edn, Academic Press, London

Ford, D. (ed.) (2001) Understanding Business Markets and Purchasing, Thomson Learning, London

Ford, D., Gadde, L.-E., Håkansson, H., & Snehota, I. (2006) The Business Marketing Course: Managing in Complex Networks, 2nd edn, Wiley, Chichester

Freeman, R. E. (1984) Strategic Management: A Stakeholder Approach, Pitman, Boston

Grabher, G. (ed.) (1993) The Embedded Firm: On the Socioeconomics of Industrial Networks, Routledge, London

Grein, A. F. & Gould, S. J. (2007) Voluntary Codes of Ethical Conduct: Group Membership Salience and Globally Integrated Marketing Communications Perspectives, Journal of Macromarketing, 27 (3) pp 289–302

Gummesson, E. (1999) Total Relationship Marketing: Rethinking Marketing Management from 4Ps to 30Rs, Butterworth-Heinemann, Oxford

Håkansson, H. (ed.) (1982) International Marketing & Purchasing of Industrial Goods: An Interaction Approach, John Wiley, Chichester

Håkansson, H. & Johanson, J. (1993) The Network as a Governance Structure: Interfirm Cooperation beyond Markets and Hierarchies, in Grabher, G. (ed.), The Embedded Firm: On the Socioeconomics of Industrial Networks, Routledge, London, pp 35–51

Håkansson, H. & Snehota, I. (eds) (1995) Developing Relationships in Business Networks, Routledge/ITBP, London

Håkansson, H. & Snehota, I. (2000) The IMP Perspective: Assets and Liabilities of Business Relationships, in Sheth, J. N. & Parvatiyar, A. (eds), Handbook of Relationship Marketing, Sage, Thousand Oaks, pp 69–93

Hoffmann, S. & Muller, S. (2009) Consumer Boycotts due to Factory Relocation, Journal of Business Research, 62, 239–47

Johnston, W. J. & Hausman, A. (2006) Expanding the Marriage Metaphor in Understanding Long-Term Business Relationships, Journal of Business & Industrial Marketing, 21 (7), pp 446–52

Lau, M. & Moon, K. K. (2008) Adoption of Strategic Networks: Evidence from the Hong Kong Clothing Industry, Journal of Business & Industrial Marketing, 23 (5), pp 342–9

Leek, S. & Mason, K. (2009) Network Pictures: Building an Holistic Representation of a Dyadic Business-to-Business Relationship, Industrial Marketing Management, 38 (6), pp 599–607

Mattsson, L.-G. (1997) 'Relationship Marketing' and the 'Markets-as-Networks Approach' – A Comparative Analysis of Two Evolving Streams of Research, Journal of Marketing Management, 13, pp 447–61

Morgan, R. & Hunt, S. (1994) The Commitment-Trust Theory of Relationship Marketing, Journal of Marketing, 58, (July), pp 317–51

Nadeem, S. (2009) The Uses and Abuses of Time: Globalization and Time Arbitrage in India's Outsourcing Industries, Global Networks, 9 (1), pp 20–40

New Strait Times (2008) Global Meet to Discuss Future of Palm Oil, Biz News, 9 (September), p 34

Pearce, F. (2008) Confessions of an Eco-Sinner: Travels to Find Where my Stuff Comes From, Eden Project Books, London

Ransom, D. (2006) The No-Nonsense Guide to Fair Trade, New Internationalist Publications, Oxford

Sadler, I. (2007) Logistics and Supply Chain Integration, Sage, London

Shell Sustainability Report (The) (2006) online at http://sustainabilityreport.shell.com

Sohail, M. S. & Alashban, A. A. (2009) Industrial Buyer-Supplier Relationships: Perspectives from an Emerging Middle-East Market, International Journal of Business and Emerging Markets, 1 (4), pp 341–60

Theingi, Purchase, S. & Phungphol, Y. (2008) Social Capital in Southeast Asian Business Relationships, Industrial Marketing Management, 37, pp 523–30

Tokatli, N., Wrigley, N., & Kizilgun, O. (2008) Shifting Global Supply Networks and Fast Fashion: Made in Turkey for Marks and Spencer, Global Networks, 8 (3), pp 261–80

Turnbull, P., Ford, D., & Cunningham, M. (1996) Interaction, Relationships and Networks in Business Markets: An Evolving Perspective, Journal of Business & Industrial Marketing, 11 (3/4), pp 44–62

Umar, I. (2008) Corporate Social Responsibility in the Petroleum Industry: An Ethnographically-Grounded Analysis of Ascriptions of Responsibility amongst Various Stakeholders in the Nigerian Oil Industry, unpublished Ph.D. thesis, University of Leicester

Wells, T. (2007) Trigger Issues: T-Shirt, New Internationalist Publications, Oxford

Westerlund, M. & Svahn, S. (2008) A Relationship Value Perspective of Social Capital in Networks of Software SMEs, Industrial Marketing Management, 37, pp 492–501

Wilkinson, I. F. (2006) The Evolution of an Evolutionary Perspective on B2B Business, Journal of Business & Industrial Marketing, 21 (7), pp 458–65

Part Three
Business Marketing Planning

Part One: The Organizational Marketing Context

1. The Significance of B2B Marketing
- Significance of B2B Marketing
- Supply/Demand Chains
- Organizational Markets
- Significance of Relationships & Networks
- Supply Chain Ethics

2. Organizational Buying Behaviour
- Types of Markets
- Organizational & Consumer Buyer Behaviour
- Influences on Demand
- Organizational Decision-Making

Part Two: Inter-Organizational Relationships & Networks

3. Inter-Organizational Relationships
- Market & Relational Exchange
- CRM
- Partnerships & Alliances
- How IORs 'Work' in Different Contexts

4. Marketing Channels & Supply Chains
- Structure & Role of Channels
- Flows & Blockages in Channels
- From Channels to Chains
- Marketing Logistics

5. Industrial Networks
- The Interaction Approach
- From Channels & Chains to Networks
- Learning from the Industrial Network View

Part Three: Business Marketing Planning

6. B2B Marketing Planning & Analysis
- Planning & S/DCM
- The Planning Process
- Situation Analysis
- Sources & Assessing Market Potential
- B2B Market Segmentation

7. B2B Strategies & Implementation
- Market Positioning
- B2B Branding
- Making Strategy Decisions
- Issues of Implementation

These 6 chapters can also be effectively combined as the 'marketing mix'

Part Four: Business Marketing Programmes

8. Business Products
- Classifying Business Products
- Managing Business Products
- New Product Development

9. Business Services
- Classifying Business Services
- Characteristics of Business Services
- B2B Services Marketing Management

10. Value & Pricing
- Value in Organizational Markets
- Making Pricing Decisions
- B2B Pricing Strategies (incl. Web-based activities)

11. Marketing Communications
- Communication Strategies
- Elements of the Communications Mix
- Relative Effectiveness of B2B Media (incl. the Internet)

12. Personal Selling & Sales Management
- Personal Selling in B2B Markets
- Organizing the Sales Force
- Key Account Management (KAM)

Chapter 6
B2B Marketing Planning & Analysis

Introduction & Learning Objectives

Chapter Six discusses some of the planning models and processes associated with the strategic management of B2B marketing. It emphasizes the importance of undertaking careful analysis and drawing up some sort of structured plan before attempting to establish a distinctive market positioning and/or network position. Do not forget, however, that it may be a little naive to claim that one can 'manage' relationships in industrial networks at all. This means there is a degree of tension in providing any theoretical justification of what marketers should know about B2B planning.

What do we mean by this? Well, by now, you should appreciate that B2B marketing is as much about 'interacting in' (or even 'coping in') networks as it is about 'managing' inter-organizational relationships (IORs) (Håkansson and Ford, 2002). Yet, the vocabulary of marketing planning tends to suggest that people can plan and manage in quite a linear and decisive way. As we saw in the job adverts in Chapter One, this vocabulary can be seductive, lulling B2B marketers into a false sense of security regarding their ability to steer the future direction of their firm. Instead, coping in IORs, supply/demand chains, and industrial networks is full of paradoxes. You should remember that other actors, and their resources and activities, need to be considered, too. Effectively, you have to appreciate your firm's presence in an IOR, chain, and network before you then try to 'strategize' either to accommodate your position or to change it.

It is, nevertheless, still fair to say that there are some strategic concepts of which every B2B marketer needs to be aware, but you should bear in mind that many of the planning models offered in this chapter are rather idealized versions of what can practically be achieved. For instance, the case in Box 6.1 illustrates the influence of the external environment on

---

Box 6.1 Mini case
B2B planning problems in an unconventional market

Theingi, Assumption University, Bangkok, Thailand

Nay San, the CEO of the AOM Company, was thrilled when his firm was chosen in 2002 as an authorized and sole distributor from among more than 200 applicants in the Burmese (also known as Myanmar) market by a well-known multinational company

---

manufacturing electronic products in Japan. Due to his expertise in distributing a variety of products and people's familiarity with the brand name, Nay San was convinced that it should not be hard to penetrate the Burmese market. Yet, after several years, profits were declining despite the high profit margin on the products that had been factored in as a precaution against currency risk.

The first difficulty AOM faced for importing products was one of the requirements of the manufacturer in Japan; the bank the manufacturer deals with in any market must be one of the top 500 banks in the world. Unfortunately, neither of the two state-owned banks in Burma which had legal permission to handle foreign exchange met this criterion. Hence, AOM had to use transactions with the HSBC bank (located in Singapore) to make payments to its manufacturer supplier. Consequently, since AOM did not use a local bank to do its financial transactions, the products the company imported were technically illegal in Burma despite the fact that the company was the authorized dealer. The manufacturer shipped the products to Singapore from where the products were delivered to Burma. The cost of shipment as well as bribes to custom officers added to the cost of transportation.

Another issue was payment. As AOM was a new and sole dealer in a market with high uncertainties, the manufacturer required AOM to make payments prior to the delivery of goods, but AOM had to use consignment selling (i.e. without getting payment 'up front') to the wholesalers, and only obtained monies three to four months after delivering the products to wholesalers. This process was found to be necessary because products from the same manufacturer had been available in Burmese markets for decades through 'grey' cross-border trade with Thailand and China. As a result, there was an established channel through two dominant distributors who had been acting as wholesalers specializing in electrical and electronic products. They had built up long-term relationships with retailers who thus tended to favour them over AOM.

Lowering the price was not an option for AOM due to the declining profit. At the same time, Nay San could not compromise on the quality of the product as he was just the distributor and was not in a position to suggest this to the very powerful manufacturer. Spending more on promotional strategies did not seem to be a viable option, both as it would worsen profitability and any promotional expenditure would probably benefit the competing distributors who handled the same products. In addition, due to the continuous innovation of electronic goods, products like digital cameras became obsolete very quickly which led to a sudden decline in price levels. In the meantime, new brand names from Taiwan and South Korea were also launched in the market, increasing competition. Thus, having got himself into the marketplace in Burma, poor Nay San was wondering how he could have avoided being in this situation in the first place.

activities carried out by the AOM Company in Burma. Factors making marketing planning difficult here include: legal issues, financing problems, competing 'grey markets', power imbalances, and shortened product life cycles. As you read the case, ask yourself whether a more careful approach to planning with respect to the network in which his firm is embedded might have helped the CEO of AOM.

Chapter Aims

After completing this chapter, you should be able to:

- Appreciate the need for a degree of strategic planning in B2B marketing, and how to take into account issues of supply/demand chain management

- Identify the key external and internal areas that should be analysed when formulating plans, including an awareness of network links

- Evaluate the role of market research and other information sources regarding the development of sales forecasts in business markets

- Recognize the main bases for B2B market segmentation.

6.1 The Planning Process & Supply/Demand Chain Management (S/DCM)

Perhaps the first thing a B2B marketer needs to ask is whether their organization has a market orientation. This may seem obvious, but many firms in business markets retain a strong emphasis on technical and functional product attributes. They have often developed their reputation from years of superior expertise, which can lead to an obsession with production issues at the expense of keeping abreast of customer needs and the activities of competitors.

Firms with a strong market orientation tend to use information about the market to anticipate customer requirements ahead of the competition. They are also able to develop stronger relationships with their customers and their channels of distribution, often involving more direct lines of communication between key personnel on the buying and selling sides, such that end user needs are more comprehensively addressed. Research conducted in countries as diverse as the US, Australia, India, Japan, and Hong Kong suggests that this sort of market orientation provides firms with the opportunity to charge higher prices and hence improve profitability (Pelham, 1999; Sin and Tse, 2000).

Marketing management & supply chain management

Closely linked to marketing orientation in business markets is the notion of supply/demand chain management (S/DCM) that was introduced in Chapter One. Recall that, while SCM tends to focus on efficient, low-cost supply, marketing looks more closely at revenues arising from the demand side of the organization. An effective marketing strategy is likely to be dependent on the distribution issues associated with SCM (Juttner et al, 2007). The more demanding customers become, the more companies will need to be able to adjust their supply to meet demand. In this way, firms should be able to achieve a sustainable competitive advantage if they can offer superior customer value and have the business system to support it. Thus, as Min and Mentzer (2000, p 782) argue, 'market orientation, relationship marketing and SCM are not separate but inextricably intertwined'. This view is captured in the quote in Box 6.2.

Such inter-functional linkages are not simple to coordinate, however. As well as excellent information flows, the influence of marketing activities on supply, and vice versa, have to

Box 6.2 Voices

Recognizing relationships as links in the supply/demand chain

Here is what the marketing director of a UK office-furniture manufacturer has to say about the relationships necessary for his products to reach his business clients who tend to buy from furniture dealers: 'The dealer, by the very nature of his name, that's what he does. He doesn't actually make anything. He buys and sells. Without their connection, between the dealer and the end user, we don't exist because we're not selling direct. It's as simple as that. So you need to make the middleman choose you first.' When drawing up his marketing plans, this manager is acutely aware of the importance of maintaining good relationships with his dealer customers.

Source: Ellis (2008)

be accommodated, for example in the way that marketing mix decisions can influence delivery times and supply chain costs. This integration needs to extend beyond the single firm, encompassing relationships throughout the entire supply/demand chain, in order to create a 'customer-centred supply chain', a chain that starts with the end-user customer and works backwards up to the raw-material supplier (as we saw in Chapter Four). Full-scale S/DCM includes all the activities an organization undertakes in its aim to create and deliver needs-based customer value offerings. For instance, the Co-operative retailing group in the UK has responded to its customers' demands for cheaper prescription medicines by working with its wholesale subsidiary, Santa, to source these drugs from a joint venture with China's Tasly Group, which will lead to the construction of a new production facility in the city of Tianjin (www.co-operative.coop; Network, 2008). We thus see a form of vertical integration that is driven from the end-user consumer back up the chain.

Whether the end user is a consumer or an organization, this level of planning requires careful alignment of customer segments (see section 6.5 ahead) and supply chains. For example, Juttner et al (2007) describe a paper production firm serving five different customer segments which decided to develop supply chains for each segment rather than trying to push on to the customer a standard range of products and delivery terms. In a further example, showing an even greater focus of resources, an engineering firm serving two large truck manufacturers invested in setting up a completely new supply chain for each of these customers. In other words, these firms have ensured that integration takes place between those functions that define demand (marketing) and those that fulfil it (SCM). Figure 6.1 outlines how marketing management relates to S/DCM.

Figure 6.1 shows how B2B marketers need to form strategies alongside supply chain managers in order to:

- Improve their awareness of any operational limitations
- Convert marketing initiatives into supply chain drivers
- Create new ways to access the market.

SCM should be a consideration at early stages in the marketing planning process, with managers having sufficient understanding of supply chain issues to be able to reject marketing decisions that may promise higher sales but which are not financially viable. Nevertheless,

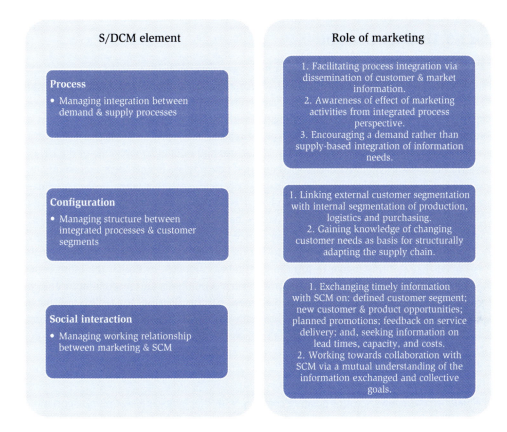

Figure 6.1 The roles of marketing within S/DCM
Source: Adapted with permission from Juttner et al (2007, p 389)
U. Juttner, M. Christopher, & S. Baker (2007) Demand Chain Management – Integrating Marketing
and SCM, Industrial Marketing Management, 36, pp 377–92, copyright Elsevier

organizations should take care to ensure that S/DCM and strategic marketing management do not become embroiled in internal battles for power: they should be mutually beneficial functions that work together to help guide IORs such that customer needs are met. For instance, research has shown that manufacturing enterprises in China achieve competitive advantage when they allow managers to meet customer expectations via the rescheduling of production orders and materials supply while also planning aggregate customer demand and providing timely deliveries (Ling-Yee and Ogunmokun, 2008).

Managing in global supply chains

A further layer of complexity for the B2B manager comes when we consider global supply chains (Sadler, 2007). Some of the issues that can occur when relationships exist with organizations in many countries include:

- Being in a position where you understand the priorities of the overall supply/demand chain but do not speak the language of local operators.

- Realizing that to shift production to a low-wage country may need to be balanced with potential skills shortage in that country.

Box 6.3 Food for thought

The demand/supply chain for timber

Papau New Guinea (PNG) is an important source of merbau, a timber that can fetch up to £250 per cubic metre. Of the timber that leaves PNG, 80% ends up in the timber yards of China, unfortunately much of it illegally logged, with estimates suggesting that the country's forests will be depleted in 15 years. Greenpeace reports that many of the merbau products made in China's workshops are sold in the DIY stores and builder's merchants of the UK in the form of plywood. The British Timber Federation now advises its members against buying PNG timber, but it is difficult for timber yards to comply with this when timber products are just labelled 'Made in China'. The Rain Forest Trust therefore wants to establish a 'chain of custody' for timber, arguing that DIY stores have the power to demand that Chinese timber mills are more transparent about the source of their wood. Moving down the supply chain, they advise consumers to look for the certification of the Forest Stewardship Council. It is hoped that as firms merge to form larger timber combines in China, the more high-profile companies involved will want to protect their reputations and respond accordingly. For instance, Happy International (who make veneer, parquet flooring, and table tennis bats) are thought to be concerned over the fact that many of their logs reach China via Pacific King Shipping of Singapore, a firm known for its transportation of logs from PNG.

Source: Pearce (2008); www.therainforesttrust.org; www.china-happygroup.com

- Balancing the lower cost of offshore sourcing with the increasing cost of transportation and logistics: it could be that the latter start to undermine your S/DCM advantage.
- Needing to become familiar with a new set of customs and laws regarding transport limitations, health and safety, product regulations, etc., for every extra country involved (see the end-of-chapter case study in Chapter Four for some examples of this).
- Possessing limited knowledge of supply chain processes in one part of the world which adds uncertainty to decisions in your part of a global chain.

Some of these issues can certainly be seen in Box 6.3, where you should also note the impact consumer decision-making can potentially have on B2B strategies throughout a global supply chain. Marketers may find that they can turn such a situation to their advantage by the careful market positioning of their firm (see Chapter Seven), whether logger, transporter, furniture manufacturer or retailer, as a more environmentally responsible actor.

6.2 The Marketing Planning Process

As we have noted, the usefulness of attempting to provide B2B marketing managers with some sort of generic marketing planning advice is a topic over which there is some debate. Nevertheless, it is generally agreed that a common format to marketing plans is a sensible way to anticipate, influence, and interact with future markets. The planning system we shall briefly outline here is a structured process by which managers can:

- Identify a range of options for their organization.
- Make them explicit in written form that can be communicated across the company.

- Establish marketing objectives that are consistent with the company's overall direction.
- Schedule and budget the activities most likely to bring about the objectives sought.

This process attempts to plot in advance the particular competitive stance that an organization intends to adopt in the business market. There are a number of benefits thought to come from the pursuit of formalized marketing planning (Ryals, 2000):

- The identification of expected developments.
- A preparedness to cope with change when it occurs.
- Improved communication amongst managers.
- Coordination over time of individual activities.
- The minimization of conflict between individuals with potentially differing goals.

A formal, rational approach to marketing planning

The planning aims and benefits listed above are based on the idea, exemplified in the work of McDonald (1996), that a formal planning process is the best way to reach strategic decisions. This approach puts forward a series of logical steps through which organizations may be able to arrive at their optimum strategy. A structured planning framework for marketing that summarizes these steps and indicates how they are related is shown in Figure 6.2.

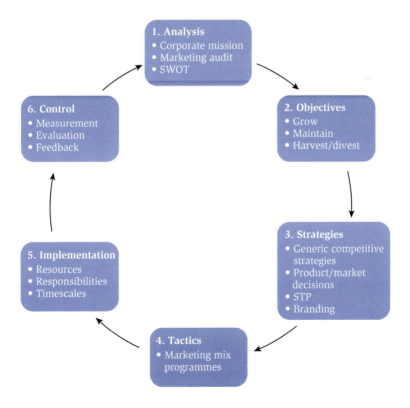

Figure 6.2 Elements of a typical marketing plan

The steps include:

1. The analysis of the organization's current situation via a combination of an external and internal audit of the firm's competitive environment and its own capabilities, in order to arrive at a SWOT analysis (see section 6.3 on the components of such an analysis, and 6.4 for some of the information sources needed to conduct it).

2. The setting of appropriate marketing objectives based on this analysis. Organizations can decide to try to consolidate their market share or sales levels, or attempt to increase them. For example, in order to meet its objectives of increasing its Asian market share from 50% to 70%, Japanese copper-foils manufacturer Mitsui built a new plant in Malaysia (www.mitsui.co.jp; Yunus, 2008).

3. The identification and evaluation of possible strategies by which these objectives might be achieved. This key stage includes considerations over how to compete, what products and services to offer to which markets (for more on both these issues, see the discussion below), the market segments to target (see section 6.5 on B2B segmentation), and the positioning of the firm (market positioning is addressed in Chapter Seven).

4. The selection of the appropriate tactics to support these strategies, typically involving the use of marketing mix programmes or the '4Ps' (see Chapters Eight to Twelve for detailed discussions of products/services, pricing, and promotion; Chapter Four has already addressed the 'place' P by looking at marketing channels).

5. The implementation of the chosen strategy via operational planning systems. This involves allocating the appropriate resources to the intended strategies and tactics (we have discussed some Implementation issues relating to the integration of S/DCM and marketing in section 6.1 above; see Chapter Seven for more).

6. The control of marketing activities, which entails assessing the degree to which objectives have been met, and then providing feedback into the analysis stage, so that the planning cycle can begin once again (some typical control measures are indicated in the Internal Audit represented in Figure 6.5 ahead).

We shall not be discussing all the elements of the traditional marketing planning cycle in detail; however, certain topics which are not explored in other sections or chapters (such as segmentation, positioning, and the marketing mix itself, as indicated above) merit further consideration here. B2B marketers should be aware of the following concepts when drawing up plans: generic competitive strategies; product/market decisions; and how tactics relate to strategies (see Figure 6.3).

The idea of generic competitive strategies is credited to Porter (1985), who identified three broad ways in which firms can compete. When you consider these alternatives, you should note that it is generally thought that firms which attempt to combine low cost and differentiated approaches run the risk of being 'stuck in the middle', resulting in less effective strategies:

- Cost leadership: Here, the organization keeps its cost as low as possible, enabling it to compete on price if it desires without sacrificing profits. As we have seen, a good grasp of S/DCM processes can help the marketer to achieve this goal. Firms can aim this approach at the whole market or choose to target a certain customer segment.

- Differentiation: The selling firm aims to make its products or services as different as possible from those of its competitors, thereby enabling it to charge a premium price.

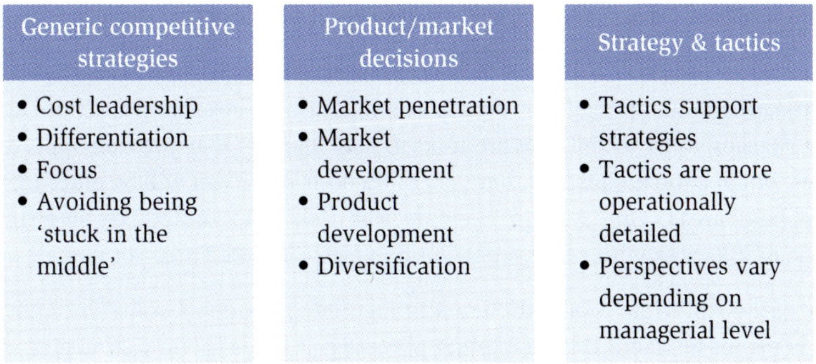

Generic competitive strategies	Product/market decisions	Strategy & tactics
• Cost leadership • Differentiation • Focus • Avoiding being 'stuck in the middle'	• Market penetration • Market development • Product development • Diversification	• Tactics support strategies • Tactics are more operationally detailed • Perspectives vary depending on managerial level

Figure 6.3 **Some strategic issues in marketing planning**

This strategy is one that many B2B marketers aspire to as it can involve the skilled coordination of the marketing mix as well as the careful management of customer relationships. However, it only works if customers perceive the differences that you are trying to construct. Again, differentiation may be aimed at the entire market or at one organizational segment.

- Focus: Here, the organization concentrates its marketing efforts on one (or a few) narrowly defined segment(s). In this way, the focus strategy is really a variant of each of the preceding approaches. It often allows firms, perhaps selling technically complex products, and/or those with high margins, to specialize in particular niche markets.

Having determined the generic manner in which your firm can compete, product/market decisions are also core to formulating marketing strategy. After all, answering the question: 'what organizational markets do we serve, and with what products?' pretty much establishes the mission of all firms in business markets. A helpful way to look at products offered and markets served is to consider the strategies suggested by Ansoff (1988), who highlights the main ways in which a firm can meet its growth objectives. Broadly speaking, the potential returns increase as you move through the four approaches listed below but, at the same time, so do the resources needed and the financial risks involved:

1. *Market penetration*: this involves attempting to gain a higher share of the markets in which your firm is already selling its products. This can be achieved by encouraging higher usage rates amongst existing customers, gaining new customers from competitors, or converting non-users into users in the same market. Marketing communications can have a major role to play in these activities (see Chapters Eleven and Twelve).

2. *Market development*: here, existing products are sold in new markets. These new markets could represent new industrial sectors, such as targeting governmental purchasers as well as private sector clients, and/or geographical locations, say by exporting. The approach will often entail building relationships with members of new distribution channels (see Chapter Four).

3. *Product development*: this involves trying to serve customers in markets where you already have a presence with new products. These products need not be totally 'new'; they can also include product modifications via new features or higher quality levels. The success

of such an approach is clearly dependent on how good your organization is at new product development (or NPD – see Chapter Eight).

4. *Diversification*: this strategy represents a combination of the second and third approaches above. The decision to try to sell new products to new markets may provide opportunities for high returns, but is it the highest risk-strategy of the four since you will be entering unknown territory in both areas. One way to alleviate this risk is to undertake diversification in partnerships or alliances with other organizations (see Chapter Three for some examples).

In terms of the shift from Step 3 to Step 4 in Figure 6.2, students sometimes get confused over what is meant by 'tactics' in marketing planning. It helps to view strategies and tactics as different levels of planning activity: tactics are really only more detailed versions of strategies. It depends on the level you are working as a B2B manager. If your role is a senior one involving an overview of the firm's entire marketing plan, then you will probably be making strategic decisions over how to gain competitive advantage and determining the most appropriate customer segment to target. The marketing mix programmes which support these decisions will typically then be viewed by you as tactics (and perhaps even as activities that can be delegated to other people in your organization, depending on its size).

Your perspective could vary, however, if you are working at a different level in the management hierarchy, say as a marketing communications manager. Here, you may well view a promotional strategy as the decision to use direct marketing to support your firm's attempts at targeting a new segment of organizational customers with your engineering products. The tactics you then employ to raise awareness may include a combination of a glossy 'mailshot' to the CEO of each prospective client and an email campaign sent to production managers at the same firms. In each case, the tactics serve to support the strategy.

The planning framework depicted in Figure 6.2 is of course relatively generic. To see how elements of such a framework might be related to the B2B context, see Box 6.4 where the marketing director quoted earlier in Box 6.2 explains how his firm undertakes marketing planning. The case shows how many of the management practices within the speaker's firm correspond to the steps you might expect to be followed in a marketing plan. It also illustrates the situation analysis process (see section 6.3).

Box 6.4 Mini case

B2B marketing planning in action

Declan MacManus is marketing director for 'Trust Seating Ltd' (names have been disguised), the UK's third-largest office-chair supplier. Trust Seating had a turnover of more than £10 million in 2001. It has nearly 200 staff. The firm makes a variety of office chairs, including those for boardroom, clerical, and operational roles. Here, Declan describes how Trust Seating undertakes its B2B marketing activities. His quotes have been assembled under headings that illustrate planning in action.

External audit

Market: 'In the public sector you're dependent on how well you network through the organizations to find out where the decision makers are, then you have to find out if they're going to spend.'

Customer: 'The Post Office is going to be privatized, so for every piece of expenditure they look at, their philosophy this year is best value, lowest cost.'

Supplier: 'From one fabric supplier we can order up to 4 o'clock today, any permutation, any length. It's here tomorrow morning, so it's very flexible.'

Competitor: 'We have a chair at £40. Our nearest biggest competitor brings one out at £38.60. So we've just had the chair tested to a very strict European Standard, to justify that extra £1.40 because they (competitor) won't bother.'

Environment audit

Legal factor: 'If we say we're ISO 9002 certificated, I have to produce the certificate. If I put a chair forward that's tested to a European standard, I have to produce that certificate.'

Internal audit

Sales: 'When we introduced the computer system it was only the most basic analysis of sales history. We've had to have special programmes written for account analysis.'

Costs: 'Our number of units of production has probably dropped 20,000 a year, but we're getting much higher value per unit.'

SWOT analysis

Strengths: 'This business is almost self-sufficient in that we have our own wood-working, our own engineering, so in key areas like mechanisms, we stock it in depth.'

Opportunities: 'Any contract over about £140,000 that involves the spending of the public purse has to appear in the *European Journal*, which means that anybody can apply for it.'

Objectives (and control)

'If we promise a Tuesday delivery, service means that, without fail, we deliver, on that Tuesday, 100%. And 98.6% of the time we hit those targets.'

Customer segmentation

'We're a business that sells into four channels (segments). The dealer channel which represents about 70% of our turnover; we then sell to the public purse, where we hold the Inland Revenue and Post Office contracts; we sell to OEMs; and we make bespoke ranges for desk companies who don't have their own seating.'

Product/market strategies

'At the moment we've got four new products being launched, so we've segmented the customer base, depending on the product. One's a contract-type product, one's quite a highly specced [specified] product. So we'll be looking for new accounts for the highly specced product.'

Market positioning

'If you can imagine a dealer salesman out there with a proliferation of literature of (rival) products to sell, he will invariably take the line of least resistance. So, if we can offer them good value for money, good products, and excellent service, then we tend to do well.'

Tactics/marketing mix programmes

Product (and price): 'We've developed more ranges to hit more price points, more specification of products, and offered things like soft seating for waiting rooms.'

Place/distribution: 'You get an awful lot of exposure through 350 dealers promoting our products day in, day out.'

Promotion: 'We've invested a lot in literature targeting the dealer market.'

Personal selling: 'There are five people in my sales team on the dealer side . . . (and) I've got a guy who looks after our public sector business.'

Implementation

Resources: 'The PR consultancy did nothing for this business, so I brought it in my own team.'

Responsibilities: 'I make sure when we get the big customers here, they meet the production people. It's a lot harder to say no to somebody you've met than to a voice on the phone.'

Ironically, at the end of the interview, Declan said, 'It's totally reactive. . . . In terms of the marketing plan, um, there isn't one. OK, we've got a new product. We just ask: do we like it, where does it fit in the marketplace, um, who are our competitors?'

Source: Ellis (2006, 2008)

It has been argued that few firms actually formalize their planning to the extent suggested in Figure 6.2, and the director's final comments in Box 6.4 tend to support this assertion. However, the framework still provides an idealized form of planning towards which the B2B marketer can aim. The overall notion of selecting an appropriate strategy based on a thorough analysis is still a worthy ambition. If this is not undertaken, then managers may miss important threats in the business environment such as strikes in a customer's production plant, as several US-based suppliers to Boeing discovered when they were forced to lay off staff temporarily due to the suspension of production by the aircraft manufacturer (Weitzman, 2008).

Other approaches to marketing planning

Some alternative approaches to strategic planning in the highly rational manner outlined above have been suggested, two of which are mentioned below. These should not necessarily be seen as replacements for the rational planning model, but more as perspectives that can compliment it. Some ways in which the three main approaches to marketing planning discussed in this section can be compared are summarized in Figure 6.4.

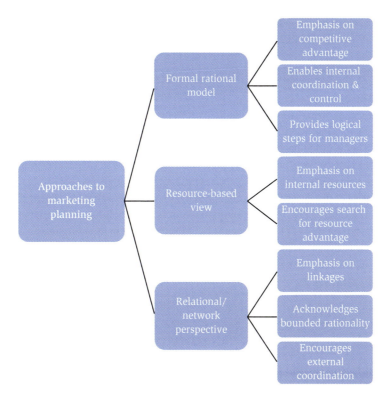

Figure 6.4 **Some approaches to marketing planning**

- As we discussed at the beginning of the chapter, one approach that is particularly pertinent to business markets is to consider the possibility of 'managing' relationships and networks. Although this approach to planning does not really provide a convenient generic set of stages to be followed, or an optimum way for the B2B manager to select the single best way forward, it does reinforce to organizations the vital fact that they do not act independently of other network members (Johanson and Mattsson, 1992). Indeed, a network perspective acknowledges that:

  - firms have a restricted view of the network in which they are embedded because there are so many organizations with which they will be directly and indirectly linked (this is known as 'bounded rationality');

  - the outcomes of their actions will be dependent on the actions of other network members; and

  - strategy formulation is concerned with more than competitive advantage, since two organizations may well be simultaneously competing and cooperating within the same relationship (e.g. in the aircraft sector where manufacturers competing in the same end user market may also collaborate on the development of a new standardized jet engine).

Thus, no matter how strategically capable a firm might be, its own success is inevitably closely related to the actions of other firms in the network. Taking this view encourages the B2B marketer to focus less on the internal resources at their firm's disposal, and more on how the firm links its activities and resources to other actors, including customers, suppliers, and competitors. For more on the challenges that this view presents to managers as they try to design strategies, see Chapter Seven.

- A further approach to planning is the resource-based perspective of the firm. This assumes that firms are fundamentally different regarding their control of strategic resources and that these resources are not perfectly transferable between firms (Barney, 2001). The resource-based view argues that an organization is only able to build a sustainable competitive advantage when it controls assets (e.g. physical or human capital) that are valuable and difficult to copy or substitute. It suggests that, instead of the primary focus of the rational planning approach on the external environment, firms should concentrate internally on their unique resources and look for opportunities that allow them to exploit these. This is thought to help managers in avoiding taking any strategic decisions that may inadvertently damage their resource advantage, especially if this is based on forms of capital that are harder to reproduce, such as the relationship-building skills of its managers.

An example of two firms responding to both internal and external issues is provided in Box 6.5. Note how the relationship (in the form of a joint venture) is seen by the two firms as a pooling of their internal resources in response to market conditions.

Relationship portfolios in planning

The key relationships for B2B planners are clearly those which a firm forms with its customers, but 'strong' relationships are not always beneficial. Some long-term customers are actually not worth retaining because they are too demanding or will not pay a fair price. Customer portfolio analysis can provide a strategic input into a firm's planning process by encouraging managers to scrutinize their current customers and segments for maximum profitability (Rajagopal and Sanchez, 2005). Managers should use their judgement to decide

Box 6.5 Mini case
Investing in chicken processing markets

Astute B2B organizations respond to market conditions and make the most of their network connections in forming strategies. Japanese firm Ajinomoto Frozen Food and the Thai Betagro Group formed a joint venture to open the largest chicken processing plant in Asia. The plant is located in Lop Buri in Thailand and will have a full capacity to produce 30,000 tonnes of grilled and fried chicken per year. The Japanese partner was basing its decision on the confidence of its food sector customers (such as retailers and restaurants) in Thailand's high-quality production and their concerns over food safety in China. For its part, Betagro's CEO recognized the need to 'satisfy consumer demand' via the 'increased production capacity made possible by the new plant'. He added that the plant 'helps us to maintain high production quality and food safety to beat competitors'.

Source: Pratruangkrai (2007); www.ajinomoto.com; www.betagro.com

the optimum spread of customers, including the conversion of high-potential or low-profitability customers into more profitable relationships.

Portfolio analysis need not be confined to customer IORs, however. Your knowledge of the S/DCM perspective will remind you that the analysis of a firm's supplier portfolio may also fall to B2B marketers, probably in close cooperation with their purchasing colleagues. For some examples of these sorts of decisions, see Figure 12.3 in Chapter Twelve on customer portfolio analysis and Figure 3.8 in Chapter Three on supplier portfolios (in the form of 'extended enterprises').

Relationship portfolios can be especially important in a network context. As we have seen, the resource-based view assumes either ownership or complete control of crucial resources by a focal firm. In an industrial network setting, however, the control of resources is more likely to require a number of actors to coordinate their resources in a partnership of multiple owners. A long-term perspective to resource accumulation through IORs can help managers to develop successful relationships in their portfolio planning, e.g. a firm may decide to pursue network relations that extend beyond immediate IORs by using their direct links with either customers or suppliers for the purpose of acquiring valuable technical knowledge from third parties (Eng, 2008).

Before reaching any decisions over relationship portfolios, the formalized approach to planning we have set out above suggests that a strategic audit should be carried out. The following section outlines some of the analyses necessary to get a comprehensive picture of an organization's situation.

6.3 Situation Analysis

Whether a firm adopts the formalized, rational planning model or an approach more influenced by a network or resource-based perspective, it is likely that better strategic decisions will be made by marketers who have a sound understanding of their current situation. You should bear in mind, however, that the compilation of all the desired information to make the 'perfect' decision may be extremely demanding and time consuming. Nevertheless, even if we accept that a completely holistic picture is impossible to obtain, a reasonably comprehensive situation analysis is still desirable.

The marketing audit

To this end, B2B managers should be aware of the components of the marketing audit summarized in Figure 6.5, with the proviso that many organizations treat the audit as an annual data collection exercise, designed to be modified at intervals during the year so that planning can remain flexible and responsive to market changes. For example, in March 2009, Xerox (www.xerox.com) warned that it might be forced to make financial cuts due to a fall in revenues of 18% experienced at the outset of the year due to corporate customers slashing their expected spending on office technology (Clark, 2009).

As the headings in Figure 6.5 indicate, a full marketing audit comprises an external and internal set of analyses. The former includes monitoring market trends and researching the behaviours, competences, and strategies of key players in the firm's network such as customers, suppliers, and competitors. The external audit also involves scanning the firm's business environment, which is usually organized under the headings of the 'SLEPT' factors

Figure 6.5 Elements of a marketing audit

(social/cultural, legal/regulatory, economic, political, and technological). These factors are sometimes grouped together under the term 'macro environment'. For an illustration of the impact on B2B marketing strategies of the environment surrounding an international airport, see Box 6.6. The case also shows how external forces were mediated by links in the network in which the airport's investors were embedded.

Box 6.6 Mini case

Environmental forces affecting airport modernization

Bella Butler, Curtin University of Technology, Perth, Western Australia

Ekaterinburg Koltsovo International Airport is the most rapidly developing airport in Russia. Over 30 Russian and foreign airlines provide air links to 104 cities, and connections at international hub airports enable passengers to travel anywhere in the world. It is expected that the passenger traffic via Koltsovo will grow by 15–20% annually.

As a result of market transformation in Russia since the early 1990s, the business network and surrounding airport infrastructure have undergone some important changes. Koltsovo Airport was established in 1993 as a result of privatization of the state-owned enterprise, Aeroflot. That year also saw the first international flights to land at the airport. Indeed, a favourable geopolitical position of Koltsovo on the border between Europe and Asia, close to the capital city of the resources-rich Ural region, Yekaterinburg, created the potential for this airport to become an international logistics terminal. However, in order to provide competitive services to attract international airlines, the airport urgently needed to update its infrastructure. During the mid 1990s, the regional government, led by Eduard Rossel, developed a plan for the reconstruction and modernization of the airport.

The proposed redevelopment of the airport could not proceed due to financial restrictions. Although Koltsovo Airport generated $US 2 billion surplus in 2000 from the sale of aviation kerosene to airline companies, it was barely profitable because airlines were slow to pay their bills. Moreover, Russian finance companies only offered investments for a maximum period of five years, which was far too short for the redevelopment project. From 2000, Governor Rossel did a lot of networking to organize finances into a public–private partnership. As result, in 2003, the RENOVA Group, an international diversified company with strong connections in the resource and industrial sector of the Ural region, became the major investor in the airport, largely due to the long-term relationships of the group with the region and its state authorities. During the same year, a new general manager of Koltsovo Airport was appointed who was a former employee of RENOVA. In 2007, this person was promoted to a key position in the regional government – further expanding RENOVA's reach. The process of modernization of Koltsovo Airport was successfully completed in 2009. These network changes illustrate a new stage in the relationships between business and power in Russia, and show how these changes can affect business planning.

Source: www.expert.ru; www.koltsovo.ru; www.renova.ru

The internal audit entails the collection of data on the firm's financial performance by customer, product line, etc., as well as market share data. It also demands a rigorous assessment of the firm's management systems for coordinating the marketing mix and of the resources intended to support any strategic decisions. For B2B-related examples of some of the internal and external elements listed in Figure 6.5, recall the extensive quotes from the director of the office furniture supplier in Box 6.4.

SWOT analysis

In order to facilitate the move from Step 1 (analysis) of the planning cycle to Step 2 (objectives) it is common to arrange the findings of the marketing audit into a framework that can assist objective setting. The widely recognized 'strengths, weaknesses, opportunities, and threats' (or SWOT) framework is helpful here. A good SWOT analysis should prioritize issues under each of these headings in order of their potential impact and their likelihood of occurrence:

- Strengths: Internal skills and resources which the organization should seek to exploit.
- Weaknesses: Internal shortcomings which should be addressed.
- Opportunities: External market possibilities in the firm's environment which should be pursued using strengths.
- Threats: External forces against which the organization should protect itself.

It can, however, be difficult to gather the necessary data to make some of assessments suggested in the analytical frameworks given in this section. For instance, many organizations do not have sufficiently comprehensive systems to calculate the 'cost to serve' for individual customers. Let us now look at some sources of information that can help the B2B planner.

6.4 Information Sources & Assessing Market Potential

Whatever approach to B2B planning is taken, if organizational processes are to meet customer requirements, the allocation of a firm's resources should follow from an understanding of the current and the anticipated needs of customers. While data on all aspects of a network's actors, resources, and activities will aid planning, what is needed most of all is accurate and up-to-date information on markets, customers, and the firm's competitive positioning. This is dependent on the organization's marketing information system (MKIS).

Maintaining an MKIS

This is an integrated approach to generating, storing, and accessing information from all appropriate sources. An MKIS will use more than just data gathered by market research; it will also draw upon data that exists in internal and external data sources. These may include, for instance, the firm's sales records and details of marketing costs as well as sales force feedback about marketplace developments, perhaps from attending trade fairs. Any data thus collected should be converted to information that is useful to managers and is stored in a user-friendly 'data warehouse' that can be used to inform decision-making (see also the discussion of CRM in Chapter Three). Such warehouses may involve quite complex IT-based network systems in large organizations, while in SMEs they may be paper-based, but no less effective, as long as information can be sensibly sifted to highlight opportunities and potential problems in the firm's strategic forecasts.

A good MKIS will exploit existing data sources before undertaking any market research since this can be an expensive exercise. Often, however, the necessary depth of information about a business market will not be available without recourse to some research, whether this is undertaken 'in-house' or by hiring a specialist agency. Owing to the cost of maintaining an in-house market research department, and the ad hoc nature of many research projects, most firms will choose to use outside suppliers. This is a form of 'make or buy' decision (see Chapter Two), although of course in this case, you are the buying firm, not the supplier of market research services. A potential risk with this approach is the loss of control over any commercially sensitive information that might be generated as an unscrupulous research agency could sell the information to a firm's competitors.

B2B market information is becoming increasingly available on the Internet, especially in the form of secondary data. Marketing managers should be cautious, however, in taking advantage of the convenience, and often low cost, of secondary data since these sources may not present a very up-to-date, or accurate, picture of the marketplace under consideration. This is especially true of international markets, as shown by the services offered by a typical agency called 1 Stop Data. This firm sells an 'International Executive File' for sales leads that includes a range of data, from industry type and location to contact name and job title (www.1stopdata.com). This information appears to be pretty comprehensive for what the agency terms its Major Companies database, but if we take a closer look at its Middle East

Box 6.7 Food for thought

Assessing market potential in challenging contexts

Although it may be difficult to do so, the importance of gaining good information about potential markets is shown by the significance of Iraq. The country is the UK's fastest-growing export market for public-sector contracts. Organizations marketing their goods and services there include 25 firms employing 4,000 private security contractors as well as oil and construction firms. If they and other market entrants are to take advantage of these business opportunities, they need to gather data about a complex region where Western organizations (and governments) have a lot to learn about the workings of the public sector, commerce, and society in general.

Source: The Marketer (2007)

Email data, we find that the information contained here does not include company turnover, number of employees, or even telephone numbers and addresses. Moreover, of course, while lists are undoubtedly useful, much more contextual information is normally required to make good strategic decisions about potential markets – see Box 6.7.

B2B market research

It is beyond the remit of this book to outline the generic market research process, or to explain the various techniques open to the market researcher, especially as most readers will have encountered these topics in their previous studies. What is important, however, is to explain some of the issues most commonly found in conducting research in B2B contexts when compared with B2C markets. Based on suggestions by Katz (1979), you should be aware of the following differences, as summarized in Figure 6.6.

- The universe (market population): This is typically small compared to consumer markets, especially when confined to a narrowly defined industry category.

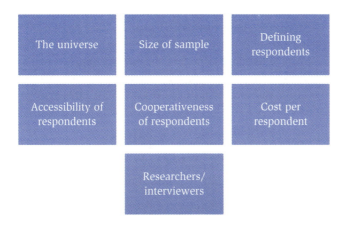

Figure 6.6 Comparing B2B with B2C market research

- Size of sample: Again, usually much smaller than that required for statistical confidence in consumer research (assuming that it is a survey you are conducting; this is not necessarily an issue in most forms of qualitative research).

- Defining respondents: Making sense of the buying centre can be difficult, particularly as the user and the buyer will rarely be the same person, and the former can sometimes have little influence on the purchase decision.

- Accessibility of respondents: Often quite difficult, as managers will be preoccupied with other priorities. They may also only be available during standard office hours.

- Cooperation of respondents: The key decision makers in most organizations can become 'over-researched' by rival researchers as there are basically so few of them in any one marketplace; this can lead to 'research fatigue'.

- Researchers/interviewers: It is important to find interviewers skilled in approaching managers, some of whom may be quite senior executives. Also, for some research projects a fairly high level of technical knowledge may be necessary.

- Cost per respondent: Due to the issues listed above, although sample sizes will typically be smaller, the cost per interview (whether conducted by email, phone or in person) for B2B research can be considerably higher than in consumer markets.

Assessing market potential

The outputs of a firm's MKIS are often used to estimate the market potential for a product or service, typically in the form of a sales forecast. Managers usually begin by assessing the overall market, and the likely market segments that the firm should be targeting (see section 6.5 ahead). Although we have made much of the need for objective data sources in the planning process, you should not forget that there is often no substitute for the experience of long-serving managers within your organization who can have vast reservoirs of knowledge about market potential. These may be senior executives or less high-ranking managers who, nevertheless, have worked 'in the field' for some time. It is good practice to combine a 'top-down' with a 'bottom-up' approach since sales representatives can be a little over-optimistic in their predictions.

Taking objective and subjective evaluations into account, predictions are then made of the market share that the firm could expect to gain in the segments that appear to be the most attractive. The resulting sales potential can then be allocated across the firm's sales force, perhaps by territory (see Chapter Twelve). To achieve the most accurate forecasts, B2B managers should attempt to use both secondary and primary data sources, especially if clear pictures are to be built up of customer's buying behaviours in particular market segments. Such information is key to the success of firms like Larsen & Toubro – see Box 6.8.

Box 6.8 Number crunching

Meeting objectives in India's construction market and beyond

AM Naik, the Chairman of India's largest engineering and construction firm, Larsen & Toubro (with sales exceeding £4 billion p.a.), claims that his company is poised to take advantage of the subcontinent's urgent need to improve its infrastructure. As the country's economy expands, there are increasing demands to rebuild decaying airports, roads, and power plants. Although the firm projected a 35% increase in orders in 2009 from domestic markets, Naik also hopes to increase the firm's international work to 25% of its revenues within two years. To achieve this, the firm will need to be able to make decisions about which market segments to enter in India, and in countries across the Middle East.

Source: Forbes Asia (2008); www.larsentoubro.com

So how can managers decide which segments are the most viable in what look like attractive business markets?

6.5 B2B Market Segmentation

A major facet of marketing strategy is the notion of segmentation, where large overall markets are broken down into more manageable 'chunks' towards which the selling organization can better target its marketing efforts. Once a particular segment (or segments) has been targeted, marketers need to position their organizations and their offerings to the target market in a way that differentiates them from the competition. We shall explore the challenges of market positioning in B2B markets in more detail in Chapter Seven.

Bases for segmenting B2B markets

Although the broad process of segmentation/targeting/positioning (STP) should be familiar to you if you have studied marketing in the past, the bases for segmenting business markets are not quite the same as those used in B2C contexts. Business markets can be segmented based on two core sets of characteristics, summarized in Figure 6.7:

1. *Market characteristics, such as organizational size and location*: more commonly used when transactional relationships abound in a market.

Market characteristics	Buyer characteristics
• Customer location	• Purchasing strategies
• Customer size	• Purchasing policies
• Market served by customer	• Importance of purchase
• Usage rates	• Attitude to risk
• Purchase situation	• Personal characteristics of buyer

Figure 6.7 **Some bases for business market segmentation**

2. *Buyer characteristics, such as the decision-making process found in each segment*: more commonly used when collaborative relationships are the norm.

Some of the most common bases for segmenting by market characteristics are arranged below, ranging broadly from the simple geo-demographic factors that are often available via secondary sources or by observation, to those more difficult to establish by sellers without some market research:

- Location: This can help smaller suppliers focus their efforts on a manageable territory, especially if they intend to use sales representatives as part of the marketing communications mix. Geographical awareness will often also be useful in establishing the viability of providing logistics support to some customers.

- Size: At its most basic, this approach allows suppliers to determine which customers may have the greatest potential spending power. A more nuanced consideration may suggest differences over issues such as service levels, with SMEs perhaps having less demanding expectations. Having said this, some large firms take their marketing to SMEs very seriously, as shown in Box 6.9.

- Market served by customer: Again, a fairly basic approach, where identifying the nature of a customer firm's business helps narrow the possibilities for the supplying firm. If the seller can determine what use their products (say, hydraulic components) may be put to, then they can target the appropriate customer segment (e.g. truck manufacturers) or develop new products and services that support their core offering. It is common to use Standard Industrial Classification (SIC) codes to get a preliminary indication of the nature of a segment's business.

- Usage rates: Customers may usefully be categorized based on the rate of consumption of the supplier's products. Low or medium user segments could then represent opportunities to be targeted and turned into heavy users.

- Purchase situation: Is the situation faced by customers a new task, a modified rebuy or a straight rebuy? As we saw in Chapter Two, an understanding of the buying situation can indicate the likelihood of acceptance by the buyer of a new approach from an 'out-supplier'.

Segmentation by buyer characteristics can involve the following criteria. It is generally more difficult to explore a market segment on the basis of these 'internal' factors that try

Box 6.9 Mini case
Targeting the SME segment

Sun Microsystems has a separate page on its website for this segment, telling these customers that they can offer them 'powerful, open innovations – starting as low as $895 – that can drive revenue and add bottom-line value'.

Software provider, SAP, adopts a similar strategy, making it clear on its website that, while the company provides 'suite offerings for global organizations', it also offers 'distinct solutions addressing the needs of small businesses'.

Source: www.sap.com; www.sun.com

to predict buyer responses than it is to use market characteristics. The closer the relationships B2B marketers can develop with firms in the marketplace, the greater their chances of maximizing the accuracy of such criteria in the segmentation process:

- Purchasing strategies: It is helpful to know whether a customer is an 'optimizer' or a 'satisficer'. Optimizers tend to evaluate a large number of potential suppliers before coming to a careful selection, whereas satisficers typically prefer to deal with a limited range of familiar suppliers and reach a quick decision that meets their basic buying requirements.

- Purchasing policies: As we saw in Chapter Two, organizations may have particular policies on purchasing. These can include rules about who holds the decision-making authority, whether (in the case of larger organizations) buying has been centralized, or whether it is driven by notions of value or simply a desire to get the best deal.

- Importance of purchase: Understanding the level of importance of a purchase to the customer may enable the supplier to appreciate the impact of the decision and thus the perceived risk for the buyer. Importance may be ascertained by the sheer cost of an item and/or its strategic significance to the operations of the buying firm.

- Attitude to risk: There may also be a general attitude to risk that pervades the customer firm's decision-making process to which B2B marketers should remain attuned.

- Personal characteristics of buyers: If marketers can get an insight into the education, personality, loyalty, and even lifestyle of key members of the buying centre this may help in segmenting business markets, especially in assisting sales people to target their efforts more effectively (see Chapter Twelve).

Making segmentation decisions

With so many different potential ways in which to divide up a market, how should B2B marketing managers start to go about the segmentation process? Perhaps the most widely accepted approach is that outlined by Bonoma and Shapiro (1983), who propose a 'nested' perspective, starting with the simplest, more macro variables (typically market characteristics) and then probing ever more deeply into those more micro variables (typically buyer characteristics) about which less is usually known. The marketer then needs to select the most appropriate segments to target – see Box 6.10, where both these organizations have decided to focus on building relationships with customers in the public sector.

Box 6.10 Mini case
Public sector segments

Western Australian shipbuilder Austal's list of defence and security customers includes Australian clients like the Royal Australian Navy and the New South Wales Water Police, as well as Middle Eastern customers such as the Kuwait government and Yemen's Ministry of Defence. Still focusing on institutional or governmental business segments, the firm has recently extended its geographical segmentation to include the Caribbean, with the announcement of a new contract to supply patrol craft to the Coast Guard of the Republic of Trinidad and Tobago.

UK construction management company Concept Project Management is basing its growth on an increasing amount of work on public-funded projects in health and education. The firm targets clients like colleges and universities and National Health Service Trusts, and has won the contract to handle the £38 million relocation of South Leicestershire College. Building on its experience in the public sector, Concept is also extending its market coverage to private sector segments where the hotel and leisure trade has been targeted, including the Ramada Encore chain of hotels.

Sources: Baker (2008); Dunkin (2008); www.austal.com; www.conceptpm.co.uk

Making these sorts of choices means asking questions about:

- The distinctiveness of the segment (do customers share a high degree of similarity, yet remain distinct from the rest of the market?)
- The future attractiveness of the segment (will it remain sufficiently large or grow? What is the level of competition within the segment?)
- The resource demands of serving the segment (does the supplier have the necessary technologies, people, and finances to target the segment?)
- The selling firm's strategy (is the segment congruent with the firm's overall corporate mission?).

For example, a niche supplier of high-quality computer components may establish that a segment of potential customers (such as mass-market laptop manufacturers) clearly exists, is attractive in terms of growth and can be served without stretching the firm's resource too far. However, it may decide that the 'fit' is not appropriate, since it risks cheapening its brand values by association with original equipment manufacturers (OEMs) that are not perceived by existing clients, or indeed end users, as sufficiently 'top end'.

Even though segmentation is one of the most important decisions a B2B marketer must make, there is sometimes a lack of understanding amongst managers of how to do this most effectively. The process is rarely as clear-cut as the one outlined above – a useful description of some of the main ways to approach the task can be found in Mitchell and Wilson (1998). An important point to note about segmentation is that it is not a static approach; instead, it should reflect current market conditions (Freytag and Clarke, 2001). Changes in economic cycles, levels of competition, and technological advances could affect customer characteristics and attitudes towards relationships with suppliers, and so managers must remain open to reexamining the bases for segmentation on a regular basis. Furthermore, of course, taking a network perspective means that managers should also try to take into account the links between competitors and their own customers and suppliers when assessing the potential of a segment.

Having segmented the business market and decided on which segment (or segments) it is most appropriate to target, B2B marketers must consider how to position their firm in the minds of customers. This will form the opening topic of Chapter Seven.

However, before you move on to explore market positioning and other strategies in more detail, take a look at the end-of-chapter case study ahead. This describes how an SME software supplier undertakes its planning activities in the construction sector. You will see that a formal B2B planning approach does not necessarily need to be present to underpin strategic success. Moreover, the case shows how the focal firm combines its resources with those of another in order to move forward.

Summary

The key points to take from this chapter are as follows:

- How business marketing planning should go hand in hand with S/DCM in order to meet customer needs.
- The main elements of a marketing plan for B2B organizations.
- Debates around the relevance of a formal planning approach to marketing 'management' in a network context.
- The significance of external and internal factors in conducting planning analyses.
- The challenges to B2B marketers of gathering appropriate market information in order to take appropriate strategic decisions.
- The market and buyer-based variables by which organizational markets may be segmented.

Discussion questions

1. Why might firms without a proper marketing orientation struggle to make appropriate marketing plans?
2. What contribution is made to B2B marketing planning by the formal (rational) planning approach? Is this the only way to undertake planning for business markets?
3. List some marketing audit elements that a firm making heavy-duty construction equipment planning to sell its products to a country like Zimbabwe might need to analyse.
4. Under what circumstances might it be more appropriate for an organization exploring new business markets to undertake their own market research activities rather than to buy these services?
5. Will all the bases for B2B segmentation discussed in this chapter necessarily apply across different countries and regions?

Case study
KMS Software: CRM for Construction Professionals

Angela Vickerstaff, Nottingham Trent University, Nottingham, UK

Introduction

Its founder, Dr Jonas Dahlkvist, established KMS in 1990 with a view to providing sales software to the engineering sector. The first product, called Market-base, was aimed at organizations with a long and complex sales process. It was designed to store, track, and manage the sales cycle for any organization that sold a typically high-value, high-involvement product or service.

Having made its first few big sales, KMS was approached by some manufacturing companies who were involved in the construction industry. Key features of construction projects are that there are multiple parties associated with a project, often with each party having numerous decision makers. Furthermore, by their very nature, construction projects involve complex sales processes, multiple bids, and numerous revisions. So, from a manufacturer's point of view, it needed to be able to relate multiple histories to a particular project. However, the existing Market-base product didn't do this effectively. Jonas saw this as an opportunity to create a bespoke solution, named Project-base. At the time (early 1990s), KMS didn't envisage a large market for this product, and estimated it would only contribute 10% of company turnover. Within two years, it was apparent that the market potential was much larger than envisaged. Project-base took over as the lead product and Market-base was soon dropped. Having taken this strategic decision, the company naturally became focused on the construction industry. What started off as a sales tool evolved to become sales and marketing software, and then into Customer Relationship Management (CRM).

Understanding the need for CRM in the construction industry

Companies operating in the construction industry fall broadly into two groups: contractors and product suppliers, and vary in size from global players to local firms. Companies compete, but also work together with project teams comprising lead contractors, subcontractors, professionals (quantity surveyors, architects, etc.), and product suppliers. Thus, the industry can be seen to be complex in nature, involving multiple relationships between different types of firms, and across project teams. Hence the need for CRM systems to enable construction companies to share customer data across the company, access data remotely, track opportunities, write quotes, track sales, report on activities, and manage customer interactions effectively.

KMS now has customers in virtually every sector of the construction industry, including contractors, developers, engineers, materials manufacturers, and suppliers. In essence, it provides project-tracking CRM systems that add value by offering companies an efficient and cost-effective means of managing their business, and enhancing their productivity across areas such as business development, marketing, work winning, and support functions. KMS has built up a very healthy customer base, and it is testament to its solutions, and commitment to customer service, that over 30 companies have been using its solutions in excess of ten years. In fact, one customer has now been using its solutions for over 17 years – virtually unheard of in the software industry!

KMS today

KMS is based in central London. Its main markets geographically lie in the UK and Ireland, but it has global reach with customers as far away as Australia. KMS has grown organically and remains privately owned, with annual turnover moving towards £1m. The company is run by a team of four directors: the managing director, sales and marketing, technical, and financial. In terms of organization, as an SME, it has a very flat organizational structure and staff are flexible in their roles. There is a technical team which is responsible for ongoing developments of the software, a commercial team who handle the delivery of the software (installation, training, consultancy, and ongoing technical support), a sales and marketing team who are responsible for the finding and winning of work, and ongoing relationship management, and a small administration team who handle invoicing and general office duties.

By virtue of its relatively small size and niche market approach, KMS is very versatile and can respond quickly to market opportunities and threats. As such, strategy is very much evolutionary and, over the years, can be seen to have been driven by core factors such as the aims and ambitions of the directors, emerging technological opportunities, and of course changing demands of customers.

Evolving market strategy

In contrast to the advice in many marketing textbooks, marketing strategy at KMS is seen to evolve in an ad hoc yet dynamic way. There is no formal marketing department; instead, marketing and sales activities are interwoven. Marketing activities are undertaken on a 'suck it and see' basis. For example, to supplement traditional marketing techniques, the team have recently introduced 'webinars' and a series of blogs, showing that the firm is not afraid to trial new technologies and means of communicating with prospects and existing customers.

Whilst there is no formal process of strategy making, there is an annual budget-planning meeting which coincides with the financial year end. At this point, the directors discuss and agree targets for sales, costs, staffing levels, and profit. These targets emerge from past experiences and their understanding of market and competitor activity. The directors would not identify with standard textbook terms such as the 'marketing audit' or 'external analysis'. When these terms were explained by this case's author, the response from the sales and marketing director was, 'We don't have time for all that stuff!' By virtue of strong market orientation, nearly all staff engage with customers every day; they know what is happening in their markets; they check data on the construction industry regularly; they know what competitors are doing as they keep their ears to the ground; and know how technology is moving on – the most important factors for the future of their industry.

The company is proactive and responsive. Directors work as a close team and discuss issues as and when they emerge. So, whilst the general direction is understood and shared, and targets are set each year, directors are comfortable in changing direction as opportunities appear. Once decisions are made by the directors; there is no need for any formal 'implementation plan' – people just go away and do it. If things aren't working out in a particular area, the directors have a discussion and try to identify alternatives before it becomes a problem.

Strategic decision-making

To illustrate, up until 2005, KMS had focused on selling and marketing its main offering, Project-base, a software package developed entirely in-house. Customers bought the basic software solution under licence, but through the purchase of consultancy the software was configured and set up for their individual business needs – i.e. customized.

During 2005, it became apparent that Microsoft was entering the CRM marketplace. Awareness of this new player emerged gradually from various sources, such as customers, prospects, and the Internet. The directors naturally took it upon themselves to investigate what was, at the time, perceived as a competitive threat. By 2006, the directors had changed their mind and reclassified the Microsoft offering as a market opportunity. Microsoft operates a partner network, which allows software companies such as KMS the opportunity to customize its generic product to better fit differing markets. So this gave KMS the chance to build a solution around the Microsoft Dynamics CRM product – which it calls Project-CRM.

The decision to enter this market was never part of a formal marketing plan, but an emergent strategy. Initially, KMS decided that its developers would invest some time assessing the system to see if they could make it work and meet the needs of the construction industry. Early feedback was positive, so the directors sat down and worked out how to move forward. Discussions followed and gradually a sales and marketing strategy has emerged, with marketing communications materials developed, partnership opportunities explored, and the product launched. It is testament to its development skills and competencies within this technology arena that KMS attained Microsoft Gold Certified Partner Status early in 2009, the highest level of certification offered within the partner network. Sales of the new offering are buoyant, it adds a new dimension to KMS's product offering, and KMS is maintaining a healthy sales pipeline, despite the challenging market conditions generally and in the construction market in particular.

Over the years, KMS's mission has remained constant: 'To be the construction industry's first choice for CRM Systems, by supplying superior products, service, and support that empower construction professionals to achieve more.' The way in which this is achieved has evolved over time, as market opportunities have emerged. There has not been a fixed marketing plan in place, or formal marketing processes. Instead, the directors have worked their way through the changing market conditions, incrementally building on successes. Consequently, the company has become more service-led, but remains very innovative. As the Microsoft product and technology generally evolve, KMS continually adds more features to its offerings, working with customers to better meet their needs for the future.

Source: www.kms-software.com

Case study questions

1. Identify key events in the history of KMS and explore how they have influenced KMS's strategy.

2. Compare marketing planning processes at KMS with the traditional marketing planning processes explored in this chapter.

3. Offer a critique of KMS's marketing planning processes. What do you consider would be the benefits and drawbacks of KMS adopting a more formalized approach to marketing planning?

Further Reading

Beverland, M. B. & Lindgreen, A. (2007) Implementing Marketing Orientation in Industrial Firms: A Multiple Case Study, Industrial Marketing Management, 36, pp 430–42

This study examines the creation of a market orientation (MO) in two New Zealand agricultural organizations, identifying that moving the firms towards an MO involves changes in the role of leadership, the use of market intelligence, and organizational learning styles, underpinned by supportive policies that form closer relationships between the organizations and the marketplace.

Eng, T.-Y. (2008) Customer Portfolio Planning in a Business Network Context, Journal of Marketing Management, 24 (5/6), pp 567–87

The author develops a customer portfolio framework that integrates four levels of relationship and integrates a resource-based view as well as determinants of competitive advantage. The framework is applied in the UK food service sector, with findings suggesting that a firm can enhance its competitive position with knowledge of network effects and interdependencies.

Faria, A. & Wensley, R. (2002) In Search of 'Inter-Firm Management' in Supply Chains: Recognising Contradictions of Language and Power by Listening, Journal of Business Research, 55, pp 603–10

This complex but fascinating study looks at how managers talk about issues relating to the use of power in the supply/demand chain, and reveals their moral judgement on the nature of 'management', not only in supply networks, but in more general terms. The authors claim that managers often feel excluded from full participation in decisions that directly or indirectly affect their activities and lives.

Vrontis, D., Kogetsidis, H., & Stavrou, A. (2006) Strategic Marketing Planning for a Supplier of Liquid Food Packaging Products in Cyprus, Journal of Business & Industrial Marketing, 21 (4) pp 250–61

This article offers a very readable case study. It shows how, through an internal and external analysis of the environment, the case company is able to decide upon an effective strategic direction and draw up an appropriate B2B marketing plan. Although restricted largely to the classic rational planning model, the article illustrates the importance of a market orientated approach to planning.

References

Ansoff, I. (1988) The New Corporate Strategy, John Wiley & Sons, Chichester

Baker, R. (2008) A Healthier Outlook at Tricky Time, Nottingham Evening Post, 21 May, p 54

Barney, J. B. (2001) Is the Resource-Based 'View' a Useful Perspective for Strategic Management Research? Yes, Academy of Management Review, 26 (1), pp 41–56

Bonoma, T. V. & Shapiro, B. P. (1983) Segmenting the Industrial Market, DC Heath Co., Lexington, M.A.

Clark, A. (2009) Xerox Warns of Cuts as Revenue Slumps by 18%, The Guardian, 21 March, p 23

Dunkin, R. (2008) Austal's $78m Caribbean Deal, The West Australian, 23 April, p 59

Ellis, N. (2006) (De)constructing Organizational Relationships, unpublished Ph.D. thesis, Lancaster University

Ellis, N. (2008) Discursive Tensions in Collaboration: Stories of the Marketplace, International Journal of Sociology & Social Policy, 28 (1), pp 32–45

Eng, T.-Y. (2008) Customer Portfolio Planning in a Business Network Context, Journal of Marketing Management, 24 (5/6), pp 567–87Forbes Asia (2008) Fab 50, 15 September, p 114

Freytag, P. V. & Clarke, A. H. (2001) Business to Business Segmentation, Industrial Marketing Management, 30 (6), pp 473–86

Håkansson, H. & Ford, D. (2002) How should Companies Interact? Journal of Business Research, 55 (2), pp 133–9

Johanson, J. & Mattsson, L.-G. (1992) Network Positions and Strategic Action – An Analytical Framework, in Axelsson, B. & Easton, G. (eds), Industrial Networks: A New View of Reality, Routledge, London, pp 205–17

Juttner, U., Christopher, M., & Baker, S. (2007) Demand Chain Management – Integrating Marketing and Supply Chain Management, Industrial Marketing Management, 36, pp 377–92

Katz, M. (1979) Using Same Theory, Skills for Consumer, Industrial Marketing Research, Marketing News, 12 January, p 16

Ling-Yee, L. & Ogunmokun, G. O. (2008) An Empirical Study of Manufacturing Flexibility of Exporting Firms in China: How do Strategic and Organizational Contexts Matter? Industrial Marketing Management, 37, pp 738–51

Marketer (The) (2007) Fact of the Month, October, p 7

McDonald, M. (1996) Strategic Marketing Planning: Theory, Practice and Research Agendas, Journal of Marketing Management, 12, pp 5–28

Min, S. & Mentzer, J. (2000) The Role of Marketing in Supply Chain Management, International Journal of Physical Distribution and Logistics Management, 30 (9), p 766–87

Mitchell, V.-W. & Wilson, D. F. (1998) A Reappraisal of Business-to-Business Segmentation, Industrial Marketing Management, 27 (5), pp 429–45

Network – The Co-operative Membership Magazine (2008) Healthcare in Focus, September, p 29

Pearce, F. (2008) Confessions of an Eco-Sinner: Travels to Find Where my Stuff Comes From, Eden Project Books, London

Pelham, A. (1999) Influence of Environment, Strategy and Market Orientation on Small Manufacturing Firms, Journal of Business Research, 45, pp 33–46

Porter, M. E. (1985) Competitive Advantage: Creating and Sustaining Superior Performance, Free Press, New York

Pratruangkrai, P. (2007) Largest Chicken Plant Opens: Ajinomoto and Betagro Team up for Supply, The Nation: Business, 24 November, p 1

Rajagopal, B. & Sanchez, R. (2005) Analysis of Customer Portfolio and Relationship Management Models: Bridging Managerial Dimensions, Journal of Business & Industrial Marketing, 20 (6), pp 307–16

Ryals, L. (2000) Planning for Relationship Marketing, in Cranfield School of Management (eds), Marketing Management: A Relationship Marketing Perspective, MacMillan Press, Houndsmill, pp 231–48

Sadler, I. (2007) Logistics and Supply Chain Integration, Sage, London

Sin, L. & Tse, A. (2000) How does Marketing Effectiveness Mediate the Effect of Organizational Culture on Business Performance? The Case of Service Firms, Journal of Services Marketing, 14, pp 295–309

Weitzman, H. (2008) Strike Shuts down Boeing Operations, Financial Times, 8 September, p 18

Yunus, K. (2008) Malaysia to be Hub for Mitsui Copper Foils, New Straits Times, 12 September, p 33

Chapter 7
B2B Marketing Strategies & Implementation

Introduction & Learning Objectives

The contents of this chapter follow on directly from Chapter Six; thus we shall be discussing in more depth how planning objectives can be achieved. This will include building on your knowledge of B2B segmentation to suggest ways in which organizations may position themselves in terms of how they are perceived by customers. A host of strategic options are open to B2B marketers, so we shall weigh up some of the most important. We shall also examine problems faced by managers when implementing marketing plans. By exploring more of the strategic elements of marketing planning, this chapter, along with its predecessor, forms a bridge between the understanding of organizational buying, relationships, and networks you will have gained in Parts One and Two of this book, and the detailed advice over marketing programmes contained in Part Four.

Even in the most stable of environments, marketing planning is a tricky business, but in countries like the Lebanon, with its recent history of unrest, the challenges are huge. Yet, some Lebanese entrepreneurs seem to thrive in organizational markets, as the case in Box 7.1 shows. Note how the firm has positioned itself in the marketplace. Note also the resources, including money, time, and knowledge (i.e. the network understanding held by the owner), which the firm has drawn upon to ensure success.

Box 7.1 Number crunching

The perfect mushroom

In 1996, the sugar mill opened by Nazem Ghandou's father in Tripoli, Lebanon to process high-grade imported beet closed after the price for sugar suddenly fell thanks to subsidies offered to domestic growers by the Lebanese government. Having lost his father's business, Nazem opened two restaurants, hoping to exploit the economic boom following a respite in the country's civil unrest. Unfortunately, the boom did not last, so he had to think again.

He drew upon his experience in running a restaurant, where he had observed that the biggest problem for organizations in the catering trade was the need to import speciality products like fresh vegetables and meat. Realizing that he had a cold storage area that had accompanied the old sugar refinery, Nazem thought it would work well for a key ingredient: mushrooms. He invested in a copy of a mushroom-cultivating guide at $65 through Amazon, and after an initial investment in imported seeds of $2,000 and several months of experimenting, he was harvesting his first batch of white button mushrooms. He took the strategic decision to position the firm at the top end of the market, and named it 'Le Champignon Parfait' or The Perfect Mushroom. Nazem discovered that the trick to growing the perfect crop was in the compost used, so he spent a considerable amount of time with his technician, Tarik, to develop the right mix of chicken and horse manure from local farms to ferment at the correct temperature. This was so complex to control that the firm chose to purchase a $7,000 computer system from Danish suppliers, Janssen Kessel, to run the whole process.

This high-quality approach seemed to appeal to the country's catering establishments. By 2002, the company was Lebanon's biggest mushroom producer, employing 21 people (largely retrained staff from the sugar refinery) and generating average annual revenues of $4,000,000 by supplying mushrooms to catering organizations nationwide. The company even claims to have achieved this without a marketing team – much has rested on the shoulders of Nazem and his network of contacts in the food industry. Nazem wants to boost sales by exporting but the licensing procedures for this are time consuming, so that route to growth represents a further strategic challenge to come.

Source: Glain (2003)

Chapter Aims

After completing this chapter, you should be able to:

- Consider some of the alternatives open to organizations seeking to strategically position themselves in business markets
- Assess the potential significance of branding in industrial marketing
- Understand some of the choices facing B2B marketing managers in designing appropriate strategies
- Identify problems encountered when implementing plans that attempt to integrate different functional activities of the organization.

7.1 Market Positioning

Following on from the segmentation and targeting issues discussed in Chapter Six, this final stage of the segmentation, targeting, and positioning (STP) process is a core element of strategic marketing planning. The aim of market (or competitive) positioning is to encourage buyers to view a supplier as different from other suppliers in elements of their offering that the customer perceives as adding value. Successful positioning entails establishing a clear distinction between your organization's products and services, and those of the competition. It is important that the attributes on which you choose to differentiate yourself are actually important to customers: there is little point basing your position on a low-cost strategy, when what is valued by customers is high-quality components or flexible delivery.

Box 7.2 Voices

Market positioning by specialization

UK company, Powder Systems Ltd, makes valves and containers to handle toxic chemicals. Its customers are mainly pharmaceutical firms such as GlaxoSmithKline and AstraZeneca. The company positions itself against the competition by producing specialist (and expensive) high-quality goods. Director Barry O'Gorman says, 'We make extremely high-quality products for an extremely high-quality, demanding market.' He can charge up to £1 million for some of his firm's most sophisticated instruments, and adds, 'If you're not making something very niche or specialist then . . . you will feel the pressure. The strength of manufacturing depends on doing things better rather than doing things cheaper.'

Source : Balakrishnan (2007); www.p-s-l.com

This represents a key role for the B2B marketing manager – it is up to the marketing function to represent the market and the customer's point of view so that the rest of the organization can define the characteristics of its offer and decide upon its position. The boss of the firm in Box 7.2 clearly believes he has got this right.

Positioning by value proposition

In line with the generic differentiation strategy outlined in Chapter Six, there are three ways in which managers can use what are termed 'customer value propositions' in order to position their organization (Anderson et al, 2006). These are represented in Figure 7.1, showing how each approach is more targeted than the last.

1. *The all benefits approach*: here, suppliers just list all the potential benefits they believe their product or service might provide for target segments. Although this is a relatively undemanding position to construct, simply asserting all these benefits has the danger of making claims that are not actually deliverable to individual customers, as well as doing little to distinguish the firm's offering from the next-best competitive alternative.

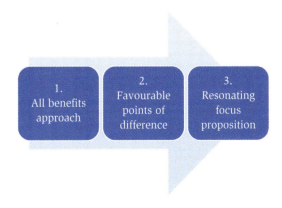

Figure 7.1 **Positioning by value proposition**

2. *The favourable points of difference approach, which aims to answer the customer's question*: 'Why should our company buy your offering rather than your competitor's?' This means managers need more detailed knowledge of their offering in order to be able to differentiate it from the next-best alternative. Managers still often fall into the trap of listing as many favourable points of difference as possible, and presuming that these points must be valuable to the customer.

3. *The most targeted approach, the resonating focus proposition*: here, the selling firm makes its offerings superior on the few elements where performance matters most to customers. Managers must be able to demonstrate this superiority and communicate it to buyers in a manner that suggests the supplier understands the customer's business needs regarding these one or two key issues. This avoids the assumption that 'more is always better'. In order to construct a position that resonates, however, the supplier will often need to conduct research to provide the necessary insights into customer perceptions of value (for more on value, see Chapter Ten).

Repositioning

Given that business markets are fairly dynamic, another important aspect of strategic positioning is repositioning, where organizations attempt to change the way they are perceived by customers. This can be achieved by changing market offerings and/or buyer–seller relationships. Penttinen and Palmer (2007) suggest a two-by-two matrix to examine alternatives for positioning (see Figure 7.2), with the horizontal axis describing the nature of the relationship from transactional to relational, and the vertical axis describing the 'completeness' of the offering. This refers to the degree to which customer problems are solved. A more

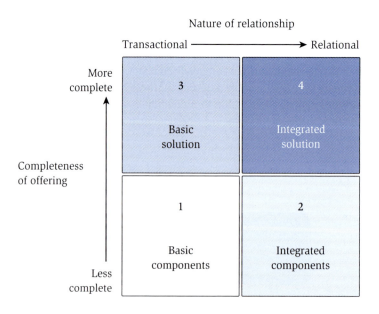

Figure 7.2 Framework for B2B repositioning
Source: Adapted with permission from Penttinen and Palmer (2007, p 554)
E. Penttinen & J. Palmer (2007) Improving Firm Positioning through Enhanced Offerings and
Buyer–Seller Relations, Industrial Marketing Management, 35, pp 552–64, copyright Elsevier

complete offering tends to contain higher levels of service and the application of specialist knowledge.

Taking each cell in Figure 7.2 in turn, we can see that:

- Cell 1 involves the most basic offering, and a limited relationship with the customer (e.g. the sale of components such as nuts and bolts). The advantages of this position are its simplicity and low cost.

- Cell 2 entails offering a slightly more integrated set of components with a likely requirement of a closer relationship (e.g. integrated sub-assemblies for cars or aeroplanes). This may spur product development and enhance customer relations, but is likely to incur relationship management costs.

- Cell 3 involves a more complete product, although with no commitment beyond a transactional relationship (e.g. 'bundling' offerings like service applications and tele-communication support). This allows the offering to become more differentiated, and keeps relationship costs low, but increases costs in coordinating the more complex products and services required.

- Finally, Cell 4 entails making a complete offering and developing a close relationship with the customer (e.g. full-service contracts in industrial maintenance). This can bring the maximum degree of differentiation, but brings higher relationship management costs.

The matrix allows firms which are struggling to make themselves stand out in a business marketplace to consider meeting customer requests and securing a steadier revenue stream via repositioning. Managers can identify their current position and search for potential differentiators to move to other quadrants, e.g. to reach Cell 4 from Cell 1, resources permitting.

Positioning using marketing mix programmes

The remaining chapters of this book, with their examination of B2B products, services, pricing, and marketing communications, provide detailed programmes on how such market positioning might be achieved. For now, this chapter maintains a more strategic overview of these programmes, programmes which can be seen as tactics in a hierarchy of planning activities (see Chapter Six). With this broader perspective in mind, we need to understand how the tactical 'tool kit' of what many textbooks call the 'marketing mix' (see the structural overview of this book in the Preface) can be combined to maximum effect in B2B markets. For instance, having chosen a position, the selling firm then needs to communicate this to all relevant stakeholders or 'publics' (see Chapter Eleven). Several approaches which are not, you will notice, confined to marketing communications tools like advertising, can be taken to signify a firm's positioning, including:

- By product feature: Where the product features that distinguish a company's offering from the competition are highlighted. These features may be changed as the product is perceived to pass through its 'product life cycle' (see Chapter Eight for more on this managerial concept).

- By benefit: This extends the features approach by making more explicit how the product or service can meet the needs of the customer. This is typically expressed in terms of 'solutions' whereby, for instance, road haulage companies describe themselves as 'providers of logistics solutions'.

- By price/quality: Where price itself can often be used to indicate relative quality. Inexperienced buyers in business markets may seek reassurance by choosing the more expensive option.

- By existing user: Where customers are reassured by being reminded of the types of user that already purchase the product. A classic example is IBM's boast that 'no-one ever got fired for buying IBM'.

- By experience and reputation: Where firms remind customers of their history and levels of expertise in a particular field. For instance, GE's website makes much of the firm's beginnings in 1892 and the amount it invests annually in R&D (a figure of almost £4 billion in 2007 – www.ge.com).

Benchmarking

Benchmarking can be seen as a method for guiding positioning. It shows how important the gathering of information can be to a firm's strategic planning. The process basically involves identifying 'best practices' for particular business processes, and then learning from and adapting these practices for the benefit of your own organization. Benchmarking is thought to be popular amongst large Western firms (Naylor et al, 2001). It is usually done against firms in non-competing industries, as this facilitates the sharing of potentially sensitive practices, but it can also be undertaken against competitors as part of a market research project.

One way of positioning is through your customer service levels, or rather on how these are perceived by your customers in relation to the competition. As we saw in Chapter Three, Christopher (1992) argues that, while many factors will influence the quality and longevity of a customer relationship, it will usually be the case that superior service performance is a key determinant of customer retention. This can be illustrated by examining the contribution which marketing logistics can make to organizational customer retention. Of course, it is no good being better than your competitors at certain things if those things are not valued. This is shown graphically in Figure 7.3, which presents the results of a customer survey carried out by a hypothetical supplier (the focal firm).

We can see that at a first glance (on the right-hand side of the figure), the focal firm appears to be performing overall at a similar level to its competitor, since each company has some relatively good scores from customers on some elements of its service provision, as well as some poor scores. However, when we look (on the left) at the importance customers attach to different elements of logistics service, a less optimistic picture emerges. Unfortunately for the focal firm, it is on all the most important criteria that it is found to be underperforming compared to the competitor company, e.g. time, reliability, and frequency. Such benchmarking clearly suggests areas for management action if B2B relationships are not to suffer. More on business services like logistics provision can be found in Chapter Nine.

7.2 B2B Branding Strategy

Branding can form an important part of an organization's attempt at market positioning. However, thanks to the popular perception that buying behaviour in business markets is much more 'rational' than in consumer markets, many B2B marketing managers are convinced that branding strategy is not relevant to their role. This is a shame, since a strong

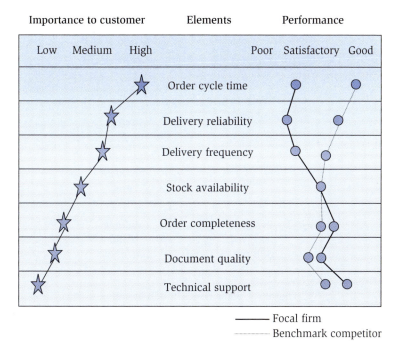

Figure 7.3 Customer service benchmarking in marketing logistics
Source: Adapted with permission from Christopher (1992, p 93)
M. Christopher (1992) Logistics and Supply Chain Management, p 93,
copyright Pearson Education Limited

brand can help to position a firm in the minds of customers and reduce the perceived risk associated with organizational purchases. For example, the UPS campaign headed 'What can Brown do for you?' used the main colour in the company's livery to position UPS as a choice that would make the buyer look good in the eyes of management (www.ups.com). Some strategic issues in branding for B2B marketers are summarized in Figure 7.4.

Branding can provide quality assurances, enhance the anticipated level of satisfaction with a purchase, and facilitate further purchases. These sorts of risk reduction factors can be more influential in industrial markets than small price differentials, thus allowing the selling firm to recoup the cost of investing in branding. As well as the implicit promise of quality that a brand brings, it can also be viewed as a valuable asset or resource for the firm, alongside more conventional measures of worth such as premises, inventory, and cash.

If you are still not convinced, think of these organizations: Microsoft, GE, Cisco Systems, SAP, FedEx, Dell, and Boeing. They show how some of the world's strongest brands are, in fact, B2B brands. Although most also operate in B2C contexts, their main business is concentrated on B2B (Kotler and Pfoertsch, 2007). For instance, one of Dell's (www.dell.com) magazine advertisements proclaims simply, 'Dell: Number One in Business', stating that 99% of the Fortune top 500 firms use Dell computers (Business Week 2008).

A number of questions should be asked by marketers pondering B2B brand building, including: what is our aspirational brand identity and does it support our overall business strategy; what value proposition is most valuable to our customers; and how do I align

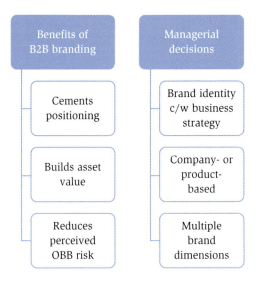

Figure 7.4 **Some issues in B2B branding**

my organization to make the brand and value propositions into realities (Morrison, 2001)? Some sort of action plan needs to be in place to address each of these questions before embarking on any brand-building initiatives. The questions flag up the fact that communicating a brand image involves a lot more than just a high-profile advertising campaign (see Chapter Eleven) – much depends on the marketing orientation of the entire organization. Indeed, for industrial products, branding is a multidimensional construct that incorporates not only how the customer views the product but also the quality of customer support that accompanies it and the firm's image (McQuiston, 2004).

Nevertheless, the image you wish to portray in your firm's marketing communications is crucial. It can be effective to link non-product-related images to your branding strategy, even in business markets. Social benefits such as 'ease of doing business' or 'peace of mind', which are hard to estimate in economic terms, can affect purchase decisions. It is these sorts of perceptions that a branding strategy can help to build, especially when combined with a demonstration of technical and monetary benefits. In some buying situations for non-essential items, a formal assessment of value is not undertaken and brand image may act as the key basis for purchase, such as a firm deciding to use 3M's Post-it notes when they perceive a need to buy repositionable self-adhesive notes for their offices. Even for more important components like electrical parts, building contractors have reported that they will buy a preferred brand more than 65% of the time (Gordon et al, 1993).

The Post-it note example shows how a firm can decide to invest in either company-based branding (3M) or product-based branding (Post-it), or both. Some industrial organizations such as ABB and Siemens follow a single brand corporate strategy. This approach involves a focus on communicating the underlying values of the company (e.g. innovation, reliability, safety, etc.). The decision whether to have one or several brands is often based on industry behaviours, tradition (such as nationalistic brand associations, e.g. JCB's claim to represent '100% British muscle' based on the 'hard work' of the people who make their construction machinery – www.jcb.com), management risk profiles and product portfolio considerations where numerous brands can help spread the risk for the seller. Sometimes, local variations are inevitable, but standardized global brand strategies can lead to significant economies of scale in terms of brand investments.

Investing in B2B branding

In order to get a full picture of ROI for a branding strategy, Ohnemus (2009) argues that any analysis of brand investment should take into account a wide range of B2B marketing expenditures, including distribution and sales-related costs, together with direct and indirect marketing expenditures like sales promotions and advertising. Based on this overall measure, Ohnemus's research shows that companies achieve the highest return when investing 5–10% of their turnover in branding.

B2B branding thus appears to be an attractive way forward for marketers, even though it is not a cheap option. Ultimately, of course, the effectiveness of industrial brands depends a great deal on the significance of brands to the buyer. Mudambi (2002) believes there may be three types of B2B customers, differentiated by the importance they attach to branding in the buying decision process:

- The brand-receptive segment: These customers need messages and a brand image that stress a highly reputable supplier, along with the emotional and social benefits of the purchase.

- The highly tangible segment: This group of customers require communications messages that emphasize the functional and quantifiable benefits of the product and company.

- The low interest segment: These customers tend to respond more positively to messages that highlight the significance of the purchase decision and the ease with which orders can be placed and goods delivered.

Recent studies tend to confirm Mudambi's assessment of the utility of B2B brands. In an examination of the logistics sector, Davis et al (2008) show how brands help to differentiate the offerings of logistics service providers, and that a degree of 'brand equity' exists for what they describe as this relatively 'commodity-like' business service. Brand equity represents a perception of superior value amongst brand-receptive customers for your brand compared with the competing brands. Look at the research findings reported in Box 7.3 and consider what goes towards building brand equity.

Box 7.3 Food for thought

Where should B2B brand investment be placed?

Logistics service firms are constantly looking for ways to distinguish themselves from other firms providing similar services in order to improve their chances of being included in potential customers' consideration sets. One way logistics firms have sought to achieve this is by developing strong brands. The investment made by marketers in various marketing mix elements aims to create awareness and a positive, unique image, resulting in brand equity. B2B brand image tends to centre on firm attributes like experience or reputation, such as the claim of Cat Logistics, a subsidiary of Caterpillar, to have 'the know-how that helped build the legend'.

Service providers and their customers have different perspectives on the relative influence of brand image and brand awareness on equity. An important realization is that, for logistics buyers, the firm's name effectively is the brand. This means that service providers with names similar to the competition or that are hard to recall may need to invest in a company name change to help customers identify them. Moreover, customers perceive brand image to be more significant than mere awareness. This suggests that managers need to consider carefully where they invest in their brands: expenditure may be better placed in staff training to ensure a consistent brand image is built via service interactions rather than just spending more on advertising.

Source: Davis et al (2008); http://logistics.cat.com

Do not forget, however, that there are some things that a branding strategy simply cannot influence. Over 60% of brand defection in B2B financial services can occur due to business closures or head office decisions as well as dissatisfaction with fees and charges or the attractiveness of competitors' offers (Bogomolova and Romaniuk, 2009). Beyond encouraging their firm to match competing offers, there is little else a marketing manager can do in terms of branding to retain these customers.

7.3 Making B2B Strategy Decisions

In this section, we highlight some ways in which different types of organizations can design B2B marketing strategies. The options put forward here are based on research which has explored organizations operating in Eastern as well as Western markets, and SMEs as well as large companies. A number of strategic considerations will be discussed, as summarized in Figure 7.5.

Managing in business networks

As we suggested in the previous chapter, an appreciation of the workings of industrial networks brings with it a new series of challenges for B2B marketing managers as they try to

Figure 7.5 **Some considerations in B2B strategy-making**

formulate strategies. Möller and Halinen (1999) have put forward a 'network management framework' to discuss the managerial implications of the webs of firms that extend beyond immediate inter-organizational relationships (IORs). This framework comprises a number of different levels which are represented in Figure 7.6.

1. *Level 1, known as 'network visioning'*: views whole industries as networks. This assumes that networks form the environment in which actors (or firms) are embedded, and recognizes that understanding network structures, processes, and evolution is crucial for any attempts at network management. Key managerial challenges from this perspective include: how to develop a comprehensive view of relevant networks and the opportunities they contain; and how to analyse strategic groups of firms, e.g. for understanding the nature of network competition.

2. *Level 2, termed 'net management'*: views actors in a particular network. It involves analysing firms' strategic behaviours by looking at the 'focal nets' they belong to. It entails considering the positions they hold in these networks, networks which are usually smaller than the whole industry networks considered at Level 1. This requires the capability to mobilize and coordinate the resources and activities of other actors. Managerial challenges here include: how to develop and manage 'supplier nets' and 'customer nets' (which are equivalent to the supplier and distribution networks highlighted in Chapter Five); and how to enter new networks, e.g. for new market entry or to launch a new product line.

3. *Level 3, or 'portfolio management'*: looks at relationship portfolios (see also Chapter Six). This explores which key activities are best carried out internally and which are better undertaken via different IORs. The capability to manage a portfolio of the necessary IORs is crucial. Challenges for B2B marketers at this level include: how to develop and manage optimal customer and/or supplier portfolios, e.g. knowing in which IORs to invest the most resources (for instance, in the allocation of sales approaches, as discussed in Chapter Twelve).

4. *Level 4 is termed simply 'relationship management'*: and as the name suggests, focuses on individual IORs between the focal firm and its suppliers or customers. The firm must possess the core skill of being able to build IORs. Managerial challenges include: evaluating the lifetime value of an IOR; and creating, managing, and terminating a relationship effectively (for numerous examples see Chapter Three).

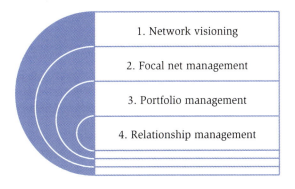

Figure 7.6 **Levels of network management**

At the more micro level of the individual manager's perspective, the concept of the 'network picture' can be related to Level Two of Möller and Halinen's (1999) framework. Network pictures are based on the different subjective understandings that social actors possess as they try to make sense of the network (or focal net): 'These perceived network pictures form the backbone of managers' understanding of relationships, interactions, and interdependencies, and therefore constitute an important component of their individual decision-making processes' (Henneberg et al, 2006, p 409). Such pictures can be seen as an indication of what individual managers feel is important about the environment in which their organization operates. The sorts of network properties that can form part of a network picture include boundaries, exchange relationships, information flows, and actor relevance, power, and centrality. You may recall that these elements correspond to the discussion in Chapter Five regarding how a B2B trade marketer working for a shaver manufacturer might define the network.

A further strategic consideration for some growth-orientated B2B organizations is how to trade internationally. An organization's network position can be a critical factor in making decisions here. For instance, there has been a considerable expansion in the cross-border activity of professional service firms (see Chapter Nine) over the last 30 years. As an example of this activity, Winch (2008) explores recent developments in the internationalization of English and French architectural practices by studying the strategies deployed by such companies for foreign market entry – see Box 7.4. Note how some firms seem to favour approaches that involve close associations with either their existing clients or a network of

---

Box 7.4 Mini case

Internationalization strategies in B2B services

In the construction industry, international trade is focused on the high-value-added design and project management elements of the building process. Architects often work as part of project coalitions which are networks of firms chartered by clients to provide specialist design services and project execution services on site. Research has identified four distinct market entry strategies used by architect firms to gain business internationally:

1. *Following a client*: after becoming the 'house' architects for French retailer, Carrefour, and taking responsibility for 90% of their work, Architectes CVZ were commissioned by the firm to build in 15 different European countries as Carrefour expanded globally.

2. *Winning a* concours: a *concours* is an architectural competition between rival practices. Much of the international work of Foster and Partners is obtained by responding to invitations to take part in international competitions, e.g. the reconstruction of the Reichstag in Berlin.

3. *Marketing*: in this context, this term covers a variety of ways in which firms get work, including being commissioned on the basis of reputation. For instance, the John

R Harris Partnership has experience in designing over 30 hospitals around the world, including massive projects in the Far East, and has thus built up an enviable reputation in the sector.

4. *Via network partners*: this can involve an association of practices bidding for business. For example, under the European Economic Interest Grouping (EEIG) structure, which is a set of rules facilitating cooperation, the practices of EPR (London) and Groupe Daviel (Paris) became founder members of Architecturo which now has partners in Lisbon and Brussels. The EEIG arrangements allow practices working in one country to import specialist skills from another, thus tapping into EPR's skills in office developments and Daviel's experience with social housing projects.

Source: Winch (2008); www.cvsa.com; www.fosterandpartners.com

other practices, while others adopt a more independent route to achieving their international goals. (For more on international marketing strategy, see the end-of-chapter case study).

Managing risk and tracking value

Recall that we noted the issue of financial risk briefly in our discussion of product/market decisions in Chapter Six. Assessing and managing the relational risks involved in any strategic decision are also an important part of marketing planning, especially when your clients are internationally based, as we often find in the B2B outsourcing sector. Aundhe and Mathew (2009) provide a study of risks from the perspective of a service provider in the major offshore IT outsourcing industry based in Bangalore, India. There are relation-specific risks in this sector associated with client misperceptions over the level of service that the vendor will be able to supply over a project's development. This can result in subsequent disagreements which may sour an IOR. Managers in Indian service provider firms have therefore learnt that it is worth investing the time to try to convince the client of the need for a collaborative 'requirements-gathering' phase at the outset of any project. During this phase, it is important for the client and the service provider to operate in a partnership mode rather than a transactional one. Encouraging as full as possible a dialogue over potential operational issues at the start of an IOR can be a crucial risk-mitigation strategy when the task complexity is high.

The requirements-gathering phase is a particularly effective strategy when the service provider has misgivings about the client's corporate culture (which may mean that the customer is used to conducting relationships in quite an arm's-length manner) or their limited experience in offshoring. Indian IT firms will often attempt to educate their client in the processes of outsourcing in order to develop a high level of involvement with managers at the customer organization, thereby managing their expectations about the quality of service on offer (see Chapter Nine). Some of the tensions in IORs in this sector are captured in the quote in Box 7.5. You can see how client guidance on the part of the service provider regarding the benefits of being more flexible and open throughout the relationship life cycle (see Chapter Three) might alleviate the risks inherent in deciding to trade internationally in this sector.

Once strategic collaborations are underway, it is important to monitor the value created for the parties concerned. Tracking value is a way of minimizing risk by catching problems before they get out of hand. It can also be seen as part of the control element of B2B

Box 7.5 Voices

Relationship-specific risks

This is how one Indian manager describes the problems he has experienced with the culture prevalent in organizations seeking to purchase offshore IT outsourcing: 'The Asia-Pacific clients do not accept collective requirements gathering' at the early stages of a relationship. He goes on to explain that purchase decisions 'are still largely based on the lowest bid. Clients are overcautious regarding agreements. . . . [They] try to cover everything under the original [contract] and would not easily sign a "change request". They have an attitude of haggling with service providers.'

Source: Aundhe and Mathew (2009)

marketing planning (see Chapter Six). Carrying out regular progress reviews with customers can reinforce each relationship's value. It can also provide opportunities for suppliers to see where they might increase the value of what is currently being offered. Moreover, if the supplier has a detailed understanding of an IOR's profitability, this helps them to handle customers seeking discounts.

For this approach to be effective, appropriate measures need to be in place, such as sales and profitability levels, as well as gauging the impact of strategies on the supplier's costs and on the customer's satisfaction levels. To get a holistic view of how the IOR is progressing, these yardsticks can be combined with a focus on intermediate outcomes and activities, e.g. the number of projects in the pipeline or the strength of relationships with a customer firm's senior management. If objectives are not being met, the organizations have the chance to rethink their strategies on an ongoing basis, rather than reach the end of a project only to find that resources have been inappropriately invested.

Control initiatives can support marketing strategies throughout relationships in the distribution channel. For example, Hancock et al (2005) report that a consumer goods manufacturer decided to combine its detailed end-consumer research with predictive, industry-wide analysis and inputs from its retail and wholesale customers. This enabled the manufacturer to track the impact of its activities on each of its organizational customers' target consumer segments. Within a year of acting on the results of this monitoring approach, the manufacturer's net profits increased by over 10%.

Strategies for SMEs

While lacking in some of the capital resources of larger corporations, SMEs also have many possibilities to develop successful B2B strategies. They can make the most of opportunities in their relationships by focusing on the development of capabilities that are seen as valuable by customers. A study of firms in Denmark's metal industry (Philipsen et al, 2008) shows how, since small suppliers do not always possess a large range of customer relationships in their portfolios to choose from, marketing managers must categorize their relationship-building options carefully. By focusing on one type of supply offering, SMEs have been able to take better and quicker decisions over investments in capability when opportunities with customers arise. Three types of supply are identified in the study:

1. *The first is classified as standard supply*, where basic products or services can be offered from a catalogue or list. This involves an internal managerial focus on technical skills in production.

2. *The second, traditional supply*, means that products are developed from customer specifications, and requires the careful management of information and component flows between buyer and seller.

3. *The third is termed partnership supply*, and involves a similar set of managerial skills as the traditional style, but with the additional need for careful management of relationships and collaboration.

SMEs perform best when they consistently adopt one of the above approaches. However, one drawback is that some firms tend to settle into 'comfort zones' as a result of always dealing with the same type of customer. Several Danish examples from Philipsen et al's (2008) study illustrate these SME B2B strategies. In each case, you should remember that these strategies only work because the offering of each firm is valued by its customers:

- Standard supply has been adopted by a firm known as BMWorks, a machine manufacturer in the arena of cutting and punching to produce standard components in various metals. Most of the firm's offerings are components made to stock and sold in simple transactions via the company catalogue. Like the textile machinery case firm at the end of Chapter One, BMWorks has gained a competitive edge by offering details of its technical capabilities, including information about the suppliers of its machines, to customers.

- JGL engineering makes a variety of parts in aluminium, brass, and other materials, and takes a traditional supply approach. It mainly manufactures components based on customers' drawings, but does not actively contribute to customers' product development. The firm tends to compete on price and has built its success on good relationships with customers' purchasing and production departments.

- Partnership supply is the style used by IntercityCom who produce communication systems for public transport. The firm is an active partner in product development with its customers, which include bus and train manufacturers. Relationships are characterized by a high level of informality with several different departments in IntercityCom's customer organizations.

SMEs in China are also making effective strategic marketing decisions in business markets (Tang et al, 2007). These firms account for almost 70% of the nation's overall employment, so it is vital that they perform well. A particularly important group of SMEs is small construction firms, which are operating in one of the fastest growing industries in China. Although many building requirements are fairly basic (e.g. apartments with bare walls and concrete floors), there is an increasing demand from property developers for better-designed apartments with a higher standard of finish. This means that construction companies which focus on innovation appear to outperform their competitors. Improved business performance is associated with long-term strategies of differentiation as well as higher R&D spending as

Box 7.6 Food for thought

Strategy issues for Minority Business Enterprises

Supplier diversity is an increasingly important element of S/DCM in the US. It involves the buying of goods and services from businesses owned and operated by minority groups, including blacks, Asians, Hispanics, and Native Americans (as defined by the US National Minority Supplier Development Council – MSDC). Such suppliers are termed Minority Business Enterprises (MBEs), many of which are relatively small. Fortunately, buyers' strategies are starting to reflect the belief that supplier diversity may help these buyers' organizations build their customer base. A vice president from IBM says, 'We want our supplier base to look like our employee base and the market we're trying to attract,' and a Johnson Controls director acknowledges, 'It gives us a competitive advantage.' Despite this goodwill, marketing managers of MBEs should not be complacent. Their firms' success depends on their ability to develop continually their knowledge and skills, and to build strategic alliances amongst themselves and with their business customers. The contribution of intermediary organizations such as local supplier councils can be crucial in helping MBEs to gain a competitive edge, especially with larger corporations.

Source: Adobor and McMullen (2007); www.nmsdcus.org

a proportion of sales, both of which lead to the development of new housing products that better serve market needs. For more on new product development (NPD) in B2B marketing, see Chapter Eight.

Box 7.6 highlights another group of SMEs, those run by minority groups in the US. Despite some open-minded purchasing policies from their business customers, these firms still need to think hard about their marketing strategy. Note how the firms' relationships with other organizations in their customer and supplier networks play a major part in their success.

7.4 Issues of Implementation

This final section flags up the frustrating fact for marketing planners that, despite their best-laid plans, strategies can still be difficult to implement. These difficulties typically stem from the trickiest resource of all to manage, the human resource. As we have noted before in this book, it is people that make decisions in B2B markets, and it is people who can get things wrong, whether a seemingly logical plan is in place or not.

The credibility of the marketing function

We began Chapter Six by highlighting the importance of a marketing orientation, and we return to this issue now. A lack of marketing orientation is perhaps the biggest stumbling block still to be found in many organizations selling to business markets. It is not unusual, for instance, for engineers to be promoted by a well-meaning CEO to marketing roles, but to be given no training in marketing. This is bad news for the firm and highly unfair to the managers concerned, who are likely to struggle to convince their colleagues of the need for investment in marketing planning activities. In fact, some organizations offer workshops in accountability to marketers to help them overcome these problems (e.g. B2B Marketing Events, 2010).

In a firm that has a strong product orientation, for example, a marketing manager may find it hard to get the funds needed to conduct up-to-date market research, something that could be crucial in B2B marketplaces undergoing rapid change. This can happen in both large and small firms: in the former case, marketers may be called 'managers' but find themselves with no place on the board and little influence on strategy; and in the latter, marketing is often an extra role added to the already heavy workload of, say, a product designer or an administrator.

What this can boil down to is that the marketing function is not taken seriously as a profession, unlike R&D, accounting, production, etc. This lack of status can have consequences for inter-functional relations within the organization. For instance, sales people may feel threatened by passing on customer information to a marketing department who they do not trust, while marketing in turn may feel powerless to gain access to this vital data. Power tussles may also develop between R&D departments and marketing over who should make final decisions about NPD commercialization.

Ideally, when a firm selects a particular business marketing strategy, decisions should be made at every level and in every functional area of the organization to support that strategy. If this does not occur, then there is a danger of inconsistencies occurring across key business processes. This all too often happens between marketing and sales, for instance where marketing intends a selective, high-price, low-volume approach to be taken in the launch of a new product, but the sales force adopts a mass-market, price-cutting approach in order to boost volumes. This sort of conflict can undermine the positioning that the firm is trying to communicate to the marketplace and the rest of the network (Strahle et al, 1996).

Planning and internal relationships

Organizations wishing to adopt a market orientation need to have adequate spanning processes that link internal processes with the customer. As you will see in Chapter Eight, an example of a spanning process is NPD since it links market requirements with internal processes like manufacturing. If internal processes are well managed, and any conflicts between functions such as purchasing and production are resolved, then the firm should benefit. Thus, it is logical to extend collaborative strategies not only to external actors such as suppliers, customers, and rivals but also to internal functions/departments which are in exchange relationships with each other. To make this happen, it may be necessary for senior managers to facilitate partnerships between different functional areas of their organization by encouraging them to view each other as 'customers' and 'suppliers' within the notional boundaries of the firm.

Figure 7.7 suggests some ways in which different functional areas might provide inputs to the strategic decisions taken by a B2B marketing department. Note the wide range of exemplar contributions from 'outside' the immediate marketing department that can facilitate marketing decisions. For instance, consider that while the marketing manager may be focused on meeting a customer's exact requirements over the immediate shipping of made-to-order products, they should not forget that manufacturing tends to be concerned with producing goods at the lowest cost and so will often want little customization and low inventories of raw materials. Marketing managers may therefore have to advise sales people of the need to negotiate compromises between what customers want and what manufacturing can deliver. Of course, if market research shows that the competition can deliver what the marketer's

Purchasing Dept	• e.g. Monitors alternatives in the supply environment • e.g. Evaluates partnerships with key suppliers
Production Dept	• e.g. Monitors quality of incoming component parts • e.g. Forecasts cost of manufacturing various volumes
R&D Dept	• e.g. Supports new product development • e.g. Assesses need for external expertise
Finance Dept	• e.g. Calculates desired ROI on new products • e.g. Evaluates viability of marketing budget
Accounts Dept	• e.g. Monitors settlement of customer accounts • e.g. Provides cost history of each market segment
Logistics Dept	• e.g. Ensures responsive deliveries to customers • e.g. Maintains good relations with distributors
Customer Service Dept	• e.g. Monitors customer complaints & feedback • e.g. Provides after sales service & training

Figure 7.7 Functional inputs to B2B marketing planning

firm cannot, then it may become necessary to advise senior management accordingly about the potential need to invest in changes to the firm's production processes.

Similarly, determining price is not done entirely by the marketing department since, although marketers will wish to reflect the value a product delivers to customers in its price, it will be the finance department's responsibility to manage the organization's cash flow and profitability. Moreover, the purchasing department will need marketing management to present the customer's definition of quality (e.g. in terms of the type of components an OEM's customers expect to see in the assembled product) in a way that can enhance the purchasing process in a cost-effective manner. Some scholars, such as Sheth et al (2009), even argue that integrating marketing with purchasing is inevitable as a result of a shift from product- to capability-focused commerce (or the provision of 'solutions' – as in the end-of-chapter case study ahead). The list of functional departments in Figure 7.7 thus reinforces the need for B2B marketers to work with colleagues from across the management spectrum.

Some ways in which an organization can try to ensure that functional integration occurs in their B2B marketing efforts are listed below, after Hutt (1995). These approaches are summarized in Figure 7.8.

• Making clear strategic decisions: Although we have pointed out that reaching a single 'best' strategic decision is particularly difficult in business networks, once a direction has been adopted for the organization, clarity in implementation is important. Problems can surface when there is a lack of decisiveness amongst senior marketing managers and an inability to communicate any decisions internally. Without clarity, marketing and sales investments can be wasted, and relationships with customers damaged, if these two key functional areas pursue contrasting strategic directions.

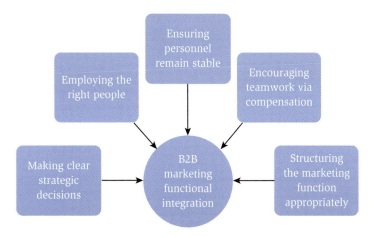

Figure 7.8 Ensuring functional integration in B2B marketing

- Employing the right people in marketing: B2B marketers need to be acutely aware of broader functional issues, probably even more so than their B2C counterparts. It is also important for those people brought into the marketing function to possess good communication and analytical skills. Even more important, however, is a deep knowledge of customer needs, typically acquired during sales or technical development work. In some cultures, however, the 'right' person may not necessarily be the most appropriately qualified – see Box 7.7. Are these sorts of business practices really fair or, more importantly, are they effective? The study reported here suggests not.

- Ensuring personnel remain stable: Relationships between organizations, and between the people representing those organizations, take time to build. So moving key staff

Box 7.7 Food for thought

Personal business networks

A study undertaken amongst business people in France has shown that there is often pressure to hire or promote managers at French firms based on their social connections. This is especially prevalent amongst people who have attended the nation's elite civil service training schools. Unfortunately, companies run by former civil servants who have maintained their links to government underperform those run by managers with private-sector backgrounds. Moreover, because established organizations are cautious about who they do business with, it appears that these traditional networks make it hard for new firms to emerge in France. One of the study's authors says that this means 'You often see that successful young firms are business-to-consumer rather than business-to-business.' He believes that online networks make collecting information on firms and their employees easier and more transparent, but if a manager wants to influence an important decision, he claims, 'It's still the old networks that really count.'

Source: The Economist (2009)

around the organization too rapidly can destabilize your firm's attempts at building long-term relations, externally with key customers and internally with other functional areas.

- Encouraging teamwork via compensation: For instance, if marketing managers have contracts with pay incentives based on contribution margins, they should work more closely with the sales force. Similarly, if sales people are rewarded for building relationships with clients that can benefit the entire selling organization, then they may balance their efforts at driving sales volumes with attempts to gain vital market information (see also Chapter Twelve).

- Structuring the marketing function appropriately: The B2B marketing planner might adopt a centralized functional organizational structure where marketing staff are classed by their roles (e.g. sales, product development, marketing communications, etc.); or take a market-orientated approach designed around geographical or product-related characteristics that help marketing teams serve their customers more closely. These choices can be crucial to meeting the needs of the marketplace.

So who'd be a B2B marketing manager? It's a tough job, as Box 7.8 suggests: in order to present a coherent relational strategy to customers, the marketing manager of the case firm here has to ensure as much consistency exists as possible between the senior management's perspective of the marketplace and that held by the sales team.

As well as maintaining internal cohesion, consistency is also necessary throughout the supply/demand chain. Firms operating in business markets are increasingly reliant

---

Box 7.8 Voices
Managing B2B marketing in the animal feeds sector

Note how these two managers describe their firm's activities in the arena of animal feed supply where the firm's route to market consists of specialist merchants selling on to farmers. In both quotes, one from the notional top and one from the bottom of the management hierarchy, you can see how much uncertainty there can be when attempting to plan in B2B markets.

The first speaker, the managing director of a feeds manufacturer, suggests that planning for his firm's supply chain is not easy: 'We're very much a hand-to-mouth supply chain, in that our merchants have tended to de-stock, and farmers are not reaching very far forward, so we're tending to order now for yesterday. So it does take a lot of toing and froing to establish what the true needs are and how you can satisfy them.'

The second quote comes from an area sales representative from the same firm, and shows how staff in the 'front line' view the relationship management task: 'The relationship is good, but if you dug deeper, I'd suggest that when [merchant customers] are on the phone, you're thinking, what are they going to complain about next? Is it an order or a problem?'

Source: Ellis et al (2005)

on their own suppliers and distributors, and even their customers (e.g. for inputs to the NPD process), in order to implement marketing strategies. Moreover, B2B marketing almost always means more than just making and keeping a single promise to your customer. Instead, both the offering and its implementation will evolve over the duration of the relationship.

The end-of-chapter case study on cinema ticketing management systems highlights a number of issues that may need to be considered when formulating B2B marketing strategies for international market entry in the service sector. By addressing topics that we have discussed in Chapters Six and Seven, it shows how relationship management decisions need to go hand in hand with more conventional marketing planning approaches like segmentation, targeting, and positioning.

Summary

The key points to take from this chapter are as follows:

- How to evaluate the possibilities open to B2B marketing managers when choosing how to position their organization in the marketplace.

- The potential benefits and limitations of B2B branding as a strategic approach at both the company and product level.

- What network-related perspectives a manager should be aware of when making strategic decisions.

- How to relate B2B marketing strategy to the value sought by your firm and your customers, and, indeed, their customers.

- The problems that need to be overcome in order to implement marketing plans successfully.

- The importance of the internal partnerships that must be forged by B2B marketing managers if strategic planning is to be effective.

Discussion questions

1. Why is it so important to achieve a distinctive competitive positioning for supplying organizations? What are some of the ways this can be done?

2. How would you respond to a colleague in your manufacturing firm who claimed at a board meeting that 'branding in B2B markets is a waste of our valuable resources'?

3. Why is a network vision necessary for a manager attempting to determine a B2B marketing strategy?

4. 'SMEs will always be at a disadvantage compared with larger corporations when trying to design effective business marketing strategies.' Debate this statement.

5. What sorts of internal relationships might it be necessary for a B2B marketing manager to maintain?

Case study

Vista Entertainment Solutions Ltd – Market Entry Strategies for India

Michel Rod, Carleton University, Ottawa, Canada and Sarena Saunders, Victoria University of Wellington, Wellington, New Zealand

Introduction

Vista Entertainment Solutions (Vista) is a New Zealand-based joint venture between a management company owned by some of its key staff, and Village Sky City Cinemas. Vista develops and supplies specialized software to organizational customers in the entertainment industry, especially cinemas, both multiplex and independent. This software enables cinemas to run virtually all of their different business activities (selling tickets, paying royalties, and the sale of refreshments) from one suite of software. The company employs 25 staff, and its software is presently sold in 23 countries.

India is the second-largest cinema market in the world, after the US. With a population of 1 billion, India has 12,000 individual cinemas (mostly family-owned, and almost entirely run on a manual basis). The development of the digital movie format has meant that new releases can be simultaneously released throughout the country through a proportion of these individual cinemas (around 3,000), but at only 70% of the original resolution and sound quality. This paved the way for the rapid development of large multiplex cinemas in the mid 2000s. These developments made India seem like an attractive potential marketplace for Vista, though determining the best strategies for entering this challenging market (read on to discover some of the hassles of this business environment) was crucial.

Vista's growth in India

Vista first entered the Indian market in 2000 through Village Sky City Cinema's overseas connections. About the same time, a new Indian company, Bigtree Entertainment, approached Vista. Bigtree was owned by three young MBA graduates seeking to develop their own business who believed that automated cinema ticketing systems would be a future growth area. In late 2000, Bigtree became Vista's agents in India, a role which continues today. Initially, Bigtree acted simply as a client of Vista's by purchasing Vista technology, but then moved into more of a partner relationship. Bigtree set about automating and linking up cinemas, by assisting Vista to customize its ticketing product for the Indian market and by acting as a value-added reseller of the Vista product in India (necessary because of the government regulations with respect to ticketing and reporting).

After injections of capital by various investors, Bigtree was able to establish the nation's first call centre for cinema ticket sales, linking eight larger urban centres and 180 cinemas. In these eight large markets, people wishing to see a movie could call up and order their tickets, after which the tickets would be delivered to their homes and they would pay cash upon delivery. This system is necessary as government bureaucracy is such that there is a need to account for all ticket sales generated, to ensure that the requisite taxes are being paid. However, Vista has been able to turn this complexity to its advantage by being ready to adapt its software to the needs of clients in meeting these bureaucratic requirements. Today, Bigtree still maintains its full service call centre and now a Web-based ticketing business and, in partnership with Vista, also provides integrated software packages to assist with all aspects of running multiplex cinemas, including ticketing, concessions, and office management.

As of 2006, there were 80 cinema multiplexes in India, and this number was forecast to grow to 350 to 500 within the following four years. Bigtree/Vista technology is present in 90% of these multiplexes. Today, any film released in India generates approximately 30% of its revenues from multiplexes. This is expected to increase to 75% by 2010. Bigtree is now looking to work with Vista to expand into the rest of the digital movie release segment amongst individual cinemas.

Success factors

The appointment and maintenance of Bigtree as Vista's agent were perhaps the most critical strategy that the firm has taken in India. All Vista's sales to India are made through Bigtree. The enthusiasm, commitment, and technical skills of Bigtree have been essential to Vista's ongoing success in the Indian market. The three founders have become good personal friends of the key Vista staff. They have also become thoroughly knowledgeable about the technical aspects of the Vista software. They carry out all the servicing that is required in the Indian market. Vista says that without Bigtree, it could not have bridged the huge gulf of understanding with respect to the intricacies of the market, cultural sensitivities, and the numerous regulatory hurdles, or been able to deal with the associated 'red tape'. Bigtree has worked hard in lobbying the federal and state authorities on relevant matters. Without this relationship, there would have been major cost problems in trying to deal with such issues as seconded or visiting New Zealand-based staff.

Another major success factor for Vista in India has been its willingness to adapt its products to suit the requirements of individual customers. For example, Vista has developed its software to work with the automatic ticket-vending machines now appearing in some Indian cinemas and has been ready to lower the price to encourage volume in what it sees as a market with huge potential. While all its main research and development has been carried out in New Zealand (and always will be), Vista has had one of its software modules further enhanced in India and the company is prepared to consider further such modifications as the market develops.

The company has not had any significant issues with intellectual property as India has some strong laws relating to information technology. Vista also notes that liberalization trends in the Indian economy have definitely been of assistance to its business there. For instance, the relaxation of foreign currency regulations has made it much easier for the company to be paid directly. The chief executive officer visits the market at least annually, often in association with cinema industry conferences, and while there will seek to meet both existing clients and prospective new ones. However efficient the local agent is, customers still like to meet the 'face' behind the product. The company also brings all its overseas agents together at least once every 18 months or so.

Bigtree has now built a good business from its involvement with Vista, employing 20 staff on Vista work alone, with a further 50 working in the call centre largely relating to the Vista products. A big success factor for Bigtree was having the innovative Vista product to work with, as well as the assistance of Vista's chief software architect, who spent 25 days in India working with Bigtree to customize the product to meet Indian requirements. An additional success factor relates to the common language spoken between New Zealand and India, enabling the coding of software to be much easier than it is, for example, in China.

Bigtree attributes the success of the partnership to mutual trust. Vista has full trust in Bigtree's local knowledge and Bigtree's founders have complete trust in Vista's technological capability. Bigtree's owners like working with similar-sized New Zealand companies because they feel that success lies in each partner feeling as important as the other. They believe that partnerships work better when there are no power/size asymmetries – when there is 'a marriage of equals', as one manager put it.

A barrier to the development of Vista's trade with India has been the much higher degree of regulation of the cinema industry than in New Zealand. State governments, in particular, derive significant revenues from an entertainment tax on every cinema ticket sold and employ armies of inspectors to pursue that funding. Complex requirements, often varying between states, have to be dealt with in this process. Vista agrees that Indian business people are very hard negotiators and will argue every point of a contract. Once the discussion is completed, however, negotiations are final. Bigtree uses the analogy of doing business in India as driving along an old, dug-up, detoured road, but one which, if you persevere, will ultimately get you to your destination. Key lessons learnt by Vista in the Indian market focus on the importance of choosing an excellent agent, being flexible in relation to meeting the particular needs of the market, and recognizing that there are many differences in India that New Zealand companies need to adjust to.

What next for Vista?

Vista now has a significant proportion of the software market for multiplex cinemas in India and its brand is well recognized. With almost all of the regulatory requirements now addressed, it anticipates further expansion into the Indian market. For instance, its Indian customers generally start with just a few of the 15 modules available under the Vista system. Once they become accustomed to those, they may then wish to buy further modules. Moreover, existing customers often open more cinemas. In addition, the company has developed and just launched a new product especially geared towards the thousands of single-screen cinemas, which are going to get a boost from the advent of digital cinema. In future, the company imagines that because of its sound reputation in the cinema market in India, it could expand into other areas of the entertainment industry.

Source: Next Stop India (2008)

Case study questions

1. List the factors which an analysis of the cinema business environment in India in 2000 would probably have suggested as opportunities and threats for Vista. What segments did the firm decide to target, and with what main strategies?

2. How would you describe the market positioning of Vista? What activities has the firm undertaken to ensure that this positioning is valued by its customers and then communicated to them?

3. What B2B marketing management skills has Bigtree shown in handling its relationships: (*a*) 'upstream' with Vista; (*b*) 'downstream' with the cinema/multiplex-owning customers; and (*c*) with the wider business network in India?

Further Reading

Baraldi, E., Brennan, R., Harrison, D., Tunisini, A., & Zolkiewski, J. (2007) Strategic Thinking and the IMP Approach: A Comparative Analysis, Industrial Marketing Management, 36, pp 879–94

This paper notes that the overall contribution to the strategy literature by the IMP Interaction approach has been relatively small. It compares the IMP approach with five major schools of thought in strategy (including the rational planning approach and the resource-based view), noting where they differ and suggesting where IMP studies can yield insights into the strategy process.

Dadzie, K. O., Johnston, W. J., & Pels, J. (2008) Business-to-Business Marketing Practices in West Africa, Argentina and the United States, Journal of Business & Industrial Marketing, 23 (2) pp 115–23

These authors extend an ongoing international study of contemporary B2B marketing management practices by looking at some under-explored national contexts and comparing them with the US. They show how most companies questioned practise both transactional and relationship marketing simultaneously, although some firms in Argentina and West Africa do not practise marketing very intensely and rarely use database marketing.

Harrison, D. & Prenkert, F. (2009) Network Strategising Trajectories within a Planned Strategy Process, Industrial Marketing Management, 38, pp 662–70

This article uses the IMP group's ARA Model to analyse how the effects of network connections are considered within a strategic planning process. The analysis results in three overlapping 'network strategizing trajectories' revolving around actors, resources, and activities, and brings a dynamic process dimension to the study of network strategy.

Hutt, M. D. & Speh, T. W. (2007) Undergraduate Education: The Implications of Cross-Functional Relationships in Business Marketing – The Skills of High-Performing Managers, Journal of Business-to-Business Marketing, 14 (1), pp 75–94

A paper which explores the collaborative skills that successful B2B marketing managers should possess, and the resulting implications for the teaching of the subject. It stresses that students need to be taught the importance of relational skills to manage across functions in order to create value for customers. In providing these insights, the authors claim that a B2B marketing course can add much to the standard marketing curriculum.

Kalafatis, S. P., Tsogas, M. T., & Blankson, C. (2000) Positioning Strategies in Business Markets, Journal of Business & Industrial Marketing, 15 (6), pp 416–37

This article suggests that, although market positioning is largely determined by 'hard' criteria (e.g. product quality) and relationship-building factors (e.g. personal contact), other considerations such as company structures (e.g. geographical coverage), breadth of offerings, and degree of integration (i.e. location in the distribution chain) also play an important part.

References

Adobor, H. & McMullen, R. (2007) Supplier Diversity and Supply Chain Management: A Strategic Approach, Business Horizons, 50, pp 219–29

Anderson, J. C., Narus, J. A. & van Rossum, W. (2006) Customer Value Propositions in Business Markets, Harvard Business Review, March, pp 90–9

Aundhe, M. D. & Mathew, S. K. (2009) Risks in Offshore IT Outsourcing: A Service Provider Perspective, European Management Journal, 27, pp 418–28

B2B Marketing Events (2010) Marketing Effectiveness through Measurement – One-Day Workshop, as publicized online at www.b2bm.biz, accessed January 2010

Balakrishnan, A. (2007) Specialist Firms Show even Bleach can be Hi-Tech, The Guardian, 4 September, p 24

Bogomolova, S. & Romaniuk, J. (2009) Brand Defection in a Business-to-Business Financial Service, Journal of Business Research, 62, pp 291–6

Business Week (2008) 18 August, p 80

Christopher, M. (1992) Logistics and Supply Chain Management, FT Pitman, London

Davis, D. F., Golicic, S. L., & Marquardt, A. J. (2008) Branding a B2B Service: Does a Brand Differentiate a Logistics Service Provider? Industrial Marketing Management, 37, pp 218–27

Economist (The) (2009) Joining the Club: LinkedIn v Freemasons, 27 June, pp 14–15

Ellis, N., Higgins, M., & Jack, G. (2005) (De)constructing the Market for Animal Feeds: A Discursive Study, Journal of Marketing Management, 21, pp 117–46

Glain, S. G. (2003) Dreaming of Damascus: Arab Voices from a Region in Turmoil, John Murray, London

Gordon, G. L., Calantone, R. J., & di Benedetto, C.A. (1993) Brand Equity in the Business-to-Business Sector: An Exploratory Study, Journal of Product & Brand Management, 2 (3), pp 4–16

Hancock, M. Q., John, R. H., and Wojcik, P. J. (2005) Better B2B Selling, online at www.mckinseyquarterly.con – accessed July 2005

Henneberg, S. C., Mouzas, S., & Naudé, P. (2006) Network Pictures: Concepts and Representations, European Journal of Marketing, 40 (3/4), pp 408–29

Hutt, M. (1995) Cross-Functional Relationships in Marketing, Journal of the Academy of Marketing Science, 23 (4), pp 351–7

Kotler, P. & Pfoertsch, W. (2007) Being Known or Being One of Many: The Need for Brand Management for B2B Companies, Journal of Business & Industrial Marketing, 22 (6), pp 357–62

McQuiston, D. H. (2004) Successful Branding of a Commodity Product: The Case of RAEX LASER Steel, Industrial Marketing Management, 33, pp 345–54

Möller, K. K. & Halinen, A. (1999) Business Relationships and Networks: Managerial Challenges of Network Era, Industrial Marketing Management, 28, pp 413–27

Morrison, D. P. (2001) B2B Branding: Avoiding the Pitfalls, Marketing Management, September–October, pp 30–4

Mudambi, S. (2002) Branding Importance in Business-to-Business Markets: Three Buyer Clusters, Industrial Marketing Management, 31, pp 525–33

Naylor, J., Hawkins, N., & Wilson, C. (2001) Benchmarking Marketing in an SME: The Case of an Italian Kitchen Furniture Manufacturer, Marketing Review, 1, pp 325–39

Next Stop India: A Guide for New Zealand Business (2008) A Report to the Asia New Zealand Foundation from the School of Marketing and International Business, Victoria University of Wellington

Ohnemus, L. (2009) B2B Branding: A Financial Burden for Stakeholders? Business Horizons, 52, pp 159–66

Penttinen, E. & Palmer, J. (2007) Improving Firm Positioning through Enhanced Offerings and Buyer–Seller Relationships, Industrial Marketing Management, 36, pp 865–71

Philipsen, K., Damgaard, T., & Johnsen, R. E. (2008) Suppliers' Opportunity Enactment through the Development of Valuable Capabilities, Journal of Business & Industrial Marketing, 23 (1) pp 23–34

Sheth, J. N., Sharma, A., & Iyer, G. R. (2009) Why Integrating Purchasing with Marketing is both Inevitable and Beneficial, Industrial Marketing Management, 38, pp 552–64

Strahle, W., Spiro, R. L., & Acito, F. (1996) Marketing and Sales: Alignment and Functional Implementation, Journal of Personal Selling and Sales Management, 14 (Winter), pp 1–20

Tang, Y., Wang, P., & Zhang, Y. (2007) Marketing and Business Performance of Construction SMEs in China, Journal of Business & Industrial Marketing, 22 (2) pp 118–25

Winch, G. M. (2008) Internationalisation Strategies in Business-to-Business Services: The Case of Architectural Practices, Service Industries Journal, 28 (1), pp 1–13

Part Four
Business Marketing Programmes

Part One: The Organizational Marketing Context

1. The Significance of B2B Marketing
- Significance of B2B Marketing
- Supply/Demand Chains
- Organizational Markets
- Significance of Relationships & Networks
- Supply Chain Ethics

2. Organizational Buying Behaviour
- Types of Markets
- Organizational & Consumer Buyer Behaviour
- Influences on Demand
- Organizational Decision-Making

Part Two: Inter-Organizational Relationships & Networks

3. Inter-Organizational Relationships
- Market & Relational Exchange
- CRM
- Partnerships & Alliances
- How IORs 'Work' in Different Contexts

4. Marketing Channels & Supply Chains
- Structure & Role of Channels
- Flows & Blockages in Channels
- From Channels to Chains
- Marketing Logistics

5. Industrial Networks
- The Interaction Approach
- From Channels & Chains to Networks
- Learning from the Industrial Network View

Part Three: Business Marketing Planning

6. B2B Marketing Planning & Analysis
- Planning & S/DCM
- The Planning Process
- Situation Analysis
- Sources & Assessing Market Potential
- B2B Market Segmentation

7. B2B Strategies & Implementation
- Market Positioning
- B2B Branding
- Making Strategy Decisions
- Issues of Implementation

> These 6 chapters can also be effectively combined as the 'marketing mix'

Part Four: Business Marketing Programmes

8. Business Products
- Classifying Business Products
- Managing Business Products
- New Product Development

9. Business Services
- Classifying Business Services
- Characteristics of Business Services
- B2B Services Marketing Management

10. Value & Pricing
- Value in Organizational Markets
- Making Pricing Decisions
- B2B Pricing Strategies (incl. Web-based activities)

11. Marketing Communications
- Communication Strategies
- Elements of the Communications Mix
- Relative Effectiveness of B2B Media (incl. the Internet)

12. Personal Selling & Sales Management
- Personal Selling in B2B Markets
- Organizing the Sales Force
- Key Account Management (KAM)

Chapter 8
Business Products

Introduction & Learning Objectives

The marketing mix issues that form the last five chapters of this book (as well as the 'place' P, or distribution, considerations of Chapter Four) are crucial in positioning each product line that an organization intends to market. In this chapter, we begin by looking at the management of what is probably the best-known 'P' of the marketing mix, the product itself. The exchange of products between firms is, after all, the prime reason that B2B markets exist. Although business services will be discussed to a limited extent in this chapter, for a full explanation of the nature of services and key elements of the management of services in organizational markets, see Chapter Nine. In fact, Chapters Eight and Nine should really be read in close conjunction.

Product management in business markets, especially new product development, is characterized by the need for the B2B marketer to handle a series of internal and external relationships (see Chapter Three). The case in Box 8.1 shows how innovation at the 'top' of the supply/demand chain in furniture manufacture can benefit all members of the supply chain. Thus, the managers in Cargill's marketing department will require a good understanding of the needs of firms that extend beyond the company's immediate customers, as well as an appreciation of the competencies of Cargill's own production department.

Box 8.1 Mini case
Investments and rewards from new product development

The Minneapolis-based manufacturer of cushioning material, Carpenter Co., has introduced a type of foam cushioning made with a soy-based polyol supplied by Cargill, the international provider of agricultural products and commodity processing services that we were introduced to in Chapter One. Polyols are chemical compounds derived from natural vegetable oils such as soybean oil. They help flexible polyurethane foam manufacturers like Carpenter reduce their environmental footprint by replacing petrochemical-derived foam components. Cargill have spent four years researching and bringing this product to the global market. Such is the supplier's commitment to this technology that it announced the opening of a $5.5 million polyols R&D facility in 2007, as well as the scaling-up of its manufacturing capabilities with the construction of a $22 million polyol plant in Chicago.

The adoption of Cargill's polyols by Carpenter allows it to produce consistent quality products without sacrificing end-user comfort, and means its organizational customers do not have to reengineer their processes, according to the firm's President, Stan Yukevich. The new cushioning is available in a wide range of firmness and densities, and has the added benefit to customers of being fully recyclable. Carpenter's website is proud to proclaim its 'eco-friendly solutions'. The firm sells its products to organizations in the furniture-making sector, such as La-Z-Boy and a variety of bedding manufacturers.

Source: www.cargill.com; www.carpenter.com

Chapter Aims

After completing this chapter, you should be able to:

- Recognise ways of classifying business products
- Appreciate how to manage business products, including what are sometimes called 'commodities'
- Understand some new product development (NPD) issues in organizational markets
- Consider how a broader network perspective can be brought to product management decisions.

8.1 Classifying Business Products

Fundamentally, B2B marketing managers must recognize that organizational buyers are focused on helping their firms (or institutions) to increase sales or lower costs, often via improving efficiency or performance, and sometimes by purchasing cheaper goods or services. It is important for marketing managers to understand exactly how the buying organization intends to use the products that they are trying to sell, and thus what attributes are likely to be the most important to them. Some firms try to capture the essence of their offering via the slogans used in their marketing communications – see Box 8.2.

Box 8.2 Voices

Conveying product quality in a slogan

TECO (Vietnam) Electric and Machinery Co Ltd is a manufacturer of motors and a subsidiary of the TECO Group of Taiwan. It has invested $4 million in synchronous production systems and claims its products to be of 'international standard'. The firm's general director, Mr Wang Ching, is quoted as saying, 'TECO owns technological advancements, high standards of quality control, and superior services.' The corporate slogans that Mr Ching's company displays internally and to external stakeholders include: 'Quality First, Technical Base and Service Utmost' and 'Renovation to Create New Visions, Innovation to Meet the Future'.

Source: Trung (2007); www.tecomotor.com.tw

Of course, it is essential that the firm 'delivers' on its claims, otherwise such slogans will not be believed by potential customers. Nevertheless, even given some slightly clumsy translation, you can see how important product issues are to TECO's success. The significance of products, support services, and innovation to B2B marketers will be explored in the rest of this chapter.

Business product classifications

There is a huge variety of products offered for exchange in B2B markets, so how can marketers make sense of them all? Figure 8.1 provides a helpful way of classifying offerings for the business market in terms of how they are used by customers, particularly in a manufacturing-orientated context. Note how the offerings that are integral to the manufacturing production process itself have been classed as input products: this represents the 'flow' of these goods 'into' the firm from upstream suppliers (see Chapter Four). Foundation products, some of which can represent significant capital investments, tend to be used to perform the manufacturing process, as well as being utilized in administrative tasks; while facilitating supplies tend to support the process or take the form of business services. They are often termed MRO goods, meaning maintenance, repair, and operational items.

Facilitating supplies in the area of business finance are illustrated by the products offered by General Electric who, in addition to technology and energy infrastructure products, provide commercial loans, operating leases, and fleet management programmes (www.ge.com). An example of a foundation product is the printing machinery sold by firms like Duoyuan Digital Press Technology Industries of China. This Beijing-based company makes medium- and large-sized presses for customer organizations printing leaflets, newspapers, and packaging materials (Dekkers, 2009). B2B input goods, including raw materials and manufactured

Input products

Raw materials
Agricultural products (e.g. soya)   *Natural products* (e.g. copper ore)

Manufactured materials & parts
Component materials (e.g. aluminium)   *Component or OEM parts* (e.g. disc drives)

Foundation products

Capital equipment or installations
Buildings & land (e.g. factories)   *Fixed equipment* (e.g. machine tools)

Accessory equipment
Light factory equipment (e.g. bar code scanners)   *Office equipment* (e.g. furniture)

Facilitating or MRO supplies

Tangible supplies
Operating supplies (e.g. lubricants)   *Maintenance items* (e.g. fastenings)

Business services
Maintenance/repair services (e.g. PC repairs)   *Advisory services* (e.g. consultancy)

Figure 8.1 Classifying offerings in business markets

parts that generate significant levels of global sales for some nations, can be found in a variety of sectors, as you can see in Box 8.3.

Another way of looking at business products is by examining the manufacturing approaches of organizations and their strategies regarding new product development (NPD) – see section 8.3 for more on this key area of B2B marketing. This is particularly interesting in what are sometimes termed 'newly industrializing economies' like South Korea or Taiwan. Leading manufacturers in these economies are thought to expand their competencies along a route described as 'OEM–ODM–OBM' (Hobday, 2000). This means a shift from the simplest original equipment manufacturing (OEM) to the more complex activities involved in original design and manufacturing (ODM), and on to even more committed product development, manufacturing, and marketing in own-brand manufacturing (OBM). The route reflects some organizations' strategies to develop technological capabilities. First, they develop process capability, followed by design capability, and finally new product development capabilities.

Taiwanese organizations have tended to operate in global supply/demand chains via OEM and then ODM strategies, contracting for international brand vendors such as Dell and Hewlett-Packard. More recently, however, Taiwanese firms such as Acer are investing higher levels of resource into brand development (Hsu et al, 2008). The shift in how products are viewed by these manufacturers is significant for their marketing activities. B2B marketers working for OEMs tend to focus their efforts on the standard manufactured parts or assemblies that constitute input products for other manufacturers; ODM marketers need to be aware of more specialist customer needs and how their firm can help design products to be used by those customers in their manufacturing and NPD efforts; while OBM marketers require greater understanding of end-user buying behaviours and the extent to which it is worth their firms pursuing their own NPD strategies.

Some firms will attempt to maintain capabilities at every stage of the route outlined above, as shown in the case study in Box 8.4. Note how this organization appears to be comfortable in marketing existing products to other firms as well as developing its own new products for consumers, thus displaying expertise in B2B and B2C marketing.

Box 8.3 Number crunching

The importance of input products to the Thai economy

Here are two examples:

1. The steering racks for automobiles made by Siam NSK Steering Systems in Thailand are key component parts for car manufacturers based in the US, Europe, China, and India, with 50% of the company's sales coming from overseas.

2. An important raw material in the production of a huge variety of goods, from aircraft and truck tyres to slippers and condoms, is rubber. This agricultural product is a vital export for countries such as Malaysia, Indonesia, and Thailand, where companies like Sri Thang Agro-Industry contribute to bringing in some $2 billion a year to the Thai economy from rubber sales to factories around the world.

Source: The Nation (2007), Hopkins (2005)

Box 8.4 Mini case

The business model of a Taiwanese manufacturer

The experiences gained by some manufacturers in providing OEM or ODM products and services for international brand vendors have allowed them to develop a competitive advantage in manufacturing know-how and often R&D as well. Makalot Industrial Co Ltd was ranked the 71st fastest-growing company in Asia by Business Week in 2006. It manufactures clothing such as underwear, jackets, sportswear, and other knitting and weaving products. The company is also involved in the development of materials, the design of garment styles, and the supplying of information regarding fashion trends and other related services. It supplies a variety of these OEM/ODM products and services to several high-profile customers like Sears, Du Pont, and Wal-Mart. Building on this success, Makalot has established its own brand, opening a flagship retail store in Taipei in 2006. Using its new OBM capacity, the firm intends to continue its B2B production for its organizational clients as well as extend its B2C marketing into China over the next few years.

Source: Wen (2007), www.makalot.com.tw

Product attributes

We have seen how some firms offer a combination of products and service to their customers. To understand how customers might value the different elements of their offerings, it is helpful for B2B marketers to apply notions of 'tangibility' and 'intangibility' to the various products that are exchanged in business markets. Tangibility refers to the physical attributes of a good, something in which a service is obviously relatively lacking. We can relate the idea of tangibility to core products, augmented products, and additional elements such as the services which can support a conventional product. The three main groups of product attributes are depicted in Figure 8.2.

- Tangible core attributes: These represent the basic functional capacity of a product. An example can be found in the ice-cream-making machines produced by the Italian

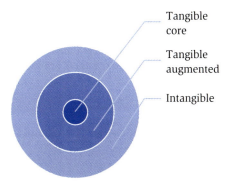

Figure 8.2 Levels of product attributes

manufacturer Carpigiani, which we encountered back in Chapter One (www.carpigiani. com). The firm's website markets one line of its machines as having 'a big production capacity in order to provide ice cream even during busy periods' and an 'electronic control and refrigeration system built taking into account current international standards' (Carpigiani, 2008).

- Tangible augmented attributes: These features are added to core attributes, either to enhance the product's performance or to provide something (such as brand or a design feature) that helps distinguish it from competitors' offerings. For instance, Carpigiani claims that its Holiday S3 SuperTRE product represents a 'powerful electronic machine . . . ideal in order to create specialized offerings where, if requested by the customer, the ice cream can have different toppings'.

- Intangible attributes: These are what customers perceive as enhancing the product, including warranties, financial services, delivery, staff training, and the corporate reputation of the vendor. Such attributes are becoming increasingly important to help sellers differentiate their offerings in the marketplace, especially as so many manufacturers can now provide goods with very similar levels of operational excellence. As well as 'rapid, real-time telephone assistance to resolve technical issues', Carpigiani provides its organizational customers with 'support options' such as personalized luminous display signs and T-shirts for their retail staff.

The above list of attributes represents a way for managers to analyse their firm's offerings at the three different 'levels' depicted in Figure 8.2. This can enable them to gauge which level of attribute best allows them to outperform the competition. For instance, Carpigiani's specialist technical augmentations may be what sets it apart in the eyes of certain customers.

In terms of the intangible level of attributes, we shall explore the implications of service characteristics like intangibility for the marketing of more purely service-orientated 'products' such as legal or financial advice in Chapter Nine.

Commodity products

Understanding the attributes of their product offering and what customers value from them can help marketers trying to cope with supposed 'commodity' markets. As products mature (see the product life cycle discussion in section 8.2) and customers gain extensive experience of using them, offerings over time tend to become undifferentiated in buyers' minds. This can happen in markets for manufactured goods like office stationery or hospital supplies, just as much as in more primary sectors like farm produce or construction materials. At this stage, price very often becomes the sole basis for deciding between competitor offerings: this is the definition of a commodity. To overcome this tendency, B2B marketers must continually seek new ways in which to show customers how their products offer extra value. Despite the common belief that a lot of business organizations just operate in a commodity market, some scholars argue that 'there is no such thing as a commodity. All goods and services are differentiable' (Levitt, 1980, p 83).

So what does Levitt mean by this claim? He cites the example of durum wheat, which is primarily used to make pasta and is often seen as a commodity. However, the price growers receive can vary quite widely, depending on the properties of the wheat, such as its protein, water, and gluten content. By carefully analysing how subtle variations in the core product's attributes provide incremental value to specific customer segments (such as pasta manufacturers for the catering industry) suppliers can find ways to differentiate their offering

(MacMillan and McGrath, 1997). Even when the core products of alternative suppliers are essentially interchangeable, augmenting services still present ways for vendors to position themselves. Thus, before assuming they are in a commodity business, marketers should examine market and internal data (see Chapter Six) to establish what differences exist between their products and those of their competitors.

It can, however, sometimes be expensive to achieve a difference in the core product that customers would perceive as significant. In such cases, it is usually the service element of the offering that can change the way the customer values the firm's offering. For example, the world's number-one supplier of cement, Lafarge, offers logistical support for orders and deliveries so that customers receive their cement at the right time and place, as well as providing demonstrations and training to clients in the characteristics and correct use of the company's cements (www.lafarge.com).

8.2 Managing Business Products

In addition to marketing individual products and services, B2B marketers need to consider the organization's overall portfolio of products. This involves looking at the whole product range of offerings and assessing the contribution that individual goods and services make to the firm's strategic direction. The aim is to enhance the long-term profitability of the total portfolio. Sometimes, trade-offs have to be made when, for example, a particular product may have been superseded by a technological advancement from a competitor, but because of a key customer's preference for the original product, it has to be maintained as part of the portfolio. Similarly, if too many of the firm's products risk becoming obsolete, the resources devoted to maintaining existing products may have to be diverted into new product development (see section 8.3).

A manager must appreciate the impact of such decisions on the overall contribution of the firm's product portfolio. Portfolios comprise four elements:

- Product items: each individual product offering
- Product lines: combinations of individual products (and often services) offered to particular market segments – for an example of product lines marketed to organizations in the healthcare sector, see Box 8.5
- Product mix: the number of product lines
- Depth of line: the number of products offered within each line.

Box 8.5 Mini case

Product lines at Fisher & Paykel Healthcare

Fisher & Paykel Healthcare designs, manufactures, and markets products used in the provision of respiratory care by public and private hospitals. The firm defines its business in terms of three product groups which it sees as quite distinct:

1. *OSA*: solutions for the treatment of Obstructive Sleep Apnoea (OSA), including a range of continuous positive airway pressure (CPAP) units.

---

2. *Respiratory humidification*: a range of heated humidification systems that create, control, and deliver gases at the physiologically normal level to the patient's airways.

3. *Neonatal*: a range of devices, branded 'Tools for New Life' for warming, resuscitation, and respiratory support designed to facilitate babies' breathing immediately after birth.

Source: www.fphcare.com

Viewing a firm's portfolio of products in these different ways allows marketers to allocate more carefully resources to each element of their organization's product offerings. It also helps managers to monitor the return on their investment decisions, decisions which can be substantial and complex, often necessitating setting up separate business units for different parts of the portfolio. For instance, if the firm is aiming to serve many segments, then it may offer a large number of product lines, resulting in an extensive product mix; e.g. The Dow Chemical Company which supplies a host of products for sectors including agriculture, transportation, construction, adhesives, electronics, textiles, furniture, medical, oil, packaging, plastics, and cables (www.dow.com). If, within each segment served, customer needs are highly specialized, the depth of line can also be considerable, e.g. Dow's plastics portfolio comprises a wide range of polyethylene resins, polystyrene, polypropylene, and engineering thermoplastics.

Categorizing product lines

While it is often less costly to develop standardized, mass-produced product lines, the demands of individual customers may make it necessary to customize offerings that maximize value for the buying organization. This will typically involve the commitment of greater resources but the pay-off should be increased sales, loyalty, and a sustainable competitive advantage for the selling firm. To help make these sorts of decisions, it is useful to categorize product lines based on the level of customization involved (Shapiro, 1977), as summarized in Figure 8.3.

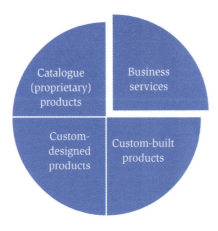

Figure 8.3 **Categorizing business product lines**

- Catalogue (or proprietary) products: These products are made in advance of orders in a standard format in anticipation of demand. The level of customization is very limited. For instance, the Shanghai Diesel Engine Company Ltd (SDEC) produces natural gas engines for commercial vehicles (www.sdecie.com). It sells dozens of its standard units, measuring 280 horsepower (for 20–30-tonne trucks), to clients such as Tiong Nam Logistics Holdings Bhd in Malaysia and the Bangkok Public Transportation Company in Thailand (Damodaran, 2008). Following the provision and analysis of comprehensive market research data in order to assess demand, key product line marketing issues for firms like SDEC involve ensuring adequate stock levels and availability (see Chapter Four).

- Custom-built products: These products are custom-assembled for customers from preformed parts and components. The final configuration is then made to meet a specific client need. Marketing decisions here involve liaison with supply/demand chain managers to ensure the appropriate level of components is held (again, see Chapter Four) and the careful presentation of the (limited) number of configurations available to customers. An example of a firm that offers custom-built products is Shanthi Gears Ltd of India. The company advertises gears from 'a few grams to more than 20 tons' and claims that it can make gear assemblies 'for any industry' (www.shanthigears.com).

- Custom-designed products: As their name suggests, these products are much more individualized than the previous two categories. They are designed to meet the very specific needs of a few customers (or perhaps only one), and are often highly expensive new-task purchases (see Chapter Two). For instance, Asea Brown Boveri (ABB) designs and coordinates the construction of large-scale projects like power plants and paper mills, some costing in excess of £50 million (www.abb.com). Marketers' product line responsibilities in this case include developing excellent understanding of the needs of individual customers and being able to recognize whether the technical and production skills of their firm can meet those needs.

- Business services: Although many organizations offer a product, they almost always offer a service element in support of this product, such as technical advice or service contracts for machine installations. Some of these services will inevitably be highly customized to fit the customer's needs, as we saw with Lafarge above. Of course, other firms (including professional service providers such as lawyers and accountants) offer business services as their core activity – these firms will be discussed in Chapter Nine. The intangibility of such services means that part of the marketer's role is to ensure that quality is maintained, even though the service may differ each time it is delivered.

The product life cycle

One widely recognized guide to the management of product lines is the product life cycle, often referred to as the PLC. This metaphoric concept suggests that products have a limited 'life' just like people, in that they gestate, are born, grow, mature, and then die (Barksdale and Harris, 1982). This cycle can be plotted in terms of sales revenue against time – see Figure 8.4.

There is some debate about what the PLC actually shows: is it depicting an industry (such as business computers), a product line (such as laptops) or a particular brand (such as the Toshiba Portégé)? All these interpretations can be relevant but it is clearly important for managers to recognize which level is being discussed at any planning meeting, since the

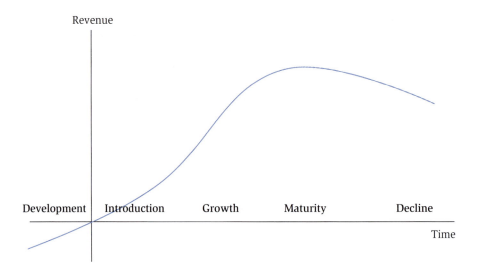

Figure 8.4 **The product life cycle**

shape of the curve can vary across the three levels of analysis. In general, however, it is at the level of the product line that the PLC is used to suggest what is going on in the market-place (and what B2B marketers could do) at each stage. The five stages have managerial implications as follows:

1. *Development*: the revenues at this stage of the PLC are shown as negative due to the investment in time and other resources required to bring a product to market. The complexity of new product development decisions will be explained in section 8.3, but for now you should recognize that costs can include materials testing, field-testing prototypes, staff training, and assessing market potential. These activities can occur inside the selling firm or within partnerships up and downstream (see Chapter Three).

2. *Introduction*: here, the product enters the market for the first time, typically with low levels of customer awareness and thus a need for considerable investment in marketing communications, both in business media (See Chapter Eleven) and in personal selling efforts (Chapter Twelve). Moreover, changes in the supply chain processes for the production of the new product, as well as in the distribution channel reconfigurations that may have to take place, can impact on the profitability of the launch. Customer reaction to the new product will need to be carefully monitored at this stage in order to refine the marketing mix. Refinements can include the use of demonstrations at trade shows, recruiting an expanded sales force, and enlarging the distribution network.

3. *Growth*: if customers accept the new product, sales are thought to expand at this stage with a concurrent growth in the overall market, especially as competitors may now enter the market by taking advantage of the lower risks involved in delivering 'me-too' offerings. Of course, should competitor offerings prove to be as popular, the rate of growth for the original vendor will slow down. This means marketers will need to think of ways in which their products can be differentiated, perhaps by offering modified/upgraded product lines or supporting services. As part of a continued heavy expenditure on promotion, satisfied customers

should be encouraged to provide referrals (see Chapter Three). B2B marketers will also need to be aware of production and supply/demand chain issues in meeting increased demand. Such issues are exacerbated in industrial network contexts, where modifying products can also affect the buyer's customers and other suppliers, as the case in Box 8.6 shows. The case illustrates how important it is for any firm planning to initiate changes to its products to interact with all the other organizations likely to be affected by the potential changes. Success in product modification will depend on getting as many of these network actors 'on board' as possible.

4. *Maturity*: at this stage, most potential buyers have adopted the product, and sales will reach their highest point. Marketing strategy often becomes focused on maintaining the volume of production in an attempt to achieve economies of scale. Competitive practice at this point can include price cutting, which may achieve short-term results against the competition, but runs the risk of devaluing how the product is perceived by customers in

---

Box 8.6 Mini case

Upgrading a product in the steel industry

As we saw in Chapter Three, relationships between firms are ideally characterized by continuous problem-solving and the co-creation of value. Steel suppliers are increasingly aiming to become more attractive business partners by upgrading their products and thereby making them appear more valuable to their customers.

Here, we outline the case of a Swedish steel producer who upgraded its core product so that the steel's strength and flexibility were enhanced. The firm's main customers were in the automotive sector, although they were not the car assemblers that you might expect. Rather, these firms had outsourced component manufacture to subcontractors, and it was the subcontractors that proved to be the target segment for the upgraded steel. One key German subcontractor, which had previously used standardized products from another supplier, was approached by the steel producer. As discussions about the adoption of the modified product began, the subcontractor also involved two external parties: a steel service centre and a press shop that would potentially process the imported steel locally. Also, since the high-strength steel would require new production tools, the Swedish steel producer had to establish relations with the manufacturer of these tools. Finally, the adoption of the modified product needed the approval of the car assembler (i.e. the subcontractor's customer).

All these different network actors (or stakeholders) had to be persuaded that the shift to the new type of steel would be viable in terms of technical, financial, administrative, and logistics issues. After two years of complex negotiations, production began. However, even at this stage, the steel producer had to liaise closely with the German press shop and the tool maker over production problems, eventually leading to an upstream change of the raw steel supplier to the Swedish producer. Ultimately, the subcontractor was highly satisfied with the performance of the modified steel. This led the producer to explore possibilities of using the product in other applications and in other countries – strategies which are still ongoing.

Source: Skarp and Gadde (2008); Woertler et al (2002)

the longer term (see Chapter Ten). As well as trying to increase customer loyalty, marketing managers may also try to reposition their products, perhaps with investments made in technical support, customized solutions, and other relational factors, or by creative marketing communications. If these strategies work, the maturity stage of the PLC can last for a considerable time. It may, however, be impossible to revitalize business products which have been technologically superseded, and thus sales and profits will begin to fall. Costs may be lowered by focusing on telesales efforts instead of a field sales force or by limiting the depth of some product lines.

5. *Decline*: here, the market consolidates and underperforming products may have to be withdrawn, or some distribution channels closed. Expenditure on any further R&D or promotion is usually severely curtailed. The focus for those firms remaining in the market is often on ensuring efficient production, especially if a key customer purchases this declining product while at the same time buying a host of other products from the selling firm. If the relationship between buyer and seller is strong, there may be cooperative arrangements put in place, perhaps over jointly funded production facilities and staff training, to ensure the continued supply of the product (and any spare parts or repair services) for the mutual benefit of both parties.

Despite the intuitive appeal of the PLC to managers, and the fact that most business marketers can easily discuss strategies in terms of the model's vocabulary, there is a risk that the PLC is taken too literally. As an overall guide to what B2B marketers might consider at each stage it can be useful, but we can never really predict what shape the curve will take or when a product has passed from one stage to the next. Furthermore, it can become a self-fulfilling prophecy such that, for example, managers assume their product is in the growth stage without appreciating that introductory awareness still needs to be built; or they may believe that their product is in decline and so withdraw the funding necessary for differentiating strategies, when, in fact, there is still potential for maintaining the maturity stage. It may even encourage managers to neglect (or 'terminate') existing product lines prematurely and turn too quickly to new product development (Wood, 1990).

Having said this, the dynamic nature of business markets means that new product development is often crucial to business product management, and it is this area we shall now explore.

8.3 New Product Development

New product development (NPD) is becoming ever more complicated. For instance, shorter life cycles and broader product assortments driven by consumer demands (e.g. for 'high-tech' goods such as global positioning systems), mean that the need for coordinating supply/demand chain activities is growing. Moreover, as manufacturers cannot always afford the investments in R&D to stay abreast of all the required technologies in their production processes, suppliers are increasingly being asked to contribute to the technical development of new products.

As we saw in Chapters Three and Four, in trying to manage NPD there can be considerable benefits to having good relationships with your suppliers. Firms that integrate with their suppliers can achieve reduced cycle times and costs, and improved product quality. Companies may agree to share capital investment for manufacture of the product, as well as sharing the risks and rewards from the NPD process. These outcomes can be positively influenced by 'socialization mechanisms' (Cousins and Lawson, 2007), a phrase which refers to processes by which people are introduced and integrated into the organizations aiming to work together. These include activities like supplier conferences, joint workshops, on-site visits, and social events to help establish communication and information-sharing. A study of the relationship between Fujitsu and ICL showed that, while formal mechanisms like documentation, training, and demonstrations are appropriate for such relationships, approaches such as secondments and face-to-face interactions were also necessary to share knowledge effectively between the two firms (Lynskey, 1999).

A phased approach to NPD

Most organizations adopt a phased approach to NPD, as shown in Figure 8.5. You should not assume, however, that these phases always occur in every NPD decision or that they necessarily occur in a simple linear fashion. Nevertheless, rather like the PLC, the generalized stages do provide managers with a sort of checklist of issues to consider when attempting to bring a new product to market.

We can consider the six stages in the order depicted in Figure 8.5.

1. *Idea generating*: a number of sources can be drawn upon for the generation of ideas for new products. These include internal sources such as R&D departments, the sales force, and customer service staff; and external sources such as competitor analysis, market research, and relationships with customer firms who encourage the vendor to participate in joint problem-solving initiatives (see Chapter Three). To encourage innovation, it is necessary to have a supportive corporate culture that welcomes ideas from all levels and functional areas of the firm. Getting people to think widely about possible forms of innovation, some more radical than others, is also important – see Box 8.7.

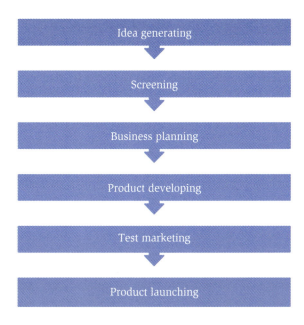

Figure 8.5 The traditional new product development process

Box 8.7 Food for thought

Stimulating ideas for B2B products

Here are some questions managers might ask themselves at the outset of the NPD process:

Can we change the physical, electrical, chemical, thermal, or mechanical properties of the product?

Can the standard components of the product be changed?

Can we make the product smaller?

Are there any new electronic, mechanical, optical, hydraulic, or magnetic ways of performing a current product function?

Has every step possible in the product's function been computerized?

Is the product's core function really necessary at all?

Can we change the power source of the product?

How can we use the Internet to improve the product or service?

Source: Crawford and Di Benedetto (2003)

2. *Idea screening*: screening should take place in relation to predetermined criteria in order to 'weed out' the most unrealistic prospects from the idea generation stage. These criteria should meet the objectives of the selling firm in terms of potential market reaction and the firm's current positioning strategy. Products that are innovative but which may necessitate a large-scale repositioning by the firm (for instance, from a low-cost, mass-market producer to a capital-intense, customized approach) may not be suitable. Concept testing with a reliable set of close customers may take place at this stage in order to gauge their attitudes to the planned product.

3. *Business planning*: at this point, an outline business plan should be developed in order to determine the likely profitability of the new product at an early stage. As well as predicted sales patterns, managers will need to look at profit forecasts, manufacturing costs, supply chain issues, and potential competitor responses. If these analyses suggest that the product, despite any technical attractiveness, will not be viable financially, the NPD process should be stopped.

4. *Product development*: here, prototypes are refined and tested in terms of their functional performance, design, and manufacturing requirements and any support required from members of the distribution channel. This stage can take time, something that is not always available in fast-moving, high-tech markets. Managers thus need to be able to evaluate the trade-offs in the risk between not being 'first to market' and launching an inadequately tested product that may fail. For instance, Danish company Secure-Globe Pty Ltd (www.secure-globe.com) is confident that its innovative security solution to the increasing threat of pirate attacks on ships in global waters will be well received by organizations shipping combustible cargoes like oil and explosives. The invention entails installing pipes around a ship's perimeter that can shoot out water at 90° Celsius. The manufacturer has rushed to market this design, optimistic that customers will appreciate the novelty of their approach to such an urgent problem (*New Straits Times*, 2009).

5. *Test marketing*: this aims to test the product in a limited marketplace but under real market conditions. Marketers can test their proposed marketing mix within a particular geographic region or amongst a specific segment of customers in order to refine their tactics before releasing the product onto the whole market. Of course, if the product has been developed in close partnership with a customer, then the test marketing would be unlikely to take place outside the existing inter-firm relationship. In this case, the test market would be used to fine-tune the final product offering to the customer's satisfaction, perhaps in one location before rolling its use out to a global set of business units.

6. *Product launching*: this stage will usually involve a launch plan that takes into account the needs of a series of stakeholders such as end users, distributors, logistics providers, and advertising agencies. It will also consider the needs of internal stakeholders such as the procurement and production departments of the selling firm and the provision of the appropriate information to the firm's sales force. Depending on the technical sophistication of the new product, communication may be required to educate all these people about its features and the benefits it can bring to customers. Without this support, there is a danger that adoption rates will be slow during the introductory stage of the PLC.

It is interesting to compare this idealized model of the NPD process with a real case of a firm attempting to improve its rate of new product success – see Box 8.8. Printing machine manufacture in China represents a fascinating context to study innovation when you consider that printing was invented by the Chinese. Note how the lack of success of the case firm seems to reflect a rather mystifying decline in the innovative culture necessary to stimulate commercially viable NPD in this sector and, arguably, the nation as a whole. In this firm, and perhaps in industries across China, the case shows that there are a number of management issues that need to be addressed if innovation, rather than just low-cost labour, is to be a future source of competitive advantage.

Box 8.8 Mini case
Innovation processes at a Chinese printer manufacturer

The maker of foundation products whom we encountered earlier in this chapter, Duoyuan Digital Press Technology Industries, is keen to improve its NPD. This reflects a frustration with the Chinese marketplace, where printing and publishing companies have become increasingly dependent on imported printing equipment which is perceived as being more competitive in terms of value (not cost – see Chapter Ten) than Chinese products. Domestically and in the global marketplace, Chinese printers offer only a low-cost advantage. The latest available sales data show that $675 million was spent on a variety of offset printing machines and spare parts by Chinese firms in 1999, representing an increase of 26% from the previous year. This is a large and capital-intense market: sales of medium-sized offset presses stood at around 2,200 per annum each year from 1999 to 2003, with top-end machines costing hundreds of thousands of US dollars.

Duoyuan is based in Beijing, where it employs 1,500 people, of which about 50 work in product development, and just one in the marketing department. The firm mainly produces medium-sized printing presses, but some larger models are also made, along with pre-press machines and post-processing equipment in an attempt to offer customers complete printer solutions. Duoyuan's processes for innovation management include two phases: initiating NPD and project management. For initiating NPD, employees are encouraged to generate ideas on a monthly basis. Each idea is followed by a limited amount of marketing research based on sources that include the Internet, sales people, international exhibitions, and trade journals. The R&D manager then writes an official proposal, which is sent to be assessed by a panel of managers including those from sales, production, and a technology specialist. Only after panel approval, which is based on profitability, the level of differentiation from the competition, and the degree of labour-intensiveness of production, can the R&D department begin the project. For project management, a team of R&D staff is deployed to meet the deadline specified by the approval panel. It then transfers 'completed' projects to the production department, with R&D input thereafter limited to the first ten presses produced. Team members are dispersed to existing or other new projects after completion, which can affect team cohesion. Control mechanisms during NPD projects focus only on meeting the set deadline, with no team managing their own budget. If there is any external expenditure required, a request must be made to Douyuan's general manager.

As a result of these rather inflexible innovation processes, the firm rarely succeeds in launching new products that are taken up by the market. This appears to be due to number of factors, including: the lack of customer involvement or sufficient market research in the initiation of projects; an inappropriate organizational structure for managing innovation projects; and a mismatch between the actual and required operational capabilities of Duoyuan, particularly in terms of 'time to market'.

Source: Dekkers (2009); www.made-in-china.com/showroom/duoyuanshuma

The stage-gate approach to NPD

Although the conventional stages in the NPD process are undoubtedly a useful reminder for managers (such as those representing Duoyuan), you should note that research from North America and Europe has shown that the mere existence of a formal process for NPD has no effect whatsoever on a firm's performance in B2B product innovation (Cooper, 1993). Thus, companies that believe that they can 'go through the motions' in structuring (and often just documenting) their new product processes to conform to the above six stages are unlikely to succeed. It is the quality and nature of the NPD process that drive performance, especially in industries where 'time to market' (see Chapter Four) is important.Several problem areas in B2B NPD are summarized in Figure 8.6.

To overcome any complacency in these key areas, Cooper (1996) recommends what he terms 'the stage-gate system' of NPD. The system breaks the innovation process down into a predetermined set of stages, with each stage comprising a number of prescribed, cross-functional, and parallel activities:

- Stage 1 (preliminary investigation): Typically involves a small team of technical and marketing people to gain a quick assessment of any proposed project.

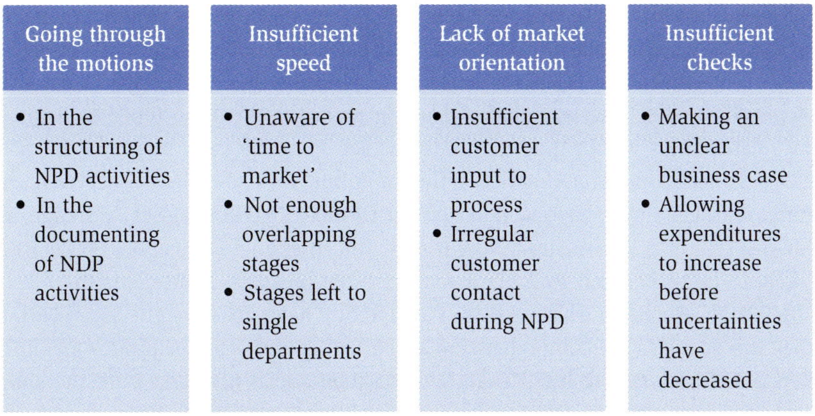

Going through the motions	Insufficient speed	Lack of market orientation	Insufficient checks
• In the structuring of NPD activities • In the documenting of NDP activities	• Unaware of 'time to market' • Not enough overlapping stages • Stages left to single departments	• Insufficient customer input to process • Irregular customer contact during NPD	• Making an unclear business case • Allowing expenditures to increase before uncertainties have decreased

Figure 8.6 Some problem areas in B2B NPD

- Stage 2 (detailed investigation): Entails a much more detailed set of analyses leading to the making of a business case for the product. Here, the manufacturing department usually comes on board.

- Stage 3 (development): Is equivalent to the fourth stage in the conventional NPD process above and involves a full team of managers from marketing, technical, manufacturing, purchasing, sales, and finance departments.

- Stage 4 (testing and validation): Corresponds to the fifth stage above and aims to deliver a fully tested product ready for commercialization.

- Stage 5 (full production and market launch): Sees the implementation of the full launch plan and any post-launch activities such as monitoring of sales performance and any marketing adjustments that may be necessary. The core development team remains in place for this stage in order to see their project through.

The 'entrance' to each stage is a 'gate' which controls the process and serves as a quality-control checkpoint, determining whether the product should be given the go-ahead or terminated. You may notice that the stages are similar to the traditional approach recommended for NPD above, with each stage designed to gather the information required to progress the project to the next gate. Unlike the tendency in the traditional model to allocate stages to the control of certain functional departments, however, each stage is multifunctional, consisting of a set of parallel activities carried out by individuals from different departments but working together as a project team. Each stage entails greater costs than the preceding one, so the gates attempt to ensure that as uncertainties decrease, expenditures are allowed to increase. The system is flexible, meaning that in order to accelerate NPD, stages can overlap each other, long lead time activities such as prototype testing can be brought forward from one stage to an earlier one, and stages can even be combined. Regular customer contact and a market orientation should underpin all five stages. Effective gates are crucial to the success of this accelerated NPD system. They ensure the funnelling of projects, where less-promising ideas are 'culled' (in keeping with the PLC metaphor) as each successive gate is encountered (Cooper, 1996).

The influence of managers from different functional areas can be significant in the NPD process. Research shows that in high-tech industries, decision-making is often dependent on technical expertise, so that R&D managers have more influence in organizations that are technologically driven. The way that marketing managers in these types of firms handle personal relationships within the internal teams set up at the early stages of the NPD process may need to be moderated across different cultures. In so-called 'collectivist' cultures like China, marketers may have to defer power to their R&D colleagues, although in more 'individualist' cultures like Australia, the market information expertise held by marketers is more likely to be recognized by R&D managers. This means that attempts to assert themselves by B2B marketers in Chinese firms can actually have negative effects on NPD teams, since they can decrease the comprehension of marketing issues by the project team. Instead, marketers should attempt to build coalitions via their social networks with the support of senior management, who should facilitate as much marketing–R&D interaction as possible (Atuahene-Gima and De Luca, 2008).

Network considerations in NPD

Viewing product development from an industrial networks perspective (see Chapter Five), flags up a number of further issues for B2B marketing managers, as summarized in Figure 8.7. The first can be termed 'getting into the mud' and the second, 'getting though the mud' (Håkansson, 1997).

The first of these issues suggests to managers that a network must be learned about by working within it. Although analysis of the network's actors, activities, and resources is still important, it does not compensate for the necessary experience gained from becoming a network actor yourself. Sometimes, NPD activities can be treated as more of a reconnaissance activity than a commercial project. They are a good way of gaining entry to a new network and to see how other actors react and whether they would be suitable partners for future projects. As a firm explores the possibilities for NPD partnerships, investments will need to be made by the newcomer but also by existing network members: the greater these investments, the more likely that the newcomer firm will become embedded in the network.

Some of the activities that lead to this sort of embeddedness have been termed 'open innovation' (Prahalad and Krishnan, 2008) or 'distributed co-creation' (Bughin et al, 2008). This involves delegating more of the management of innovation across networks of suppliers

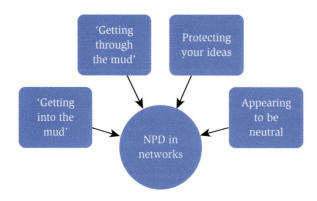

Figure 8.7 Network considerations in NPD

and other third parties, as well as customers. Thus, many of the ideas and technologies that result in new products emerge from a number of participants in the value chain. For instance, while Boeing designs its own aircraft, its suppliers make many of the components, for which they also hold the intellectual property rights (www.boeing.com). Specialization encourages focus and innovation in value chain roles so that, for example, an automobile manufacturer's suppliers should be able to make parts like headlights at a lower cost and of better quality than the OEM. Downstream co-creation also takes place. For instance, firms like the software specialist SugarCRM work with their corporate clients to customize the firm's open-source customer relationship management packages to suit their particular industries (www.sugarcrm.com).

The second NPD issue in industrial network contexts (getting through the mud) indicates a need for 'staying power' in pursuing activities. It is vital to have sufficient resources to push projects through and to persuade other network actors of their viability (see Box 8.9). It is therefore usually better to focus on just a few projects and commit resources to those, rather than attempting to 'juggle' too many new product projects across the network of cooperating forms involved in the NPD process. It may also be necessary to put some less optimistic projects 'on hold', but not to abandon them completely, in the hope that the network may change in the future (perhaps by gaining access to new materials, technology or knowledge) in such a way that the innovation becomes commercially viable once again.

The benefits of sharing NPD activities with partner organizations can be great since cooperation can mobilize joint resources. However, cooperation with other network actors can create problems in terms of sharing in-house knowledge and in maintaining a 'neutral' position in the network (Håkansson, 1997). Thus, we have third and fourth issues that should be borne in mind.

Third, working closely with another organization on NPD can make it difficult to protect your own ideas. If, at the prototype development stage of the process, you share your plans for developing a new component with a supplier on whom you rely to provide the appropriate raw materials, there is a risk that that supplier may then reveal your plans to your competitors in order to gain favourable orders from them in the future, however unethical such behaviour may appear. It is sometimes necessary to abandon a relationship, leaving one firm to continue the process alone, if the project moves too much into the territory of the unique technical core skills of one of the firms. One way around this is to divide the project into sub-projects that can be completed internally.

Fourth, the neutrality issue is one that can affect relations with other network actors since they may perceive your firm to be too closely allied with their customers, suppliers

---

Box 8.9 Voices

Getting through the NPD mud

Here is what an R&D manager in a successful Swedish organization says about the NPD process: 'It is never a question of how good, useful, or profitable the idea is from the beginning, but how to make it useful, and in this way profitable, by hard work. Thus, product development without endurance is worth nothing!'

Source: Håkansson (1997, p 492)

or even competitors. This may make them less likely to work with you in the future. One way to handle this is to participate in several NPD projects involving a number of different partners so as to appear unbiased in your innovation plans, and thus to lessen the risk of jeopardizing future network relations.

Having provided a host of examples of fairly 'high-tech' and manufacturing-orientated products from around the world, the chapter concludes with a case study that focuses on a crucial raw material in the supply/demand chain by exploring the B2B marketing of agricultural products. The case shows how relationships with a wide network of different stakeholders must be considered by marketers upstream in the food chain.

Summary

The key points to take from this chapter are as follows:

- How different ways of classifying business products help us to make sense of the complexity of the product offerings in industrial marketing.

- Why an appreciation of product attributes can help B2B marketers in commodity markets.

- How categorizing business products based on the level of customization involved in their production indicates what sort of marketing activities are most relevant for the firms involved.

- The utility (and limitations) of the product life cycle concept in managing business product lines.

- The guidelines for managing the new product development (NPD) process offered to managers by conventional and 'stage-gate' approaches to NPD.

- How taking a network perspective on NPD can raise some important issues for the B2B marketer, including matters of confidentiality and neutrality.

Discussion questions

1. What might be the most important attributes to organizational customers of the product lines supplied by a manufacturer of office photocopiers?

2. What measures could a firm that manufactures microchip components for electrical goods take to avoid the risk of their products being perceived as commodities?

3. What advice would you give to a B2B sales force manager whose firm had products at each stage of the product life cycle, including the development stage?

4. Do you think that all NPD activities must result in completely new innovations? Justify your answer with reference to some examples of incremental additions to business product lines or better versions of existing products.

5. Turn back to the Duoyuan mini case study in this chapter. What recommendations would you make to the management of this firm to improve their NDP processes?

6. Are there any potential ethical issues in developing new products via knowledge inputs from: (*a*) customers; or (*b*) suppliers?

Case study
Marketing Agricultural Products from Transition Economies

Peter J. Batt, Curtin University of Technology, Perth, Western Australia

Introduction

In the highlands of Papua New Guinea (PNG), smallholder coffee farmers produce some of the world's best coffee. As the coffee ripens, the cherries are harvested and pulped, washed, and fermented to produce 'parchment'. After several days, the parchment reaches the desired moisture content when it is stored in the farmer's home until sold. For most smallholder subsistence farmers, coffee is their only source of income.

Selling coffee parchment

In deciding when to sell and to whom they will sell the parchment they have produced, smallholder coffee farmers consider the prevailing market price and the immediacy of payment. Prices are readily available from one of the many roadside traders who set up weighing stations at strategic points along the main arterial roads, making verbal offers to the farmer. The farmer is paid in cash and the farmer's parchment is aggregated with other purchases the trader has made that same day.

Where the farmer is able to transport his own coffee, he may take his parchment directly to the factory door. While parchment prices generally increase with closer proximity to the processing factory, for security reasons most factories pay by cheque. At the processing factory, the parchment is dried, skinned, and polished to produce the green bean coffee that is subsequently sold to traders and exporters.

At the factory door, parchment prices change on almost a daily basis as a result of fluctuations in the price of coffee on both the London and New York futures market. While PNG produces and exports around 1–1.2 million 60-kg bags, which represents just 1% of the world production, the prices growers receive are very much dependent upon the quantity of coffee produced in Brazil, the world's largest producer, Colombia, and Vietnam. Recently, price volatility has dramatically increased as commodity traders continually re-evaluate their decisions either to invest in or to divest from the coffee futures market. Furthermore, modern technology and concentration and aggregation at all levels of the supply chain are putting more downward pressure on price.

Product quality issues

The other key determinant of price is the quality of the coffee parchment. At the factory door, the parchment is assessed on the basis of its moisture content, colour and smell, and the level of defects. For the processors, parchment quality has a direct impact on recovery rates and thus the profitability of their operations.

Quality, however, is ultimately determined by taste and this is where the coffee produced by smallholder farmers is compromised. As these primary producers use a variety of different techniques to prepare the parchment, a variety of different tastes is introduced. Due to significant variations in taste from one shipment to another, smallholder 'Y grade' coffee is heavily discounted on the New York coffee exchange, largely due to the risk that some lots will fail to meet buyers' expectations. By comparison, plantation 'A grade' coffee from PNG receives a price premium of US 25 cents per pound.

The difference between the generic Y grade smallholder coffee and the plantation A grade coffee is not so much the source of the coffee, but rather the way in which the parchment has been processed. Rather than purchase parchment, the plantations buy cherries, which they purchase and process on the same day of harvest.

Selling coffee cherries

The plantations ordinarily pay a 35% price premium to purchase smallholder cherries. The farmer needs to harvest the cherries and bring them to a designated collection point where they are rigorously inspected. However, again because of security issues, the farmers are seldom paid at the time of collection. If the quality is acceptable, the coffee is weighed and the farmers issued with a receipt. Upon the presentation of these receipts at the buying office, the farmer will be issued with a cheque which they can then take to the bank.

Not unexpectedly, when the farmers transact directly with the processing factories and plantations, a considerable amount of trust is inherent within the exchange. With little knowledge of the factors influencing the world coffee market, smallholder farmers rely upon their preferred downstream buyers to treat them fairly. While these exchange transactions might be best described as transactional, personal relationships play a significant role in the PNG coffee industry. As production is highly seasonal, farmers often need cash advances to meet household expenses and to purchase some of the inputs required to reinvigorate their coffee trees.

Quality assurance schemes

International buyers worldwide are progressively introducing quality assurance systems. The most widely known of these is Café Practices, introduced by the Starbucks restaurant/café group (www.starbucks.com). Café Practices require each component of the supply chain (growers, processors, and exporters) to meet minimum economic, social, and environmental standards. Before a supply/demand chain can be evaluated, it must meet two prerequisites: the product must meet Starbucks's quality requirements; and there must be economic accountability along the entire supply chain, meaning financial transparency, equity, and ongoing financial viability. Suppliers who have met the prerequisites are listed on the Café Practices approved supplier roster, and those with the highest evaluations are afforded first consideration when Starbucks procures coffee.

Every smallholder coffee farmer who delivers cherries to the factory for processing must be registered to ensure traceability and financial accountability. Furthermore, Starbucks expects continuous improvement from its suppliers. This demands that smallholder farmers minimize water pollution and the application of fertilizers, and implement safe and equitable working conditions. By necessity, this requires downstream processors and traders to build enduring relationships to secure a regular and reliable supply from smallholder farmers. It also requires them to deliver training programmes and, in the early stages of certification, to provide financial incentives, even though none will be forthcoming until the chain is formally accredited.

For those smallholder farmers who are too isolated or otherwise unable to supply cherry to the processors, opportunities also exist to enter the speciality market through organic and Fairtrade certification.

Organic schemes

Organic agriculture is a production method that relies on the use of natural resources and the management of the ecosystem rather than external inputs such as agrochemicals. Certification is a formal and documented procedure by which a third party assures that organic standards have been followed. Certification leads to consumers' trust in the production system and its products, giving organic farming a distinct identity.

Achieving full certification as a primary producer is a long process. Producers need to be aware of the potential for some loss of income in the first year as conventional farming methods are phased out and converted to organic. Following at least three years of consecutive organic management, full certification may be granted. However, compliance with organic production standards must be maintained for the certified status to be ongoing and thus annual re-inspections of the farm are required.

In PNG, as the majority of producers are smallholders, rather than for each producer to be certified, a grower group scheme is implemented, where a marketing or development company works closely with a network of village-based growers. These systems require every member of the group to be registered, and group members collectively operate under a binding agreement which specifies their commitment to comply with applicable organic standards. If one member of the group fails, the whole group fails.

Fairtrade schemes

Fairtrade is an organized social movement and market-based approach for empowering developing country producers and promoting sustainability. Fairtrade seeks to work with marginalized producers in transitional economies to assist them in achieving economic self-sufficiency. The principles of Fairtrade espouse: a minimum floor price and an additional premium for certified organic products; fair labour conditions; direct trade through eliminating unnecessary middlemen and empowering growers to develop the business capacity to compete in the global market; democratic and transparent organizations; community development; and, environmental sustainability (e.g. www.fairtrade.org.uk).

Fairtrade certification provides an economic benefit to producers in the form of a guaranteed minimum price and a social premium for community investment. This premium is payable thanks to the higher prices end users are prepared to pay for their fairly sourced coffee. It provides economic incentives to growers to improve the quality of their production, protect the environment, and to reinvest in their farms. Fairtrade certification also promotes enduring long-term relationships between buyers and sellers and greater transparency throughout the supply chain. However, farmers must be organized into democratic, transparent organizations where the members collectively vote on the use of the Fairtrade premium to fund community-based projects like schools, or to provide low-interest loans.

In 2007–8, Fairtrade and organic coffee accounted for only 3% of PNG coffee exports, even though the coffee was sold at a premium well above the Y grade parchment price.

Although Fairtrade offers a minimum price of US 121 cents per pound, when prices exceed this level, registered growers receive a Fairtrade premium of US 15 cents per pound. Organic coffee adds a further US 15 cents per pound premium.

Problems for supply/demand chain members

Significant additional costs are associated with Fairtrade and organic coffee, including hand-sorting of the green beans, assisting cooperatives, and facilitating annual inspections. Not unexpectedly, few exporters are willing to invest the time and effort required to achieve certification, for there is every possibility that growers, individually or collectively, will forgo any such arrangement in the short-term pursuit of higher prices.

At the farm level, the major constraint is the need for growers to actively participate in collaborative marketing groups. Regrettably, relatively low levels of education among village growers and cultural issues generally lead to the failure of cooperatives in NPG due to conflict, poor management, and corruption. The costs associated with certification are an additional problem for smallholder coffee growers.

Another issue that must be addressed is the inconsistent taste and appearance of the coffee, for in reality, both Fairtrade and organic coffee are Y grade coffee. Customers are likely to complain about the inconsistent quality, especially when they are paying a premium price.

Case study questions

1. As the marketing manager for Volcafe (www.volcafe.com), one of the world's foremost coffee traders and exporters, what are the key issues affecting your firm as it seeks to increase the global market share of smallholder coffee produced in PNG?

2. How would you go about building long-term relationships with upstream smallholder farmers?

3. Would you consider implementing a quality assurance system for the generic Y grade coffee? Think of the implications of such a product positioning strategy for your firm's downstream organizational customers, including brand manufacturers (such as Nestlé) and retailers.

Further Reading

Conway, S. & Steward, F. (2009) Managing and Shaping Innovation, Oxford University Press, Oxford

This book includes a network perspective on innovation which provides a distinctive lens and approach for understanding this key aspect of product marketing within and between organizations. The text encourages readers to evaluate research and theory, and gives explicit attention to developing areas like social networking in business markets.

Gressetvold, E. & Torvatn, T. (2006) Effects of Product Development: A Network Approach, IMP Journal, 1 (2), pp 41–55

The authors use the case of an electronics company to examine the wider effects of NPD at the network level and over time. They show how, while some effects of product development are highly visible to the participating companies and thus easy to plan for, others are less visible.

The occurrence of these effects is not predetermined, meaning that the NPD process cannot be fully planned in advance.

Homburg, C., Kuester, S., Beutin, N., & Menon, A. (2005) Determinants of Customer Benefits in Business-to-Business Markets: A Cross-Cultural Comparison, Journal of International Marketing, 13 (3), pp. 1–31

The authors of this paper examine the concept of customer benefits, distinguishing between core and add-on benefits. They discuss product quality, service quality, flexibility, trust, joint action, and commitment of the supplier. The results of their study suggest significant cultural differences with respect to the impact of different determinants on perceived customer benefits.

Woodside, A. G. & Biemans, W. G. (2005) Modelling Innovation, Manufacturing, Diffusion and Adoption/Rejection Processes, Journal of Business & Industrial Marketing, 20 (7), pp 380–93

This paper uses a number of case studies and a systems-modelling approach to make recommendations for managerial actions in order to manage successfully new products built using radical new techniques. The authors argue that identifying individual factors in NPD success or failure is insufficient: instead, a systems view is necessary in order to move beyond overly simplistic checklists.

References

Atuahene-Gima, K. & De Luca, L. M. (2008) Marketing's Lateral Influence Strategies and New Product Team Comprehension in High-Tech Companies: A Cross-National Investigation, Industrial Marketing Management, 37, pp 664–76

Barksdale, H. C. & Harris, C. E. (1982) Portfolio Analysis and the Product Life Cycle, Long Range Planning, 15 (December), pp 74–83

Bughin, J., Chui, M., & Johnson, B. (2008) The Next Step in Open Innovation, McKinsey Quarterly, online at http://www.mckinseyquarterly.com, accessed July 2008

Carpigiani (2008) Floor Standing Machines for the Production of Soft Ice Cream, online at http://carpigiani.com/eng/splfoor.htm, accessed August 2008

Cooper, R. G. (1993) Winning at New Products: Accelerating the Process from Idea to Launch, Addison-Wesley, Reading, MA

Cooper, R. G. (1996) Overhauling the New Product Process, Industrial Marketing Management, 25, pp 465–82

Cousins, P. D. & Lawson, B. (2007) The Effect of Socialization Mechanisms and Performance Measurement on Supplier Integration in New Product Development, British Journal of Management, 18, pp 311–26

Crawford, C. M. & Di Benedetto, A. (2003) New Products Management, McGraw-Hill, New York

Damodaran, R. (2008) China Engine Maker Keen to Set up Plant here, New Straits Times, 11 September, p 34

Dekkers, R. (2009) Endogenous Innovation in China: The Case of the Printer Industry, Asia Pacific Business Review, 15 (2), pp 243–64

Hakånsson, H. (1979) Product Development in Networks, in Ford, D. (ed.), Understanding Business Markets: Interaction, Relationships and Networks, 2nd edn, Dryden Press, London, pp 475–98

Hobday, M. (2000) East versus Southeast Asia Innovation Systems: Comparing OEM- and TNC-led Growth in Electronics, in Kim, L. & Nelson, R. R. (eds), Technology, Learning and Innovation – Experiences of Newly Industrialising Economies, Cambridge University Press, Cambridge, pp 129–69

Hopkins, J. (2005) Thailand Confidential, Periplus Editions Ltd, Singapore

Hsu, C.-W., Chen, H., & Jen, L. (2008) Resource Linkages and Capability Development, Industrial Marketing Management, 37, pp 677–85

Levitt, T. (1980) Marketing Success through Differentiation – Of Anything, Harvard Business Review, January–February, pp 83–91

Lynskey, M. J. (1999) The Transfer of Resources and Competencies for Developing Technological Capabilities – The Case of Fujitsu-ICL, Technology Analysis and Strategic Management, 11 (3), pp 317–36

MacMillan, I. C. & McGrath, R. G. (1997) Discovering New Points of Differentiation, Harvard Business Review, July–August, pp 133–45

Nation (The) (2007) Business: New Plant to Boost Siam Motors Exports, 24 November, p 1B

New Straits Times (2009) Hot Shower to Deter Pirates, 4 December, p 13

Prahalad, C. K. & Krishnan, M. S. (2008) The New Age of Innovation: Driving Co-created Value through Global Networks, McGraw-Hill, New York

Shapiro, B. P. (1977) Industrial Product Policy: Managing the Existing Product Line, Marketing Science Institute, Cambridge, MA

Skarp, F. & Gadde, L.-E. (2008) Problem Solving in the Upgrading of Product Offerings – A Case Study from the Steel Industry, Industrial Marketing Management, 37, pp 725–37

Trung, X. (2007) Innovations Drive Company Success, Vietnam Economic News, 44, p 30

Wen, H. (2007) The Challenge of Reform: How does Taiwan's Textile Industry Shift from OEM/ODM to OBM? Taiwan Money Weekly, 361, pp 62–3

Woertler, M., Jones, B., Mouton, J., Schmiedeberg, A. Shanahan, M., & Young, D. (2002) Breaking the Stalemate: Value Creation Strategies for the Global Steel Industry, Boston Consulting Group, Boston

Wood, L. (1990) The End of the Product Life Cycle? Education Says Goodbye to an Old Friend, Journal of Marketing Management, 6 (2), pp 145–55

Chapter 9
Business Services

Introduction & Learning Objectives

An extensive network of service providers surrounds most organizations. This network has always included firms offering services that have traditionally been purchased by client organizations such as transportation, banking, and market research. Now, however, it also includes more and more firms specializing in activities that might once have been carried out 'in-house' such as staff recruitment, security, cleaning, and IT advice. This shift in the purchasing of services means that as many B2B marketers can be found working for service providers as for manufacturers. This makes it important for marketing students to have a good understanding of the range and nature of business services, and of how to maintain sufficiently high levels of service quality for increasingly demanding business customers.

The case in Box 9.1 shows how a well-designed business model, as well as attention to service quality issues, has helped a logistics service provider stand out in the organizational marketplace. Note how Pall-Ex's network approach makes freight shipments more efficient for its clients and note, too, how the firm justifies its expenditure on new premises in terms of the positive impact this has had on its image.

Box 9.1 Mini case

A network approach to B2B freight services

The business freight company Pall-Ex was only formed in 1997, but has already celebrated handling its 12-millionth pallet. The firm uses a pallet network business model which enables organizational customers seeking to ship goods between UK locations to avoid having to pay for a full truckload one way, or having to wait for enough freight to be accumulated to make it worth the haulier's while. The average vehicle fill for pallet networks is 73% compared with a conventional UK average of 51%. The network allows Pall-Ex to deliver individual pallets by using a hub system where freight is brought from outlying locations and then sent on to its final destination in locally consolidated loads, rather than transferring it from point to point. This is achieved by drawing on members of Pall-Ex's network. These members are local hauliers who deliver freight from their own regions to the hub from across the UK. When at the hub, these hauliers collect and distribute freight bound for their area.

Pall-Ex conducts its business from extremely smart offices, linked to a newly built logistics hub. The firm's commercial director designate, Tony Mellor, believes these premises help to differentiate Pall-Ex from its competitors: 'Quality of the premises reflects quality of the service.' Another way in which the firm stands out is by ensuring that a proportion of all its members' trucks carry Pall-Ex livery and logos. The new premises are designed to minimize exhaust fumes from waiting trucks, and all the firm's forklifts run on natural gas. These 'green' initiatives also help to distinguish Pall-Ex in the eyes of potential customers. While some of these firms may not care too much about environmental issues, they do care if pallet loads get wet or dirty from poor warehousing conditions. Also, for sensitive electric goods, pharmaceuticals, and foodstuffs, a fume-free environment can be important. There has been a significant investment by Pall-Ex in these premises, leaving the firm little flexibility to compete on cost. This, however, says Mellor, is not its aim: 'We're certainly not the cheapest. . . . What we sell on is offering a bespoke service to corporate customers.'

Source: Allen (2008); www.pallex.co.uk

Chapter Aims

After completing this chapter, you should be able to:

- Recognize ways of classifying business services
- Appreciate how business services differ from business products in terms of some key characteristics
- Understand some service management issues in organizational markets
- Reflect on the significance of personal relationships in professional business services.

9.1 Classifying Business Services

B2B services can be classified most conveniently as support services and 'pure' services. As you will have gathered from Chapter Eight, many firms in organizational markets offer products combined with a certain level of service support. Support services include storage, delivery, installation, staff training, maintenance, credit facilities, and product guarantees. In contrast, pure services are not offered in support of a tangible product; instead, the core service generally stands alone. Pure services include market research, management consultancy, financial services, and legal and accountancy advice.

Product–service combinations

As a bridge between this chapter and the last, we begin by looking at how firms have attempted to introduce new product–service combinations in their offerings to customers. The trend away from more traditional product-orientated marketing towards a combined product–service strategy has been termed 'servicization' (van Looy et al, 1998). Firms pursuing such strategies are thought to pass through three stages, as represented in Figure 9.1:

1. *First*: the firm must possess the capability to manufacture or distribute goods.

Figure 9.1 Stages of servicization

2. *Second*: it starts to offer additional services that complement the product portfolio.

3. *Third*: it practises servicization by marketing different product/service combinations.

In this final stage, a shift has been seen by researchers from an 'old' to a 'new' service model, such that firms have moved from providing services which support their products to providing services which support the client (Mathieu, 2001). For instance, a truck manufacturer who might once have claimed that it sold and serviced trucks will now assert that it can help its clients reduce their life-cycle transportation costs; and a chemical producer who may once have been in the business of providing a wide range of carefully designed lubricants will now seek to increase the machine performance of its clients. The differences in proposition are subtle, but these promised solutions represent a more customer-orientated approach to B2B market positioning (see Chapter Seven).

Three cases of product–service combinations are explored by Johnstone et al (2008): 'EngCo', which is a leading power and IT firm, with clients in the chemicals, oil, minerals, paper, and utility sectors; 'ConstructionCo', which builds infrastructure projects and provides maintenance mainly for the highways sector; and 'JetCo', which provides power systems and service to the civil and defence aerospace sectors. Strategies at EngCo saw a move towards 'cradle to grave' asset management over product life cycles rather than the more conventional product sale with a series of routine maintenance contracts attached. JetCo recognized the opportunity for a 'total service package' model that supports clients requiring considerable spare parts and maintenance activity. ConstructionCo, in contrast, saw 'through-life service' as more of a pragmatic response to market conditions in the UK where there had been an increase in government-funded projects that were partially invested in by private organizations seeking better 'whole-life costing' on projects.

All three of these firms claimed to have adopted a 'product–service' strategy; however, the use of this term and the varied vocabulary that can be seen in the three cases indicate that usage varies by industry and organization. Each firm has always provided some sort of service, but there are differences in their current approaches. These differences include the rationale for product–service provision (i.e. EngCo and JetCo versus ConstructionCo); new timescales (through-life versus ad hoc); strategic importance (central versus peripheral); and potential value (high versus low). Indeed, it might be argued that the espoused theoretical shift towards more developed product–service models just captures what organizations have always done (Johnstone et al, 2008). Nevertheless, in general, there does seem to be a belief in each case firm that servicization will lead to more long-term relationships between the firms and their clients.

You should note, however, that the proportion of manufacturer revenues generated via support services is difficult to determine (Gebauer and Fleisch, 2007). The sales volume of service deals is clearly important for firms like Rolls-Royce and KONE (see Box 9.2), but their profitability needs to be monitored.

Business service classifications

We can classify business services as shown in Figure 9.2. The first (i.e. left-hand) column in this figure represents mainly support services such as those offered by Rolls-Royce and KONE, while the remaining four columns group together a number of different services available to organizational customers, the majority of which could be described as pure (although, clearly, they can still be related to products, such as the provision of capital to assist product purchases).

In order to ensure the appropriate resources are made available to deliver any service promises, it is important for the B2B marketer to be aware of some of the operational considerations that can affect each of these groups of services (Majewski and Srinivas, 2003). These often centre on 'make or buy' decisions on the part of the customer:

- Product-related services: For these support services, purchasing managers may have to weigh up the pros and cons of a number of options such as using the firm's own logistics resources, or hiring in a third-party provider; providing repairs via a network of local maintenance staff, or a centralized hub; encouraging the firm's own sales force to provide customer training, or using a separate team of field workers; and handling warranty claims via a dedicated team of employees or drawing upon an external call centre to take customer calls. Marketers representing business service providers should try to gain a close understanding of their potential clients' operations in order to be able to

Box 9.2 Number crunching
Service business in the aircraft engine and elevator sectors

In 2009, the UK aero engine manufacturer Roll-Royce announced that it had extended its contract to maintain engines for the German Condor Airline – an extension worth £92 million. Such service contracts are significant for Rolls-Royce, as shown on its website which claims that a total of 194 new 'Corporate Care' contracts were signed in 2007.

The Finnish company, KONE, makes elevators (lifts), escalators, doors, and loading bays. Its offerings include design, manufacture, and installation, as well as maintenance and modernization. KONE employs what it describes as '30,000 dedicated experts' around the world to provide localized service in 49 countries. Nevertheless, even though about 60% of KONE's business is service-based, the profitability of this part of the business is hard to pin down. This is due to the high cost of maintaining a technical service presence under the KONE brand in so many locations. Achieving the rapid response rates that clients with broken elevators require can involve complex subcontracting arrangements with many local service engineers.

Sources: Nottingham Evening Post (2009); Wendelin (2009); www.kone.com; www.rolls-royce.com

Product-related	Marketing services	Professional services	Information services	Financial services
Delivery services	Market research services	Consulting services	Inventory management	Financing for product purchases
Installation & maintenance	Advertising agencies	Accountancy services	Supply chain management	Managing billing processes
After-sales training	Export advice	Legal advice	Data aggregation	Credit evaluation
Warranty services				Banking & insurance

Figure 9.2 Classifying services in B2B markets

present a good justification of the value the services firm can add to the client's product support activities. This is exactly what ChemChina has done in the industrial cleaning sector (see Box 9.3). This may not be a very glamorous service but look at how big the business has become by the way it highlights to clients how they could save money by using ChemChina's services.

- Marketing services: B2B marketers representing these service providers must recognize what aspects of the marketing planning process (see Chapters Six and Seven) their clients are likely to be able to perform in-house, and which they may need to purchase from external service providers. While secondary market research data are often available

---

Box 9.3 Mini case
It's a dirty job but someone's got to do it

China BlueStar Chemical Cleaning, China's first industrial cleaning company, has 90% of the domestic market, overcoming competitors from Japan and Germany. Domestic growth and international acquisitions have given the firm, now known as ChemChina following a merger with companies affiliated to the Ministry of Chemical Industry, annual revenues of $17.4 billion. The firm's president, Ren Jianxin, says that after he discovered in 1984 that 8 million tons of coal were wasted each year due to boiler incrustation, he had the idea of offering a solution to companies by bringing a particular chemical cleaning agent to bear on the problem, thus improving his clients' heating efficiency. The new technology extended BlueStar's business from boilers to commercial pipes and on to petroleum pipelines and the launching facility for China's first spaceship. The firm also holds service contracts for most of China's ethylene and large chemical plants.

Source: Koch and Ramsbottom (2008); www.chemchina.com.cn

to clients, research specialists and export advisors should be able to offer more focused studies of certain sectors or regions. The more creative aspects of the marketing communications role (see Chapter Eleven) are unlikely to be performed in-house by most industrial firms, thus service providers typically seek to persuade buyers of the need to invest in the promotional design and media expertise of their particular agency. This may be easier when the buyers are marketers themselves, but can present some issues of credibility when buyers are heavily product-orientated with a degree of scepticism towards what might be perceived as 'frivolous' costs like advertising. This can occur in small high-tech client organizations where there is no such thing as a marketing department. Marketing services are often argued (not least by marketers themselves!) to be dependent on such an extensive knowledge base that they should be classified as professional services (see below), thus giving marketing experts the same level of social status as other more traditional professionals (Ellis, 1999).

- Professional services: A similar set of considerations affects the marketing of these services to business clients as for marketing services. Marketers have to be able to persuade customers that they need the service on offer (sometimes, of course, this is a legal obligation, such as with end-of-year company accounts and tax returns), and that their firm is the best choice of provider and, moreover, that the delivery of the service will be of good quality. A particularly tricky area for the client can be evaluating the service provided. Unlike, say, checking that a component part is sufficiently well made to fit into the assembly of OEM products, it is hard to know in advance of purchases (or even during the time the service is being delivered) that the consultant, accountant, or lawyer the customer has hired really knows what they are doing – the buyer often simply cannot judge. Marketers representing these sorts of firms must work closely with the professionals themselves to ensure that the client's perceptions are positive. The characteristics of pure services can make this a difficult task, as we shall see in a closer look at professional services in section 9.2.

- Information services: Suppliers of these services often contribute to channel or supply/demand chain management performance by helping client organizations to manage the information flows necessary for efficient supply chain operations (see Chapter Four). The services on offer can range from designing stockholding record systems and electronic networks that link warehouses to manufacturing facilities, to parcel-tracking technology to help firms plot the whereabouts of urgent deliveries to their customers. Data aggregation is a service that might be offered to clients with a large and varied customer base who wish to improve their CRM efforts (see Chapter Three). These clients benefit from having user-friendly summaries produced of transaction records, costs, and customer details that are maintained via software and data 'silos' managed externally.

- Financial services: While some of these could be included within the services offered by accounting and information management firms, this category of business service is more to do with allowing sellers to facilitate access to capital for buyers, especially buyers of large capital items like production machinery or other installations. Financial services firms can also help operational processes such as billing and the assessment of a potential client firm's credit rating. Finally, the provision of banking and insurance to organizations is a major service industry, for instance in the granting of loans and the protection of stock and premises as well as financial guarantee schemes in higher-risk trading contexts, such as might be found in international markets.

Some organizations are turning to outsourcing as a way of managing their operations, with outside service suppliers increasingly called upon to help them create and deliver value to their end customers (LaPlaca, 2009). Outsourcing refers to subcontracted relations for services (and products) that extend beyond the organizational boundaries of the contracting firm. Typical areas in which outsourcing occurs include support activities such as IT infrastructure development and maintenance, payroll management, data entry, and staff training. In this way, client firms can lower their fixed and variable costs, reduce their headcounts, increase their flexibility by being able to change service supplier if necessary, and gain access to enhanced capabilities from more specialist service providers, leaving them to focus on their core business. There are many opportunities for service suppliers whose B2B marketing efforts can promote these advantages to potential clients.

Box 9.4 highlights an interesting case of marketing in the outsourcing arena, showing how an 'offshore' service provider has sought market opportunities in the US. Note how

Box 9.4 Voices

Russian service firms 'onshoring' in the US

Offshore Russian suppliers of IT services face particular challenges when marketing to the onshore US marketplace. There is no link to Russia through the entrepreneurs that often return from the US to countries such as Taiwan or India, nor are there many organizational links to large US firms that could facilitate outsourcing relationships. This makes it difficult for Russian service providers to establish a profile in the US as they frequently lack a social network to build upon. Software firms based in St Petersburg have embarked on a number of activities across borders to create new linkages between post-Soviet and Western economic systems. These include creating contacts through travel to the West, localizing services in the US by establishing onshore offices or agents, outsourcing their own marketing and PR needs to firms located in the US, and creating a legal presence onshore. Some of these activities are captured in the following quotes from Russian managers:

'Probably after a week of visiting several companies, I was spending my time without any result, so . . . I opened the telephone book and called all the companies in the computer software list. I probably made 150 calls . . . I [finally] reached a company where their secretary said, "OK, our general manager is from Russia."'

'What makes sense is establishing a professional office that is two-armed . . . a marketing department with salesmen who know what they are doing . . . and, very important, the other arm is project development . . . to come and convince this guy that they can do the job.'

'This American [marketing] company helped us a lot . . . they helped us to express ourselves in the right words. Thanks to them, I met many senior people . . . responsible for global programmes for offshore development. They were really professional, making telephone calls and sending positioning statements.'

Source: Feakins (2009)

245

much harder it can be for offshore suppliers to begin relationships with business customers when there is little or no history of a social network between individuals in the 'onshore' (customer) and offshore (supplier) countries.

9.2 Characteristics of Business Services

Services, especially pure services, differ from conventional products in that they are essentially acts or processes (Gronroos, 2000). In IMP Group terminology (see Chapter Five), these processes comprise a series of activities in which customers interact directly with suppliers, and which draw upon resources from both sets of actors (for instance, clients will need to commit time as well as money to the service interaction). The resource implications of service interactions are generally thought to depend on a number of characteristics that differentiate services from product offerings (Gronroos, 2000; Lovelock et al, 1999; Zeithaml and Bitner 2000) – summarized in Figure 9.3. Taking each in turn, we can relate these characteristics to a variety of business services.

- Intangibility: This prevents customers from touching, seeing or even owning the offering. It means that business services are difficult to evaluate prior to purchase and have to be experienced at the point of consumption. Service firms should try to provide tangible 'clues' to customers about what the service may entail and the quality involved. These include brochures outlining the service, physical evidence in the form of staff uniforms, or an attractive reception area to a company's offices, and corporate logos on

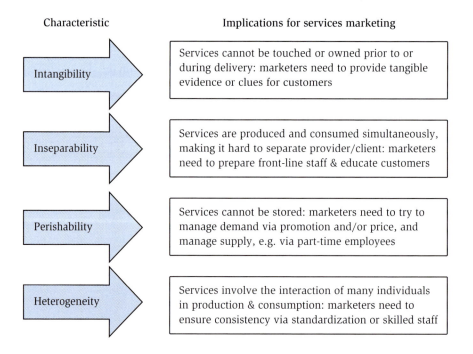

Figure 9.3 The characteristics of business services

the side of well-maintained delivery trucks (e.g. the well-known Eddie Stobart fleet of vehicles in the UK which has become so popular that the firm even sells toys and other consumer goods now, emblazoned with its logo – www.eddiestobart.co.uk). Even the most intangible of services such as consultancy can still contain a tangible element in the form of a report submitted at the end of the consultancy contract or a summary of market research data gathered.

- Inseparability: Service providers and customers must interact at the point of consumption since services are produced and consumed simultaneously. This characteristic is, therefore, sometimes termed 'consumed when produced'. It means that every member of a service organization's staff that might interact with the customer becomes important to the impression made, to the extent that they have been described as 'part-time marketers' (Gummesson, 1991). Ideally, the marketing department should have an input into the recruitment and training of 'front-line' service staff to ensure that these people manage customer relationships properly in addition to performing their functional role. For instance, industrial cleaning operatives need to make sure their clients are satisfied with their punctuality and communication skills as well as ensuring that the equipment they are required to clean is left immaculate.

- Perishability: Services cannot be stored due to the characteristic of inseparability. This means marketers need to understand both the demand and supply sides of their firm's business in order not to under-commit resources, resulting in demand that cannot be met, while at the same time not overcommitting resources that go to waste. This can be a significant problem in e.g. the transport sector, where airlines offering seats in business travel must plan their capacity carefully. Failure to predict passenger numbers can have disastrous consequences as evidenced by the collapse of the business class airlines, Silverjet, MAXjet, and Eos. These firms suffered as many organizations chose not to send their executives around the globe at premium prices at the onset of the recession in 2008 (Bokaie, 2008). Predicting demand can be difficult to achieve when the economy is volatile, thus B2B service marketers will often try to control either demand or supply:

  1. *In terms of demand*: using promotional pricing in order to dampen demand at peak periods and stimulate it at quieter periods is a common approach (e.g. the high room rates charged by hotels to business people midweek when managers are often on the road and require overnight accommodation, compared with the weekend when many rooms will become cheaper).

  2. *In terms of supply*: hiring staff on part-time contracts to work only at peak times, or training staff so that they can 'multitask' can enable service levels to be maintained in one area of the business where customer queues may form, should another area become slack (e.g. a call centre business will staff its phone lines with differing numbers of people at different times in order to cope with expected customer requests, typically busiest in office hours; but think of how carefully managers must plan this if the call centre serves countries in different time zones).

- Heterogeneity: Since so many individual actors (including the part-time marketers we noted above) can be involved in the delivery of a service, each service interaction is likely to be different. This characteristic, also known as 'variability', means that customers may not always experience consistent service quality. This need not cause problems in a well-run service firm, especially a creative business like advertising where you would not expect the outcome of the service to be the same for each client, but it does have the potential for the delivery of the service to be jeopardized by, for example, staff who do not meet the client's expectations over deadlines or even politeness. One management response is to standardize as much of the service as possible, perhaps by automation (as in electronic order-taking mechanisms for 'rebuy' situations) or by providing 'scripts' to service personnel that guide them about what to say to customers in different circumstances. A criticism of this approach is that it can leave individuals less able to respond to unexpected customer queries or problems. While often leading to lower costs for the supplier, service standardization is particularly difficult to achieve in professional service contexts (see ahead).

Taken together, these characteristics make the purchasing of business services a relatively high-risk decision for potential customers. Some customers, especially those facing new-task situations, lack the knowledge needed to make the appropriate judgements over which service provider is best for them or sometimes even whether they really require the service in the first place. Drawing upon the knowledge of a B2B marketer can be crucial for firms offering business services since it is the marketer that acts as the 'voice' of the customer within the firm – if their grasp of customer needs and concerns is not passed on to the people actually delivering the service, then the interactions that comprise service-based relationships between organizations may founder on the poor interpersonal relations between the staffs of the supplier and customer firms. If these processes are handled properly, then long-term relationships between organizations should blossom. For instance, look at how the HSBC bank markets its business services. The mini case in Box 9.5 shows the significance the bank attaches to relationship building through personal contact.

Coping with the characteristics of professional business services

As we have seen above, professional services often involve customers paying fees for extremely complex services that they do not always understand. The marketing of these services presents quite a challenge, even when clients are organizational buyers who are supposedly more expert than their consumer equivalents (see Chapter Two). This holds true

---

Box 9.5 Mini case

Business relationships in banking services

The commercial banking arm of the HSBC bank is keen to stress in its advertising that it understands how important relationships between business and their suppliers can be. In messages aimed at corporate clients during 2009, it even refers to its own sponsored research, contained in a report entitled, 'The Value of Relationships', to support this claim. The advertisements state that the bank is 'actively supporting business' by ensuring that its relationship managers are 'proactively spending 30% more time than they did last year meeting customers'. This contact is designed to help customers comprehend issues such as cash flow management, business planning, and gaining access to governmental financial guarantee schemes for enterprise.

Source: www.hsbc.co.uk/businesssupport; The Guardian (2009)

---

across a wide variety of professional services which are becoming increasingly important to the performance of modern organizations (Lian and Laing, 2007). Some of the key issues affecting how these types of service are marketed are summarized in Figure 9.4.

Research suggests that the most important selection criterion for buyers is prior experience of services like architectural and engineering expertise. During the progress of any assignment, the supplier's capabilities in understanding customers' needs and interactive relationship management take equal precedence, especially in terms of the 'personal chemistry' between service firm personnel and their clients (Day and Barksdale, 1992). For legal services, the outcome of what has been delivered is rated as the most important indicator of service quality, but, again, interactive factors such as a sense of confidence in the lawyer's expertise and keeping the client informed of progress are almost as significant. As the main corporate buyers of professional services, CEOs place considerable weight on word-of-mouth (WOM) referrals made by their peers (File et al, 1994). This suggests that marketers of professional firms should focus on improving the communication skills of client contact and service provision staff to enhance the service experience, rather than taking their traditional approach of investing solely in promotional tactics like brochure production and public relations (Ellis and Watterson, 2001).

The role of professional service staff as boundary spanners in the formation of inter-organizational relationships is highlighted by Lian and Laing (2007). They show how the purchasing of occupational health services by public and private sector organizations in the UK is characterized by a high degree of intangibility, comprises non-standardized offerings, and involves much interaction between the supplying firm and the purchaser. In these circumstances, the personal relations between client and occupational health professional become crucial, even to the degree that there is some debate whether clients are purchasing the health services or a mixture of services and personal relationships. If the latter is the case, then the stability of the relationship can be used as a platform to build jointly developed services in the future. This depends on the service firm's ability to retain its professional staff – a high turnover of key personnel can be very damaging to any professional service firm, whether it is involved in delivering health advice or legal, accountancy, and other types of expertise.

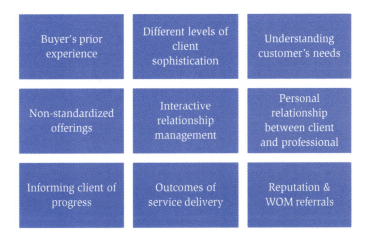

Figure 9.4 Issues in the marketing of professional services

Sometimes, of course, as is the case for many SME providers or self-employed consultants, the professional and the marketer are the same person. In such instances, consultants and people in similar occupations must perfect their relationship marketing skills as much as their professional expertise. To help overall perceptions of service quality, in creative business services like advertising, architecture, and design, service personnel can cultivate impressions about likely creative output by remaining attentive to the wide range of client feelings and uncertainties about the service on offer. This requires a high level of interpersonal skills 'in order to respond appropriately to what they think their clients think they know' (Davies 2009, p 116). Moreover, service providers could consider segmenting their clients by their degree of sophistication, in order then to match service levels to clients' knowledge and need for reassurance, for instance by ensuring that some customers receive more in the way of explanations and progress reports regarding the assignment than others.

This all places considerable responsibility on the heads of individual members of staff in professional service firms, making it vital to attract the right recruits in the first place – see Box 9.6. These sorts of relationships between professional organizations and universities are especially common in the accounting and finance sector, as you may have noticed by the high visibility of such companies at graduate job fairs.

The key role of individual actors in the service sector is also illustrated by the 'headhunting' (or executive search) part of the staff recruitment industry. For firms selling this type of service to organizations on an increasingly global scale, the ability to draw upon the resource of the personal reputation of certain key people in the sector is helping to drive the process of internationalization in Europe (Hall et al, 2009). Thus, names like Russell Reynolds and Richard Ferry (who both founded firms in 1969) are commonly evoked, which is equivalent to talking about high-profile advertising agencies like Saatchi & Saatchi. These individuals and their brand-leading firms (e.g. Korn/Ferry International – www.kornferry.com) are referred to by other, competing, service suppliers to legitimate headhunting as an industry and educate new geographical markets on the benefits of hiring a headhunting firm for executive searches. This has been an important strategy as headhunting has only recently

Box 9.6 Mini case

Gaining access to the key resource in business services

As the consulting engineers Arup appreciate, the quality of a professional service firm is maintained by the quality of the individual professionals who represent it. The firm, which is famous for working on landmark projects such as the Bird's Nest stadium in Bejing, thus devotes a lot of attention to graduate recruitment. For example, from its Nottingham regional offices, where staff have been responsible for developing the Trent Bridge Cricket Ground and the widening of the M1 motorway, Arup has established an international reputation for its staff's expertise in certain areas of construction such as pavement engineering. The firm's growth in Nottingham has been facilitated by a steady supply of graduate talent from universities in the surrounding region in cities like Nottingham, Leicester, and Loughborough. Arup's senior local manager, Dr Robin Lee, says that 'this is one of the great strengths of being in the city'.

Source: Baker (2008); www.arup.com

been recognized as a 'stand-alone' professional service industry. It allows all the members of the same industrial network to gain from the opportunities of the stable market that it helps create by reinforcing, promoting, and celebrating competitors rather than challenging them.

9.3 B2B Services Marketing Management

The characteristics of services have led to different approaches being taken to the implementation of service delivery in business markets (Gronroos, 2000). Several of these management approaches are summarized in Figure 9.5 and are outlined below.

- Service concept development: This involves expressing the service in terms of the customer problems that the supplier must address, i.e. what the service will do. Defining this, in turn, guides investment decisions by the supplying firm over the resources and activities necessary to deliver the service. You should remember that the service element of a firm's offering rarely exists in isolation, but is combined with other, more tangible, product offerings. Thus, being able to combine creatively services with products where appropriate to maximize the value available to organizational customers is an important part of the marketer's role. For example, a bank may offer a basic savings and loan service to its corporate clients, while also providing tax advice and insurance, with the latter incorporating guidance on the physical equipment necessary to secure premises and stock.

- Service outcome management: This involves determining how the service will solve the customer's problem, i.e. how the service will be delivered. In B2B markets, this often involves agreeing specific, measurable performance criteria with clients, such as a logistics firm agreeing to meet strict time targets for the transportation of goods between factories and local depots. This offers a degree of tangibility regarding the service, making it more possible to ensure outcomes. Note in Box 9.7 how Italian firm, ZenAsia, offers reassurance to its customers through a host of logistics checks. Such is the success of its approach that the firm is planning to open a new branch in Spain where it has determined that wholesalers are interested in drawing upon their logistics services to support sourcing from the Far East.

- Customer expectation management: For relationships between service providers and customers to be successful, it is important to manage customer expectations. Buyers may

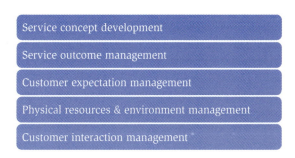

Figure 9.5 Management approaches to B2B service delivery

> **Box 9.7**
>
> **Managing logistics services throughout the supply/demand chain**
>
> ZenAsia serves Italian SME manufacturers and distributors who import goods from China, Vietnam, and India across a wide range of sectors from electro-mechanical and wooden furniture components to clothing and metal tools. The firm trades with 350 separate Asian suppliers, though its focus is on Chinese manufacturers from whom it guarantees a continuous monitoring for its organizational clients in Europe. The list of logistics-related services provided by ZenAsia is extensive, and covers many potential problem areas for its clients from the start to the finish of the entire order process: product sourcing, vendor search, document acquisition, consultation over contractual terms, control of pallets and packaging, online quality control, manufacturing time checks, pre-shipment inspection, shipment of materials, customer assistance, complaint handing, and reorder assistance. The detailed audit reports and quality controls that ZenAsia applies at every stage of the process provides its Italian clients with a high degree of reassurance that things are working well in the relationship between themselves and vendor.
>
> *Source: Nassimbeni and Sartor (2006); www.zenasia.com*

need to be advised over any unrealistic expectations they have regarding the ability of the supplier to deliver the service. If we return to our transportation example, it might be quite impractical for a firm to get goods to certain isolated parts of the world as fast as others; thus customers will need to appreciate that service levels may vary, depending on how far they wish their goods to be shipped. If the customer is not 'educated' up front about the reasonable limitations of the offering, there is a danger they will perceive the service supplier as breaking its promises.

• Physical resources and environment management: These elements of service delivery must provide the appropriate technological base for operations and support interaction with the customer. Marketers need to ensure that systems put in place to check resources (staff levels, equipment, information systems, etc.) are sufficient to enable service promises to be met and that locations such as reception areas, meeting rooms, or technical laboratories where customer interactions may take place are maintained to a high standard. For instance, the business aircraft manufacturer Hawker Beechcraft ensures that it can provide global customer service via what it claims is the largest customer support network in the industry, available on a round-the-clock basis, comprising over 100 factory-owned and authorized service centres staffed by over 3,000 people worldwide (www.hawkerbeechcraft.com).

• Customer interaction management: Since any relationship will be the outcome of interactions between customer and supplier, it is difficult for managers to have complete control of the service delivery. The behaviours of both parties play a role in creating the atmosphere of the relationship (see Chapter Five). In addition to attempting to influence the performance of their own staff, marketers from business service providers can also attempt to guide customers on how to get the best out of the service on offer. This can range from quite basic issues such as encouraging the phasing of order placements so that queues do not build up at busy times, through to more complex matters like explaining the need for openness and information sharing during a consultancy or audit exercise.

Delivering service quality

The above approaches suggest that the three most important functional departments of a service organization are marketing, operations, and human resources (Lovelock, 1992). These departments contribute to two 'sides' of service delivery: the 'front' stage and 'back-stage', the latter so called because it is largely invisible to the customer. Front-stage activities are the interactive part of the service offering, such as service personnel, physical resources, and interaction systems, whereas backstage activities involve providing the necessary supervisory, physical, and systems support. Much of this support is provided by the human resources and operations functions of the firm. B2B marketing contributes to service delivery but also to other components such as market analysis and customer satisfaction research, and the more visible activities of advertising and sales efforts (Gronroos, 2000).

Such is the importance of distinguishing a company from its competitors by providing good service that some marketers try to measure service quality as a way of assessing client satisfaction. The most well-known set of dimensions used to determine customer perceptions of quality are those developed by Parasuraman et al (1985) – see Figure 9.6.

Even if the formal mechanism for measuring these dimensions (known as the 'SERVQUAL' scale) is not employed, it is widely believed that the dimensions can serve as a useful checklist for managers to ensure that their firm is meeting customer expectations; expectations which may, of course, have been raised by the firm's own marketing communications. The dimensions reflect many of the characteristics of services and issues in business service management that we have discussed in this chapter so far:

- Tangibles: This refers to the physical appearance of staff, equipment, facilities, and communication materials. Note how the marketing efforts of Pall-Ex in the case at the start of the chapter reflect the use of tangible clues.
- Reliability: This is the ability of the provider to perform the promised service dependably and accurately. This is the single most important dimension of service quality – failure to deliver here can have serious consequences in terms of bad word of mouth from

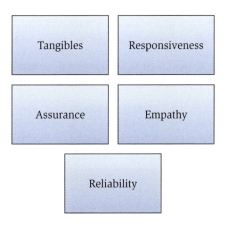

Figure 9.6 Some dimensions of service quality

dissatisfied customers. Some business service providers focus on this dimension in their advertising, e.g. the Malaysian B2B express delivery service City-Link claims, 'We live by the rule of quality service: reliability' (www.citylinkexpress.com.my).

- Responsiveness: The willingness to help customers and provide prompt service, particularly in response to unforeseen problems or service breakdowns.

- Assurance: The ability of service staff to convey trust and confidence via their knowledge and courtesy.

- Empathy: Providing individualized, caring attention to customers.

If we accept that the level of quality in the way a firm delivers its services to industrial customers is central to building relationships (see Chapter Three), then a means of measuring the perceptions of customers' experiences becomes attractive. Some researchers, however, question the applicability of the SERVQUAL dimensions to B2B services. Durvasula et al (1999) surveyed organizations in Singapore which regularly utilized ocean freight services for their export needs. They found that, due to differences between consumer and industrial contexts, the scales used in SERVQUAL need to be specifically tailored to the sector under investigation. Moreover, they concluded that the dimensions themselves may not be universally relevant across different types of business service. Indeed, it might be argued that a qualitative data gathering approach, where customers are interviewed about critical incidents during the provision of the service, may be more valuable in building a holistic picture of perceptions of service quality (Johns and Tyas, 1997).

Internal marketing

Due to the need for the interaction between people that underpins most services, internal marketing is particularly important in the service context. Three internal stakeholders, summarized in Figure 9.7, are involved in this process:

1. Front-line staff who are key to the quality of service provision and hence customer satisfaction

2. Management (including marketing management) who design the appropriate service offering and communicate this to potential customers

3. Other staff in the service firm who act in a supporting role to assist the service personnel as necessary (e.g. mechanics who maintain a transport firm's truck fleet, or clerks who provide customer address information for logistics delivery schedules).

In effect, managers have to treat staff as their internal 'customers' to whom the message of customer relationship building through service quality must be 'marketed'. In order to

Figure 9.7 Internal stakeholders in service marketing

ensure the consistency between promises made and actual service delivery implied by the reliability dimension of service quality, all employees need to 'buy in' to the marketing orientation of the firm. To help them do this, managers must make sure staff are convinced about the firm's market positioning, listened to if they have any concerns over their abilities to match this positioning, and given the necessary resources (and sometimes incentives) to meet customer expectations.

Research has shown that there is a direct link between employee satisfaction, retention, and productivity and customer satisfaction, which in turn relates to the service firm's financial performance (Heskett et al, 1994). Moreover, a satisfied customer is not just loyal but may well also act as an advocate of your firm (see Chapter Three). As part of ensuring employees are suitably motivated to turn their clients into advocates, internal marketing programmes should use the input of B2B marketers to explain the concepts underpinning the firm's offering and to help train staff about their key role in delivering this offering. More on internal marketing can be found when we discuss the role of marketing communications in Chapter Eleven.

New service development

Just as with product offerings, there is often a need for B2B marketers to design new services in order to maintain overall sales as different service offerings within a firm's portfolio reach the maturity stage of their life cycle (see Chapter Eight). In organizational markets, there appear to be a number of types of new service projects that succeed (De Brentani, 1995). Basically, new offerings that make the most of the supplier's capabilities, are closely matched to meet customers' needs and are introduced with careful planning have the greatest potential for adoption by the marketplace. Projects that incorporate these features include:

- Customized expert services: As the name suggests, this approach involves fitting the firm's capabilities very closely to the specific needs of individual customers. To make this work requires skilled front-line personnel who can accurately determine client needs, e.g. an IT consultant able to recommend to his/her firm's software engineers the appropriate elements of an inventory-control package that supports a customer's manufacturing operations.

- Planned pioneering services: This approach involves developing a new service around the firm's core capabilities, but doing so in a new competitive context. Careful planning of the launch of such a service is necessary to convince potential clients to try it out, e.g. via appropriate tangible evidence (perhaps via a demonstration at a trade show – see Chapter Eleven) to a new-task buyer of the benefits the service can bring.

- Improved service experiences: Here, an existing service offering is enhanced using new resources, for instance in the form of new technical equipment to boost the speed of the process; e.g. the addition by a logistics firm of an electronic tracking system that enables a customer's warehouse and delivery staff quickly to scan bar codes on goods as they pass through the transportation network.

On the other hand, new service developments that typically fail tend to exhibit these characteristics:

- Peripheral low market potential services: These sorts of supposed innovations are, unfortunately, fairly common in B2B markets. While such services might provide a relatively rapid way to add to the service portfolio, they fail because they are launched with minimal attempts to understand customer needs and demand levels, and without taking into account the service provider's core capabilities.

- Poorly planned industrialized clones: Here, service firms are guilty of just copying the innovations of competitor firms, but doing so without really verifying whether the new service is what their customers want, or even whether or not they are too complex for the firm's staff and physical resources to deliver properly. They thus fail to provide any sustainable competitive advantage.

Front-line employees are potentiality good sources of innovative B2B service ideas picked up during service delivery. This is due to their external network of personal contacts from which they can gather better-quality information – see Box 9.8.

However, for firms to benefit from any ideas acquired at the customer–supplier interface, the ideas generated from the sorts of interactions described in Box 9.8 need to be brought into the company and developed further. Research has shown that service staff are sometimes unsure of what to do with ideas for innovation generated this way and who to go to in their firm to initiate the new service development process. In fact, some service firm managers can be guilty of showing a lack of interest and encouragement towards suggestions made by front-line employees, with inadequate feedback, few incentives, and no mechanism for distributing ideas internally (Neumann and Holzmüller, 2007).

In an attempt to address these sorts of problems, Nätti and Ojasalo (2008) describe a number of organizational practices that can encourage internal customer knowledge utilization in professional B2B service firms. They suggest developing a relationship coordination system, with a manager who collates feedback from the customer (perhaps via front-line staff) and interprets it for the organization. The coordinator's role is to link different experts to their customer contacts, combining different types of expertise in order to create the best possible value-added offering for the client. This depends on the coordinator having as strong an internal network (e.g. amongst the firm's professional staff) as external. It is also important that this manager is seen as a 'neutral actor' at the customer interface, keeping themselves separate from any internal politics in the organization. The coordinator should be

Box 9.8 Voices

Sources of innovation for business services

Here are a German manager of a technical service firm and a front-line member of service staff explaining how their interactions with people in customer organizations have led to innovations:

'When our consultants work on-site for the customer, they become our eyes and ears there. There is huge potential there. We can see what other problems and ideas the customer is working on.'

'It's important to not just talk to the purchasing people but also to the people actually working with the machines. . . . They often have a lot of ideas: "You should do this" and so on.'

Source: Neumann and Holzmüller (2007)

responsible for adding customer-specific knowledge to data that can be stored on common IT systems that support CRM (see Chapter Three). This can facilitate the creation of a matrix structure that combines functional expertise and client expertise in project teams for each client's service needs as required. Once again, therefore, we see how sensitive relationship management underpins much of B2B marketing.

The chapter concludes with a case study that looks more closely at the relationships between people in service firms and their clients in the context of the advertising industry. The case represents an alternative way of looking at marketing practice as it shows how some subtle behaviours of individual professional service providers have the potential to influence corporate clients.

Summary

The key points to take from this chapter are as follows:

- The strategic shifts important in adopting a combined product–service approach to business markets.
- The extensive range of business services available to client organizations.
- How services differ from business products in terms of some key characteristics and what these characteristics mean for B2B marketers.
- The challenges of managing marketing in professional services firms where the supplier's key asset is each individual member of the professional staff.
- How a number of different strategic approaches can lead to success in business service provision.
- The significance of service quality and internal marketing for firms operating in organizational markets.
- Some of the ways in which new service development can be carried out successfully.

Discussion questions

1. How can a manufacturer of machinery for garment making generate increased revenue through its business service offerings?

2. What would you advise a newly appointed marketer representing a corporate conference venue about what it may need to take into account regarding the key characteristics of business services?

3. Imagine you work in marketing for a large accountancy firm with many organizational clients. Explain to your human resources department why 'part-time marketers' are so important in B2B services marketing.

4. How do buyers of business services tend to evaluate the quality of what they are provided?

5. How would you carry out an internal marketing programme for a road haulage firm with clients based across Europe?

Case study

Constructing Credibility in Working with Organizational Clients in a Swedish Advertising Agency

Peter Svensson, Lund University, Lund, Sweden

Introduction

The advertising industry is a particularly interesting kind of business service. Some parts of the service offering are tangible, e.g. the actual advertisement, brochure, or film that the agency creates for the client. However, the creative expertise and know-how offered by the advertising agency are difficult to capture and evaluate. Moreover, marketing services – and perhaps advertising in particular – are often looked upon with a great deal of suspicion, both with respect to their relevance for organizational performance and their wider, societal consequences.

Given these factors, a major challenge for marketing service providers is that of creating and maintaining a certain level of legitimacy and trustworthiness in client relations. Much of the legitimacy work takes place in the direct interaction between providers and buyers. At the end of the day, inter-organizational relationships (IORs) boil down to relations between flesh-and-blood people interacting, meeting, talking, arguing, and negotiating. This is shown in the following example taken from the Swedish advertising industry (Svensson, 2004, 2007).

ADEXP and the lawn mower campaign

ADEXP was a typical Swedish creative advertising agency. The work at the agency was organized in teams, comprising a project leader, art director, and copywriter. Garden Inc. had been ADEXP's client for several years. The company produced lawnmowers. A new gardening season was approaching, so a fresh advertising campaign for lawnmowers was needed. Therefore, a meeting was organized at which ideas for the upcoming campaign were to be discussed. Present at the meeting were: Sven, CEO of Garden Inc.; Victoria, project leader at ADEXP; Anders, art director; and Bill, newly employed copywriter at the agency.

During the meeting, the advertising team worked intensely to present themselves as credible and trustworthy. One way of doing this is to appear professional. Professionalism can function as a clue that removes client uncertainty and doubts about their business service provider. Despite efforts to become a profession, marketing does not enjoy the kind of professional status held by doctors or lawyers. Traditional professions such as these gain legitimacy through various credentials, certifications, titles, and compulsory degrees. 'Marketer', however, is not a state-controlled title and you do not need a university degree in order to refer to yourself as a 'marketing person'.

Consequently, the professional credibility of marketing work needs to be created by other means. Marketing service providers must accomplish credibility and trust on a daily basis in interactions with their clients. The task for the marketer, then, becomes that of appearing professional in everyday communications. Professional credibility can thus be seen as a local and situational accomplishment that emerges in ongoing interactions with clients rather than as a pre-existing resource to be utilized.

Note that while the meeting in this case concerned the design of a campaign aimed at end-user consumers, it is the marketing practices of the agency in relation to the corporate client, Garden Inc., that we are interested in. ADEXP's team members presented themselves in two main ways: one that emphasized proactivity and control over consumers; and one that focused on market orientation and responsiveness.

Portraying oneself as expert in manipulating consumers

The art director and copywriter constructed themselves several times as experts on the manipulations of symbols. The knowledge of how to use symbols in advertisements in order to evoke certain (profitable) emotions and desires in the minds of consumers was brought to the fore as one of the professional competencies offered by the agency. One example of this was when the advertising team presented the idea of letting a factory worker 'sign' individual lawnmowers in order to create a sense of genuineness and high quality:

'I would like to emphasize that Garden Inc. is a domestic company,' Sven, the Garden Inc. CEO declared.

'I think it is possible to go even further than that,' Anders said. 'We can let the person who has made the particular lawnmower sign some kind of note that we attach to the machine: "This is made by Nils."'

'Quality,' Bill said.

Sven also had some ideas of his own. 'We could take some photos of the factory. Well, first we have to clean it up a bit, of course. But some pictures of the factory floor. . . . Then we could reinforce this thing about high-tech at the same time as we emphasize genuineness. It shouldn't be "high-tech-ready to-deliver-to-the-factory". It must be "handmade", right?'

'Yes, it is part of our (i.e. consumers') nature,' Anders agreed, 'that we think that handmade is high quality.'

In the excerpt above, Bill and Anders from ADEXP presented their competence as one of handling symbols. Note how Sven, the client, responded positively to this idea.

Another example is offered in this excerpt:

'We must turn "it is expensive" into "security and durability", that the lawnmowers last for a long time,' Sven made clear. 'After all, Garden Inc. lawnmowers are 15 to 20% more expensive than other lawnmowers.'

Anders nodded. 'Yes, we could use that; that you cannot produce a good lawnmower cheaply.'

In this short interaction, Anders responded approvingly to the client's wish to 'turn' one association ('it is expensive') into another more desirable one ('security and durability'), and assured Sven that this is something the advertising agency is able to do.

In emphasizing symbolic management as a unique professional marketing skill, the marketing services offered were portrayed as a proactive enterprise, and consumers' desires and emotions were described as objects of control and manipulation. Needless to say, the competence to create or at least stimulate consumers' demands for the client's products is an expertise that in most cases is considered highly valuable. From the client's point of view, this may be a competence that is well worth purchasing from a marketing service provider like ADEXP.

Portraying oneself as responsive to end-user customers

A second mode in which the advertising team tried to perform professionally in relation to the client was by means of emphasizing the importance of market orientation.

Anders informed Sven about what the advertising team had discussed before the meeting:

'Yesterday, Bill and I talked about having some clues for the consumer; what kind of lawnmower you are in need of.' He told Sven about the idea of constructing a lawn-mower guide on the Internet, where the potential buyer could specify his or her requirements for lawn mowing, for instance by answering questions dealing with the size of the lawn and preferred time spent on the task. In doing so, the idea was that Garden Inc. would help the consumer to find the lawnmower that best suited his or her unique demands.

Sven presented a sceptical face. 'Well, we want to avoid specifying too much. We want to lift them up, to a higher assortment level. Then we make more money, right? It is a trick, you see? We don't want to lower them to a lower assortment level, like: "Ok, then I don't need more than this."'

Bill, the copywriter, responded, 'Yes, but most important is what kinds of needs you (i.e. the consumers) have, isn't it?'

In this interaction, the advertising team presented an idea based on the premise of market orientation. The needs of the consumers were thus stressed as an important point of departure for the definition of the client's business. However, the client was a bit nervous that this would lead to the consumers choosing a cheaper type of lawn-mower (in a 'lower assortment level'). Thus, whereas the client stressed his wishes to control his customers ('lift them up'), the ADEXP team assumed the opposite position, promoting the idea of listening and adapting to the individual needs of the client organization's consumers.

This brief tension was a moment in the meeting when the advertising agency people presented themselves as professionals with integrity and insights that exceeded the client's knowledge. Market orientation is a fundamental cornerstone of marketing management knowledge and the professional marketing service provider needs to show that he or she is well acquainted with this formula for business success. In contrast to the presentation of themselves as manipulators of symbols, the emphasis on market orientation suggests a more responsive view of marketing on the part of the agency personnel.

Conclusions

To sum up, at the meeting between ADEXP and its client, two different viewpoints on marketing services were presented. Whereas the first emphasized possibilities to control and manipulate the consumers by means of symbol management, the second stressed the responsive aspects of marketing work. This polarization of viewpoints is a part of the advertising agency's local accomplishment of professional credibility. In order to qualify as a professional provider of marketing services, manipulation and responsiveness are here presented as crucial competencies.

In these types of daily interactions with clients, the professional credibility of the advertising agency is locally accomplished. Professional credibility and trust are not stable phenomena but need to be incessantly accomplished in everyday interactions such as in the meeting discussed above. The marketing professional is, as it were, created and recreated over and over again in these mundane situations.

More generally, IORs are practically handled in the small and mundane interactions with partners of different sorts on a day-to-day basis. Consequently, it can be argued that IORs are best understood as local accomplishments, taking place via interactions in daily work, rather than as results of grandiose and visionary top management strategies.

Source: Svensson (2004); Svensson (2007)

Case study questions

1. The case suggests relations between advertising agencies and their clients are based upon mundane, everyday interactions in meetings and conversations. Do you think this is also the case for more 'traditional' professions such as lawyers and accountants, or even doctors?

2. Do you think it is possible to plan and manage these 'moments of truth' in which service providers deliver – and to some extent simultaneously produce – marketing services? How could this be done?

3. Two main representations were used by ADEXP in order to create a sense of professional credibility and trust: expertise in symbol management and market orientation. Are there other themes or clues that the advertising agency personnel could have used? And might these clues change in importance for corporate clients in different national cultures?

Further Reading

Alvesson, M., Karreman, D., Sturdy, A., & Handley, K. (2009) Unpacking the Client(s): Constructions, Positions and Client-Consultant Dynamics, Scandinavian Journal of Management, 25, pp 253–63
This paper argues that client organizations are heterogeneous assemblies of actors and interests involved in multiple ways in consultancy projects. It emphasizes three issues: client diversity; processes of socially constructing 'the client' and the client identities which are thereby produced; and the dynamics of client–consultant relations in the provision of consultancy services.

Gronroos, C. (1998) Marketing Services: The Case of a Missing Product, Journal of Business & Industrial Marketing, 13 (4/5), pp 322–38
The author discusses the case of an elevator (lift) repair and maintenance service firm which conducted research to explore why it was losing business to competitors. The findings provided a valuable lesson, as they showed that although the outcome of the work was satisfactory, customers indicated that they were not happy with the way the service was being carried out.

Yanamandram, V. & Whaite, L. (2006) Switching Barriers in Business-to-Business Services: A Qualitative Study, International Journal of Service Industry Management, 17 (2), pp 158–92

This article investigates the determinants of behavioural brand loyalty amongst dissatisfied customers in the B2B services sector. The findings are useful for those firms which have many prospective switchers because it is important to understand why these customers stay, and to what extent such firms, in both positive and negative ways, can discourage such customers from leaving.

Zeithaml, V. A., Parasuraman, A., & Berry, L. L. (1985) Problems and Strategies in Services Marketing, Journal of Marketing, Spring, pp 33–46

These authors compare issues in the service marketing literature with those reported by actual service providers, including those in the commercial banking, transportation, construction, and consultancy sectors, as well as some consumer services. They discuss several themes that emerge, including the interesting finding that B2B service providers appear to be more customer-orientated than B2C firms.

References

Allen, A. (2008) Delivering Success, The Marketer, December–January, pp 24–7

Baker, R. (2008) Taking Talents around Planet, Nottingham Evening Post, 24 September, p 49

Bashford, S. (2008) People Protector, The Marketer, November, pp 24–7

Bokaie, J. (2008) OpenSkies Axes Economy Option, Marketing, 8 August, p 4

Davies, M. (2009) Service Quality Tolerance in Creative Business Service Relationships, Service Industries Journal, 29 (1), pp 91–110

Day, E. & Barksdale, H. C. (1992) How Firms Select Professional Services, Industrial Marketing Management, 21, pp 85–91

De Brentani, U. (1995) New Industrial Service Development: Scenarios for Success and Failure, Journal of Business Research, 32, pp 93–103

Durvasula, S., Lyonski, S., & Mehta, S. C. (1999) Testing the SERVQUAL Scale in the Business to-Business Sector: The Case of Ocean Freight Shipping Service, Journal of Services Marketing, 13 (2), pp 132–50

Ellis, N. (1999) A Disco(urse) Inferno: The Pitfalls of Professionalism, Marketing Intelligence and Planning,17 (7), pp 333–43

Ellis, N. & Watterson, C. (2001) Client Perceptions of Regional Law Firms and their Implications for Marketing Management, Service Industries Journal, 21 (4), pp 100–18

Feakins, M. (2009) Offshoring in the Core: Russian Software Firms Onshoring in the USA, Global Networks, 9 (1), pp 1–19

File, K. M., Cermack, D. J., & Prince, R. A. (1994) Word of Mouth Effects in Professional Services Buyer Behaviour, Service Industries Journal, 14 (e), pp 301–14

Gebauer, H. & Fleisch, E. (2007) An Investigation of the Relationship between Behavioural Processes, Motivation, Investments in the Service Business and Service Revenue, Industrial Marketing Management, 36, pp 337–48

Gronroos, C. (2000) Service Management and Marketing, 2nd edn, Wiley, Chichester

Guardian (The) (2009) 11 April, p 40

Gummesson, E. (1991) Marketing Orientation Revisited: The Crucial Role of the Part-Time Marketer, European Journal of Marketing, 25 (2), pp 60–75

Hall, S., Beaverstock, J. V., Faulconbridge, J. R., & Hewitson, A. (2009) Exploring Cultural Economies of Internationalization: The Role of 'Iconic Individuals' and 'Brand Leaders' in the Globalization of Headhunting, Global Networks, 9 (3), pp 399–419

Heskett, J. L., Jones, T. O., Loveman, G. W., Sasser, W. E., & Schlesinger, L. A. (1994) Putting the Service-Profit Chain to Work, Harvard Business Review, 72 (2), pp 164–74

Johns, N. & Tyas, P. (1997) Customer Perceptions of Service Operations: Gestalt, Incident or Mythology? Service Industries Journal, 17 (3), pp 478–88

Johnstone, S., Dainty, A., & Wilkinson, A. (2008) In Search of 'Product-Service': Evidence from Aerospace, Construction and Engineering, Service Industries Journal, 28 (6), pp 861–75

Koch, T. & Ramsbottom, O. (2008) A Growth Strategy for a Chinese State-Owned Enterprise: An Interview with ChemChina's President, McKinsey Quarterly, online at http://www.mckinseyquarterly.com, accessed July 2008

LaPlaca, P. J. (2009) The Impact of Outsourcing on B2B Marketing, Industrial Marketing Management, 38, pp 373–5

Lian, P. C. S. & Laing, A. W. (2007) Relationships in the Purchasing of Business to Business Professional Services: The Role of Personal Relationships, Industrial Marketing Management, 36, pp 709–18

Lovelock, C. (1992) Managing Services, Prentice Hall, Englewood Cliffs, NJ

Lovelock, C., Vandermerwe, S., & Lewis, B. (1999) Services Marketing, FT Prentice Hall, Hemel Hempstead

Majewski, B. M. & Srinivas, S. (2003) The Services Challenge: Operationalizing your Services Strategy, IBM Business Consulting Services Executive Brief, Somers, NY

Mathieu, V. (2001) Product Services: From a Service Supporting the Product to a Service Supporting the Client, Journal of Business & Industrial Marketing, 16 (1), pp 39–58

Nassimbeni, G. & Sartor, M. (2006) Sourcing in China: Strategies, Methods and Experiences, Palgrave Macmillan, Houndsmill

Nätti, S. & Ojasalo, J. (2008) What Prevents Effective Utilisation of Customer Knowledge in Professional B-to-B Services? An Empirical Study, Service Industries Journal, 28 (9), pp 1199–214

Neumann, D. & Holzmüller, H. H. (2007) Service Delivery Encounters in Business-to-Business Contexts as a Source of Innovation – A Conceptual and Explorative Study, Journal of Business Market Management, 1 (2), pp 105–34

Nottingham Evening Post (2009) Rolls-Royce Deal, 17 June, p 21

Parasuraman, A., Zeithaml, V., & Berry, L. (1985) A Conceptual Model of Service Quality and its Implications for Future Research, Journal of Marketing, Fall, pp 41–50

Svensson, P. (2004) Setting the Marketing Scene: Reality Production in Everyday Marketing Work, Lund Business Press, Lund

Svensson, P. (2007) Producing Marketing: Towards a Social-Phenomenology of Marketing Work, Marketing Theory, 7 (3), pp 271–90

van Looy, B., Gemmel, P., Desmet, S., van Deerdonck, R., & Seernels, S. (1998) Dealing with Productivity and Service Quality Indicators in a Service Environment: Some Field Experiences, International Journal of Service Industry Management, 9 (4), pp 359–76

Wendelin, R. (2009) Developing Total Business Solutions in B2B from Product to Solution Sales: Possibilities and Challenges, Comments in Presentation at 4th Meeting of the IMP Group in Asia, Kuala Lumpur, 10–12 December

Zeithaml, V. A. & Bitner, M. J. (2000) Services Marketing, McGraw-Hill, New York

Chapter 10
Value & Pricing in B2B Markets

Introduction & Learning Objectives

This chapter covers one of the classic 'Ps' of the marketing mix, price, but moves beyond the sometimes rather restrictive notions of pricing and costs to discuss value in more detail. The concept of value highlights some of the complexities faced by the B2B marketer in determining the significance of costs compared with benefits for buyers. Research has shown that there are often more important issues than price for organizational customers (Laric, 1980). As B2B scholars have increasingly acknowledged the significance of inter-organizational relationships (see Chapter Three), there are indications that cooperative price negotiations are becoming the norm, leaving the aggressive practices of 'zero-sum' haggling behind. It is probably naive, however, to imagine that all organizations and individual purchasing managers will give up their desire to strike cost-driven deals, especially if we see a growth in electronic reverse auctions (see section 10.3).

The case in Box 10.1 shows how value creation is important for firms working together to market their resources in the form of competencies or skills. The approach taken by this network of Tuscan spinners reflects their appreciation that non-monetary value is a key part of a customer's incentive to purchase, making price far from the only consideration in buyers' minds.

Box 10.1 Mini case
Marketing competencies to add value for business customers

The case of the textile industry in Italy illustrates how suppliers can market competencies that are relevant for their customers, both in order to revitalize existing relationships and to influence the buying behaviour of prospective customers. In the 1990s, a group of small but high-quality yarn manufacturers in Tuscany embarked on a strategy to align themselves more closely with fashion producers. The success of their strategy, which has helped firms like Florence-based Lineapiu fend off low cost competition from the Far East, can be attributed to their approach to value creation. This success has continued as the firms' premium-pricing position allows them to focus their marketing efforts on luxury brand manufacturers: Lineapiu's revenues for 2008 were expected to exceed €88 million.

Together, Tuscan yarn spinners possessed valuable knowledge-based skills regarding the fashion trend-setting process, i.e. by their collective understanding of consumption trends, designers' ideas, and the utility of different materials, thereby being able to incorporate future fashion into their yarns with great flexibility. This depended on the different firms in Tuscany being able to maintain relationships amongst themselves, thus bridging 'know-how' located in different organizational actors in their regional network. These firms' joint strategy involved three stages. First, they had to be able to anticipate the buyers' skills gap prior to the establishment of a relationship, and then align their own business processes accordingly. This entailed the supplier taking a risk in investing in competence development. Second, the competencies needed to be promoted to raise customers' awareness of the value potential of the resources on offer. This necessitated some sort of 'live' demonstration of the skills, especially as the intangibility of knowledge exchange can be difficult to convey. Third, the suppliers had to apply specific competencies to the customer's business processes.

Taking each of the above stages in turn: the Tuscan spinners first funded joint research teams to pool the expertise of each firm in the region in forecasting the fashion adoption process, thus enabling them to adapt their innovation to future market needs despite their position near the 'top' of the supply/demand chain; they then organized what one of their customers described as 'a learning experience' for prospective organizational buyers attending a major trade fair, based on displaying tangible clothing and fashion prototypes; finally, they attracted new customers by selling yarn that already incorporated some of the forecasted fashion trends. The value added for customers was not just the high-quality yarn, but the ability of the spinners to anticipate future fashion and to collaborate with their clients in NPD and reducing time-to-market.

Source: Zerbini et al (2007); www.lineapiu.com

Chapter Aims

After completing this chapter, you should be able to:

- Recognize the significance of value perceptions in B2B marketing
- Understand how a number of internal and external factors can affect price setting in organizational markets
- Identify different strategies for managing the price element of the marketing mix.

10.1 Notions of Value in Organizational Markets

Pricing in B2B marketing is inextricably linked to notions of value. For a business customer (and, indeed, an individual consumer), value is determined by the net satisfaction derived from any transaction, and not simply the costs of obtaining the goods or services concerned. Thus, value can be defined as the worth of the economic, technical, service, and social benefits a customer firm receives in exchange for the price it pays for a market offering (Anderson et al, 1993). In this definition, 'benefits' indicates net benefits, in other words allowing for any costs (except the purchase price) incurred by the customer in obtaining the desired benefits. The weighing of costs against benefits is represented in Figure 10.1.

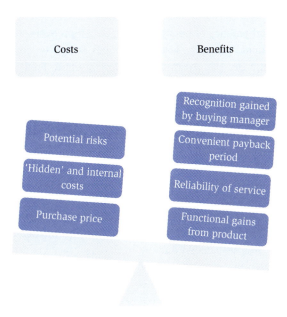

Figure 10.1 Value as benefits vs costs: some examples

In organizational markets, value is relative to the customer's expectations and experience of other offerings within any product category, such as alternative (perhaps cheaper, but not as high quality) sources of components, or even deciding to make the goods concerned in-house. As we saw in the Tuscan spinners case (Box 10.1), value can be found in areas like the knowledge-exchange relationship between buyer and seller, and the reliability of inter-firm logistics links, as well as in the quality of products. Competing firms attempt to offer enhanced value to their potential customers through activities such as product design, flexibility of production, marketing, and service in the form of delivery and after-sales support. Box 10.2 shows how international buyers of stationery may value such offerings, even when price is what appears to be the most important factor in certain markets.

Box 10.2 Mini case
Understanding the value perceptions of global business customers

Sid Lowe, Kingston University, Kingston Upon Thames, UK

Nancy was an executive director of a Hong Kong company manufacturing stationery and greeting cards for the US and UK markets. She had secured a very large American contract in 1995, which she regarded as a lifeline to the company. She attributed her success in securing the contract to 'modern' management techniques which she had introduced to the company after having completed a part-time MBA from an Australian university.

Instead of the usual practice of passive order taking from overseas buyers and Hong Kong trading companies, Nancy had actively sought buyers by conducting extensive market research in the US, UK, Australia, and New Zealand. From this, she had concluded that while price competitiveness was the essential prerequisite for all of these markets, subsidiary requirements were different in each country, so making it difficult to standardize the marketing mix. Nancy had decided to target mainly buyers not seeking the lowest price, but requiring punctual delivery and good quality standards for volume products and, secondly, to develop new high-value-added products for less price-sensitive niches.

The aforementioned American contract was with a direct marketing company. This organization was seeking high-quality personalized greeting cards for specific customers. It entered into an agreement in which bespoke designs for each customer were transmitted via the Internet to Nancy's company from the American buyer. The order was then produced and despatched directly to the customer via a bulk distributor in the US. Nancy believed that her value-added approach to business had been crucial to securing this contract.

Benefits and costs

It is thus important for marketers to be aware of how customers might perceive the costs and benefits, and hence value associated with a particular purchase. For every purchase decision, there are a number of attendant costs that must be weighed up against any potential benefits. For the purchase of a large piece of machinery, for example, there can be a myriad of further costs that occur well after the initial purchase price has been paid, ranging from the costs of maintaining the equipment to the cost of training the firm's staff in how to operate it.

- Benefits to the customer organization in such a situation may include: the functional and operational gains offered by the physical aspects of the product, or the reliability of any attendant service; financial benefits such as a convenient payback period; and the personal benefits gained by the purchasing manager who is recognized for making a good decision.

- Costs can include: acquisition costs which can comprise the initial purchase price minus any discounts, plus delivery and installation; internal costs such as training, lost production as the new piece of machinery is installed, and the disposal of any obsolete equipment; and potential risks arising from a poor purchase leading to interrupted operations and personal damage to a buyer's status.

Note how some of these issues may not be immediately obvious to the outside observer, such as the personal benefits and risks for the buyer associated with the decision (see Chapter Two). Similarly, you can see there can be many 'hidden' costs associated with a purchase in B2B markets. Figure 10.2 captures some of these in the metaphorical form of an 'iceberg', the majority of which is hidden beneath the surface. Nevertheless, the clearer the picture that B2B marketers have of the cost/benefit considerations that affect the customer, the better able they will be to advise their firm on setting the most appropriate price.

Marketers need to keep a close eye on their own organization's costs, too. Any assessment of a buyer–seller relationship should include an attempt to determine the true profitability

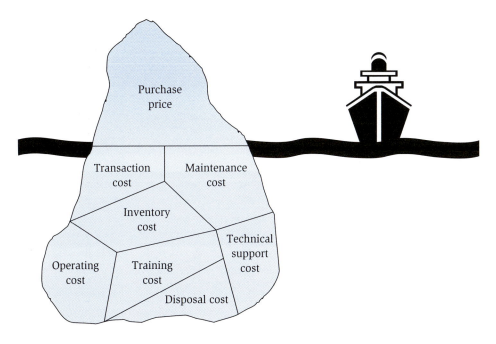

Figure 10.2 The total cost of ownership

Source: Adapted with permission from Christopher (1997, p 49)
M. Christopher (1997) Marketing Logistics, Elsevier, p 49,
copyright M. Christopher

of serving that customer, as shown in Figure 10.3. Note how the overall profitability of trading from the supplier's perspective is reduced by a series of costs, including those from the activities of production, marketing, and distribution.

We shall return to the significance of costs in price setting in Section 10.2 below, but for now, it is worth considering the idea of 'de-featuring' or cooperative pricing (van Weele, 2002). This occurs when managers from suppliers and customers work together in identifying superfluous product features and additional services that are not strictly required in order to meet a customer's requirements. Eliminating some of these 'extras', such as overly ornate design features, very short delivery times, or 24-hour parts availability from a warehouse, can enable a lower price to be agreed. Mutual benefits should arise from this negotiation as the customer achieves an offering at the best value possible, while the supplier is still able to achieve a reasonable profit since it has stripped some unnecessary costs out of serving this customer.

An accurate assessment of how value is perceived by its customer base can help a supplier to segment the market and target certain segments with appropriate offerings (see Chapters Six and Seven). A key part of organizational marketing management is recognizing that the value of an offering can vary, depending on the importance different segments attach to different exchange elements. It enables the supplier to target their resources appropriately, for instance in not pursuing a high-price, high-quality approach towards all segments when not all customers desire this. In practice, however, we can only ever estimate how value is seen by the marketplace. Quite often, the supplier may overestimate the value of their offering to

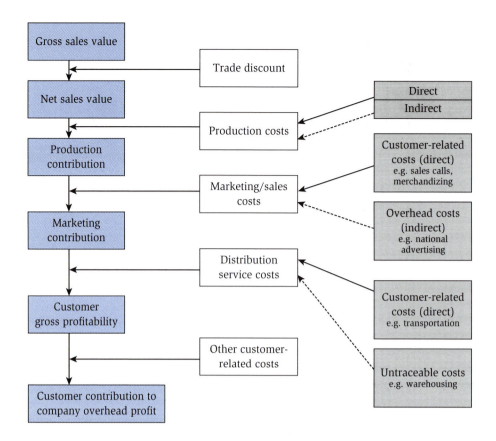

Figure 10.3 Customer account profitability
Source: Adapted with permission from Christopher (1997, p 67)
M. Christopher (1997) Marketing Logistics, Elsevier, p 67,
copyright M. Christopher

a particular customer, while the customer may underestimate the value. This suggests the importance of close relationships between suppliers and potential buyers in organizational markets so that the appropriate information can be exchanged, and an understanding of both parties' needs reached, to ensure the best possible matches to be made between seller and buyer perceptions of value.

Equipped with this understanding, B2B marketers need to translate product features into potential benefits that their customers can easily understand, and, moreover, into benefits that are worth something in use, i.e. to demonstrate their value in the customer's own setting. Much vital work at the final stage of this process is carried out via marketing communications and by the firm's sales force (see Chapters Eleven and Twelve). Moreover, a firm seeking to create value in its offerings needs to manage carefully how that value is delivered, especially in a business service context where so much is dependent on the firm's staff.

One way to approach this issue is shown in Box 10.3, where a large number of Infosys staff use their technical expertise to deliver a highly successful service to a client firm. Note how they add value for the client by helping to improve business processes in an industry where time is a crucial factor in logistics implementation (see also Chapter Four).

Box 10.3 Mini case

Creating value in corporate IT services

Infosys is an Indian company which has grown into a world leader in IT and consulting over the last three decades. It offers its organizational customers a variety of 'business solutions', including technology consulting, systems integration, software development, and business process outsourcing. Infosys has offices in Europe, China, Australia, Japan, and Canada and, of course, India. The firm is proud of its client relationships, claiming that over 97% of its revenues come from existing (i.e. repeat) customers.

One of Infosys's clients is a North American subsidiary of global electronics conglomerate making semiconductors for computing, wireless, and automotive sectors. A critical success factor in these sectors in on-time delivery as the client's customer firms work on extremely short product life cycles. The problem for the electronics conglomerate was that its legacy information systems for supply chain management were not sufficiently flexible to handle market fluctuations.

Infosys tackled this problem by committing a team of 45 experts, working over an impressively short time span of 18 months, and drawing on Oracle Enterprise Resource Planning applications. These workers' efforts meant that the project achieved process efficiencies across the client's manufacturing, distribution, purchasing, and accounting activities. This resulted in significant value gains, including an improvement in ROI for the client, as well as greater transparency 'up and down' the supply chain, increased levels of automation thereby reducing costs, and major improvements in on-time deliveries to their corporate customers.

Source: Infosys Technologies Limited (2010); www.infosys.com

10.2 Making Pricing Decisions

It remains a fact that purchasing departments are often charged with cost-cutting above all else, especially in recessionary times. Thus, despite attempts to ensure that it is notions of long-term value that influence purchasing decisions, the importance of the price 'P' remains high. The B2B marketer therefore needs to remain aware of a number of different issues in setting prices in industrial markets.

Compared with B2C exchanges, there is often greater complexity in B2B marketing regarding the pricing decisions that managers have to make. This is because prices charged by suppliers or retailers to consumers are generally fixed, enabling reasonably simple comparisons to be made by buyers. Organizational purchasers, on the other hand, typically have different factors to take into account, as we have seen in our discussion of value in the previous section. So how should suppliers go about judging the best price levels for their products and services? It helps to consider the process of price setting in two ways: 'inside-out' and 'outside-in' pricing (Christopher, 2000):

- Inside-out pricing: This is also known as cost-based pricing and assumes that price should reflect the costs involved 'inside' the selling firm in making and marketing the product. This sounds logical, but it presents a few problems: first, it can be difficult to identify and measure all the costs involved (see Figure 10.3), even if the firm has adopted techniques like activity-base costing; second, it is not a very market-orientated approach and runs the risk of setting a higher price than customers are able to pay simply in order to accommodate the adding of a profit margin to the accumulated costs. This can occur when a firm's pricing objective is focused on achieving a certain minimum level of profitability. While costs are clearly relevant to setting prices, there is a risk that managers taking this approach assume that customers somehow care about their supplier's costs, when most simply do not.

- Outside-in pricing: This begins by considering the perceptions customers (i.e. 'outside' the selling firm) have of value and the appropriate price to pay for the product given these value perceptions. Pricing decisions should be based on evaluating both tangible and intangible elements that customers gain from the purchase (see Chapter Nine). An advantage of an outside-in approach is that it encourages managers to think in terms of the relationships the firm hopes to develop and thus to avoid setting what might be perceived as an exploitative price. Although this approach is market-orientated, it is also difficult to implement in practice due to the knowledge needed to get an accurate idea of customer's perceptions of value. Nevertheless, certain research approaches can enable managers to establish an idea of the sorts of trade-offs buyers may make in terms of price (see Christopher, 2000).

Price-setting decisions

The balancing act between inside-out and outside-in approaches means that reaching a pricing decision in B2B markets can depend on many factors, as shown in Figure 10.4. Note how five different sets of factors, all conveniently beginning with the letter 'C', may need to be considered by any marketers with price-setting responsibility.

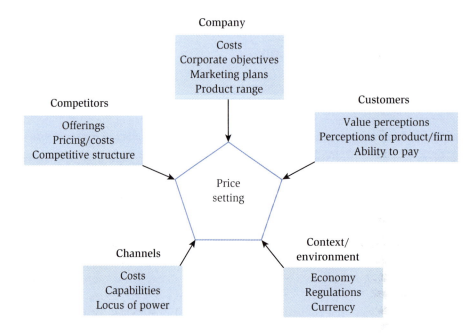

Figure 10.4 Factors affecting price setting

1. *Company*: these inside-out factors include the product-related costs incurred by the supplier, embracing development, production, and marketing expenditure, as well as noting the corporate objectives of the firm (e.g. do they take a short-term view of gaining financial returns or is the firm prepared to take a longer-term perspective?). Product range or line management issues (see Chapter Eight) can also be important; these are discussed in section 10.3 below. Some problems can arise when a number of internal stakeholders with an interest in price setting need to pool their knowledge in order to decide the best way forward. These stakeholders can include cost accountants, financial managers, buying departments, logistics managers, sales forces, and the marketing department. All may seek different outcomes since they can be evaluated on different criteria such as maintaining accurate records, or controlling operating costs, material costs, warehousing costs, etc., as well as generating high sales volumes, and the profit margins generated on those sales.

2. *Customer*: these concerns, like the rest of the Cs in Figure 10.4, are outside-in factors. Probably the most crucial thing B2B marketers must try to understand in setting prices is how customers perceive the value of their offerings. Along with this, the corporate reputation of the supplier is important, and may allow some firms to charge more than others. Finally, the customer's ability to pay may have to be carefully assessed and, if necessary, advice may have to be provided on financial services to facilitate a purchase (see Chapter Nine).

3. *Channels*: distribution considerations lead to a further set of outside-in factors. Many manufacturers require a series of intermediaries to deliver their products to the end user, and these intermediaries will have their own costs to recover in the price charged to the final customer. Suppliers need to ensure that their distributors can make a profit, yet at the same time monitor whether the resulting prices 'downstream' are not beyond those which customers are prepared to pay. If reseller margins are too low, then the manufacturer can suffer in the long term as the distributor may lack the resources to invest in its services, thereby driving dissatisfied customers to other outlets. If the value added by distributors via things like advice and repair services (see Chapter Four) is sufficiently highly regarded by customers, then accepting pricing increments within each level of the channel should not be too problematic. However, if these services are beyond the capability of a distributor, their costs may have to be borne by the manufacturer, thus affecting the price they charge.

When a manufacturer is desperate to hold market share, it can resort to rather dubious practices to gain the support of channel members in price negotiations, as you can see in Box 10.4. Do you think that the European Commission was right to penalize Intel?

Box 10.4 Food for thought

Anti-competitive practices in supply/demand chain relations

The European Commission fined microchip manufacturer Intel a record £948 million in 2009 as a penalty for what the Commission saw as anti-competitive practices. The firm was adjudged to have paid computer manufacturers and a retailer to purchase Intel chips (either as components, or to effectively resell within stocked PCs) over those of rival firm, Advanced Micro Devices (AMD). The Commission maintained that PC manufacturers Acer, HP, Lenovo, Dell, and NEC had all been given hidden rebates if they exclusively used Intel chips, and that Media Saturn, owners of Europe's largest electronics retailer, Media Markt, had been given cash if it would only stock PCs containing Intel chips. Intel is appealing against the verdict, but AMD welcomed the decision, having logged complaints against Intel in 2000, 2003, and 2006. Although the organizational customers of the firm may have gained through lower costs, the Commission argued that end users had suffered a restricted choice as a result of Intel's practices.

Source: BBC News (2009); www.intel.com; www.amd.com

---

4. *Competition*: these outside-in factors may sometimes be difficult for the marketer to judge, but the more information that can be gathered on competitors' costs, their approaches to pricing, and the overall impact of these on the value of their offerings to the marketplace in comparison with the firm's own situation, the better able the firm's marketing plans will be to achieve the desired market positioning (see Chapter Seven). If the competition 'C' in Figure 10.4 should dominate managerial thinking, however, there is a danger that control of this key aspect of your firm's marketing strategy is effectively being handed over to your competitors. Even if you believe that low price is the most important purchasing criterion, only one supplier can ever achieve this position. Firms who chase it can end up setting off a downward price spiral as a price war ensues between competitors, reducing perceptions of value across the entire marketplace. In terms of the industrial network (see Chapter Five), it thus behoves marketers to think of the impact a price change can have on other network participants. If stability is desired, perhaps precipitating a price war may not be a wise move.

5. *Context (or environment)*: a final set of more macro outside-in factors must also be borne in mind by the B2B marketer. The overall economic picture is clearly likely to influence customer spending (see Chapter Two); governmental policy regarding things like import duties and price controls will make trading in certain countries more complex than others; currency fluctuations will also affect the stability of prices quoted in global business relationships (Cavusgil, 1996). Box 10.5 illustrates an aspect of pricing and exchange that you may not have thought to be still relevant in the contemporary business context, but which loomed all too large for Russian organizations until relatively recently.

Box 10.5 Mini case

A challenging trading context

The Russian economy was a tricky place in which to do business in the 1990s. In the period 1990–6, Russia's GDP was reported to be shrinking by an average annual rate of 8%. This affected B2B trade such that it became dominated by barter as the form of exchange. Indeed, barter effectively replaced financial transactions in over half the sales completed during this period. Organizations adopted barter since they lacked the funds to be able to source from international markets, thereby making them reliant on domestic suppliers who still held a position of dominance inherited from the Soviet system.

Source: Holden et al (2008)

Inter-organizational relationships and price setting

Pricing can be more complex in organizational markets because of the typical need to agree not only a price for the particular transaction in question but also a pricing structure and associated rules that can be applied over the expected life of the relationship between the firms involved.

There can be a tension between the competitive advantages that manufacturers gain from having trusting supplier relationships with the necessity for them to push for price reductions, or at the least, for price maintenance while achieving greater value. Henke et al (2008) have examined this issue in the North American automotive industry, a sector characterized by some close working relationships but also by high OEM price reduction pressure on suppliers. They found, perhaps surprisingly, that powerful manufacturers can push suppliers to reduce prices while maintaining trusting working relationships with these same pressured suppliers. This only works, however, when the manufacturer is perceived as desiring and acting conscientiously to develop trusting relationships. Actions that contribute to this perception include sincerity and fairness in the customer's working practices, and the open sharing of timely and detailed information. Thus, B2B marketers representing suppliers may have to accept that price reduction pressure will occur during negotiations due to the need for low OEM procurement costs, even when they are working with a customer who is committed to a trusting relationship. Although the marketer may have hoped to command a higher price, in the long term such actions, if handled carefully, should benefit both parties.

Another B2B context in which there can be power asymmetries between supplier and customer firms is that of manufacturer–retailer relationships. As we saw in the case study concluding Chapter Three, many firms choose to become dependent on strong customers due to the benefits that derive from their relationships, even if the power balance is uneven. In these situations, organizations may forego the signing of formal contracts and arrange instead 'framework contracts' (sometimes called 'umbrella agreements') to balance the need for stability with the desire to remain flexible (Mouzas and Ford, 2006). Contract negotiations usually take place between the retailer's purchasing department and the manufacturer's sales team in September to December of each year. Key account managers (see Chapter Twelve) from the manufacturer visit the buying managers of the retailer in order to propose the 'listing' (stocking) of brands and offer trade 'allowances', such as fees for the distribution gained by the brands that are listed. The outcome of this process is determined by the market share of particular brands, the trade allowances paid, and the power of the retailer's own brands, all taken alongside both firms' more general expectations regarding the relationship. The joint appreciation of the other's needs that are captured in such framework contracts enables managers to use them repeatedly as a sort of test of their understanding of what they have jointly agreed. If circumstances alter for either party, they can renegotiate prices and other details. The parties may agree to arrange quarterly business reviews which allow for gradual adjustments to terms. The firms view framework contracts as strategic tools that lay down the foundations for an ongoing interaction.

Discounts

Discounting can be an important part of price setting in business markets. Some approaches to discounting are highly visible, such as those based on a promotional appeal (see Chapter Eleven) like the email messages sent to potential customers by Security Direct, an Internet-based supplier of products such as gloves, face masks, and body armour to medical organizations and security providers. Security Direct positions itself as a 'specialist business to business supplier' and offers discounts such as 'free delivery on orders over £100 on selected items', an 'extra 10% off sale price for existing customers' as well as a series of 'best buys' prominently listed on the firm's website (www.securitydirect.co.uk).

Other approaches to discounting are not so visible (as we saw in the extreme case of Intel above). One factor that makes it difficult to set prices in relation to the competition in business markets is the practice of offering discounts that result in substantially lower prices than are indicated on official price lists. These discounts, typically based on bulk buying by the customer, are termed 'file discounts' or 'trade discounts' (see Figure 10.3). The file discounts offered by some manufacturers to particular customers can be considerable. For instance, in the author's own experience of working in the purchasing department of a major UK home entertainment retailer, suppliers would agree to provide discounts of 10% over and above any list price that might appear on an invoice. These discounts were negotiated annually by the firm's head office and meant that the organization's stores could operate at a greater profit than might initially appear possible. The retailer had the power to negotiate these terms due to its high overall market share amongst end-user consumers, meaning that smaller retail organizations with lower marker share would pay considerably closer to the list price for their products. Such is the sensitivity of these types of pricing arrangements that they present problems for a market analyst: although list prices, sometimes in the form of business catalogues, are reasonably easy to establish, the details of specific negotiated price agreements are often highly confidential (Blois, 1994). Price setting by rival suppliers in these circumstances necessarily has to be undertaken with a degree of uncertainty.

The preceding discussion raises some issues of ethical behaviours on the part of powerful customer firms. Ethical considerations work both ways, however, and Box 10.6 shows how suppliers of business services view price setting in terms of ethics. Note how an approach that balances internal and external issues seems to be the most highly regarded, and most likely to gain customer appreciation.

Box 10.6 Food for thought

Pricing and ethics

A recent study of firms selling transportation and IT services found that most managers associate ethical considerations with pricing. Respondents indicated that setting prices which lead to excessive profits or took advantage of a customer's needs was seen as unethical behaviour. The study suggested that managers believed initiatives to reduce non-ethical behaviours should come from the firms themselves, perhaps in the form of a corporate culture that encourages a customer orientation, and not from governmental sources. Companies that took ethics into consideration when setting their prices tended to follow a 'systematic approach' which focused on both internal and external issues. In order to ensure that they are perceived to be acting in a socially acceptable manner, the study concluded that managers responsible for setting prices within their organizations will enhance how they are seen by B2B customers by avoiding pricing practices that raise ethical concerns.

Source: Indounas (2008)

10.3 B2B Pricing Strategies

Now let us explore some pricing strategies in more detail, beginning with some broadly outside-in approaches and then a number of tactics that correspond to a more inside-out view of pricing. These are summarized in Figure 10.5. We will then move on to discuss some important topics that lend themselves to discussion under a 'pricing' heading, including competitive bidding, leasing, and price negotiations in different types of relationship.

Outside-in orientated strategies

Taking the product life cycle (PLC – see Chapter Eight) into consideration in pricing often entails an outside-in approach. These strategies will only work, however, if there are target organizational segments who value the price positioning that your firm adopts at that particular time. This could, of course, change as products are perceived to progress through the PLC:

- Price skimming often happens when a new product is launched and when the market comprises few competing offers: a high price can help a firm make a short-term contribution to cash flow. Such pricing is also used to suggest prestige positioning in relation to potential competitors.

- The opposite approach is that of penetration pricing: here, a mass-market perspective is taken by setting a low price during the introduction of a new product. It often suggests a long-term view to the recovery of initial investments. The low price can discourage competitors and lead to economies of scale if sufficient volumes are sold.

Another outside-in approach to pricing is found when suppliers have to try to respond to target pricing from purchasing organizations. This works as follows: taking a demand chain approach, buyers determine their own firm's target selling price by conducting market research amongst end users, say for an automobile; they then divide the car into different elements and estimate the proportion of the car's price that will come from each element;

Figure 10.5 **Outside-in and inside-out pricing strategies**

277

they 'drill down' into the sub-elements that comprise each main element of the car, arriving at individual parts, and the target cost that each of these must be bought at in order to arrive at the desired target price. The buyers then use this target in their negotiations with parts suppliers (Newman and McKeller, 1995). This tends to happen in sectors where buying organizations have a lot of purchasing power, such as grocery retailing or automobile manufacture, and leaves the selling firm with little choice but to ensure it can make the target price if it is to get the contract. If this squeezes margins too tightly, marketers may find themselves having to persuade production colleagues of the need to 'bite the bullet' in order to maintain the relationship with a particularly important client depending on whether a long-term partnership is desirable.

In what can be seen as a form of target pricing, some suppliers will enter into 'open-book' arrangements with customers in established relationships. Here, they disclose their costs of supply and production, and then accept an agreed margin to arrive at a price. The transparency of open-book relationships aims to prove to the buyer that the seller is not taking advantage of them. Such openness can run the risk of important proprietary information about a firm's operations being misused by unscrupulous customers but does much to show the commitment of the supplier to the relationship.

Inside-out orientated strategies

Most pricing strategies, however, tend to be more inside-out in their approach:

- Methods like mark-up pricing and break-even pricing involve relatively simple considerations like adding a set percentage to the production cost (or purchase price in the case of a distributor or retailer) in the former case, or taking a similar view but this time incorporating all direct and indirect costs in the latter case.

- If we consider the entire range of a firm's products, then a product line approach to pricing presents customers with a range of prices reflecting value across the line to choose from. This hopefully lets the supplier maximize their profits on an overall line basis rather than product by product. The approach balances out the contributions of all the products in a particular line, some of which may be more profitable than others.

- Peak load pricing takes into account varying levels of customer demand. As we saw in Chapter Nine, the marketing of business services often needs to 'smooth' demand in order to match supply to customer demand. This approach of raising prices at peak demand times encourages customers to use the service at off-peak periods.

- Also in the service context, marginal cost pricing is used by firms to overcome the perishability of their offerings. Thus, hotels, conference venues, and travel companies with high fixed costs will attempt at least to recover their variable costs in quiet periods by generating some income through cutting prices.

Another inside-out strategy is that of suggested resale pricing, where intermediaries are encouraged to maintain a certain price to pass on to their customer which effectively supports the price level (and value perception) expected by the manufacturer. For instance, the US manufacturer, Texas Instruments, announced on its website (http://focus.ti.com) in 2008 that it was about to introduce a new LED backlight driver for computer display screens. This component, the TPS61181, was claimed to 'give engineers designing medium-sized portable applications an easy path to LED design'. In highlighting the availability of this attractive-sounding component, the manufacturer explained that it could be brought from Texas and its authorized distributors, noting that 'the suggested resale price is $1.75 in 1,000-unit quantities' (Texas Instruments, 2008).

Competitive bidding and electronic marketplaces

B2B markets differ from most consumer markets in the existence of competitive tendering. This occurs in both private and public sectors. It involves buyers asking prospective suppliers to tender to provide desired products or services. An open bidding system allows rival suppliers to see one another's tenders. They can then make adjustments in an auction process with the buyer able to maximize value, either by seeing a reduction in price or through ever-more augmented offerings. Closed bids mean that only the customer will know the value of all the bids submitted. The process usually results in the lowest cost bid being selected, but not always: sometimes, the client will recognize better overall value from a particular bid that is not based solely on the lowest costs to the buying organization, but also on the degree to which the supplier promises to meet a detailed specification for the project.

The bid process is shown in the case in Box 10.7, where a particularly large contract appears to have been decided on a claimed 'best value' basis. It is quite likely that the relatively low cost promised by the supplier was a key deciding factor for the cash-strapped Panamanian government, yet technical issues could not be ignored in so crucial an undertaking.

Box 10.7 Mini case
Comparing bids for the Panama Canal

One of the world's largest infrastructure projects is the plan to expand the Panama Canal by building new locks in order to double the waterway's capacity. In July 2009, the Panama Canal Authority, an autonomous governmental agency, announced its favoured 'best-value' bid from amongst the three rival international consortia bidding for the lucrative contract. The favoured bid was from a group led by Sacyr Vallehermoso from Spain, and comprising the firms Impregilo from Italy, Jan de Nul (Belgium), and Constructora Urbana (Panama). This group's bid was considerably lower than its two rivals', coming in at $3.12 billion, which was well under the Authority's (hitherto undisclosed) target price of $3.48 billion. It also appeared to meet the technical requirements of the tender, although this will need to be confirmed before the deal is signed. The three rival consortia had submitted their proposals, including construction cost estimates and technical designs, in March. Since then, the bids, and the Authority's target price, had been held in a locked vault to allay fears over corruption. What looked like being the winning bid had not only undercut its rivals on cost (one led by US firm Bechtel of $4.18 billion, the other by the Spanish Grupo ACS of $5.98 billion), but it also scored slightly better on technical criteria – which will be an impressive feat if Sacyr and its partners can deliver their promises.

Source: Carroll (2009); www.gruposyv.com

One skill that B2B marketers working in these types of sectors need to acquire is that of managing the specification (or 'spec') process, even to the degree of advising customers what should go into a bid spec as it is being drawn up. While a firm's advisor may offer specialist knowledge to help the customer construct a suitably detailed spec, they will also attempt to influence the bid contents so that their firm has a competitive advantage in possessing the most appropriate capabilities to fulfil the spec. The development of the necessary close relationships required to facilitate this process can involve a considerable investment of staff time by the prospective supplier.

The auction process in organizational market bids increasingly takes place online via Web-based applications. This allows for dynamic pricing in real time, thereby facilitating what are known as 'reverse auctions'. By fixing terms and technical specifications in these auctions, buyers tend to lead suppliers to compete only on price. Recall that some issues about reverse auctions were raised in Chapter Three where potential opportunistic behaviour by customers over price negotiations was discussed. In general, however, it is thought that electronic reverse auctions offer purchasing organizations legitimate benefits in price reduction and increased purchasing efficiency. E-marketplaces tend to result in lower costs for market search activities by prospective customers since they can conveniently explore more alternatives by comparing sellers' electronic catalogues and lower the price via auctions. Orders from different firms for small volumes for similar products can be aggregated through the e-marketplace, thus enabling two seemingly incompatible benefits (diversity and volume) to be achieved simultaneously (Kwon et al, 2009).

E-marketplaces have been particularly effective in the trading of commodity products such as most maintenance, repair, and operational (MRO) goods (see Chapter Eight). This is because many firms find it difficult to control spending on these items from centralized purchasing departments due to their irregular demand and the need for spot purchasing. A study of the buying of MRO products in South Korea (Kwon et al, 2009) reveals that MRO e-marketplaces such as www.iMarketkorea.com and www.ServeOne.co.kr are the most active type of B2B market in terms of participant numbers and transaction volumes. As well as the search cost and price reductions mentioned above, buyers in Korea have been able to improve efficiency in their purchasing practices by electronically processing buying operations and accumulating buying records. The relative impact of the two main benefits (price reduction and procurement efficiency) depended on whether the trading relationship was market or relationally based. The greater the tendency towards the latter, the more purchasing efficiency increased, and the less the price was reduced. This suggests that e-marketplaces are not just about gaining price reductions. It indicates that B2B marketers representing MRO suppliers would do well to encourage close relationships with their organizational customers who wish to participate in such markets.

Although there appear to be benefits afforded by e-marketplaces, there are some concerns that these markets can damage competition and thus violate anti-trust legislation. It is important for suppliers taking part in B2B e-marketplaces to feel confident that a 'level playing field' exists for all parties (Pressey and Ashton, 2009). These markets are typically sponsored by a single organization (known as the 'hub firm' or 'market maker') with the purpose of matching up vendors and buyers in a sector (e.g. www.converge.com, a global e-marketplace for computer components). Some suppliers have reservations about trading in these marketplaces due to issues like: the falling prices that can be set off by reverse auctions; pressure from powerful buying firms for suppliers to join an e-market network;

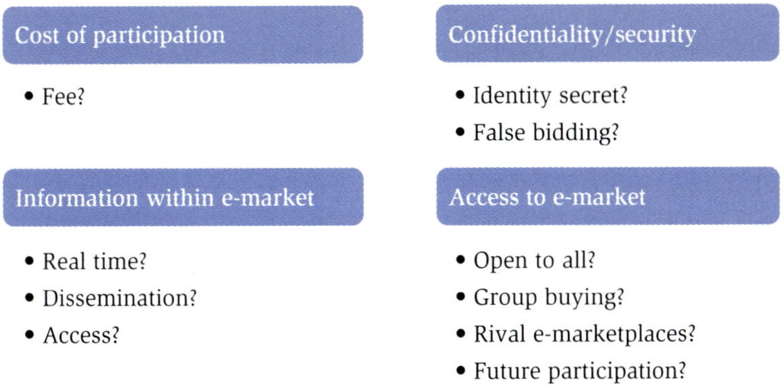

Cost of participation	Confidentiality/security
• Fee?	• Identity secret? • False bidding?

Information within e-market	Access to e-market
• Real time? • Dissemination? • Access?	• Open to all? • Group buying? • Rival e-marketplaces? • Future participation?

Figure 10.6 Participation in e-marketplaces

the ease with which buyers can compare and bypass existing channel members; and the risk of standardization where buyers can seek common terms from all their suppliers thanks to the ease with which such information can be accessed.

'Market makers' should be able to demonstrate that their operating rules and procedures do not stifle competition or hurt individual organizations. If in any doubt, marketers are advised to consider some of the following questions (summarized in Figure 10.6) before their firms agree to participate in e-marketplaces (Pressey and Ashton, 2009, p 475):

- Will we have to pay a fee to participate?
- Is the exchange open to all firms?
- How will identities be preserved?
- Will real-time posting of prices occur?
- Is group purchasing allowed?
- What provisions are in place to prevent false bidding in reverse auctions by buyers?
- How will the information my firm posts be disseminated?
- What information will I have access to?
- Will we be prohibited from participating in rival e-marketplaces if we join?
- Will there be an exit fee?
- Will we be able to participate again in the future?

Despite such concerns, it is thought that increasing numbers of firms will take up the benefits offered by electronic reverse auctions, as shown in Box 10.8 which outlines the developing situation in Italy for organizations trading in the food sector. Suppliers of both goods and supporting services to these retailers will need to keep abreast of their expectations regarding bidding practices.

Leasing

A further consideration in B2B pricing is leasing, which is a process that gives customers an alternative to outright purchase. This approach is most often used for goods which are

Box 10.8 Number crunching

The use of electronic trading in Italian supply/demand chains

The grocery supply chain is the third largest in Italy in terms of the value of total e-commerce B2B transactions, increasing at a rate that is three times greater than overall B2B trading in the country. Yet researchers argue that the level of adoption of e-procurement tools in the sector is still low, noting that e-transactions amounted to €850 million in 2004, equivalent to only 0.4% of the total grocery supply chain transactions that year. This does, however, represent an increase of 50% since 2003, with 70% of these purchases made by retailers, and 30% by producers. Retailers allocated 64% of this expenditure to goods for resale: the rest went on facilitating products, services, and packaging. It is anticipated that the adoption of electronic reverse auctions will be more rapid in future years due to the time savings promised by this medium of exchange compared to 'offline' negotiations in grocery retailing.

Source: Martinelli and Marchi (2007)

very expensive. For instance, the Porterbrook Leasing Company facilitates the leasing of rolling stock (trains and carriages) to UK railway companies (www.porterbrook.com).

Leasing can help customer organizations to focus their use of debt on the most strategically important areas of their business by reducing their exposure to debt on the purchase of certain assets. A downside is that these sorts of arrangements can also commit the customer to a particular piece of capital equipment for a lengthy period, restricting their ability to make changes if their operating environment should alter. Nevertheless, three types of lease arrangements can be offered by marketers keen to encourage customers to commit to using their firm's products (Wengartner ,1987):

- Operating leases: These financial arrangements include maintenance of the asset that is effectively 'owned', although there is no transfer of ownership of the actual product when the payment schedule has been completed.

- Capital leases: Once they have agreed a purchase price with the supplier, customers arrange a capital lease with a leasing firm. These leases involve no maintenance element.

- Sales/leaseback: Here, products are sold to a leasing firm, and then leased back to the original owners for a fee over an agreed period. This provides an injection of cash from the initial sale.

Some further relational considerations in B2B price negotiations

Provided they have a sound understanding of the atmosphere of the relationship between their firm and the buying organization, B2B marketers can adapt their pricing strategy according to the nature of the relationship (Anderson and Narus, 1991). Some important considerations in price negotiations are summarized in Figure 10.7, which also contains two relational issues discussed earlier in section 10.2 on price setting: price reduction pressure and umbrella agreements.

In transactionally orientated relationships, it can make sense in negotiations to 'unbundle' a firm's offerings by eliminating certain standard elements of the product/service package

Transactional IORs	Collaborative IORs
• Bundling goods/services • Unbundling options • 'Milking' customers • Short-term ROI vs lifetime value	• Premium pricing opportunities • De-featuring • Sharing information • Value of learning • Inertia • Price reduction pressure & trust • Umbrella agreements

Figure 10.7 Relational considerations in price negotiations

or changing them into options for the customer. Marketers then lower the price for each element that is unbundled, but ensure that the price is still more than the cost of currently performing the service, thus maintaining their firm's profit margin. A menu of options is offered to the customer organization, with services such as delivery, installation, and maintenance listed on an incremental price basis. If all the individual services are added together, then the sum of the price increments should exceed the price quoted for a 'bundled' full offering, thus incentivizing the customer to take the full service package if they wish. This approach remains marketing-orientated as it allows clients to choose the offering and arm's-length relationship that they perceive as giving the best value for them.

In more collaborative relationships, where activities are undertaken especially to add value to the exchange between the organizations, marketers may seek a price premium in return for maintaining and developing the collaborative offering. As we saw in our discussion of 'de-featuring' in section 10.1, it is beneficial for supplier and customer firms to work together in order to gain a deeper understanding of the customer's requirements. This allows the supplier to use more fully the expertise of its staff to propose modifications in the customer's product/service specifications that can enable it to lower its price, or even to redesign its offerings to provide greater functionality at the same price.

Ideally, price alone will rarely be the deciding issue in a negotiation. For instance, the supplier can make concessions on price if the customer agrees to share production schedule information, thereby facilitating better production planning by the seller; or the buyer may make concessions if the customer firm's inventories are reduced by the supplier agreeing to introduce more just-in-time methods (see Chapter Four). In both transactional and collaborative types of relationship, suppliers may choose to retain a portion of any costs saved as extra profit and pass on the remainder to the customer in order to incentivize them to adapt to any proposed changes.

The value of IORs

B2B marketers should remember that an inter-organizational relationship itself has value in two ways. First, there is the relationship's current value resulting from the learning that has taken place between the two parties about their operations. Second, the relationship has a potential value due to existing adaptations having the potential to evolve in a way that can solve future problems for the customer (Ford et al, 2006). From the perspective of both customer and supplier, value from a relationship can arise over such things as: the reduction of NPD costs via the sharing of information on capabilities and product usage; the reduction of administration costs via more integrated information systems and increased experience of each other's operations; and the application in other network relationships of what each party has learnt from their own relationship.

From the supplier's viewpoint, relationships can be seen as key assets in which the role of pricing should be to maximize the rate of return on each relationship over its perceived life cycle (see Chapter Three). A balance needs to be struck in negotiations between generating a return on the investments made in the relationship by the selling firm and maintaining the long-term (or 'lifetime') value of the relationship. Thus, marketers should resist any temptation to 'milk' customers by trying to seek short-term financial gain for their firm. It is also worth noting, however, that a certain amount of inertia can exist in relationships since customers will have invested considerable resources in the partnership and may thus face unwanted 'switching costs' in developing a relationship with a new supplier.

This concluding discussion reminds us of how 'softer' issues of relationship management are key to B2B marketing, even within the sometimes 'hard-edged' world of price and costs.

The end-of-chapter case study illustrates some dilemmas facing an SME supplier of a commodity good regarding its plans to add value to its offering via a 'green' approach. A key consideration is the product's acceptance by the organizational marketplace, especially as the firm plans to charge an increased price for its more environmentally friendly steel.

Summary

The key points to take from this chapter are as follows:

- The significance of customers' value perceptions in evaluating business market offerings, and the costs and benefits that can accrue for an organizational buyer in making an assessment of value.
- How 'inside-out' pricing approaches to price setting differ from 'outside-in' approaches.
- Five broad factors to take into account when setting prices in B2B markets.
- The impact of discounting and power asymmetries in relationships on firms' behaviours regarding B2B pricing practices.
- The variety of different pricing strategies that can be pursued by marketers, from both an inside-out and an outside-in perspective.
- How electronic reverse auctions can affect competitive bidding processes from the perspective of vendors and buyers.
- The value that an inter-organizational relationship itself may have for the parties, in addition to the nuances of price negotiation that can take place in such relationships.

Discussion questions

1. Using generic examples, explain the difference between price and value in organizational markets.

2. How might B2B marketers gain a comprehensive picture of a customer's perceptions of value regarding their firm's offerings?

3. Why do outside-in price-setting approaches suggest a more market-orientated approach to strategy than inside-out approaches?

4. What are the risks of adopting a purely competitive approach to pricesetting in terms of a discounting strategy?

5. What sorts of issues should be considered by B2B marketers intending to take part in e-marketplaces?

6. How should a marketer approach price negotiations in a collaborative relationship with a customer compared to a situation where the relationship is more adversarial?

Case study

Abbeysteel™ Ltd – Adding Value in the Material Recycling Market

Maurizio Catulli, Sustainable Business Process Research Group (SPRING), University of Hertfordshire

Introduction

Founded in 1981, AS (Abbeysteel) Ltd is a small-to-medium sized enterprise, with a turnover of circa £2.5 million and 20 employees. AS is based in the East of England and specializes in supplying steel, and steel blanks and shapes to a variety of industry sectors, including automotive, lighting, office furniture, horticulture, catering equipment, homeware, and shopfitting industries. Steel blanks are guillotined precision-cut rectangular sections of waste material cut ready for customers' first operations. Steel shapes are sections of material discarded by car companies in their manufacturing process.

The steel AS supplies is recycled from the waste material from the automotive industry. Over 10 years, AS has developed partnerships with many automotive manufacturers, for example Jaguar, Land Rover, and Honda. As part of their manufacturing activities, automotive manufacturers cut steel in order to make vehicle bodywork, and in the process, a proportion of this material goes to waste, for example when cutting a sunroof in a vehicle's top. The cuts are in such shapes that it is difficult for the manufacturers to reuse this material in their operations. The surplus steel is therefore purchased by AS, which then goes on to supply it to other companies after further processing it. This means that AS contributes to the automotive sector's efforts to reduce waste and recycle/reuse materials, thus 'leaning' their manufacturing processes.

After it arrives at AS, the steel is cut to customers' required sizes or packed and sold either to export markets or to UK manufacturers who may shear it themselves. There has been a trend in the past two years towards working with car manufacturers to get the surplus steel reused by their own subcontract presswork/sub-assembly supplier base. In this case, AS acts as a 'resource manager' and handles the commercial transaction to supply the reused steel to these companies.

The steel and metal recycling industry

Many manufacturing sectors use steel to make their products. The steel manufacturing industry is extremely carbon intensive and energy absorbing. Steel production contributes about 5% of the UK's total CO_2 emissions. However, to this we need to add: activities connected with the extraction of iron ore, which are also energy consuming; the transport of iron ore often over long distances; and the transport of the steel itself to the point of use. World production of virgin steel rose in 2008 by 5.8% to 119.5 million tonnes, while in the EU this production fell by 2.3% to 18.6 million tonnes (www.steel-onthenet.com). These declining statistics for the EU (UK statistics are rather flat) may be due to key industries ordering less of the metal, for example new car registrations were down by 9.5% in March 2008.

The metal recycling industry was estimated at £1.56 billion in 2003, equivalent to about 5.5 million tonnes. In 2003, China appeared to be the largest market in terms of demand for all types of scrap metal (Key Note, 2004). The source of this metal is divided into pre-consumer and post-consumer. The pre-consumer comes from various sectors, e.g. the metalworking industry, automotive, etc. The post-consumer metal originates from various scrap products, e.g. redundant ships, old vehicles, and household goods. Recycled iron and steel require large-scale processing equipment. Demand for steel and stainless steel has been on the increase in recent years, albeit affected by a downward trend in more recent times (Key Note, 2004). Metals are commodity products subject to price fluctuations. Recycled and reused metals tend to maintain their properties so they can be used interchangeably, which means that the commercial value of recycled material may be close to that of virgin product. Steel is apparently the most recycled metal, with 435 million tonnes being recycled every year worldwide. The recycling and reusing of metals saves natural resources, waste production, and energy.

A new growth strategy: adding value in the supply/demand chain

The advantage of the steel supplied by AS is that the material is reused rather than recycled through smelting, and therefore is a 'carbon-neutral' supply if one excludes transport to destination. Currently, AS buys surplus steel from car manufacturers for a price slightly above scrap metal price. AS is then able to supply other manufacturers of various products with this steel at a price much lower than that of virgin steel. Using this business model, AS has been reasonably successful, although only on a small scale.

In devising a strategy for the future development of AS, the firm's management have identified the current environmental issues revolving around climate change as a growth opportunity for the company. By purchasing steel supplied by AS, industrial buyers not only reduce costs; they also reduce their environmental footprint. One tonne of reused steel purchased from AS equals 5.5 tonnes of CO_2 saved, as well as all the additional CO_2 generated during the extraction of iron ore. The next step in the development of AS, in the management's view, consists in growing the company and repositioning it as a 'green' supplier. One of the key objectives is improving trading margins, making AS a more profitable company. To do this involves building a 'green brand' of steel to allow for a price level which is at least on a par with that of virgin steel.

Industrial buyers have many reasons to want to reduce their environmental footprint. One of the major drivers of these purchasing policies is the legislation and regulation on environmental impact of business – both UK and EU driven – which 'forces' all businesses to adopt environmentally sound processes (Catulli, 2008). Some research also suggests that consumers value the environmental attributes of a product when selecting goods for purchase. Manufacturers of various products therefore see an opportunity, and also a threat, deriving from being the ones left behind in adopting environmentally friendly processes: the enhancement of a company's reputation and image is therefore another strong reason for adoption of recycled and reused materials.

Many manufacturers are in the process of applying for, or obtaining, ISO14001 certification. This is a certification released by the International Standard Organization, confirming that the company has implemented environmentally friendly processes and systems. Many companies have found that this certification is increasingly becoming a necessity. Manufacturers of various products are finding that their retail customers require their suppliers to be ISO14001 certified. The retailers themselves are also seeking this certification as this enhances their image with consumers – this means that they need to 'green their supply chain' which means they have an incentive in selecting ISO14001 certified suppliers. Looking 'up' the supply/demand chain, these suppliers are also in turn encouraged to list ISO14001 certified suppliers.

Green branding

Manufacturers purchasing steel supplied by AS are awarded quarterly certificates detailing how many tonnes were recycled, together with the environmental benefits associated with their purchases. This added value has convinced the firm's management that their steel does not necessarily need to be supplied at discounted prices. So what strategy should the firm adopt? Some of the initial ideas discussed by managers on branding revolved around the concept of co-branding, 'Intel inside' style. The general thinking was that it was necessary to create a 'pull' along the supply chain – i.e. create demand for 'eco-brands' amongst consumers. However, green branding has risks; for example, companies trying to emphasize environmental values in their brand are often accused of 'green washing'.

One of the highest profile cases of green branding involved BP – their multimillion campaign, 'Beyond Petroleum', had backfired spectacularly and had become, in some commentators' views, the prototype of green washing (Monbiot, 2006).Companies such as The Body Shop and Lush had deliberately positioned themselves as 'green', socially responsible companies. Again, The Body Shop had considerable problems with this strategy when accused of lying about animal testing (www.mcspotlight.org; Monbiot, 2006). Furthermore, these companies were all marketing directly to consumers. How then could a green branding strategy be convincingly implemented by AS, a company marketing to business customers?

As an SME, AS has limited resources to promote any new brand. There is also a fundamental constraint that affects recycling and reused product markets. Vadde et al (2007) claim that recycling and reused product markets are affected by irregularity of supply. This means that as the company grows, there would be more risk of getting into 'out of stock' positions, where AS could not supply their customers with steel in a timely manner. These are only some of the issues to tackle in order to reposition AS as a 'green steel' supplier, and thus enable it to add value in a relatively imaginative way within the supply/demand chains of its customers.

Source: Catulli (2008); Monbiot (2006); www.steelonthenet.com/production.html, (accessed May 2008); Key Note (2004); www.mcspotlight.org/beyond/companies/bodyshop.html (accessed May 2008); Vadde et al (2007)

Case study questions

1. Explain why AS might want to change the market positioning of its commodity product? How is the firm attempting to add value in order to achieve this?

2. What are some of the relationship management issues the firm may need to consider in its plans to carry out co-branding with manufacturers of consumer goods?

3. Identify all the stakeholders in AS's network for value-added steel, and analyse their likely perceptions of the firm's planned value-based repositioning and the accompanying higher prices.

Further Reading

Flint, D. J., Woodruff, R. B., & Gardial, S. F. (2002) Exploring the Phenomenon of Customers' Desired Value Change in a Business-to-Business Context, Journal of Marketing, 66, pp 102–17

The authors present findings from a grounded theory study that sheds light on the nature of customers' desired value change and related contextual conditions. They discover that the phenomenon typically occurs in an emotional context, as managers try to cope with feelings of tension. This provides a reason for customers to seek, maintain, or move away from relationships with suppliers.

Matthyseens, P., Vandenbempt, K., & Weyns, S. (2009) Transitioning and Co-evolving to Upgrade Value Offerings: A Competence-Based Marketing View, Industrial Marketing Management, 38 (5), pp 504–12

This article shows how subcontractors in the metalworking industry can effectively upgrade their customer value offerings. Using qualitative methods, the research identifies 'ideal' value-added market positions and relates these to specific organizational competencies. It also reveals the need to manage coevolution with other network partners in order to make a successful transition from basic to value-added offerings.

McDowell, R., Brennan, R., & Canning, L. (2007) Price-Setting in Business-to-Business Markets, Marketing Review, 7 (3), pp 207–34

In a comprehensive overview, the authors argue that firms should be encouraged to think of pricing as a continuous process rather than a one-off decision. They discuss issues such as bid pricing and price setting within long-term relationships, as well as a number of important ethical concerns like anti-competitive pricing, price fixing, collusion, discrimination, predatory pricing (dumping), and price gouging.

Shipley, D. and Jobber, D. (2001) Integrative Pricing via the Pricing Wheel, Industrial Marketing Management, 30 (3), pp 301–14

This article introduces the concept of the 'pricing wheel' as a multistage process for effective price management. It provides a systematic means for analysing and incorporating into decision-making the strategic role of price, pricing objectives, the plethora of internal and external pricing determinants, pricing strategies and tactics, and implementation procedures.

References

Anderson, J. C. & Narus, J. A. (1991) Partnering as a Focused Market Strategy, California Management Review, Spring, pp 95–113

Anderson, J. C., Jain, D., & Chintagunta, P. (1993) Customer Value Assessment in Business Markets: A State-of-Practice Study, Journal of Business-to-Business Marketing, 1 (1), pp 3–29

BBC News (2009) EU Slaps a Record Fine on Intel, online at http://www.news.bbc.co.uk, accessed May 2009

Blois, K. J. (1994) Discounts in Business Marketing Management, Industrial Marketing Management, 23 (2), pp 93–100

Carroll, R. (2009) Unblocking Panama's Bottleneck, The Guardian, 11 July, p 35

Catulli, M. (2008) Review of the Environmental Goods and Services Sector in Hertfordshire, SPRING, http://www.environmenteast.org.uk/resources/white-papers/

Cavusgil, T. S. (1996) Pricing for Global Markets, Columbia Journal of World Business, 31 (4), pp 66–78

Christopher, M. (1997) Marketing Logistics, Butterworth-Heinemann, Oxford

Christopher, M. (2000) Pricing Strategy, in Cranfield School of Management (eds), Marketing Management: A Relationship Marketing Perspective, Macmillan, Basingstoke

Ford, D., Gadde, L.-E., Håkansson, H. & Snehota, I. (2006) The Business Marketing Course: Managing in Complex Networks, 2nd edn, Wiley, Chichester

Henke, J. W., Parameswaran, R., & Pisharodi, R. M. (2008) Manufacturer Price Reduction Pressure and Supplier Relations, Journal of Business & Industrial Marketing, 23 (5), pp 287–300

Holden, N., Kuznetsov, A., & Whitelock, J. (2008) Russia's Struggle with the Language of Marketing in the Communist and Post-Communist Eras, Business History, 50 (4), pp 474–88

Indounas, K. (2008) The Relationship between Pricing and Ethics in Two Industrial Service Industries, Journal of Business & Industrial Marketing, 23 (3), pp 161–9

Infosys Technologies Limited (2010) Oracle Implementation for a Global Electronics Conglomerate, Case Study online at http://imfosys.com, accessed January 2010

Key Note (2004) Metal Recycling, Key Note Publications, London

Kwon, S.-D., Yang, H.-D., & Rowley, C. (2009) The Purchasing Performance of Organizations Using E-Marketplaces, British Journal of Management, 20, pp 106–24

Laric, M. V. (1980) Pricing Strategies in Industrial Markets, European Journal of Marketing, 14 (5/6), pp 303–21

Martinelli, E. & Marchi, G. (2007) Enabling and Inhibiting Factors in Adoption of Electronic Reverse Auctions: A Longitudinal Case Study in Grocery Retailing, International Review of Retail, Distribution and Consumer Research, 17 (3), pp 203–18

Monbiot, G. (2006) Heat, Penguin Press, LondonMouzas, S. & Ford, D. (2006) Contracting in Asymmetrical Relationships: The Role of Framework Contracts, IMP Journal, 1 (3), pp 42–63

Newman, R. G. & McKeller, J. M. (1995) Target Pricing – A Challenge for Purchasing, International Journal of Purchasing and Materials Management, 31 (3), pp 13–20

Pressey, A. D. & Ashton, J. K. (2009) The Antitrust Implications of Electronic Business-to-Business Marketplaces, Industrial Marketing Management, 38, pp 468–76

Texas Instruments (2008) TI Brightens Notebook LCD Displays with New White LED Driver, News Release online at http://focus.ti.com, accessed August 2008

Vadde, S., Kamarthi, S., and Gupta, S. M. (2007) Optimal Pricing of Reusable and Recyclable Components under Alternative Product Acquisition Mechanisms, International Journal of Production Research, 45 (18/19), pp 4621–52

van Weele, A. J. (2002) Purchasing and Supply Chain Management, Thompson Learning, London

Wengartner, M. H. (1987) Leasing Asset Lives and Uncertainty: Guides to Decision Making, Financial Management, 16 (2), pp 5–13

Zerbini, F., Golfetto, F., & Gibbert, M. (2007) Marketing of Competence: Exploring the Resource-Based Content of Value-for-Customers through a Case Study Analysis, Industrial Marketing Management, 36, pp 784–98

Chapter 11
B2B Marketing Communications

Introduction & Learning Objectives

Given the importance accorded to communication in inter-organizational relationships (Lindberg-Repo and Gronroos, 2004) and networks (Olkkonen et al, 2000), the topic of marketing communication is vital for B2B marketers to understand. Unfortunately, the way that communication (or the promotional 'P') is so often taught to students, typically from the perspective of managing high-profile 'blue-chip' consumer brands, does not properly reflect the workings of the organizational marketplace. While a lot of the vocabulary describing the communication methods and media in B2C contexts is the same as that used in B2B markets, industrial marketing managers will often have to give quite different emphases to each element of the communication mix. They may also have to cope with considerably smaller budgets than B2C marketers have at their disposal in order to communicate with their predominantly mass consumer audiences.

For instance, in 2008, the trade journal, *Marketing*, contained a recruitment advertisement for a communications manager placed by Ceram, a specialist materials technology firm (www.ceram.com). The firm was seeking someone who could deliver a 'full external and internal marketing communications plan', and produce 'effective' materials for advertising, public relations, sales, and online media in order to target particular types of organizational customers. The ad stressed the ability to 'tackle planning, budgeting, and implementation', but nowhere did it suggest that having a B2C background would help applicants – this is quite unusual, so what is so different and demanding about managing marketing communications in a B2B context?

For some initial insight, look at what can be achieved with a relatively small marketing budget in the low-profile, but vitally important, world of security services – see Box 11.1.

Box 11.1 Number crunching
Communicating the benefits of B2B security services

The head of communications at G4S UK, Naomi Broad, acknowledges that business buyers are 'not going to go for gimmicks or BOGOFs ("buy one get one free" offers). It can take years to build a relationship with a client and to convince them that security services are worth the investment.' These services include airport security checkpoints, and cash and justice services. Broad has faced some significant challenges since her appointment in 2003, when she joined the sector with Securicor. Her company merged with Group 4 Falck the following year to create Group 4 Securicor, which has been known since 2006 as G4S. G4S is not exactly a household name, so a post-merger rebranding exercise was essential, especially in the relatively mature security market of the UK. But how was this to be achieved on an annual marketing budget of £150,000?

One approach Broad adopted was to target her competitors' institutional clients. For instance, she observed 'there are a large number of embassies in London using security services, but they weren't using ours'. She organized a campaign to bring diplomats over to G4S by inviting them to a seminar. Thanks to the production of a well-targeted Diplomatic Security bulletin, combined with follow-up telephone calls, 40 embassy officials attended. They heard three external speakers and G4S's CEO talk on diplomatic security issues. As a result, 30 appointments with decision-makers were arranged, with a potential contract value of £1.5 million. In a further ongoing initiative, Broad has sent out a booklet to shopping centre managers which emphasized the skills of G4S's security guards. Again, this mailing is to be followed up by the firm's telemarketing team to generate sales meetings.

G4S also makes sure it attends the security industry's main trade show, the IFSEC exhibition, in Birmingham every year. This involves a 'major investment' of Broad's budget and six months of planning to ensure opportunities from the four-day event are maximized. Appointments are made in advance for potential clients to visit the company's stand, and once the prospective customer has made contact, the relationship is tracked over three years via a CRM system. Broad also places expert speakers in the exhibition's seminar slots to establish G4S's credibility as a brand.

Finally, embracing the flexibility of the Internet, Broad has spent £20,000 on an email marketing tool which allows her department to create its own HTML and text emails. She says, 'For the price of one direct marketing campaign we can now regularly send out security advice and updates to prospects with no follow-on costs.' Tracking of each campaign's success rate is facilitated by links to the firm's CRM database.

Source: The Marketer (2008); www.g4s.com/uk

Chapter Aims

After completing this chapter, you should be able to:

- Identify appropriate B2B marketing communication strategies, including the integrated marketing communications (IMC) approach
- Evaluate the relative effectiveness of communication/promotional tactics
- Evaluate the relative effectiveness of communication media
- Recognize the potential benefits of the Internet as a communications tool in organizational markets.

Note that, while they form part of the communications mix, the key areas of personal selling and sales management are so important to organizational marketing that they will be discussed separately in Chapter Twelve.

11.1 Communication Strategies

A strategic perspective has tended to dominate academic thinking on marketing communication in inter-organizational relationships (IORs), with a presumption that communication can be utilized in a wide range of relationship management tasks, including persuading customers, discussing relationship investments and adaptations, showing commitment and building trust, exercising power, and managing dependence. Effective communication is thought to moderate or control the behaviour of business partners (Mohr et al, 1996). Several classification systems have been applied to marketing communication, differentiating between communication patterns or styles. These include distinctions made between: power/conflict and trust/commitment-based communication (e.g. Gaski and Nevin, 1985); managed/planned and unplanned communication (e.g. Mohr and Nevin, 1990); and, most recently, monologic (or unidirectional) and dialogic (bidirectional) communication (e.g. Ballantyne, 2004). At the most general level, a picture emerges of trustful and committed relationships that are necessarily supported by 'good' communication (Ellis and Hopkinson, 2010).

So how does a firm make sure that it is practising good communication? There are a large number of alternative (and sometimes complementary) marketing communication strategies open to the B2B marketer. You should note, however, that certain factors make B2B communication rather different from B2C communications strategies. Chief of these is the fact that there are fewer opportunities to use 'mass' media (like TV, radio, or press advertising) for targeting businesses, at least not in the same way that a TV advertisement can reach millions of potential consumers. This means that B2B marketers must think a little differently about the best way to communicate with their intended audiences.

For a comprehensive example of business marketing communication in action, see Box 11.2, which outlines the promotional and other activities undertaken by a fleet (vehicle) management firm keen to reposition itself. Recall the discussion of the importance of positioning as part of marketing strategy in Chapter Seven. Do you think that the FMG organization would have been as successful without the investments it made in marketing communications?

Box 11.2 Mini case

The contribution of marketing communications towards a repositioning strategy

In 2003, FMG Support, a fleet management group, was a relatively small operator in the UK. In order to grow, the firm's head of marketing Stefan Rodgers realized that he had to convince customers that his firm was more client focused, something that he was confident could be achieved after FMG had invested £2m in Web-based software to track their clients' processes. At this time, FMG comprised three smaller businesses that dealt separately with roadside repair, incident management, and vehicle recovery for corporate clients. These businesses were all branded separately, and were performing well, but there was no cross-selling and thus opportunities were not being maximized.

Rodgers decided that he needed to work with some external experts to achieve a complete overhaul of FMG's promotion, so he appointed creative agency Propaganda. The agency conducted some market research and concluded that clients were frustrated by seeing information from different departments from FMG, sometimes on the same day, because nothing was integrated. The decision was taken to merge the three small operations into one so that the company could use its software to offer better advice to all its clients. Propaganda also recommended introducing a loyalty programme to strengthen FMG's relationship with its supply partners.

A 12-month campaign was launched in 2004, centring on a name change from FMG Group to FMG Support – a name which made it much clearer to customers what the firm was about. Flexibility and consistency in customer relations were improved by creating inbound and outbound call centre teams which were cross-trained in each other's operations. The firm's Web-based software was also branded as Ingenium, enabling FMG to market the service benefits of this technology more distinctively. Images in the campaign's advertisements moved away from traditional pictures of vehicles and tried more eye-catching ideas such as two people kissing, which represented the close relationships the firm had with its partners. The ads were placed in the trade publication, *Fleet News*, to target key decision makers.

By 2008, FMG was on target to achieve a turnover of £88 million. The firm now manages 250,000 vehicles and has captured five large contracts since the campaign began, including Royal Mail, for whom FMG looks after 40,000 vehicles, and clients such as GE Capital and Masterlease. Rodgers concludes that he can't put all the success down to marketing communications but he believes that 'the adverts helped us immensely'.

Source: Papas (2008); www.fmgsupport.co.uk

General communication strategies

It is possible to differentiate three broad strategies of communication in business markets: push, pull, and reputation, each of which is outlined below.

1. *Pull strategies*: these have a product or service focus and are designed to influence end users lying downstream in the supply/demand chain. The intention is to generate motivation within the target audience that may prompt them to enquire about a product, sample it or make a repeat purchase. The strategy gets its name because it encourages end-user customer demand that will then 'pull' products through the channel – as shown in Figure 11.1. End users can be either consumers or organizational customers, and successful pull strategies should compel them to seek out resellers. Because of the significance of distribution channels and networks in most organizational markets, it tends to be push and reputation approaches that occupy the day-to-day activities of B2B marketers, but pull strategies are important when communicating with organizational end users. Various forms of direct marketing, as well as personal selling, are often more effective than advertising when communicating with these customers, though of course advertising can help create awareness (see section 11.2).

2. *Push strategies*: these also have a product/service focus, but this time aimed at organizational intermediaries in the marketing channel. This audience, also known as the 'trade', can

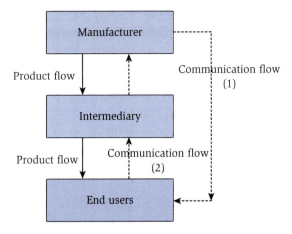

Figure 11.1 Pull communication strategy

be crucial for the successful distribution of a manufacturer's goods, whether via retailers to consumers, or via wholesalers and distributors to organizational clients (see Chapter Four). The push strategy is so called because it involves suppliers encouraging intermediaries to stock their goods for resale, thereby 'pushing' products down the supply chain by persuading distributors of the mutual benefits to be gained by taking on the manufacturer's output – see Figure 11.2. Although the push terminology has become widely accepted, your understanding of inter-organizational relationships (IORs – see Chapter Three) should tell you that the coercion implied by the word 'push' is probably not the best way to describe the cooperation necessary between the manufacturer and channel members in order to make this communication strategy work (Rosenbloom, 1999). The most significant parts of a push strategy are usually personal selling and sales promotions, with trade advertising and other elements of the communications mix playing more of a secondary role.

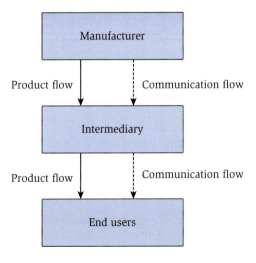

Figure 11.2 Push communication strategy

3. *Reputation strategies*: these normally have a company focus, and are designed to influence a broad range of stakeholders (or 'publics') in the company's network – see Chapter Five. The idea is to build the reputation of the supplying organization amongst audiences who do not necessarily purchase its goods or services. Different messages about the firm's role are aimed at different stakeholders, such as details of financial performance for the finance markets, and environmental issues for the local community. We shall return to these strategies, which are sometimes termed 'corporate communications', when we consider the public relations element of the communication mix in section 11.2.

Note that it may be necessary to combine all three strategies in a particular situation. For instance, a new product launch may entail using pull strategies to attract end-user interest, push strategies to ensure availability of the new product in the marketing channel, and reputation strategies to ensure that press coverage is positive and the financial impact of the (hopefully) successful product launch is recognized by shareholders and investment institutions.

Linking communication strategies to channel conditions

We saw in Chapter Four how the structure of the marketing channel can vary in different sectors. We also noted in Chapter Five how the atmosphere of an IOR can exert an important effect on how business is conducted. If B2B marketing communications managers take these issues into account when planning their strategies, it may be possible to enhance the overall performance of the channel. Mohr and Nevin (1990) stress the need to relate strategies to channel conditions. First, they define four facets of communication that should be considered:

- Communication frequency: An excess of communication can result in 'overload' where channel members are bombarded with too frequent/repetitive information or just too much of it over time, and thus become disenchanted. Too little information, however, can mean that members are deprived of the necessary operational guidance, motivation and support.

- Communication direction: Communications can be unidirectional (or 'monologic') if they only flow in one direction, typically from a powerful manufacturer to a number of intermediaries. Bidirectional (or 'dialogic') communications flow to and from organizations that are more equally powerful. There is a general belief in relationship marketing thinking that communication should be bidirectional, since one-way communication runs the risk of the 'voice' of the less powerful partner being ignored.

- Communication modality: For Mohr and Nevin, this refers to whether the communication is formal and planned (such as meetings and written reports) or informal (such as word of mouth, or WOM, communication or ad hoc conversations). The latter tends to be more spontaneous and less structured than the former.

- Communication content: Basically, this refers to what is said. For instance, direct influence strategies involve specific requests or instructions to change behaviours. Indirect strategies, on the other hand, try to change a channel member's attitudes about the appropriateness of their behaviour, perhaps by a more general discussion of business issues (Frazier and Summers, 1984).

Second, three channel conditions should be assessed:

- Channel structure: This refers to whether exchanges between channel members are predominantly relational, with a long-term perspective and a high level of interdependence, or discrete (or transactional) with a short-term orientation and low levels of interdependence – see Chapter Three.

- Channel climate: This is broadly equivalent to relationship atmosphere. It indicates the levels of trust and support between channel members.

- Power balance: This refers to whether power is held symmetrically within a channel with power equally balanced between members, or whether it is asymmetrically apportioned with a power imbalance that favours one party.

Different channel conditions suggest the need for different types of communication. Two broad strategies are identified by Mohr and Nevin. On the one hand, a 'collaborative communication strategy' corresponds to relational channel structures and supportive climates with symmetrical power, and, on the other hand, 'autonomous communication' is more likely to occur in channels with transactional structures, unsupportive climates, and asymmetrical power. In general, the more relational, supportive, and balanced the conditions, the more effective will be more frequent, bidirectional, indirect, and informal communication. B2B marketers should consider the nature of the channel conditions in which their firm operates. If marketers develop communication strategies that complement them, then levels of coordination, member satisfaction, and mutual commitment should increase. This means that the channel's performance, and that of their own firm, should improve – see Figure 11.3. Failure to match strategies to channel conditions runs the risk of ineffective communication and resources being misdirected, leaving channel performance adversely affected.

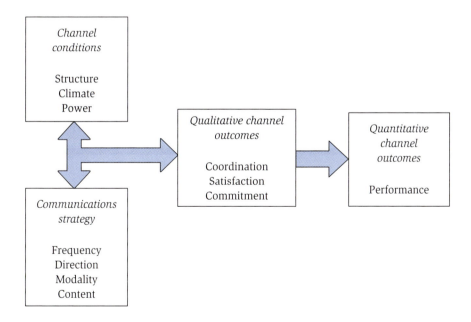

Figure 11.3 A model of communication in marketing channels
Source: Adapted with permission from Mohr and Nevin (1990, p 38)
Reprinted with permission from Journal of Marketing, published by the American Marketing Association, J. Mohr & J. R. Nevin (1990) Communication Strategies in Marketing Channels, 54 (4), pp 36–51

Do not forget that the IMP interaction approach (see Chapter Five) suggests that the way you manage your communications will also have an effect on the atmosphere of IORs in the channel. Thus, the influence is not just one way: the approach a selling firm takes to communication can also prompt perceived changes to channel conditions. These perceptions have the potential to guide management actions and thus lead to structural changes too (Ellis and Hopkinson, 2010).

Integrated marketing communications

An important development in thinking about marketing communication strategy is the concept of integrated marketing communications (IMC). Advances in communication technology, combined with increased sophistication amongst customers, have underpinned greater bidirectional communication between buyers and sellers, and the development of closer relationships. Given this operating environment, the IMC approach emerged from a recognition that organizations must now use a variety of messages and channels in order to manage a wide range of stakeholder relations effectively and consistently (Hall and Wickham, 2008). Some elements of an IMC approach for B2B marketers to consider are summarized in Figure 11.4.

IMC began as a way of maximizing the impact of an array of promotional tactics (see section 11.2) from a minimum level of investment, but has now shifted to an acceptance that the integration of all business functions is needed to achieve an IMC-based competitive advantage. Thus, IMC thinking requires commitment to marketing messages from all staff throughout the organization, and not just from those defined as marketing communications managers. Interestingly, as smaller firms have less bureaucracy and flatter hierarchies, they often find themselves better able to adopt IMC strategies than larger competitors, thereby ensuring greater consistency in their corporate communications (Low, 2000).

As we saw in Chapter Nine, internal communications may be required if the firm's own staff are to be persuaded to accept the need for changes in marketing strategy. For example,

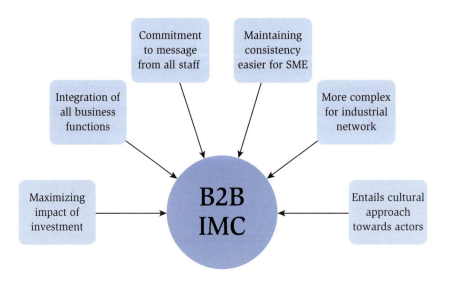

Figure 11.4 IMC in B2B marketing

when the express delivery provider, Parceline, rebranded itself as DPD (www.dpd.co.uk) in 2008, the firm had to ensure that its 4,000 workers were informed before customers were told. This was a difficult task as many employees were dispersed geographically and rarely worked in an office. The news was launched at the firm's annual motivational conference where each manager was given a pack containing a list of questions and answers for staff and samples of all external communication materials. A DVD was also sent to each employee in which DPD's chief executive reassured long-serving personnel of their continuing key role in the company's future. Such was the success of the relaunch that the firm won a trade journal award for the best internal marketing campaign of the year (*B2B Marketing*, 2009).

It is one thing for a single B2B firm to take an IMC approach, but more complex for a network of organizations to realize the benefits of utilizing IMC. As the TLSN case in Box 11.3 shows, it requires redefinition of the roles and functions of those involved in communications. This entails a 'cultural' approach to IMC (Beverland and Luxton, 2005) where network actors' behaviours are guided via education about the core network vision and values. In this way, employees in all member organizations can appreciate their role in championing the aims of the network as a whole and managing stakeholder relations, as well as relations between themselves. In fact, a significant outcome of the TLSN's IMC work was that individual firms (the majority of whose names have been disguised for reasons of confidentiality) were also able to incorporate the principles adopted by the group into their own specific marketing efforts.

Box 11.3 Voices

Managers in the Tasmanian light shipbuilding network

The Tasmanian light shipbuilding network (TLSN) originated in 1984 with the development of the world's first aluminium welding technology by the International Catamarans (Incat) company. Incat's MD realized that he needed a number of partner organizations to help construct a catamaran from this lightweight material, and thus the network began with the integration of several different product lines from members, including fire safety equipment, life rafts and innovative engineering products. By 2000, the TLSN had gained 40% of the world market for fast ferries and associated technologies, a success due in no small part to the IMC approach it had taken and continues to take. It seems that three distinct roles supported the international IMC function of TLSN.

First, the IMC champion: This role was adopted by a single member of the network, and involved information gathering and dissemination, and the coordination of IMC activities throughout TLSN. The IMC champion also attempted to integrate the marketing communication functions undertaken by individual network firms to minimize duplication of effort and to ensure that TLSN presented a consistent message to its common audiences, as shown in this quote: 'I went to Japan to sell a product. . . . All I saw was the mast maker arguing with the sail maker who was arguing with the designer, and this is all our own people. . . . So I went around every MD of the companies that were involved . . . and put the idea to them that we form a network so that if any of us go overseas, we can transfer information.' – MD, Firm A.

Second, the role of network ambassador: This was performed by various network members who were seeking to promote the benefits of TLSN's entire product range whenever possible. Network organization managers were happy to disseminate information about other network firms' capabilities and, moreover, were aware of the need for this information to be consistent, accurate, and given in a way that related directly to their customer's enquiry. These ambassadors had to deal with the promotion of maritime products at both the network and individual firm level. Note what this manager has to say: 'I always make sure I tell the group if I'm going to a trade show, or going overseas to meet with customers. . . . It's really important to know what's going on in the network . . . I mean, if I give out old information that is no good, we all look very ordinary and unprofessional.' – MD, Firm B.

Third, the government lobbyist: Again, this role was adopted by several individuals within TLSN. The role effectively involved outsourcing of those IMC functions that network members could not provide, such as the coordination of trade show presentations and the provision of marketing consultancy reports (via state government staff). The government lobbyist also took on issues that needed substantial investments in time (as opposed to just economic cost) to achieve: 'The main thing that we are lacking in is marketing internationally. . . . So the government, through the Department of State Development, helped us to the Pacific 2000 tradeshow. They helped us with uniforms, backdrops, that kind of thing. . . . We didn't have the contacts, or the time really, to organize everything ourselves.' – MD, Firm C.

Source: Hall and Wickham (2008); www.incat.com.au

11.2 Elements of the Communications Mix

This is an area that forms a core part of most introductory marketing courses and as such is something that most marketing students should feel fairly comfortable with. Nevertheless, for a useful reminder about the elements of the promotional 'P' and, crucially, how these elements can be related to the perhaps unfamiliar B2B context, it is worth revisiting them here. In particular, you should note over the course of this chapter, and the next, how there is a greater emphasis on the direct-response (or interactive) aspects of direct marketing and the use of personal selling in industrial marketing communications than in B2C settings.

Figure 11.5 summarizes the main tactical elements of the communications mix. The elements are listed in descending order of the degree to which they facilitate social interaction between buyer and seller. You can imagine the target audience positioned at the apex of the pyramid. In order to communicate with an array of audiences, B2B marketers need to understand the key tactics of the mix, and the level of communication, cost, and control associated with each. While bearing in mind their relative position in Figure 11.5, we shall now discuss the elements in the order with which they are probably the most familiar to you.

Advertising

Advertising is, of course, an important element of the mix, especially for raising awareness, but is perhaps less effective in business markets that in consumer markets such as for FMCGs. The need of buyers to seek detailed, often technical information tends to mean

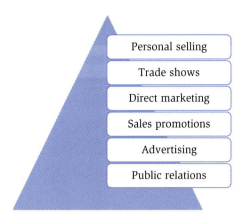

Figure 11.5 The elements of the communications mix

that the emotional and entertainment potential of advertising messages remains relatively insignificant in organizational marketing. Attempts are made by some suppliers to use B2B advertising quite creatively, however. For example, the business data provider, Corpdata (www.corpdata.co.uk), uses photographs of its research teams in trade advertisements, describing them as 'the human face of marketing data' (*The Marketer*, 2008).

Advertising is often used to inform and remind organizational customers of a supplier's offering, for example as in Canon's advertisement explaining to readers of the *Viet Nam News* (2007) that its new machines allow businesses to 'copy, print, scan, fax, network, and share' images (www.canon.com). Differentiating a product from the competition and persuading the buyer to commit to a purchase are normally delivered through other elements of the mix (see below).

An extra set of IORs needs to be taken into account by most B2B marketers when planning an advertising campaign: those between their own firm and the ad agency they may hire. Whatever the size of organization you represent, it is likely that an external firm will be needed to provide creative input and media planning, e.g. The Base One Group which offers business clients like IT outsourcing provider, Mastek, with communications expertise in advertising and direct marketing campaigns (www.baseonecommunications.co.uk). We have discussed this type of business service in Chapter Nine, but largely from the perspective of the agency selling its services to the client company. In this case, you would be taking the decision to purchase an agency's skills and then be responsible, along with the agency's account manager, for managing the relationship between the two organizations. For more on this interesting set of relationships, at both the personal and the corporate level, see the work of Haytko (2004).

Sales promotion

Although sales promotions are common in B2C contexts, they can also be important in B2B marketing. The purpose of sales promotions is typically to induce buyers to make a purchase, either by accelerating sales or by generating a change in attitude through rewarding existing customers or encouraging prospective customers. To achieve these aims, free merchandise, discounts (see Chapter Ten) or gifts are used – see the end-of-chapter case study for more details on this last method. Price-based promotions can also be extended to discounting technical support so that the buyer perceives an increase in the value of the offering. Promotions often have most effect for firms selling low-unit-value products that are bought frequently, such as office stationery. Sales promotions have less impact in markets where goods and service are of high value and where they can be more easily differentiated through technical attributes.

The use of promotional tools, typically in the form of discount 'allowances' for the customer, can be significant in dealing with the trade sector. Manufacturers offer a variety of trade promotions to encourage resellers, including the 'buying allowance' which aims to stimulate restocking or to persuade new stores to carry the product. This promotion represents a reward for specific orders placed between given dates, where the distributor is entitled to a refund of a certain percentage of the regular price. Also popular is the 'promotional allowance' which can take the form of a contribution towards the cost of an advertisement in return for stocking the manufacturer's products. Marketers need to be aware, however, that the reseller may not view promotions with the same enthusiasm as the manufacturer, particularly if it has limited stockholding capacity and is bombarded by incentives from a large number of competing suppliers. Nevertheless, B2B promotions can provide a significant return on investment, as the case in Box 11.4 suggests.

Public relations

Public relations (PR) can influence the perception of all the network stakeholders surrounding a focal firm. PR can contribute to the credibility of an organization, as what are hopefully 'good news' stories about the firm are disseminated through third-party media such as newspapers, magazines, broadcast media, and the Internet. Although there is a cost in producing

---

Box 11.4 Mini case
Promoting loyalty

MRO (maintenance, repair, and operations) products distributor Brammer has close relationships with many manufacturers such as NSK, Siemens, and Loctite. Brammer sees itself as working in partnership with its customers, helping them to achieve savings across their manufacturing processes. The company is keen to distance itself from competitors who try to win business on price alone. In order to let its target audience know of its partnership credentials, Brammer set out to engender greater loyalty from existing clients and reactivate dormant customers across its regional accounts.

Brammer worked with agency Wyatt International to choose 15,000 accounts from its customer database where buyers appeared to be spending only sporadically between competing distributors. A 'Partners programme' was set up to reward annual spend with a voucher-based 10% loyalty bonus. Direct marketing was used to launch the programme and included sending a four-colour, silk-printed box containing an explanatory booklet to recipients considered to be influential in MRO spending. The materials were produced and distributed within two weeks, and resulted in a response rate well above average, with an 'extremely high' ROI and with Wyatt staying well 'within the agreed marketing spend', according to Brammer's head of marketing, Jeremy Salisbury.

Source: B2B Marketing (2009); www.brammer.co.uk

publicity material and no ultimate control over how it will be used (or, of course, whether it will be used at all), unlike advertising, there is no media cost in gaining coverage for the firm if the material is reported.

A wide array of PR options is available to the B2B marketer. Press releases can be sent in the conventional mail, or emailed or posted on a website to attract the attention of the news media. In writing a press release, the aim is to make some report concerning a change in, for example, an organization's performance or product range into a 'newsworthy' item that will be reported as such by the media house concerned. As you will have seen, if you follow most of the Web links highlighted in this book, corporate websites often contain case studies and third-party endorsements as part of the PR communication process. Websites can be a good way of generating PR as busy journalists will search them for potential stories. For instance, engineering company Larsen & Toubro incorporates a 'media room' on its website, which lists a series of press releases under such headings as 'L&T Ranks First in Quality in *Wall Street Journal* Asia survey' (www.larsentoubro.com).

Many organizations now also have crisis management plans in place to cope with, say, a serious health and safety incident (perhaps a chemical spill at a manufacturing plant close to a housing estate). These plans try to ensure that, first, and most importantly, the firm solves the actual problem, and, second, that it can use PR to manage stakeholder perceptions of how it handled the situation – see the Mabey and Johnson mini case (Box 12.5) in Chapter Twelve. Community events such as open days or sponsored 'clean ups' of local rivers or parks can be designed to improve goodwill and understanding amongst the workforce and a firm's geographical neighbours. Sponsorship can be used to develop awareness in a target audience by enabling them to make positive associations between an event or popular group (such as a football team, or orchestra) and the sponsor.

Direct marketing

Direct marketing targets individual customers with personalized messages with the aim of building a relationship with them based on their responses. Direct marketing is often used in B2B communication to complement personal selling activities and thereby reduce costs (e.g. from wasted 'cold calling') and improve overall performance. The two main direct approaches have traditionally been direct mail and telemarketing. (We shall discuss the Internet as a separate type of direct marketing communication later in this section.) Direct mail uses the postal system to address advertising materials and brochures to named individuals within the DMU in purchasing organizations (see Chapter Two). It can generate enquiries and sales leads, as well as maintain personal relationships with customers. Telemarketing is used, like direct mail, to generate leads but also to make appointments, close sales, and to collect market information. Telephone systems can be used for handling 'inbound' calls to collect orders, and provide technical support and new product information to end users and distributors. Taking orders by phone reduces the staff and time costs associated with personal sales calls for both buying and selling organizations, although telemarketing would not normally be appropriate for more complex offerings. As we saw in Chapter Three in our examination of CRM, these sorts of marketing communications require comprehensive and easily accessible databases in order to be effective.

Personal selling

This is the single most important form of marketing communication in business markets. It involves face-to-face personal interaction between individuals representing the selling and buying firms. Personal selling, when conducted professionally, allows instantaneous feedback to be delivered to the seller, and the seller to respond equally quickly, thus setting up a true dialogue between parties. Due to the frequent need to build relationships with buying centre members and to explain complex technical specifications, the flexibility of this bidirectional flow of communication can be crucial to obtaining an order. Personal selling and sales management will be tackled in depth in Chapter Twelve.

Trade shows

Attending these events is another B2B promotional activity which involves a lot of personal interaction. We saw the importance of trade shows (or exhibitions) in the TLSN case in Box 11.3. The main aims of attendance are to meet prospective channel members, develop partnerships with customers (perhaps through the provision of corporate hospitality to key clients), build corporate identity, and gather market intelligence. Shows can also be useful to resolve conflicts face-to-face since they provide an opportunity to meet customers on relatively neutral ground. The exhibition environment allows products to be launched and demonstrated, and prices negotiated and technical problems to be discussed. Sometimes, of course, sales can be confirmed at trade shows. For instance, on a single day of the 47th Paris Air Show in 2007, Airbus took orders worth $45 billion (*Condé Nast Traveller*, 2007). All these benefits suggest that the commonly held belief that exhibitions are events that should be attended merely because one's competitors will be present is rather short-sighted (Blythe, 2002).

Other targeted methods of generating interest that involve social interaction in B2B contexts include seminars and technical or professional conferences, to which specialist users and industry experts are invited. For example, the Italian Trade Commission held a 'workshop for managers, technicians and machinery traders' in the textile sector in Ho Chi Minh City to promote fabric technologies (*Viet Nam News*, 2007).

11.3 Relative Effectiveness of B2B Media

B2B marketing tends to involve more direct methods of communication than consumer marketing where indirect mass media channels abound. This reflects the lower number of customers, the greater significance of one-to-one relationships, and the usually far larger size of individual orders in organizational markets. Given the tightly bounded market segments that make up most targets for B2B communications, it is usually too wasteful to invest in mass media methods. Nevertheless, there are several contexts in which these communication channels are also relevant to industrial contexts, such as where the organization is seeking to develop its brand (see Chapter Seven) or to build a wider public perception of its contributions to society. Large organizations have also found their company newsletter to be a useful means of communicating with external stakeholders such as potential investors.

The main forms of media open to the B2B marketer are summarized in Figure 11.6 and discussed briefly below.

Each of these has a series of strengths and weaknesses:

- Magazines: Often known as 'the trade press' in B2B markets. These offer high impact thanks to their high-quality reproduction, allow for the inclusion of detailed product information, and enable the targeting of specialist audiences. Trade press magazines are

Figure 11.6 **B2B communications media**

often perceived as credible sources of information and remain in circulation for some time (witness the piles of trade journals in the reception areas of many firms), ensuring a decent exposure for an advertisement. However, long lead times can be necessary before an ad can be produced and placed, and magazines are a moderately expensive medium.

- Newspapers: These have a wider reach and higher profile than most magazines, and much shorter lead times. Marketers should remember, though, that newspapers have a short lifespan, provide relatively low-quality reproduction, and are rarely targeted at a specialist group of business customers. Sometimes, however, newspaper advertisements can be used to help a firm make a corporate announcement as well as to cement relationships between the firm and it suppliers. For instance, 23 suppliers of Malaysian firm CSC Steel (www.cscmalaysia.com) took out a cooperative newspaper advertisement congratulating the firm on its new corporate identity (it was formerly known as Ornasteel). This full-page announcement let the general business community know of the rebranding and, at the same time, allowed these suppliers to show their commitment to CSC while raising their own profiles (New Straits Times, 2008).

- Television: This provides a very high profile and mass audience coverage, but it is difficult to communicate complex messages to your target audience, the vast majority of whom is unlikely to be interested in your business product or service. Moreover, the absolute cost of an ad campaign on TV is usually substantial.

- Radio: This is similar to TV, but often allows for more focused (regional) targeting of campaigns, and with less cost, although messages can lack the impact and detail of visual media. Note how Barclays Bank communicated its business service in the UK using a campaign that incorporated the medium of radio – see Box 11.5. The number of responses suggests that the campaign worked. Do you think this approach would succeed in every country?

- Outdoor media: Media such as posters and billboards are relatively inexpensive and can provide high reach with excellent location targeting. However, in general, the image of this medium is not very prestigious, and printing and erecting large posters involve

Box 11.5 Number crunching

Attracting new clients

The B2B arm of Barclays is keen to target small businesses. To increase the number of local UK firms using its services, the bank ran a campaign in 2007 positioning itself as the market leader for SMEs. The nine-week campaign was aimed at bringing in 17,000 new business accounts and encouraging 5,000 firms to 'switch' to Barclays. As well as providing advertising within Barclays branches containing humorous strap lines such as 'Been together years but still feel like strangers?' the campaign used radio advertising. The MD of Barclays Local Business, John Davis, says, 'Radio is a terrific way for us to reach new small business customers. Maybe this is because many of the people fitting this profile have radios on in the background while they work.' The campaign cost what the firm described as a 'relatively small' £250,000 and generated over 30,000 leads, resulting in an increase of 10% in new accounts and 21% for 'switchers' compared with the same period in the previous year.

Source: The Marketer (2008); www.barclays.co.uk

considerable lead times. Readership is also difficult to measure. Having said this, some B2B firms have used outdoor media successfully, like when outsourcing expert Mastek (www.mastek.com) wanted to stress the skills of its staff to potential clients. For maximum impact, it did so by commissioning an advertisement proclaiming the firm's 'people factor' displayed on a poster the size of a building erected alongside the busy London-bound side of the M4 motorway. This site ensured great exposure to executives who commute daily and those that might be flying into Heathrow Airport before making their way to the UK capital.

B2B communication via the Internet

A key attraction of the Internet for B2B marketer is the fact that it facilitates interactivity. The speedy, bidirectional nature of the electronic medium allows buyers to search for information, get answers to their questions from sellers, and decide whether to purchase goods with relative ease. There are a number of benefits to using the Web in business markets, which can be weighed against some limitations (Evans and King, 1999).

- Benefits of B2B websites: Enabling sellers to achieve global reach; providing '24/7' access for users; maintaining up-to-date information for stakeholders; creatively exploiting the Web's interactive and multimedia capability; cost effectiveness compared with some of the more traditional forms of marketing communication; acting as a sales channel; providing distributor support; enhancing customer service; JIT inventory planning; gathering competitor intelligence; and gaining access to commercial research.

- Limitations of B2B websites: Global differences can make pricing difficult; poor site organization may result in frustrated users; and resistance may be encountered from some buyers less keen to welcome change in buying practices with their sector. Moreover, different user-PC settings can result in suboptimal information control; website congestion can occur if too many users attempt to visit the site simultaneously;

and non-user-friendly URLs can be too long and impossible for customers to memorize, although these latter factors appear to be diminishing in significance as Web-based technology improves.

The Internet combines many strengths of other media due to its ability to handle textual data, audio, and visual messages, leading to its utility in all the promotional elements of the marketing communications mix. Two tools in particular are of relevance to B2B marketers, the use of organizational websites and email. They are summarized in Figure 11.7.

- Company websites: These have developed over the last few years from acting as static online brochures to becoming much more interactive propositions. Sites can often now accommodate e-commerce transactions and handle bidirectional communication, thereby allowing firms to offer a genuine 'dialogue' with their customers online. Well-designed B2B websites which are easy to navigate can enable suppliers to react to customers' detailed queries with focused responses and personalized solutions. This means that websites should make the most of the multimedia opportunities available to engage visitors and help them focus on the part of the site that is most appropriate to their needs, minimizing their search time. The content of websites can be used by marketers to enhance the reputation of the company and assist information exchange between the firm and its customers, thus increasing customer participation in communication flows (Karayanni and Baltas, 2003).

Some experts believe that business 'blogs' (personal online diaries) are also useful communications tools. For instance, Chaffey (2007) argues that blogs provide a good opportunity for organizations to demonstrate authority and provide information in a more personal tone of voice than most corporate websites will allow (e.g. the site of market research experts B2B International on www.b2binternational.com/b2b-blog).

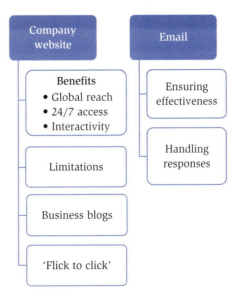

Figure 11.7 **B2B communications via the Internet**

Another website tactic is to allow your customers to 'flick to click'. This is a phenomenon that has traditionally been confined to B2C contexts but which is now making an impression in B2B marketing. Look at the example in Box 11.6 to see how this combination of using direct marketing in the form of printed catalogues with Web-based ordering seems to be taking off. Do you think that the network of firms involved in the Abacus Alliance are right to continue to place their faith in this hard/soft combination of media?

- Email: In direct marketing terms, email provides a speedy and efficient way to communicate regularly with a target audience. However, the effectiveness of such an approach

Box 11.6 Voices

Using 'flick to click' communication methods in B2B markets

Flick to click refers to the practice of customers browsing a company's catalogue and then going online to enter the product code in a search box on the company's website. According to Ginna Clark, the MD of Catalink.com (which is both a B2B and B2C catalogue portal), business suppliers like Screwfix (who offer fastenings) and Viking Direct (who sell stationery) have realized that their clients find it easier to browse through a printed catalogue to determine exactly what they need from each firm's vast array of products before engaging with the Internet to place their orders.

Some businesses work together to manage their direct marketing campaigns for sending out catalogues to customers. Abacus Alliance runs a mail-order data pool that allows organizational members who put data in to take out the data from other members for their own campaigns. They describe this as a 'business-to-business cooperative database'. Abacus's senior account director Des Wilson argues: 'The catalogue has always been an important tool for B2B firms, even before the days of the Internet.' He believes that the importance of purchasing a vital piece of equipment for an organization means that client companies demand something that can be taken to meetings and passed around so that all buying centre members can give feedback. This view is confirmed by George Karibian, MD of office supplies firm Euro office.co.uk, who says, 'We struggled with it initially. We are an online catalogue, so why print catalogues? But we have learnt now that it's an important part of the mix, especially early in the lifecycle of customers.'

Another assenting voice regarding flick to click is that of Emily Travis, head of publishing at Royal Mail. She claims that the organization's B2B catalogue is able to bring products to life in a way that is more flexible and pleasurable than sitting in front of a computer screen. Highlighting the popularity of B2B magazines, Travis points out that they 'boost brand appeal by one-quarter, with 25% of readers visiting the website as a direct result of reading the publication.' It is likely that more businesses will adopt the approach as it allows firms to keep their order processing costs low, while their customers find the purchasing process easier and quicker, having already browsed a tangible catalogue or magazine.

Source: Murphy (2007); www.abacusalliance.com

is dependent on the accuracy of the email lists available to the marketer. Failure to ensure your emails are being sent to the appropriate person leaves B2B marketers open to accusations of distributing Internet 'spam', much like the postal 'junk mail' version of direct marketing. A good place to start compiling an email list is to utilize the information held by the firm's CRM system. Email allows suppliers to send their existing and prospective customers updated catalogues, details of sales promotions, and PR material. For example, previous purchasers of Hewlett-Packard printers receive regular emails containing information about HP's latest products and price offers, typically under the heading 'Growing businesses run better on HP'. Recipients can either call a special phone line or click on links embedded in the email for further offers (www.hp.com/uk/happypeople).

- A further consideration in email marketing concerns the handling of responses. These will often be swift and the firm must be similarly rapid in replying, whether initially only to acknowledge receipt of the customer's message or to initiate some action (like despatching an order) and sending email confirmation when this has been completed. If the responses are to be processed by an outsourced call centre, then careful guidelines about promptness and accuracy will need to be given to this service provider.

Note how the relatively high-profile broadcast media of TV and radio represent areas that may not be particularly useful in communicating with key members of the buying centre, especially if the selling firm is not a large brand name. Having said this, mass media may be effective for B2B marketing communications when the target organizations are relatively numerous or widely spread, such as SMEs in industrial regions like 'Silicon Valley', or agricultural businesses in rural Australia, or when the products offered are relatively generic (e.g. office stationery or cleaning services). For most sellers, other media such as printed forms of communication and the Internet may be more appropriate than broadcast media, both in terms of cost and effectiveness.

You should also appreciate that the relative effectiveness of B2B marketing communications tools is thought to vary, depending on the stage of the purchase process (see Chapter Two), meaning that a combination of different communication tactics and media is usually necessary in marketing campaigns. For instance, while advertising and, to a lesser extent, PR are often powerful tools at the beginning of the process, in general there is a decline in effectiveness of advertising once awareness has been raised, with a corresponding rise in effectiveness of personal selling and sales promotions as the purchase decision is potentially reached, with the sales force becoming crucial in many contexts (see Chapter Twelve). Advertising and PR, however, can be useful to reassure customers post-purchase that they have made the right decision, thus building loyalty and leading to repeat purchases. Direct marketing and Internet-based approaches tend to exert a fairly consistent influence throughout the purchase decision process.

Fundamentally, despite the increasing sophistication of the media available to B2B marketers, it is the personal WOM recommendation (or condemnation) that remains the most influential medium in organizational markets (Webster, 1970). WOM is highly dependent on perceptions of customer satisfaction. Much marketing communication involves making a promise to the user, but unless the value in use of the offering is perceived as worthwhile, these promises will ring hollow, and relationships will be unlikely to develop. Nevertheless, the B2B marketer must always manage his/her firm's expenditure to make the best possible communications impact on the target audience.

The chapter concludes with a case study of a firm that produces corporate promotional gifts: in an interesting twist, you will be considering the marketing communications issues facing an organization that specializes in helping other organizations with their own communications. The case asks you to begin linking the promotional strategies in the chapter to some marketing planning issues, and to start thinking creatively about B2B communications messages.

Summary

The key points to take from this chapter are as follows:

- How the different broad approaches to marketing communications strategy (push, pull, and reputation) can be applied in B2B markets.

- The ways in which different facets of marketing communication can be linked to the nature of inter-organizational relationships in marketing channels.

- How the concept of integrated marketing communications (IMC) helps marketers to ensure the consistency of their message to a number of different audiences or stakeholders.

- The large range of promotional tactics available to the B2B marketer, and the relative effectiveness of each.

- The importance of choosing the appropriate media for your marketing message in an organizational market context.

- How the Internet can be utilized in B2B marketing communications in terms of website and email applications.

Discussion questions

1. 'A "push" marketing communications strategy is the only promotional approach that a B2B marketer needs to be concerned about.' Debate the validity of this statement.

2. What activities would you advise the marketing communications manager of an organization supplying market research services to include in an IMC programme aimed at targeting new customers?

3. How are some of the communication tactics used in B2B markets thought to differ in their relevance/effectiveness compared with B2C approaches?

4. You are the marketing manager of a manufacturer of specialist food processing equipment for firms in the retail and catering trades. How might you plan a technical seminar for the launch of your latest product? What sort of stakeholders (both internal and external) would you invite?

5. What are the main considerations in selecting the appropriate media to convey a communications message to customers for a bulk-buy discount promotion for a commodity-like industrial product?

6. What are some of the opportunities and possible limitations of using email as part of your B2B marketing communications strategy?

Case study

The Corporate Incentive and Promotion Industry

Natalia Tolstikova, University of Gloucestershire, Cheltenham, UK and Gillian Hopkinson, Lancaster University, Lancaster, UK

Introduction

Take a close look at the objects in any workplace to get some idea of the suppliers to that organization. You are likely to see mugs, mousemats, calendars, notepads, pens, and many other objects embossed with corporate logos and slogans. A long-standing tradition of gift-giving (or 'gifting') added to the recognition of the power of branding has created a massive industry in providing promotional gifts given by suppliers to industrial customers. It is an industry worth over £900 million per annum, according to industry body the British Promotional Merchandise Association (BPMA) (www.bpma. co.uk).

However, gift supplier Re-Sourceful (www.re-sourceful.co.uk) claims the promotional merchandise market is full of 'promo-tat'. A monthly competition on this organization's website invites visitors to cast their vote for the most tatty object amongst a selection of promotional products. Objects they have featured include a pack of miniature high-lighters (for someone with tiny hands, they say) and a set of pottery Wellington boots (perhaps for a teddy bear, they suggest). Comments posted on the website indicate that the company is not alone in its criticism of the promotions industry. Someone called Gemma writes, 'It makes me angry seeing this useless tat. Is anyone ever pleased to receive this stuff? Whoever approved the purchase of this in an organization should stop wasting time and do something more creative with their money!' (23 April 2009) and Jennifer comments 'promo-tat is a great initiative, I hope you manage to raise the standard of corporate gifting' (23 April 2009).

Raising the standard of corporate gifting is central to Re-Sourceful's mission: 'Our aim is to provide positive promotional gift ideas that allow businesses to say more about themselves and that have a positive impact on lives at home and abroad.' As a small company with big ambitions, how can they best go about growing their market for effective corporate gifts with a lower environmental impact? Some understanding of the corporate gift market will help you address this question.

The purpose and problems of corporate gifting

Organizations buy corporate gifts primarily to serve two different purposes. Firstly, they offer gifts as incentives and, secondly, for promotions.

An example of the former might be the promise of a gift to a sales person within the company who exceeds a certain sales target. Alternatively, a firm might offer a gift to an external purchaser, for example offering a watch to a purchasing agent if they exceed a certain quantity of purchases over a specified time period. Such gifts act to incentivize the intended recipients to behave in a certain way and can be used tactically when, for example, the gifting company wants to move an excess of stock quickly. For incentives to be effective, the gift must be something that is desired by the target group.

Secondly, gifts can be used as a form of promotion and, in this case, are often used in connection with some special occasion. Thus, promotional gifts may be sent in festival periods such as Christmas or may be sent in association with a new product launch, given out at a trade fair or presented by sales people as they visit customers. In this latter case, gifts are usually branded, carrying the logo, advertising message, and contact details of the gifting company. As a form of marketing communication, the gifts seen as most effective in these contexts are those that maximize the chance of visibility for reasons of their usefulness to the recipient or their novelty or attractiveness. Mugs and fridge magnets, for example, may be repeatedly used and viewed.

There are, however, additional considerations when organizations give gifts to their customers. Corporate gifting is ubiquitous, so providing a gift that is noticeable and genuinely welcomed is becoming increasingly difficult. Additionally, organizations with 'green' credentials may question the gifts they are giving, or, indeed, receiving. Incentives and promotional gifts must be appropriate to the gifting company – in keeping with their product or ethos and supportive of their other communication efforts – after all, through repeated use in the recipient work environment, these objects continue to 'talk' on behalf of your organization. Promotions and incentives are therefore seen by the B2B marketer in firms that utilize gifts as one element working within an integrated communication plan. The marketer in a promotional gifts company such as Re-Sourceful, is likely to be successful if they can target appropriate client companies with a total offering that maximizes the utility of promotional objects as part of a broader communication effort.

The promotional gift market

To the organization wanting to implement a gift programme, there is a bewildering array of potential suppliers. Promotional gift companies generally act as distributors for a range of manufacturers who are able to add the customer company's logo and message to their products. Sourcing from a range of suppliers, the promotional companies add value through their ability to offer a 'one-stop' ordering and delivery solution to customers. Some promotional gift companies become more broadly involved in advisory services surrounding the selection of gifts and their role in the customer's communications plan.

The seeming simplicity of the business and the absence of considerable scale cost advantages make this a fragmented market with low barriers to entry. This means that in the UK, there are estimated to be over 2,000 promotional gift companies, although about half of these have an annual turnover of less than £250,000 (www.bpma.co.uk).

Whilst organizations purchasing gifts thus have ample choice, selling organizational gifts presents several challenges. There is no one clear 'type' of organization that purchases gifts, rather, they are used by organizations of all sizes and in many sectors. Additionally, communicating with the person within an organization who is responsible for purchasing gifts can present a challenge. The corporate gift buyer is not a purchasing manager but rather a mid-level manager in a department, including sales, marketing, operations, production, human resources, or product management. In short, the purchaser can be anyone who has responsibility for motivating and recognizing key people and, moreover, will have a broad-ranging set of responsibilities of which gift buying is only one.

Many companies will also be sporadic gift buyers with changing needs, so it is difficult to predict whether an order will be small or large. Also, purchasers are often not loyal to any one promotional gift company but act according to the perceived needs of a particular situation. The recent economic downturn has led to a decrease in corporate gift purchasing: down 20% over the previous year in spring 2009, according to Sourcing City (www.sourcingcity.co.uk). Some corporate gift companies have gone out of business and those remaining note a sharp decrease in lead times, meaning that responsiveness to the customer is increasingly critical to generating business.

Green promotional gifts

To the extent that organizations wish to be recognized for their environmental policies and efforts, the eco-friendly gift market might be expected to benefit from an increased societal awareness of environmental issues. Evidence suggests that this is happening. For example, Sourcing City tracks 'click-through' Web activity on BPMA member websites and ranks these according to product groups in terms of growth and absolute share of Web activity. In spring 2009, 'green' products showed impressive growth figures. For example, the highest overall riser was eco-clothing, eco-pens ranked number 4 followed by eco-bags ranked 13. Their absolute share of activity, though, was less impressive. For example, eco-clothing ranked 36, eco-pens 27, and eco-bags 19. Thus, the total share of market of eco-products is of some note but the growth of attention such products are achieving is remarkable.

In response to this trend, many general corporate gift companies offer green products alongside their mainstream offerings. As an example, Phoenix Corporate Gifts (www. phoenixcorporategifts.com) offers 106 eco-friendly products alongside a far wider range of standard products. In general, the eco-friendly products are more expensive than their standard counterparts. For instance, in the pen range, a Flamenco Ballpoint Pen at 16p for orders of 2,000 or an eco-friendly alternative, the biodegradable Vegetal Ballpoint pen at 30p for orders of 2,000.

Re-Sourceful is, however, amongst a much more limited set of companies that offer exclusively eco-friendly products. Their extensive product range includes:

- T-shirts and toys from organic, fair trade, or recycled materials
- Pens and coasters made from recycled CDs
- Glasses made from cola bottles
- Notebooks made from recycled tyres
- Wooden memory sticks.

In addition to a sole focus upon eco-friendly products, Re-Sourceful also differentiates itself from mainstream competitors through the environmental basis of its entire communications, the depth of environmental product information provided on its website, and by what might be seen as its cheeky and involving attack on the mainstream industry.

Whilst the company seems well adapted to market trends, it nevertheless faces challenges as a small company with limited resources. In particular, it needs to decide how to communicate its unique benefits to customers who will value these to the extent that they will be prepared to pay the slightly elevated costs of the eco-friendly products in order to integrate these gifts within their communications plan.

Source: www.bpma.co.uk; www.phoenixcorporategifts.com; www.re-sourceful.co.uk; www. sourcingcity.co.uk (all accessed in 2009)

Case study questions

1. Drawing on your knowledge of segmentation bases used in B2B markets, discuss the usefulness of these for Re-Sourceful in terms of developing a communications strategy.

2. Which elements of the B2B marketing communications mix can best be deployed to allow Re-Sourceful to access gift buyers in the segments that you have defined? For advertising plans, you may be able to identify relevant media and indicative costs by searching on the Internet. How would you use elements other than advertising?

3. Focusing on one of the communications elements you have identified, elaborate on the message you would communicate. Develop a form of written words (or salesperson's speech – see Chapter Twelve) that you feel would be most effective.

Further Reading

Bengston, A., Pahlberg, C., & Pourmand, F. (2009) Small Firms' Interaction with Political Organizations in the European Union, Industrial Marketing Management, 38 (6), pp 687–707
In what can be seen as an alternative take on public relations in business markets, the authors demonstrate how small companies proactively support and influence the key stakeholders represented by political actors in the EU. Their case studies are a contrast to previous research which tends to show how SMEs have been forced to accept the political decisions made in the region.

Ellis, N. & Hopkinson, G. (2010) The Construction of Managerial Knowledge in Business Networks: Managers' Theories about Communication, Industrial Marketing Management, 38, pp 413–24
The authors use an interpretive methodology to identify elements of B2B managers' talk about marketing communication which are deployed to establish the range of communicative work, the difficulty in managing the directionality of communication, and the complexity of managing IORs. They argue that managers' understandings of communication may be better deployed than at present by the organizations they represent and in management education.

Gronroos, C. (2004) The Relationship Marketing Process: Communication, Interaction, Dialogue, Value, Journal of Business & Industrial Marketing, 19 (2), pp 99–113
The paper discusses a framework of processes in relationship marketing aimed at encouraging dialogue between IOR parties. The framework includes an interaction process as the core, a planned communication process as the marketing communications support through distinct communications media, and a customer value process as the outcome of relationship marketing.

Ling-Yee, L. (2007) Marketing Resources and Performance of Exhibitor Firms in Trade Shows: A Contingent Resource Perspective, Industrial Marketing Management, 36 (3), pp 360–70

This study argues that the main effect of trade show resources on trade show performance is contingent upon the network context in terms of the firm's internal knowledge assets and its external relationship assets. One managerial implication for exhibitor managers is the need to adjust allocation of trade show marketing resources according to the market-based assets the firm possesses.

References

Ballantyne, D. (2004) Dialogue and its Role in the Development of Relationship Specific Knowledge, Journal of Business & Industrial Marketing, 19 (2), 114–23

Beverland, M. & Luxton, S. (2005) Managing Integrated Marketing Communications (IMC) through Strategic Decoupling, Journal of Advertising, 34 (4), pp 103–16

Blythe, J. (2002) Using Trade Fairs in Key Account Management, Industrial Marketing Management, 31 (7), pp 627–35

B2B Marketing (2009) The Winners: The B2B Marketing Awards 2008 in Detail, online at http://www.b2bm.biz, accessed August 2009

Chaffey, D. (2007) Help or Hyperbole, The Marketer, July/August, pp 16–19

Condé Nast Traveller (2007) Hard Sell, September, p 28

Ellis, N. & Hopkinson, G. (2010) The Construction of Managerial Knowledge in Business Networks: Managers' Theories about Communication, Industrial Marketing Management, 38, pp 413–24

Evans, J. R. & King, V. E. (1999) Business-to-Business Marketing and the World Wide Web: Planning, Managing and Assessing websites, Industrial Marketing Management, 28, pp 343–58

Frazier, G. L. & Summers, J. O. (1984) Interfirm Influence Strategies and their Application within Distribution Channels, Journal of Marketing, 48, pp 43–55

Gaski, J. F. & Nevin, J. R. (1985) The Differential Effects of Exercised and Unexercised Power Sources in a Marketing Channel, Journal of Marketing Research, 22, 130–42

Hall, L. & Wickham, M. (2008) Organizing IMC Roles and Functions in the Business-to-Business Network Environment, Journal of Marketing Communications, 14 (3), pp 193–206

Haytko, D. L. (2004) Firm-to-Firm and Interpersonal Relationships: Perspectives from Advertising Agency Account Managers, Journal of the Academy of Marketing Science, 32 (3), pp 312–28

Karayanni, D. A. & Baltas, G. A. (2003) Web Site Characteristics and Business Performance: Some Evidence from International Business-to-Business Organizations, Marketing Intelligence and Planning, 21 (2), pp 105–14

Lindberg-Repo, K. & Gronroos, C. (2004) Conceptualising Communications Strategy from a Relational Perspective, Industrial Marketing Management, 33, pp 229–39

Low, G. S. (2000) Correlates of Integrated Marketing Communications, Journal of Advertising Research, 40 (3), pp 27–42

Marketer (The) (2008) Case Study: Barclays, February, pp 21–5

Marketer (The) (2008) Profile: Guarding her Patch, February, pp 27–9

Marketing (2008) Can you Get the Message Across? 6 August, p 40

Mohr, J. & Nevin, J. R. (1990) Communication Strategies in Marketing Channels: A Theoretical Perspective, Journal of Marketing, 54 (4), pp 36–51

Mohr, J., Fisher, R. J. & Nevin, J. R. (1996) Collaborative Communication in Interfirm Relationships, Journal of Marketing, 60 (3), 103–15

Murphy, D. (2007) Off the Page, On to the Web, The Marketer, October, pp 30–3

New Straits Times (2008), 9 September, p 37

Olkkonen, R., Tikkanen, H., & Alajoutsijarvi, K. (2000) The Role of Communication in Business Relationships and Networks, Management Decision, 38 (6), 403–9

Papas, C. (2008) Goodbye to Small Fry, The Marketer, April, pp 20–2

Rosenbloom, B. (1999) Marketing Channels: A Management View, Dryden Press, Fort Worth

Viet Nam News (2007) 21 November, Advertisement Section B

Webster, F. E. (1970) Informal Communication in Industrial Markets, Journal of Marketing, 7, May, pp 186–9

Chapter 12
Personal Selling & Sales Management

Introduction & Learning Objectives

This final chapter discusses the role of personal selling in B2B markets. It considers different possibilities for the management of industrial sales forces and examines the significance of key account management (KAM) in inter-organizational relationships (IORs). Underpinning this chapter is the notion that collaborative relationships can only really be established and nurtured through properly managed personal contact, including selling.

The examples in Box 12.1 show how B2B marketing initiatives often depend on personal interactions in order to communicate the value of the selling firm's offerings to organizational customers. While the first case involves the use of a sales force, the second illustrates the fact that some SMEs may not have the resources to employ such a team, and so other members of the management team must effectively act as sales people. Regardless of what job title the individuals charged with making personal contacts with customers are given, this chapter will go on to argue that social exchanges are fundamental to the success of almost all IORs. Marketers therefore need to know how to get the best out of these boundary-spanning members of their organization.

Box 12.1 Mini case
The importance of personal contact in the marketing communications mix

Small bio and nanotechnology companies have to work hard to get the most out of their marketing budgets, especially as they must try to distil the highly complex scientific benefits of their offerings into compelling customer propositions. Personal interactions between selling staff and customer personnel are crucial in these business markets.

For instance, the Internet and direct mail are used a great deal by firms like Lab21, a biotech diagnostics firm, to target customers in the UK's National Health Service (NHS) and private healthcare markets. However, recognizing that these elements of the communication mix are not enough to explain the operation of such specialist services, Lab21 also employs a direct sales team which focuses on key customer accounts and potential clients after these have been identified through telemarketing. The company's CEO, Jerry Walker, says, 'In selling to the NHS the key issues are performance and price benefits,' and the sales team are an 'important part' of communicating those benefits to buying contacts in the organization.

Facing a similar dilemma is the business development director of Exilca, Norman Leece. His firm's core products are tiny spherical particles or beads and hollow silica shells which are sold to organizations in the cosmetics, drugs, and household goods sectors. Explaining the company's technology is a fundamental marketing challenge, and so Leece spends a lot of his time 'demystifying', as he puts it, what Exilica's products can do for prospective clients. He achieves this by focusing on face-to-face discussions with customers' technical development teams.

Source: Gray (2007); www.lab21.co.uk; www.exilica.co.uk

Chapter Aims

After completing this chapter, you should be able to

- Identify key tasks of personal selling in organizational markets
- Evaluate alternative approaches to organizing the sales force
- Link key account management (KAM) strategy to relationship management.

12.1 Personal Selling in B2B Markets

The role of the industrial sales person is generally very important in organizational markets. Personal selling in most industrial sectors has a more significant role than in B2C contexts due to the higher order values, more complex product offerings, and the smaller number of buyers in B2B markets. In order to differentiate themselves, suppliers often feel that they must offer a personal service to potential and existing buyers, a service that is delivered by a sales force.

Not only can a professional sales person generate sales for the firm, their personal customer relationships can also result in privileged access to confidential information, hints of competitor initiatives, or even sight of tenders by rival suppliers. Notwithstanding ethical consideration over such information exchange, for instance if inducements are given to solicit this sort of marketplace data, sales force feedback can be crucial for the selling firm's strategic planning (Pitt and Nel, 1988).

Is a sales force necessary?

Although the relationships fostered by personal selling can be very effective, especially at the later stages of the buying process, the sales force is also the most expensive element of the B2B marketing communications mix (see Chapter Eleven). As Box 12.2 shows, some sales calls (visits to customers) can cost over $200 each. Note, however, that this statistic was collated in the US, so you might wonder if the cost of sales calls varies across the globe – for instance, how much would it cost a firm to maintain a sales force in a country where labour costs are substantially lower than in the US?

These sorts of costs mean that the use of a field-based sales force must be carefully considered by B2B marketers. This is especially so when you recall that many straightforward 'rebuy' purchase decisions are relatively routine (see Chapter Two), involving little need for protracted negotiation or technical analysis. Sales personnel in these situations act more like

Box 12.2 Number crunching

The cost of personal sales calls

Here are the typical average costs (in US dollars) of four different selling strategies. You can see how the cost per call increases as the complexity of the customers' demands becomes greater, necessitating a bigger investment of sales people's time and supporting resources in order to try to secure the sale.

1. Script-based selling, which uses the same presentation from customer to customer due to these organizations' needs being fairly similar = approx. $57 per call.

2. Needs satisfaction selling, which uses questioning techniques to identify client needs, and occurs in markets where customer needs can vary, although still based on a common set of requirements = approx. $143 per call.

3. Consultative selling, which also uses questioning techniques, but involves proposing a more customized solution for customers whose needs are unique = approx. $165 per call.

4. Strategic partner selling, where buyer and seller jointly create needs and cooperate in developing solutions = approx. $212 per call.

Source: Marchetti (2000) cited in Dwyer and Tanner (2002)

order takers, and their work can be undertaken by more junior sales staff located centrally and utilizing telephone or Internet-based ordering systems. In some service sectors, however, managers are reporting that their sales staff have had to switch from an order-taking role to one where they must solicit new corporate clients. This has happened, for instance, in the hotel trade following a downturn in the previously 'cash cow' Middle Eastern markets for hotel operators serving business travellers and conference organizers (e.g. www.hoteliermiddleeast.com).

Even if ordering has become a routine clerical operation, a company's sales force can still contribute significantly by reinforcing the supplier's reputation for reliability and support services. They can help to resolve conflicts and build personal relationships with key buying centre members such that buyers perceive the switching costs in changing suppliers to be too great (Biong and Selnes, 1996).

The role of the B2B sales person

As they operate in the field, the modern sales person is not only expected to act as a generator of sales and a manager of customers, but increasingly as someone responsible for the development of IORs as a part of the firm's overall customer relationship management (CRM) approach – see Chapter Three. This demanding role is reflected in the list of activities a sales representative (or rep) may be expected to perform (Guenzi, 2002). Note how it extends far beyond mere selling:

- Selling: Closing sales to prospective and existing customers.
- Prospecting: Locating new customers, both on the sales rep's own initiative and from leads provided, say, from responses to the parent firm's direct marketing campaigns.

- Pre-sales service: Ensuring customers are encouraged to feel confident enough in the selling firm and its offerings to make a purchase.

- Post-sales service: Providing reassurances and handling queries to encourage the formation of long-term IORs.

- CRM: Developing and maintaining relationships with customers (see section 12.3 below for more on this topic).

- Inbound information handling: Feeding information about the marketplace and the broader network back to the selling organization.

- Outbound information handling: Delivering information about the selling organization to the marketplace.

- Market research: Analysing and forecasting market trends.

- Sales team cooperation: Working closely with sales support staff, such as database administrators, IT technicians, and telemarketers.

The list of activities is summarized in Figure 12.1. Some of these tasks are fairly generic in that they will be performed by sales people across most sectors. These activities include selling, CRM, and communicating information to the marketplace. Other activities, like pre-sales service, market analysis, and inbound information handling, tend to be more industry-specific (Guenzi, 2002).

Finding and retaining good sales people who can cope with such tasks can be difficult, especially in competitive sectors like pharmaceuticals. For example, sales staff turnover amongst drugs companies in China is consistently above 20%. This is despite the existence of carefully designed training programmes, as shown by the firm that has set up its own 'university' in Shanghai where new sales people spend several weeks learning about products and procedures before being allowed to visit customers (Bucher, 2008).

It is interesting to compare managerial views of the selling role between different countries. Box 12.3 records some views from B2B sales personnel that reflect similarities but also some cross-country differences between managers. Do you think the perspectives of sales people in, say, India would also show such differences when compared with the US?

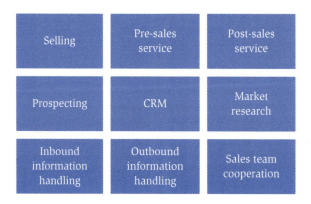

Figure 12.1 **Typical tasks of sales representatives**

Box 12.3 Voices

How sales executives view their changing role

Researchers asked sales people representing firms in a variety of industrial sectors (including capital equipment and financial services) from the US, Mexico, and France about how they saw the changing role of their profession. One reason for comparing these countries was that selling is probably a more accepted profession in the US than in the other two contexts (Tanner et al, 2008). Indeed, Mexican participants seemed to think that there was room for greater professional development of sales forces in their country than in the US. As one manager stated, a sales person should be more than just an 'everyday nice guy'. Now it was necessary for them to 'know clients in advance and have a very good understanding of their own company'. French sellers, more so than North American managers, believed that centralization of buying and consolidation of customers was leading to increased globalization among buyers. One said, 'the manufacturer's sales structure will follow the buying structure of the customer. If they are more global, we must adapt.'

One issue on which all sales people appeared to agree was the increasing fragmentation of customer responsibility, with the field sales person often having only part of the responsibility for an IOR. This can lead to difficulties for the selling firm and different parts of the sales team (see section 12.2) in maintaining a single unified perspective of the customer. Another common issue to all three contexts was the importance of value creation. One US manufacturer said that sales people have to add value to the sales process or the buyer would just purchase from the Internet. A French participant believed that managers should be asking themselves, 'What is the contribution of each person to the company?'

In general, it seems that adding value involves augmenting the product or service such that the buyer is willing to pay more in order to receive greater benefit. Mexican and French managers felt more strongly than those in the US that sales people do, indeed, add value to the selling process. However, in both of the former countries there also appeared to be concern over the selection of sales people, with the opinion being voiced that the selling role is not always seen as a positive career choice, making it difficult to hire good staff.

Source: Tanner et al (2008)

Sales force effectiveness

Although the personal contact provided by sales people is often valued in B2B communications, the reach and frequency of audience contact are always relatively low compared with other media. Moreover, to ensure the maximum amount of flexibility in negotiating with different customers, sales people are typically given a large degree of freedom over how they deliver the company's message to audiences. Although there will clearly be some guidance given to sales staff over the limits to which they must adhere to provide customer satisfaction, the individual characteristics of each sales person make it difficult to ensure consistency in marketing communications.

To achieve success in their role, sales people can take up a lot of company resources, such as salaries, commissions, statutory employment costs, IT support, and expenses (e.g. travel, accommodation, subsistence, and entertaining clients). The high cost per personal contact and, to an extent, the lower central control by the parent organization over the ultimate message communicated should be weighed up against the strengths of personal selling, especially its capacity to handle bidirectional communication and negotiation. Having said this, some sales reps misuse the personal communications media available to them, according to sales benchmarking consultants Best Practice LLC (www.best-in-class.com). Unfortunately, responding to communication tools such as instant messages, texts, and mobile email can get in the way of sales people's engagement with institutional end users. As one medical sales executive states, 'They're so distracted by doing four things at once that the quality of their work across all fronts is poor' (Reuters, 2009).

All this means that a sales force should not be the automatic strategy for reaching every business market. As researchers like Cravens et al (1991) have suggested, several factors should be considered by B2B marketers before committing to the use of a sales person (or people, depending on the resources you have available). These are summarized in Figure 12.2.

- Communication effectiveness: The B2B marketer should not forget the relative effectiveness of other elements of the marketing communications mix, as outlined in Chapter Eleven. Recall that tools like advertising cannot usually provide all the information an organizational buyer needs to make their decision. While PR and advertisements may raise awareness and encourage desire, and sales promotions may prompt actual buying, many industrial purchases require face-to-face negotiations and demonstrations before the sale can be completed. The ability of sales people to listen and respond to customer concerns, thus building a relationship dialogue, is largely beyond the capacity of mass communication media.

- Channel/network structure: When the overall communications strategy is push orientated (see Chapter Eleven), personal selling will often be required to ensure effective

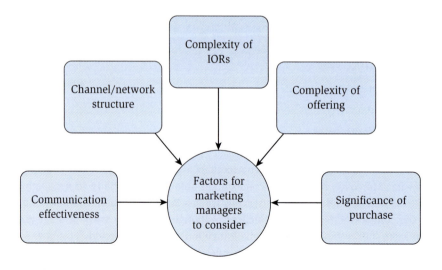

Figure 12.2 Are B2B sales people necessary?

communication with channel members. If the number of network actors is relatively small, then sales reps will be much more effective than less personalized approaches like advertising in answering distributors' questions, handling any objections, and overcoming misperceptions. If these communication tasks are professionally managed, the opportunity for forging strong relationships with other network actors can be great. As you have seen in Chapters Three and Four, these channel links can lead to significant competitive advantages for a manufacturer.

- Complexity of IORs: This may be associated with the environment in which negotiations are taking place, such as a relationship atmosphere that has previously been characterized as adversarial with low levels of trust, or a tough overall economic environment where customers are becoming increasingly cautious. The social interaction afforded by a sales person enables the selling firm to convey the reputation of the firm and the benefits of the offering more persuasively.

- Complexity of the offering: The characteristics of the product or service may necessitate a great deal of knowledge on the part of the sales person and much negotiation over technical specifications, for instance in the installation of a new bespoke software package. The expertise of the sales person and the opportunity to demonstrate the product in use to key decision makers (especially on the customer's premises) can be very important in such situations.

- Significance of purchase: The importance to the buyer of the potential purchase can indicate whether a sales person should be employed. Where the levels of risk (both financial and personal) are thought to be high, a persuasive personal contact can do much to alleviate such perceptions and to overcome resistance from members of the buying centre, making negotiations over costs less arduous. If the pricing policy of the selling firm is to use a set price list, however, then the need for sales reps may not be so great, and a telesales team may suffice.

A final point to make about the role of the B2B sales person is that managers probably need to understand better the tensions that can affect people who must operate in this boundary-spanning position. As Box 12.4 indicates, there may be some important social and psychological aspects of the role that companies can take into account when selecting,

---

Box 12.4 Food for thought
Coping with working on the boundaries of organizations

It is common to describe sales and marketing personnel as 'boundary spanners' because they are thought to operate at the boundary of the selling organization, providing the link between their own firm's needs and the needs of their customers. There is danger, however, in assuming that boundaries really exist between firms embedded in industrial networks, especially if these organizations operate within close collaborative relationships. If boundaries are 'talked up' too much, such ways of making sense of the world can impinge on the levels of communication, trust, and commitment necessary for IORs to function. Conversely, if organizational boundaries are never acknowledged, then it can be difficult to determine which firm a sales representative actually 'represents' – are their loyalties to their parent organization or to their clients? The answer, depending on the task at hand, is probably both.

This 'in-between' status is a tricky role for anyone to take on because it can undermine a manager's sense of identity (Ellis and Ybema, 2010). It is important for sales personnel, and B2B marketers, too, to be able to cope with inevitable shifts in their loyalties as they conduct their day-to-day activities.

In their daily roles, boundary spanners do more than simply follow well-defined scripts and procedures set by their parent firms. They must also cope with social emotions as they attempt to mange B2B relationships (Bagozzi, 2006). These non-rational perspectives can have positive and negative effects. For instance, a feeling of pride in a job well done by a sales person can lead to greater adaptive selling practices, harder work, and higher self-sufficiency, but if it becomes too strong, pride can be dysfunctional, resulting in overconfidence and displays of egotistical behaviour which could damage a relationship. Furthermore, some sales people experience high levels of sales-call anxiety due to negative evaluations of their self-identity in anticipation of a particular encounter with a customer, perhaps from recalling past failures, or perceived negative evaluations from clients, especially those that are high status or new. This sort of anxiety can impede communication in interactions.

Source: Bagozzi (2006); Ellis and Ybema (2010)

training, and managing their sales forces. These are just some ideas to get you thinking, but Bagozzi (2006) provides a host of suggestions in a series of studies by himself and his colleagues that begin to address this topic.

12.2 Organizing the Sales Force

The overall effectiveness of an organization's selling effort is thought to be determined by two factors: the sales manager and the sales force itself (Grant and Cravens, 1999). We have discussed the role and performance of sales people in the preceding section, so let us now turn our attention to sales management. Important decisions for managers must be made over the best way of organizing a B2B sales force in the field. This is a difficult area since, although the sales force is probably the most expensive marketing tool at a firm's disposal, it comprises independently minded people who have strong ideas on how to do their job and who are working 'out in the field', away from their managers for most of the time. So, how can a manager get the best out of the sales force?

Managing a relational sales approach

Sales activities are becoming increasingly orientated towards the need to build and maintain relationships. It is therefore important for sales managers to allocate the right sales person to the right customer IOR. Three characteristics of sales people in particular are thought to influence the outcome of a sales person's relational approach (Keillor et al, 2000):

- Customer orientation: An IOR has more chance of flourishing when the sales person occasionally sacrifices short-term sales (i.e. those that just benefit the selling firm) for a longer-term approach. This can be achieved by looking to add value over the course of the relationship by uncovering customer needs and attempting to satisfy them via the most appropriate offerings.

- Service orientation: As we have seen (in Chapters Three and Four), perceptions of good service quality can lead to customer satisfaction, which in turn has a positive impact on relationship commitment. Sales people should be able to show the customer that they are motivated to take part in selling and non-selling activities throughout the lifetime of the IOR.

- Adaptability during the sales process: This helps to maintain a dialogue with the customer such that interactions continue to the mutual satisfaction of both parties. An adaptable approach will involve careful listening, questioning, and probing to remain attuned to changing customer needs.

Managers also need to decide whether a relational approach is suitable for a firm's complete portfolio of IORs since the potential attractiveness of each relationship can vary. Sales managers will often have to make investment decisions regarding their sales force's efforts and where else to provide resources to ensure that all the different types of relationships in the firm's network are adequately serviced. This is made more complex by the wide range of marketing communication elements and media available that can facilitate sales (see Chapter Eleven). To assist managers in planning their allocation of resources, it is helpful to match the level of sales support required to the nature of the firm's different IORs – see Figure 12.3. These relationships can be considered in terms of their strength and their potential attractiveness in providing long-term opportunities. The optimum efficiency in selling effort and costs can be obtained by varying sales communication approaches with the level of investment suggested by the IOR type (Cravens et al, 1991). As you can see, some relationships will not necessarily require a sales person's attention, but can be supported in other ways.

Strength of relationship

	High	Low
High	*Invest heavily & develop accounts* • *Heavy selling for key accounts* • *Field force selling for others* 1	*Select best potential accounts & build* • *Field force selling* • *Telemarketing* • *Direct mail* • *Website* 2
Low	3 *Adjust investments & maintain* • *Field force selling* • *Telemarketing* • *Website*	4 *Reduce investments & minimal support* • *Telemarketing* • *Direct mail* • *Website*

Level of potential

Figure 12.3 Allocating sales approaches to IORs

Source: Adapted with permission from Cravens et al (1991, p 39)

D. W. Cravens, T. N. Ingram, & R. W. la Forge (1991) Evaluating Multiple Channel Strategies, Journal of Business & Industrial Marketing, 6 (3/4), pp 37–48, Emerald Publishing Group Limited

Looking at Figure 12.3 in more detail, customer IORs in Cell 1 will be crucial for the selling firm, with some even meriting designation as 'key accounts' (see section 12.3), and all requiring a significant level of personal selling. Cell 2 IORs have considerable potential but represent customers with which the selling firm has yet to forge close relationships. Investment here needs to be monitored, such that if the potential is realized following direct marketing approaches, then more will be spent on the field sales force, but if the IOR's potential does not materialize, then telesales may take over. In Cell 3, the IORs may be strong, but the potential of the relationship is not great. This suggests opportunities to alter the mix of communication approaches so that sales are maintained, but hopefully at a lower cost, perhaps by reducing (but probably not completely eliminating) the level of sales force activity. IORs in Cell 4 are not deemed worthy of receiving a sales person visit, but relations should be maintained by a number of other methods, all of which represent a reduction in investment. By adjusting the different levels of support required for each type of IOR, managers can balance cost efficiencies with selling effectiveness and relationship building.

Controlling the sales force

A sales manager needs to have the appropriate control strategy in place. This means considering the degree to which resource and process inputs are controlled, as well as how sales people are rewarded for meeting agreed targets, such as sales volumes or market share. Control can be achieved either through managing sales inputs (known as a behaviour-based system) involving a relatively high fixed salary, or through an outcome-based approach which tends to involve less managerial direction and high levels of commission that incentivize sales people to perform. Most organizations will adopt an approach that is a hybrid of the two systems, and research has shown that sales managers should balance their attention devoted to target setting, directing, and measuring results with time spent on selecting, training, and developing their sales force in order to generate positive behaviours (Baldauf et al, 2002).

But can organizations ensure that they control their sales people enough to display the right sort of behaviour? Sadly, as we have noted in this book before, ethical standards in B2B marketing can sometimes be found wanting. An example of highly questionable practices, and, ultimately, an acknowledgement of misbehaviour by the organization involved, is presented in Box 12.5. What do you think about the response of the firm to the revelations made here?

Box 12.5 Mini case

Bribing officials in order to win sales contracts

In 2009, a UK bridge-building firm, Mabey and Johnson, admitted it had paid bribes to win contracts in Jamaica, Iran, and Ghana. The UK's Serious Fraud Office (SFO) and Jamaican authorities have been investigating what they describe as 'questionable payments totalling several million US dollars' between 1993 and 2001. A Jamaican government minister has denied receiving any money. The firm has also been accused of planning to influence corruptly officials in Ghana between 1994 and 1999. Mabey and Johnson agreed to admit to the charges following a year of private investigations with the SFO. As a result, the SFO was able to 'fast-track' the case, and in return the firm will escape with a fine and will, it believes, be able to put its corrupt past behaviour behind it.

In an interesting example of crisis management, Mabey and Johnson issued a press release in which MD Peter Lloyd stated: 'Business ethics have been put at the heart of our business, and new whistle-blowing procedures introduced.' He added that all the firm's sales staff and 'associated systems' had been reviewed and would be regularly updated, while all relevant staff had been extensively trained or retrained. Moreover, 'We have also agreed to pay appropriate compensation as a further expression of our regret.' In addition, the announcement confirmed that five of the firm's eight directors had stepped down since 2008. It appears that people from the top to the bottom of the corporate hierarchy have been affected by the discovery of these sales practices.

Source: Evans and Leigh (2009); www.mabey.co.uk, accessed 11 July 2009

An important question related to controlling the sales force revolves around whether this element of the communications mix should be outsourced. The outsourcing option involves taking on a contracted sales force that is hired to perform specific duties. Members of this sales force are commonly termed manufacturers' representatives (McQuiston, 2001). Their role is often to sell non-competitive products and services which complement the manufacturers' own offerings. This allows the firm's own direct sales force to focus on more strategically important clients, leaving the independent representatives to target smaller organizational customers. The approach works well when the outsourced sales forces have extensive knowledge of the marketplace and the manufacturer shares its detailed product knowledge with its hired representatives. While outsourcing may run the risk of losing control over front-line sales activities, it does have the benefit of removing some employment overheads from the manufacturer's costs.

Setting up sales teams

Assuming senior management have decided to employ their own direct sales force, the selling firm may also need to consider if these individuals should be organized into teams to meet the needs of major organizational customers. Large corporate clients frequently have complex buying centres comprising a mixture of different functional personnel (see Chapter Two), and some authors claim that sales teams are being employed in direct response to the formation of these decision-making units (Rangarajan et al, 2004). This can mean that for a major, highly technical purchase, a single sales person's initial access to a potential customer firm may have to be backed up with a range of other experts from the selling organization, including engineers, programmers, logisticians, staff trainers, and financial advisors. Thus, the sales team can comprise employees whose chief responsibility may not be selling, but with whom the sales person must develop a good working relationship in order to present the best possible impression of the manufacturer to the customer's personnel. Should a team-based approach be adopted, then sales managers may need to alter the selling firm's internal reward mechanisms, for example in encouraging team selling by extending the allocation of sales commission to other functional areas within the firm (Piercy et al, 1998).

Making sales teams work can involve a lot of planning by selling organizations. Look at Box 12.6 to see how sales are managed by a supplier of materials to original equipment

Box 12.6 Mini case

B2B team selling in the automobile manufacturing sector

Alcoa is a world leader in the production and management of aluminium, making a range of goods and components, including flat-rolled products, forgings, and fastening systems for a wide range of industrial sectors. During the 1990s, its Wheel and Forged Products division began to focus on developing customized products for several car manufacturers, resulting in the production of distinctive new types of aluminium wheel for models like Jeeps, Ford trucks, and Hummers. By extending its collaboration with OEMs to include post-sales service and marketing, it now has 35% of this market. To facilitate the IORs with manufacturers that lie behind this success, a number of sales approaches have to be managed.

First, there is a need to engage the organizational customer. Alcoa's sales teams hold joint strategy sessions at the customer's premises where the Alcoa teams often interact with manufacturers' personnel, including R&D engineers, operations managers, and supply chain experts. Some customers, however, question the need for a team approach as they are wedded to a highly centralized decision-making process. This means that Alcoa may have to begin negotiations by persuading a senior manager within the buying firm who deals with end users and also has important functional responsibilities, such as marketing or NPD, that a diverse sales team is what is needed.

Second, the firm's sales processes have to be appropriately organized. Alcoa staff from different business units have recognized that some collaborative efforts are essential for the whole firm, even though they may harm their own unit's or department's income statements in the short term. If sales people from different parts of the company try to pitch different products or services to the same customer, this can threaten Alcoa's 'one-face' continuity with their organizational clients who value a single sales person's ability to satisfy their diverse needs.

Third, the right contact person for the relationship needs to be in place. Alcoa needs managers who have personal contacts across functions, business units, and regions that can assist them in marshalling resources for a customer on an ad hoc basis. Contact managers also need to be able to hold strategic-level discussions with the appropriate senior executives in the customer organization.

Fourth, the sales team must be developed. A typical sales team for Alcoa needs members that between them have deep product knowledge, engineering expertise, pricing knowledge to facilitate deal making, legal skills to draw up contracts across business units, as well as service experience to ensure post-sale support. These teams will rarely be smaller than ten people strong.

Fifth, there is a need to involve senior executives. Verbal commitments from senior managers may be necessary to focus people's attention on collaborative sales efforts. Alcoa maintains 'virtual teams' for its customer IORs. These teams answer to business unit senior leaders, who play an active account management role and who answer in turn to a chief customer officer. The leaders ensure that the overall running of the IORs goes smoothly by setting targets and monitoring progress.

Sources: Hancock et al (2005); www.alcoa.com

manufacturers (OEMs) based in the US, but with almost half of its business conducted internationally. The commitment to team selling by Alcoa is considerable.

One way of approaching team selling is to form 'selling alliances' (Smith and Barclay, 1997) where sales people from organizations that already have strong network ties (e.g. suppliers of computer systems, software developers, and training service providers) cooperate in making joint sales approaches to prospective customers. This is fairly common practice in major capital projects where tenders often involve coalitions of suppliers, but is becoming increasingly used in smaller, yet technically complex, purchases.

Structuring the sales force

How the sales force should be structured is another important decision for B2B managers. A number of alternatives for sales territory design exist, each with their pros and cons. Sales managers need to find the optimum approach by taking into account the number of potential customers, their sales potential, their geographic concentration, and the availability of resources. The three main options for structuring the sales force are listed in Figure 12.4.

- Geographically based: Here, sales people are assigned separate geographic regions of responsibility. They will be tasked with all the activities required to sell all of the firm's offerings to every potential organizational customer in 'their' region. This approach tends to be adopted by companies whose customers purchase a range of products and in markets where there are minimal differences in buying patterns across regions. It is a relatively simple structure to operate and can keep travel costs down. It is thus a common initial approach taken by firms new to a marketplace or those with limited resources. Many large organizations use the geographic approach successfully, too. For instance, Luxottica, the Italian sunglasses manufacturer, has a global sales network that distributes its products in around 130 countries and also operates 38 wholly or partially owned wholesale subsidiaries in major markets. Each of these subsidiaries operates its own local network of sales representatives, who look after the firm's retail clients (www.luxottica.com).

- Product based: This involves a set of different sales teams for the overall market, each responsible for a particular line of products. It is well suited to companies that offer a wide range of products that are technically complex and diverse in application. Such products typically require specialist knowledge on the part of the sales person and skilled selling techniques. The extra field costs in having each sales force covering the

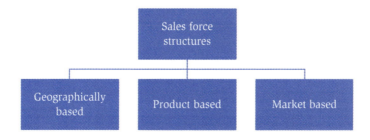

Figure 12.4 Options for structuring the sales force

entire marketplace are compensated by the potential large returns on sales of what are typically high-tech, high-value products.

- Market based: This approach reflects a high degree of marketing orientation on behalf of the selling firm. By basing the structure of the sales force around the needs of specific customer groups or segments, it facilitates the sale of products with multiple applications to a wide variety of markets. It does mean that the selling firm has to be especially in tune with marketplace dynamics, and can tie up rather more resources than the above two approaches, but should result in more focused customer attention and thus satisfaction in the long term – see the key account management issues discussed in section 12.3. The formation of selling alliances mentioned above is an extension of a market-based approach across the supplier network.

Technology in organizational selling

Technology is playing an increasingly significant role in helping to manage sales force activities, although it tends to be used more by sales people in the office, typically to prepare for sales calls and to compile reports, than in the field. The list below, based on the work of Widmier et al (2002), suggests six areas in which IT and other technologies can support the sales effort in B2B markets:

- Organizing: Compiling contact details, call schedules, route plans
- Informing: Learning about prospective customers, and details of product specification and performance
- Presenting: Aiding customized sales proposals, portable multimedia presentations
- Communicating: Using mobile telephones, email, Internet, faxes
- Supporting transactions: Order status tracking, checking stock availability
- Reporting: Assembling performance evaluations, call reports, expense claims.

The integration of these forms of sales force automation should enable increased productivity via lower costs, or a larger number of interactions of a higher quality to take place. However, this is not always the case. Successful implementation of technologies within the selling function depends on management commitment, staff training, user involvement, and the appropriate setting of expectations. If sales people perceive the introduction of IT as a threat, perhaps due to their 'technophobia', or resentment over interference in their selling activities, or the loss of their own carefully collected customer information, then implementation will be difficult (Morgan and Inks, 2001). Moreover, the impact of introducing IT into the B2B selling process should also be assessed from the perspective of customers. It is possible that some key clients may not welcome the depersonalization that they believe accompanies a greater use of technology, which could result in a subsequent negative impact on buyer–seller relationships.

Such is the apparent belief that more IT will lead to more sales, that it has been estimated that over $27 billion is spent worldwide annually on sales force-related CRM software. Rather than just possessing blind faith in the efficacy of these massive investments, B2B marketers must justify their expenditure in this area (Ahearne et al, 2007). The study outlined in Box 12.7 goes some way towards helping them to do this. Note how sales people and their managers claim that sales technology has made a difference to working practices and performance.

Box 12.7 Voices

The impact of IT on sales effectiveness

A number of B2B sales personnel were interviewed on the contribution of technology to selling (Ahearne et al, 2007). The study participants worked for a middle-sized US division of a European pharmaceutical firm, responsible for selling two product lines direct to doctors. They noted how IT can improve and facilitate information processing and communication, thereby increasing the quantity of work performed. For instance, one sales manager said, 'Technology helps [sales people's] productivity and efficiency. Based on their computer analyses, what they know about the customer, and determining the best time to see a specific customer, they can make eight calls a day.'

Increased knowledge helps sales people in targeting and presentation skills, as this sales rep states: 'I pull a lot from the Internet (e.g. articles) and sometimes put together binders for my customers. It gives me ammunition to support my arguments.' This follows tasks like analysing purchase patterns and sorting customer lists based on 'business potential' to put sales efforts into the most profitable product–customer combinations. Being fore-armed with technical knowledge allows a sales person to convey a reassuring level of expertise to customers. A sales rep explained: 'I assemble each customer's prescribing behaviour, look at the application where I have my call notes, and determine what message I want to focus on this time. I can go in and focus on their needs and wants.'

In a survey extension of their study, Ahearne et al also researched the views of sales people selling consumer goods to retail organizations as part of a push communications strategy. Their findings show how sales people who integrate IT tools into their activities can significantly improve their performance. This provides a good justification to sales managers for implementing IT initiatives. Moreover, when sales people who may have been reluctant to 'buy into' IT can see the positive outcomes of its acceptance amongst their colleagues, they will probably be more likely to value these technological aids and thus be willing to invest the necessary effort to learn how to use them.

Source: Ahearne et al (2007)

12.3 Key Account Management (KAM)

Another term for an organizational customer in B2B markets is an 'account'. 'Key' accounts (sometimes termed national or major accounts) are those deemed to be strategically important by the selling organization and willing to enter into relational exchanges. They need to be carefully handled since it is increasingly the case that a small number of these key accounts have become essential for the survival of many supplying firms. As a result, IOR participants will demand ever more professional sales people to manage their relationships. If these IORs are not managed professionally, the selling firm runs the risk of losing a long-term partner and probably one that can offer access to other key network actors or resources.

Some organizational customers can provide symbolic value as perceived by the rest of the market due to their power and reputation. For instance, the Danish provider of ERP solutions for professional service organizations, Maconomy, is proud to list amongst its key accounts one of the world's leading market research companies, Millward-Brown (www.millward-brown.com). Maconomy's website even provides an interview with a key account manager who describes his typical working day, with all its customer meetings, presentations, and project briefings (www.maconomy.com).

Organizing for KAM

In this market-based approach to selling, firms must select the appropriate customers to be designated as key accounts. Some large clients may not have needs that can be met by key account management (KAM) programmes, particularly those that have expectations of value that the firm would have difficulty in meeting over the long haul (Abratt and Kelley, 2002). Taking this into account, once the selection has been made, three possible approaches to assigning staff to key accounts present themselves:

- Forming a key account division: In order to service the major customers' needs, this approach draws on managers from different functional areas such as production, finance, and sales, much like the selling team approach discussed earlier. It can be costly since it effectively duplicates resources that exist elsewhere in the firm, but does facilitate the close integration of a range of different experts such that the customer is exposed to a highly knowledgeable set of contacts. For instance, a typical set of contacts from a supplier of large capital purchases can include the key account manager, the marketing manager, product development managers, operations and logistics managers, site service personnel, and telesales people.

- Forming a key account sales force: As noted in the market-based approach to sales force structure, this can result in resource inefficiencies, but by appointing their most skilled sales people to these roles across the whole market, it does allow the selling organization to differentiate itself through a heavily customer-orientated service. The creation of such an 'elite' sales force can, however, cause resentment amongst other sales people in the firm, especially due to the capacity for these KAM-based individuals to earn higher commissions through their key accounts.

- Assigning sales executives: Because of a relative lack of resources, smaller organizations tend to assign senior managers to the KAM role, allowing them to make decisions over much of the marketing mix in order to provide the responsive service required by key accounts. There is a risk that the sales executives can become overly focused on their key customers, neglecting the rest of their firm's marketing strategy.

Some assumptions about KAM approaches

Suppliers who operate KAM argue that their customers benefit from KAM-style sales relationships. Five 'Cs' of value have been described by suppliers, as summarized in Figure 12.5, claiming that customer organizations gain from customization, consultancy, complexity management, consistency, and continuity (Ryals and Holt, 2007).

Despite its popularity as a form of sales management, some scholars have begun to question the assumptions about KAM held by practitioners and academics alike. For instance, in a study conducted in Germany amongst purchasing managers in the packaging and market research industries, Ivens and Pardo (2008) showed that KAM programmes were thought to involve higher supplier investments and dependency, a large number of individual actors on

Figure 12.5 Five Cs of customer benefits derived from KAM
Source: Adapted with permission from Ryals and Holt (2007, p 410)
L. J. Ryals, & S. Holt (2007) Creating and Capturing Value in KAM Relationships, Journal of
Strategic Marketing, 15, pp 403–20, Taylor & Francis Ltd, http://www.informaworld.com

the customer side, and increased customer expenditure. However, several common beliefs about KAM were not supported. Some counter-intuitive results included:

1. *KAM is not always felt to lead to better process coordination*: this may be because time is needed to achieve proper coordination, and if KAM has only recently been implemented, then processes are still developing. It may also be due to the tensions faced by key account managers who must translate customer problems into solutions that their firm can provide. This requires the cooperation of other functional departments who may not be as supportive as they should.

2. *KAM programmes are not just reserved for long-term customers*: this may be explained by appreciating that if KAM means creating value through a particular approach to sales management dedicated to the customer, the choice to implement KAM can quite legitimately be made without reference to relationship duration. Thus, a prospect can be treated as key account if a KAM-style approach is thought to be the most appropriate for negotiating with this customer.

3. *KAM does not necessarily allow suppliers to push for price premiums*: this is because the objective of the approach is not to raise prices but to create value. This can entail the same or even lower prices but higher volume, such as can be achieved via cross-selling. A KAM approach could equally entail the same prices but lower costs for the supplier which is, again, a value-creating outcome (see Chapter Ten).

The key account manager

A major issue in KAM concerns who in the selling organization should be ultimately responsible for these key accounts. This is far from simple to resolve as key account managers must be able to manage large and complex organizational customers, and possess strong relationship-orientated skills. They often have to cope with lengthy buying decisions and need to facilitate these decisions by acting as a conduit of information between buying and selling firms.

This means that key account managers will often not be the sole point of contact between the parties of an IOR. Instead, they may oversee a range of contact possibilities within the customer organization that might be appropriate to pursue by members of what is effectively a selling team (see section 12.2 above). The KAM process then becomes one of coordination, ensuring that the right person in the selling organization is matched to each contact without 'overkill' or duplication from different departments, both of which can annoy the customer and run the risk of sending inconsistent marketing messages, for instance if a marketer makes a promise about delivery that is then contradicted by a logistics manager.

As interaction between individuals is so vital to successful KAM, B2B marketers should try to ensure that the social element of a relationship is enhanced through such things as multiple contact points between firms. Note that this need not necessarily involve a high degree of 'socializing' (say, dinner parties or golf tournaments), but should give managers in particular functional areas in a selling firm (e.g. R&D) the chance to communicate with managers in certain key roles within a buying firm (e.g. production). Thus, a move away from an IOR with a single point of contact (i.e. sales person and buying officer) towards a larger number of interfaces between selling and buying departments should be encouraged where appropriate. In this way, what can be described as a 'bow tie' model of KAM becomes a 'diamond', as shown in Figure 12.6. Before instigating such changes, however, marketing managers should confirm whether a single point of contact is actually what customers who value the simplicity of the bow-tie arrangement may prefer.

The two approaches represented in Figure 12.6 reflect some of the differences between what Millman and Wilson (1995) term early and mid levels of KAM, as discussed below. These views of IORs appear to be commonly understood by managers in contemporary business markets – see Box 12.8.

Linking KAM levels to IOR life cycles

Much of the thinking on key accounts revolves around the notion of relationship development stages. The idea is to match the style of KAM to the appropriate stage in the IOR life cycle. Millman and Wilson (1995), drawing in part on the work of Dwyer et al (1987) as discussed back in Chapter Three, were amongst the first authors to suggest how KAM might be implemented over the supposed stages of a relationship. Based on these authors' frameworks, a series of levels of KAM can be determined, summarized in Figure 12.7.

You should note that these stages need not necessarily be adopted sequentially, as some IORs may 'jump' to a higher level more rapidly due to their strategic significance and/or high levels of compatibility between parties (and, of course, some relationships will never move beyond the early stages):

- Pre-KAM: Here, the main role of the B2B marketer is to identify which IORs have key account potential, so that resources can be efficiently allocated. While the customer will be evaluating the value offered by the seller, managers in the supplying firm should be asking whether the buying organization can provide them with an adequate volume of sales at a decent level of profitability over the long term. If so, then marketers should try to persuade senior management within the supplier of the need to give this IOR key account status.

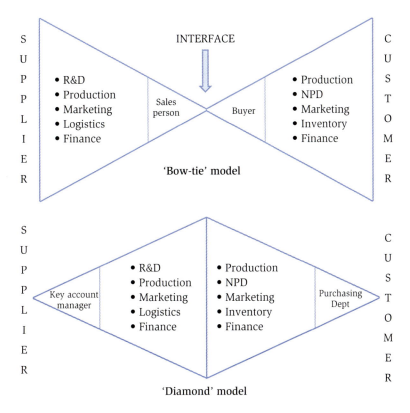

Figure 12.6 Alternative approaches to inter-organizational interfaces in KAM

Box 12.8 Food for thought

The spread of marketing management metaphors

Ellis and Mayer (2001) report the explicit use of the bow-tie metaphor by managers in a chemical supplier to explain how they saw KAM working for their firm. This seems to show how ideas circulating in marketing studies (e.g. McDonald et al, 1996) are quickly assimilated by practising managers. Of course, you could argue that academic researchers are merely reflecting what they have found from studying B2B interactions. Indeed, one of the earliest reported mentions of the bow-tie relationship was at an academic conference in 1994 by speakers representing Wal-Mart and Procter & Gamble to explain the IORs between this major retail customer and their goods supplier. With their 300 brands selling across 130 countries, P&G continue to make much of their ability to work in close relationships with key organizational partners upstream for product innovation and downstream for distribution (www.pgconnectdevelop.com). This leaves us to ponder who thought of the bow-tie/diamond terminology first. The answer is unclear, but it probably does not matter as long as the metaphors help B2B marketers to make better sense of the world.

Source: Ellis and Mayer (2001); McDonald et al (1996); Wal-Mart/Procter & Gamble (1994)

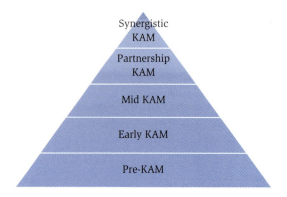

Figure 12.7 Stages in KAM

- Early KAM: This involves a fairly transactional approach to trading within the IOR, where the two parties establish their suitability as potential partners by conducting some initial sales interactions. It corresponds to the 'exploration' stage of Dwyer et al (1987). To make the best-possible first impression, the sales person or key account manager should set appropriate expectations, monitor order progress, and ensure the product or service is used properly by the customer's staff. This attention to detail by individual actors can allow social networks to develop.

- Mid-KAM: This represents a more cooperative approach where an increasing number of contacts from each organization communicate with each other (see Figure 12.6). The buying firm begins to trust the seller more and more, and may commit to purchasing a broader range of goods and services. KAM participants should seize any opportunity to add value to the relationship by identifying additional needs and recommending solutions. This corresponds to Dwyer et al's 'expansion' life-cycle stage.

- Partnership KAM: This stage reflects a high level of mutual commitment between the two organizations. The selling firm may become recognized as a preferred or even sole supplier by the buying firm, and the seller will clearly define the customer as a key account of strategic importance, signifying the level of dependence between the parties. It will be vital for the key account manger to ensure that everyone involved in the KAM process is delivering consistently high-quality service to the customer, and that all departments prioritize the allocation of resources to the partnership. More on these sorts of IORs can be found on the website of the Strategic Account Management Association where global partnerships driven by firms like DHL are highlighted (www.strategicaccounts.org).

- Synergistic KAM: Here, the value of the IOR is so great that the two firms effectively begin to act as one, exchanging significant resources, including large amounts of information and even personnel in order to solve complex operational challenges. It reflects a great deal of organizational and personal allegiance to the account on both sides. The partnership and synergistic stages broadly correspond to Dwyer et al's 'commitment' stage.

- Uncoupling KAM: At this stage (not shown in Figure 12.7), the account may disintegrate due to the realization that the IOR is no longer mutually beneficial. This can be a unilateral or joint decision. Handled sensitively, however, it need not be a damaging decision, especially when uncoupling occurs due to changes outside either firm's control, such as a significant technology shift in the overall market or a merging of two customers or suppliers at a horizontal level in the network.

A network perspective on KAM

One limitation of the stage approach to KAM is that it does not really accommodate the interactions that can occur with other actors in the industrial network in which the IOR supposedly being 'managed' is embedded. Decisions taken by other organizations can impact on the best-laid KAM plans of the selling firm and, of course, the KAM activities of the firm itself have the potential to influence the entire network, as you will see in the end-of-chapter case study based on research by Ellis and Mayer (2001).

A firm's relationship portfolio comprises relations with other types of network actors than just customers. Across these relationships, too, some have more importance than others and therefore are 'key'. In an exploration of inter-organizational alliances from the French IT sector, including those between software suppliers (e.g. SAP), hardware manufacturers (e.g. HP), and IT integrators (e.g. Cap Gemini – www.capgemini.com), Ivens et al (2009) show that alliance management has strong similarities with KAM. From the perspective of the whole network, what they term 'key relationship management' has several characteristics:

- It focuses on relationships with external actors in order to gain access to the resources (including economic, material, informational, or social) held by those actors. The organization and the relationship manager need to ensure that the right contracts, relational norms, and relationship-specific investments are in place to enable the continuity of the relationship and to protect against any opportunism.

- It takes an interaction approach (see Chapter Five) to the management of exchanges with these key external actors. This approach involves bidirectional communication and a joint learning process between relationship participants.

- It focuses on the management of strategically important relationships, based on the assumption that some relationships have different value from others in the firm's portfolio. This assumption holds for upstream relationships with suppliers, and horizontal relationships with alliance partners, as well as downstream sales relations with customers.

This has implications for any individual responsible for relationship management, perhaps as part of a B2B marketing remit. They must first assess which external organizational actors control critical resources and then determine which kind of IORs will allow the most appropriate combination of resources to be exchanged by the firm (see Chapter Five). Identifying key relationships and managing them are recursively linked. In other words, the relationship justifies the role (that of key relationship manager) which at the same time moderates the relationship which, in turn, justifies the role (Ivens et al, 2009). This makes key relationship management a significant challenge for managers since it is not just customer, supplier or partner characteristics that define 'keyness', but the nature of the ever-shifting IORs between the focal firm and these actors.

Thus, we see once more the complexities of inter-firm relationships and networks in business markets, all of which confirms the fascination of studying the world of B2B marketing!

To pull together several of the strands of thought that you have encountered in this book, this final chapter concludes with a case study showing the impact of buying behaviours and sales strategies on relationships in an industrial network in the chemicals sector.

Summary

The key points to take from this chapter are as follows:

- The many activities that make up the role of the modern B2B sales person.
- How to weigh up whether employing a sales force is actually effective for all organizational markets.
- How to prioritize investments in the sales force and other elements of the marketing communications mix, depending on the nature of current IORs.
- What is involved in controlling and structuring B2B sales force activities.
- The complexities of managing sales teams and the impact of information technology (IT) on sales force practices.
- The benefits and assumptions behind key account management (KAM) approaches.
- How to link levels of KAM to the idea of an IOR life cycle, and ensure that the appropriate interfaces are maintained between buying and selling organizations.

Discussion questions

1. Describe the role of personal selling and highlight its main strengths and drawbacks as part of a firm's B2B marketing communications mix.

2. How can sales managers decide on the relative level of investment in personal selling that is required to service their organization's portfolio of customer IORs?

3. What external and internal factors should sales managers consider when deciding how to organize and control their sales force?

4. Do you think that IT and Internet-based approaches will ever fully replace the industrial sales person?

5. Reply to your CEO who asks at a board meeting, 'Why should our company bother to invest in a key account manager – surely they are just senior sales people?'

6. Using a B2B sector of your choice, explain some of the differences between an early (exploration) level of KAM and a partnership (commitment) level.

Case study

Relationship Management and Network Construction in the Chemicals Sector

Introduction

'ChemCo' is a company operating in the global speciality chemicals sector whose name has been disguised to maintain confidentiality. Its products are chemical additives designed to enhance a base chemical's properties. These products are used by blenders/manufacturers to create branded products for the global market, including the oil and petroleum sectors. The number of major global suppliers in this sector shrank from eight in 1992 to four by 1998, including ChemCo, which was once regarded as the market share and technical leader. This had been achieved through investment in R&D and a widespread geographical coverage of local agents offering close customer liaison. Unfortunately, at the start of 2000, adverse market conditions caught ChemCo 'wrong-footed', according to one senior executive, as the sector seemed to be moving towards an aggressive price war. So how did this situation arise?

Case history

In the early 1990s, the sector represented an attractive operating environment. Demand was high and enabled manufacturers and, in turn, chemical suppliers to set premium prices via product differentiation. ChemCo defined three oil market segments: the 'global majors', the major volume purchasers with an international scale of operation; large nationally based manufacturers, with dominant positions in domestic markets, known as the 'nationals' and comprising about 40 in number; and a remaining tier of hundreds of small, local chemical blenders.

The global majors did not coordinate their buying activity, and each local subsidiary acted on its own initiative. This situation was generally welcomed by purchasing managers who felt that they had better working relationships with local representatives from ChemCo. Negotiations were typically conducted at a technical level. Once the specification was met, the chemical supplier's prices were merely passed on to the end industrial customer by manufacturers. There appeared to be a degree of complacency amongst sellers and even a recognition of opportunistic behaviour: 'If we got an exclusive approval [for a product specification], we would put a price tag on it accordingly. We have screwed them on price,' said one manager candidly. Nevertheless, despite some buyer awareness of these practices, local customers seemed largely satisfied, particularly with their regular personal contact with ChemCo's sales representatives.

Market changes

By the end of the decade, however, the marketing environment was changing. Worldwide consumption of chemicals was beginning to plateau, partly due to the fortunes of the Pacific Rim economies, leading to spare capacity amongst manufacturers. This led to a focus on cost reduction, with corresponding knock-on effects on speciality suppliers as customers demanded price reductions. Consolidation became endemic among the global oil majors: at one point, ChemCo had been able to identify over 300 local business units with whom trade was possible; however, this was now reduced to only seven core businesses (known within the sector as the 'Seven Sisters') due to global coordination of buying.

There was now a significant increase in the bargaining power of the industry's major customers thanks to centralized purchasing. At the same time, the pursuit of market share seems to have become the primary objective of chemical suppliers, leading to price-based competition becoming the norm. The 'high-tech' associations of ChemCo could not prevent the slide into a commodity-style market. In fact, there was a tendency towards the standardization of products bought centrally, depriving suppliers of opportunities for differentiation. Even though this might, on the face of it, have presented

ChemCo with the opportunity of targeting the second tier of 'national' customers, some sales managers were reluctant to do so for fear of 'fragmenting the business' – for them, at least dealing with the Seven Sisters was simple.

Yet, for many ChemCo managers, including those in non-boundary-spanning roles, coping with centralized buying was proving problematic. The practice restricted the firm's ability to negotiate over anything other than price, and prevented it meeting the needs of local customers: 'Some of the majors have driven it too far. Their local operating units now, for example in Scandinavia where they have colder weather than anywhere else, and say, in South America where the end user hasn't got the same level of sophistication, they need different things.'

Most manufacturers were addressing their costs by requesting reductions in speciality chemical prices, but this tactic failed to recognize other significant costs related to adding value in the manufacture, freight, and storage of these materials. Thus, 'cost to use' issues such as product quality, on-time delivery, and lead times were being ignored. ChemCo's lack of detailed information about its customers' operations hindered its ability to offer long-term tailor-made solutions to buyers. One frustrated manager explained: 'Our understanding is wholly dependent on our key contact's cross-functional expertise. These guys are just not aware of things like logistics. So we have to widen the network of contacts with our customers.'

ChemCo's actions

The price war was affecting all the suppliers at the same level in the supply chain as ChemCo. One bitter rival, ChemTwo, actually accused ChemCo of starting the war, something never acknowledged by ChemCo managers themselves. The price war seemed to have then escalated, as shown by the internal conflict facing a product manager within ChemCo who felt that his prices quoted to major customers were frequently 'moderated' downwards by the firm's senior sales division, with the result that, as he said: 'I don't think they realize, but this is sending a signal to our competitors that this is the appropriate price for this additive. And it's naive to think that this price level isn't filtering out to the nationals too.' Perhaps unsurprisingly, ChemTwo's response was simply to lower their own prices further.

In response to these market changes, ChemCo decided to place an emphasis on head office key account management (KAM) with the global majors. For some employees, this meant that relationships with the 'nationals' segment were being neglected. They argued that investments in relationship development were being 'steered away to the globals'. Since lower price levels would be doing little to make funds available in the first place, it seemed as though a vicious circle was in operation.

In this context, the crucial role of the firm's key account managers was explained by one product manager thus: 'The key account manager is the guy driving it. I'm one of the back-up team he would draw upon to help with the bid.' Many managers, however, felt that customers needed more than just one contact point, especially for technical queries. Commenting on the key account manager's authority to lower prices to clinch deals, one functional manager said, 'I think it's a short-term view and I think there's a lot of empire building going on amongst the key account guys.' The level of personal power apparently resting in the KAM role could well have been an explanatory factor in

ChemCo's concentration on the centralized global majors, since the sales force was able to achieve targets much more quickly by focusing on the 'Seven Sisters'.

In addition to the lack of a long-term orientation within the firm, the problem of short-termism was felt to permeate the entire chemicals industry. One senior manager claimed: 'If you look at the analysis of Wall Street of the corporation, everything is short term. That's what's driving the company. But it's not just us – I think some of the big customers take too short term an approach to the business.' Much of the buyer–seller behaviour shown in the industry's rush to reduce prices seemed to reflect an adversarial approach to relationships. This could well have been a historical legacy of customer's perceptions of earlier, exploitative marketplace negotiations.

It is noteworthy that the speciality chemical suppliers also interacted with OEMs (the end users of oil and other lubricants), especially in the area of NPD. One manager representing ChemThree, a further competitor to ChemCo, remarked: 'The OEMs and the chemical industry can't live without speciality additives. Our futures are intertwined.' The extent of ChemCo's own relationships with the OEMs was indicated thus: 'I think the chemical manufacturer's view is that we are just a link in the traditional supply chain, and they are very concerned that we often have a better relationship with end users than they do. That's because we have a technical working relationship and you'll find that lots of OEMs actually consider the chemical to be a machine part, so it's just as natural for them to talk to ChemCo as it is to talk to any component manufacturer.'

Some conclusions

Are we able to plot how ChemCo has found itself in its new, somewhat unattractive, network position? Well, it seems that the combined impacts of global economic forces and of customer consolidation and centralized buying have been significant. In particular, the case highlights the dangers of the focal firm's conflicting goals, whereby reasonably close local relationships have been overridden by the new corporate KAM strategy.

In such a context, we might question the wisdom for ChemCo of pursuing a sales approach based around market share alone and, further, of focusing on key global accounts at the expense of second-tier accounts. The dangers of adopting this narrow version of relationship management are reinforced because the global majors are adopting a coercive power stance based on short-term transactional goals offering no long-term benefit to the supplier. ChemCo's current relational approach probably has its origins in a combination of traditional industry attitudes and an overreaction to the buying policies of the majors.

Overall, the case illustrates the long-term nature of relationship building and the impact of past experience on the atmosphere of interactions between organizations. It appears that ChemCo, and its rivals ChemTwo and ChemThree, have a lot to learn about developing closer partnerships in B2B markets.

Source: This case is based partly on empirical material from Ellis and Mayer (2001)

Case study questions

1. Briefly compare and contrast the situation in this sector in the early 1990s with the one found at the end of the decade. What were the pros and cons of ChemCo's approach to relationship management in the earlier period?

> **2.** How would you describe the impact of ChemCo's present KAM-based actions on the network in which the firm is embedded? Consider every stakeholder, both external and internal to the organization.
>
> **3.** What recommendations would you make to the senior management team at ChemCo? These should be in terms of selling approaches and other vertical and horizontal (including internal) relationships.

Further Reading

Boles, J. S., Barksdale, N. C., & Johnson, J. T. (1996) What National Account Decision Makers would Tell Salespeople about Building Relationships, Journal of Business & Industrial Marketing, 11 (2), pp 6–19

This paper asks managers responsible for national account buying decisions about what sales people need to do to build relationships. Findings address a number of salesperson behaviours and attitudes – some of which had not at that point been empirically examined in the sales literature. The paper presents managerial and theoretical implications of these results for buyer–seller relationships.

Geiger, S. & Finch, J. (2009) Industrial Sales People as Market Actors, Industrial Marketing Management, 38 (6), pp 608–17

This paper explores the concept of boundaries in the context of sales people and their counterparts as they undertake work to build relationships and, as the authors put it, shape markets. It draws on a case study to show how market shaping implies a mutual development of relationships, goods and services exchanged, and boundaries.

Hutt, M. D. & Walker, B. A. (2006) A Network Perspective of Account Manager Performance, Journal of Business & Industrial Marketing, 21 (7), pp 466–73

These authors take a conceptual look at the social network represented by the relationships sales account managers draw upon in their role. They argue that by building a strong network of relationships both inside their own firm and in the customer organization, account managers can better diagnose customer requirements, mobilize internal experts, and coordinate activities in order to create more competitive customer solutions.

Ryals, L. J. & Holt, S. (2007) Creating and Capturing Value in KAM Relationships, Journal of Strategic Marketing, 15, pp 403–20

These authors believe that suppliers are increasingly adopting KAM under pressure from their customers, which can be problematic if the supplier is unable to capture value from the IOR. They provide a model of the drivers of customer lifetime value, and explore how good practice in several supplier organizations confirms the model's propositions.

References

Abratt, R. & Kelly, P. M. (2002) Perceptions of a Successful Key Account Management Program, Industrial Marketing Management, 15 (5), pp 467–76

Ahearne, M., Hughes, D. E., & Schillewaert, N. (2007) Why Sales Reps should Welcome Information Technology: Measuring the Impact of CRM-Based IT on Sales Effectiveness, International Journal of Research in Marketing, 24, pp 336–49

Bagozzi, R. P. (2006) The Role of Social and Self-Conscious Emotions in the Regulation of Business-to-Business Relationships in Salesperson–Customer Interactions, Journal of Business & Industrial Marketing, 21 (7), pp 453–7

Baldauf, A., Cravens, D. W., & Grant, K. (2002) Consequences of Sales Management Control in Field Sales Organizations: A Cross-National Perspective, International Business Review, 11 (5), pp 577–609

Biong, H. & Selnes, F. (1996) The Strategic Role of the Salesperson in Established Buyer–Seller Relationships, Journal of Business-to-Business Marketing, 3 (3), pp 39–78

Bucher, J. (2008) Retaining Pharma Salespeople in China, Heidrick & Struggles China, online at http://www.heidrick.com, accessed August 2009

Cravens, D. W., Ingram, T. N. & la Forge, R. W. (1991) Evaluating Multiple Channel Strategies, Journal of Business & Industrial Marketing, 6 (3/4), pp 37–48

Dwyer, F. R. & Tanner J. F. (2002) Business Marketing: Connecting Strategy, Relationships and Learning, 2nd edn, McGraw Hill, New York

Dwyer, F. R., Schurr, P. H., & Oh, S. (1987) Developing Buyer–Seller Relationships, Journal of Marketing, 51 (April), pp 11–27

Ellis, N. & Mayer, R. (2001) Inter-Organizational Relationships and Strategy Development in an Evolving Industrial Network: Mapping Structure and Process, Journal of Marketing Management, 17 (1/2), pp 183–222

Ellis, N. & Ybema, S. (2010) Marketing Identities: Shifting Circles of Identification in Inter-Organizational Relationships, Organization Studies, 31, pp 279–305

Evans, R. & Leigh, D. (2009) Firm Admits Bribing Officials Abroad to Secure Contracts, The Guardian, 11 July, p 10

Grant, K. & Cravens, D. W. (1999) Examining the Antecedents of Sales Organization Effectiveness: An Australian Study, European Journal of Marketing, 33 (9/10) pp 945–57

Gray, R. (2007) The Cutting Edge, The Marketer, July/August, pp 27–30

Guenzi, P. (2002) Sales Force Activities and Customer Trust, Journal of Marketing Management, 18, pp 749–78

Hancock, M. Q., John, R. H., & Wojcik, P.,J. (2005) Better B2B selling, McKinsey Quarterly, online at http://www.mckinseyquarterly.com, accessed July 2005

Ivens, B. S. & Pardo, C. (2008) Key-Account-Management in Business Markets: An Empirical Test of Common Assumptions, Journal of Business & Industrial Marketing, 23 (5), pp 301–10

Ivens, B. S., Pardo, C., Salle, R., & Cova, B. (2009) Relationship Keyness: The Underlying Concept for Different Forms of Key Relationship Management, Industrial Marketing Management, 38, pp 513–19

Keillor, B., Parker, R. S., & Pettijohn, C. E. (2000) Relationship Orientated Characteristics and Individual Salesperson Performance, Journal of Business & Industrial Marketing, 15 (1), pp 7–22

Marchetti, M. (2000) Cost per Call Survey, Sales & Marketing Management, September, p 81

McDonald, M., Millman, A., & Rogers, B. (1996) Key Account Management: Learning from Supplier and Customer Perspectives, Cranfield Research Report, Cranfield University

McQuiston, D. H. (2001) A Conceptual Model for Building and Maintaining Relationships between Manufacturers' Representatives and their Principles, Industrial Marketing Management, 30 (2), pp 165–81

Millman, A. & Wilson, K. (1995) From Key Account Selling to Key Account Management, Journal of Marketing Practice: Applied Marketing Science, 1 (1), pp 9–21

Morgan, A. J. & Inks, S. A. (2001) Technology and the Sales Force: Increasing Acceptance of Sales Force Automation, Industrial Marketing Management, 30 (5), pp 463–72

Piercy, N. F., Cravens, D. W., & Morgan, N. A. (1998) Salesforce Performance and Behaviour-Based Management Processes in Business-to-Business Sales Organizations, European Journal of Marketing, 32 (1/2), 79–100

Pitt, L. E. & Nel, D. (1988) The Weaver's Merit – A Comparison of the Attitudes of Suppliers and Buyers to Corruption in Business, Industrial Marketing and Purchasing, 3 (1), pp 30–9

Rangarajan, D., Chonko, L. B., Jones, E., & Roberts, J. A. (2004) Organizational Variables, Sales Force Perceptions of Readiness for Change, Learning and Performance among Boundary-Spanning Teams: A Conceptual Framework and Propositions for Research, Industrial Marketing Management, 33, pp 289–5

Reuters (2009), Sales Force Effectiveness: Less Texting, More Engagement, Thomson Reuters, online at http://www.reuters.com, accessed August 2009

Ryals, L. J. & Holt, S. (2007) Creating and Capturing Value in KAM Relationships, Journal of Strategic Marketing, 15, pp 403–20

Smith, J. B. & Barclay, D. W. (1997) The Effects of Organizational Differences and Trust on the Effectiveness of Selling Partner Relationships, Journal of Marketing, 61 (1), pp 3–21

Tanner, J. E., Fournier, C., Wise, J. A., Hollet, S., & Poujol, J. (2008) Executives' Perspectives of the Changing Role of the Sales Profession: Views from France, the United States and Mexico, Journal of Business & Industrial Marketing, 23 (3), pp 193–202

Wal-Mart/Procter & Gamble (1994), Presentation at American Marketing Association Educators' Conference, Chicago, 28–30 August

Widmier, S. M., Jackson, D. W., & McCabe, D. B. (2002) Infusing Technology into Personal Selling, Journal of Personal Selling and Sales Management, 22 (3), pp 189–99

344

Index